Marie Aratari

Trigonometry
Student Study Guide
A Circular Function Approach

Taken from:
*Student's Study Guide and Solutions Manual to Accompany Trigonometry:
A Circular Function Approach*
by Marie Aratari

Cover Art: Courtesy of Photodisc/Getty Images.

Taken from:

Student's Study Guide and Solutions Manual to Accompany Trigonometry: A Circular Function Approach
by Marie Aratari
Copyright © 2012, 2004 by Pearson Education, Inc.
Published by Addison Wesley
Boston, Massachusetts 02116

This special edition published in cooperation with Pearson Learning Solutions.

All trademarks, service marks, registered trademarks, and registered service marks are the property of their respective owners and are used herein for identification purposes only.

Pearson Learning Solutions, 501 Boylston Street, Suite 900, Boston, MA 02116
A Pearson Education Company
www.pearsoned.com

Printed in the United States of America

1 2 3 4 5 6 7 8 9 10 V036 16 15 14 13 12 11

000200010271280356

SP

ISBN 10: 1-256-48760-0
ISBN 13: 978-1-256-48760-9

Table of Contents

Worksheets

Appendix Exercises

Selected Solutions to Text Exercises

Answers to Appendix Exercises

Preface

Each section of the text has corresponding worksheets that are designed to be used in the classroom as an outline for the presentation of the material, or as directed by your instructor.

There are also exercise sets that coordinate to the review material in the appendices of the textbook. Answers to these appendix exercises are also included in this manual.

This manual also contains complete solutions to every odd exercise from the problem sets, and every exercise from the review exercises and chapter tests. Reading the text and the examples is necessary before you begin an exercise set. You are advised to try to work out the problem on your own before consulting this manual. Try several problems before you check your answers. If you are not successful, study the solution for one problem and then try to solve a similar one with the same technique. Remember, practice is critical in order to become good in any subject area, especially in math.

Note: As indicated in the text, solutions display intermediate steps rounded to four decimal places. But the final answer is determined by calculations that are not rounded until the last step. Best wishes for a great semester in Trigonometry!

Worksheets

Chapter 1
Circular Functions

Worksheet 1.1   Fundamentals

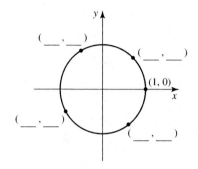

1. **a)** Label the quadrants with the appropriate name:
    QI, QII, QIII, and QIV.

    b) Indicate the positive or negative nature of the
    coordinates of the points in each quadrant
    by filling in the blank with $+$ or $-$.

    c) Name the quadrant in which the y-coordinate
    is positive and the x-coordinate is negative.   _____

2. The equation $x^2 + y^2 = 1$, graphed above and below,
    represents a circle whose center is at (0,0) with a radius
    of one unit. It is called the **unit circle**.

    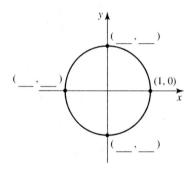

    a) Fill in the coordinates of the points representing the
    x- and y-intercepts of the unit circle.

    b) What are the smallest and largest values of x on the unit circle?   _____

    c) What are the smallest and largest values for y?   _____

3. Given a point P on the unit circle, if you know one of the coordinates you
    can find the other coordinate using the equation $x^2 + y^2 = 1$.
    If $y = \dfrac{3}{5}$, find x.

    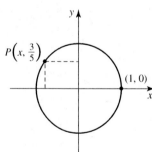

4. Find the circumference of the unit circle.   _____

Worksheet 1.2 Circular Functions

1. On the unit circle, draw the arc t with initial point $(1, 0)$ and name the quadrant that contains the terminal point of the arc. Use an arrowhead at the terminal point of the arc to indicate direction.

   a) $t = \dfrac{7\pi}{4}$

   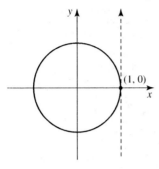

   b) $t = 2.3$

   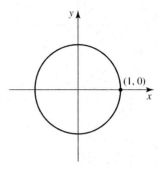

   c) $t = -\dfrac{5\pi}{3}$

   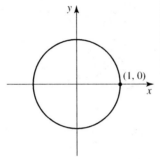

   d) $t = -1$

   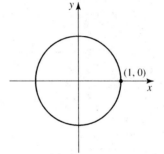

2. For arc t, t represents its length and _____. Arcs that are represented by a positive real number wrap the circle in a _____ direction while arcs represented by a negative real number wrap the circle in a _____ direction.

3. Fill in the blanks to complete the definitions of the **circular functions**.

   The **cosine** $t = \cos t$ is defined to be the ____-coordinate at the _____ point of arc t whose initial point is (____ , ____) on the unit circle.

   The **sine** $t = \sin t$ is defined to be the ____-coordinate at the _____ point of arc t whose initial point is $(1, 0)$ on the _____ circle.

   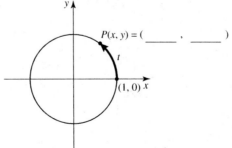

   The domain of both the cosine function and sine function is _____.

   The range of the cosine function and the range of the sine function is: _____ $\leq \cos t \leq$ _____

   _____ $\leq \sin t \leq$ _____

4. Translate the equation of the unit circle, $x^2 + y^2 = 1$, into the language of trigonometry using the definitions of the circular functions.

_____

This is called the _____ identity.

5. Translate the following algebraic question into the language of trigonometry. Then answer the question.

"Where is the x-coordinate negative and the y-coordinate positive?"

_____

6. Complete the table with $+$ or $-$.

Quad	$\cos t$	$\sin t$
QI		
QII		
QIII		
QIV		

7. If $\sin t = -\dfrac{1}{2}$ and $\cos t > 0$, find the following.

a) The quadrant that contains the terminal point of t. _____

b) $\cos t$

c) $\dfrac{\sin t}{\cos t}$

d) $\dfrac{1}{\sin t}$

Worksheet 1.3   Functional Values for Common Arcs

1. Fill in the coordinates at the terminal points of the indicated **common arcs** on the unit circle. Then, complete the table of the common arc functional values.

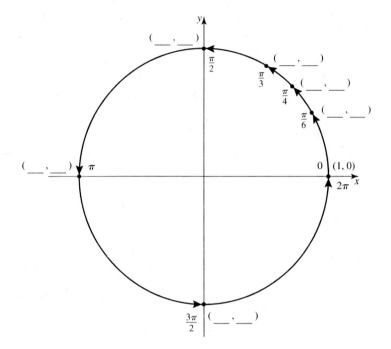

t	$\cos t$	$\sin t$
0		
$\dfrac{\pi}{6}$		
$\dfrac{\pi}{4}$		
$\dfrac{\pi}{3}$		
$\dfrac{\pi}{2}$		
π		
$\dfrac{3\pi}{2}$		
2π		

2. Evaluate each expression, if defined. Give *exact values* for your answers.

a) $\cos \dfrac{\pi}{3} + \sin \dfrac{3\pi}{2}$

b) $\sin^2 \dfrac{\pi}{3} \cdot \cos^2 \dfrac{\pi}{4}$

c) $\sin \left(\dfrac{\pi}{2} - \dfrac{\pi}{3} \right) + \sin \dfrac{\pi}{3}$

d) $\dfrac{\sin \dfrac{3\pi}{2}}{\cos \dfrac{\pi}{2}}$

3. Use a calculator in radian setting to find an approximation to four decimal places for the following expressions. (Watch parentheses!)

a) $\sin \dfrac{\pi}{8}$

b) $\dfrac{\sin 1.8}{\cos(-2.669)}$

4. Are the following statements true or false? If the statement is false, explain why or give an example that shows why it is false.

_____ **a)** $\dfrac{\pi}{9}$ is a common arc.

_____

_____ **b)** $\cos^2 t = \cos t^2$

_____

_____ **c)** Parentheses are unimportant when evaluating expressions like $\cos\left(\dfrac{\pi}{2} + \dfrac{\pi}{6}\right)$.

_____

_____ **d)** A calculator should be in radian mode to approximate $\sin \dfrac{\pi}{7}$.

_____

_____ **e)** $\cos^2 a + \sin^2 t = 1$

_____

_____ **f)** The functional value $\cos t$ is defined to be the y-coordinate at the terminal point of arc t whose initial point is $(1, 0)$ on the unit circle.

_____

_____ **g)** $\cos t$ and $\sin t$ can never be larger than 1.

_____

_____ **h)** $\cos t$ and $\sin t$ can never be smaller than -1.

_____

_____ **i)** $\sin \dfrac{\pi}{2} = \sin^2 \dfrac{3\pi}{2}$

_____

_____ **j)** The arc $\dfrac{3\pi}{2}$ is coterminal with arc $-\dfrac{\pi}{2}$ because they have the same initial and same terminal points on the unit circle.

_____

Worksheet 1.4   Reference Arcs and Functional Values for $\cos x$ and $\sin x$, $x \in \mathbb{R}$

1. Using the symmetry of the circle, along with the coordinates of the common arc indicated in the first quadrant, fill in the coordinates at the terminal point of each arc in the remaining quadrants. State the reference arc $\hat{x}$ for the arcs in the remaining quadrants.

a)

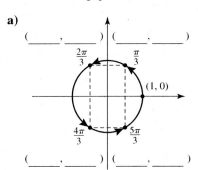

(___ , ___) (___ , ___)

(___ , ___) (___ , ___)

$\hat{x} =$ _____

b)

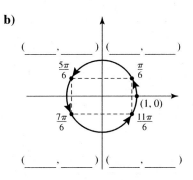

(___ , ___) (___ , ___)

(___ , ___) (___ , ___)

$\hat{x} =$ _____

c)

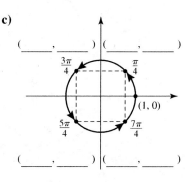

(___ , ___) (___ , ___)

(___ , ___) (___ , ___)

$\hat{x} =$ _____

2. Use the diagrams above to assist you in finding the exact functional value.

a) $\cos\left(\dfrac{2\pi}{3}\right) =$ _____

$\sin\left(\dfrac{2\pi}{3}\right) =$ _____

b) $\cos\left(\dfrac{7\pi}{6}\right) =$ _____

$\sin\left(\dfrac{7\pi}{6}\right) =$ _____

c) $\sin\left(\dfrac{7\pi}{4}\right) =$ _____

$\cos\left(\dfrac{7\pi}{4}\right) =$ _____

3. Sketch the arc x on the unit circle, state the reference arc $\hat{x}$, and then find the exact functional value.

a) $x = \dfrac{5\pi}{3}$

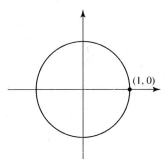

$\hat{x} =$ _____

$\sin\left(\dfrac{5\pi}{3}\right) =$ _____

b) $x = -\dfrac{3\pi}{4}$

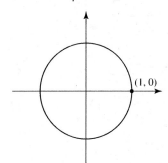

$\hat{x} =$ _____

$\cos\left(-\dfrac{3\pi}{4}\right) =$ _____

4. Find arc x on the unit circle that has the indicated terminal point and direction.

a) $x =$ _____

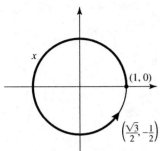

b) $x =$ _____

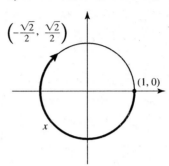

5. Find the arc x with initial point $(1, 0)$ within one counterclockwise wrap of the unit circle that makes each statement true. Draw the arc.

a) $\cos x = -\dfrac{1}{2}$, $\sin x = \dfrac{\sqrt{3}}{2}$

b) $\cos x = 0$, $\sin x = 1$

$x =$ _____

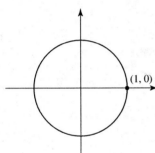

$x =$ _____

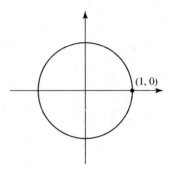

6. Find arc x with initial point $(1, 0)$ within one clockwise wrap of the unit circle that makes each statement true. Draw the arc.

a) $\cos x = \dfrac{\sqrt{2}}{2}$, $\sin x = \dfrac{\sqrt{2}}{2}$

b) $\cos x = -1$, $\sin x = 0$

$x =$ _____

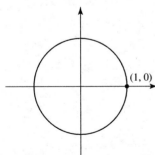

$x =$ _____

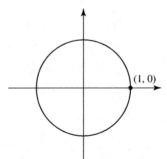

7. a) Why would you need to use a calculator to find $\cos \dfrac{5\pi}{9}$?

_____

b) Use a calculator to find an approximation rounded to four decimal places. $\cos \dfrac{5\pi}{9} \approx$ _____

Worksheet 1.5   Four Additional Circular Functions: Tangent, Secant, Cosecant and Cotangent

1. Complete the following definitions.

                                                      Domain

a) _____ $x =$ _____ $x = \dfrac{\sin x}{\cos x}$, where $x \neq$ _____

b) _____ $x =$ _____ $x = \dfrac{1}{\cos x}$, where $x \neq$ _____

c) _____ $x =$ _____ $x = \dfrac{1}{\sin x}$, where $x \neq$ _____

d) _____ $x =$ _____ $x = \dfrac{\cos x}{\sin x} = \dfrac{1}{\tan x}$, where $x \neq$ _____

2. Fill in the table with exact functional values and the blanks on the right with $>$ or $<$.

x	$\cos x$	$\sin x$	$\tan x$
0			
$\dfrac{\pi}{6}$			
$\dfrac{\pi}{4}$			
$\dfrac{\pi}{3}$			
$\dfrac{\pi}{2}$			
π			
$\dfrac{3\pi}{2}$			
2π			

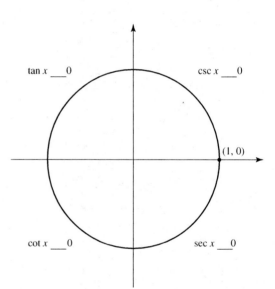

$\tan x$ ___ 0 $\csc x$ ___ 0

$\cot x$ ___ 0 $\sec x$ ___ 0

3. Determine the quadrant where $\sec x > 0$ and $\cot x < 0$. _____

4. Sketch the arc on the unit circle, state the reference arc and then find the exact functional value.

a) $\tan \dfrac{5\pi}{6}$

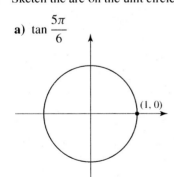

b) $\sec \dfrac{4\pi}{3}$

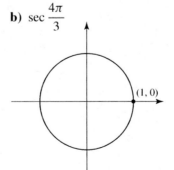

c) $\csc \left(-\dfrac{7\pi}{4} \right)$

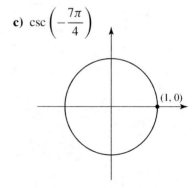

_____   _____   _____

5. Find an approximation to four decimal places.

   a) $\tan(-26.4)$　　　　　　　　**b)** $\sec\left(5 - \dfrac{\pi}{5}\right)$　　　　　　　　**c)** $\cot\dfrac{9\pi}{11}$

   _____　　　　　　_____　　　　　　_____

6. If $\sin x = \dfrac{24}{25}$ and $\cos x < 0$, find the following.

   a) The quadrant that contains the terminal point of x. _____

   b) $\cos x =$ _____　　　**c)** $\tan x =$ _____　　　**d)** $\csc x =$ _____

   e) $\sec x =$ _____　　　**f)** $\cot x =$ _____

7. Rewrite the right side of the following equation in terms of $\cos x$ and $\sin x$. Then simplify to determine if the statement is an identity (true for all values for which it is defined).

$$\sin x = \tan x \cdot \cos x \cdot \dfrac{1}{\sin x} \cdot \dfrac{1}{\csc x}$$

Worksheet 1.6 Negative Identities and Periods for the Circular Functions

1. Draw arcs $\dfrac{5\pi}{6}$ and $-\dfrac{5\pi}{6}$ on the unit circle. Label the coordinates at the end of each arc. Then determine if the statement is true or false.

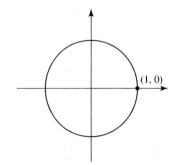

     a) $\cos \dfrac{5\pi}{6} = \cos\left(-\dfrac{5\pi}{6}\right)$ _____

     b) $\sin \dfrac{5\pi}{6} = \sin\left(-\dfrac{5\pi}{6}\right)$ _____

     c) $\tan \dfrac{5\pi}{6} = \tan\left(-\dfrac{5\pi}{6}\right)$ _____

2. Are the values of $\cos x$ and $\cos(-x)$ the same or opposites? _____

3. Are the values of $\sin x$ and $\sin(-x)$ the same or opposites? _____

4. Are the values of $\tan x$ and $\tan(-x)$ the same or opposites? _____

5. Generalize what you have answered above to complete the following **negative identities**:

     $\cos(-x) =$ _____

     $\sin(-x) =$ _____

     $\tan(-x) =$ _____

6–8   Draw the arcs to determine if the following statements are true or false.

6. $\sin\left(\dfrac{\pi}{4}\right) = \sin\left(\dfrac{\pi}{4} + 2\pi\right)$ _____   **7.** $\cos\left(\dfrac{2\pi}{3}\right) = \cos\left(\dfrac{2\pi}{3} + 2\pi\right)$ _____   **8.** $\tan \dfrac{\pi}{6} = \tan\left(\dfrac{\pi}{6} + \pi\right)$ _____

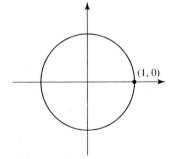 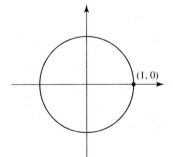 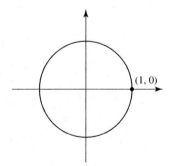

9. Complete the definition:

     If f is a function and there is a number $p > 0$ that is the smallest value such that $f(x + p) = f(x + k \cdot p) = f(x)$

     for all x in the domain of f, where $k \in \{\dots -2, -1, 0, 1, 2, \dots\}$, then f is a _____ **function** and p is

     the _____ of f.

10. What is the period of $\sin x$? _____ $\cos x$? _____ $\tan x$? _____

              $\csc x$? _____ $\sec x$? _____ $\cot x$? _____

11–12 **a)** Find the values of x within one wrap ($0 \leq x < 2\pi$) of the circle that make the statement true.

b) Then use the periodic property to find all values ($x \in \mathbb{R}$) that make it true.

11. $\cos x = -\dfrac{1}{2}$

12. $\tan x = 1$

a) _____

a) _____

b) _____

b) _____

13. A spring is weighted on one end and is bouncing up and down with initial displacement of 3 inches. The displacement is given by the equation $d(t) = 3\cos\left(\dfrac{\pi}{8}t\right)$, where t is in seconds and $d(t)$ is in inches. Find the displacement and draw the position of the spring for the indicated time.

a) $t = 0$ **b)** $t = 8$ **c)** $t = 12$

Chapter 2
Graphs of the Circular Functions

Worksheet 2.1 Graphs of Sine and Cosine Functions

1. Graph the circular function.

a) $y = \sin x$

x	$\sin x$
0	
$\frac{\pi}{4}$	
$\frac{\pi}{2}$	
$\frac{3\pi}{4}$	
π	
$\frac{5\pi}{4}$	
$\frac{3\pi}{2}$	
$\frac{7\pi}{4}$	
2π	

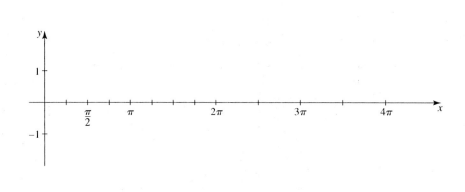

b) $y = \cos x$

x	$\cos x$
0	
$\frac{\pi}{4}$	
$\frac{\pi}{2}$	
$\frac{3\pi}{4}$	
π	
$\frac{3\pi}{2}$	
2π	

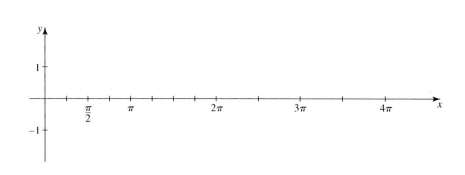

2–4 Fill in the blanks to make a true statement.

2. The graph of the sine or cosine function is called a _____ wave. The graph of one period of the sine or cosine function is called a _____, and each cycle consists of four identically shaped arc sections. There is an x-intercept at one end of each arc section with either a maximum or a _____ y-coordinate at the other endpoint. The endpoints of the arcs are called _____ points.

3. On the graphs above, label the critical points for one cycle of each function. Using their periodic property, graph another cycle for both the sine and cosine by first plotting the critical points. Then, connect the critical points with four more arc sections ("copy and paste").

4. Amplitude is defined to be: $\frac{1}{2}|$ _____ $-$ _____ $|$.

The amplitude of $y = \sin x$ is _____, and $y = \cos x$ is _____.

5. List similar and different characteristics of the ***pure form*** of $y = \sin x$ and $y = \cos x$.

similar characteristics	different characteristics

6. Graph the following for $-2\pi \le x \le 2\pi$, and label the critical points of one cycle.

a) $y = 2\sin x$

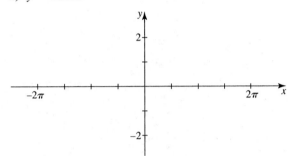

b) $y = -\dfrac{1}{2}\cos x$

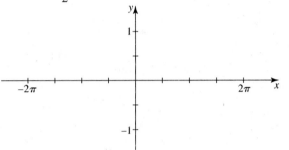

c) For $y = A\sin x$ or $y = A\cos x$, $|A| =$ _____.

d) What effect does $|A| > 1$ have on the graph? _____ $|A| < 1$? _____

What affect does $A < 0$ have on the graph? _____

7. Find an equation of the form $y = A\sin x$ or $y = A\cos x$ that represents the graph. Check your answers with a graphing calculator.

a) $y =$ _____

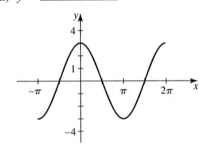

b) $y =$ _____

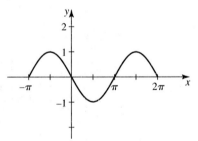

8. Below are two attempts to graph an equation of the form $y = A\sin x$ or $y = A\cos x$. Find at least one error for each attempt.

a)

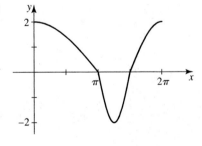

_____

_____

b)

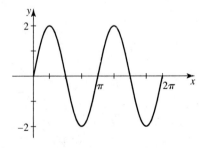

_____

_____

Worksheet 2.2   Period, Phase Shift and other Translations

1. To compare the pure form of $y = \cos x$ with $y = \cos(2x)$, dot in the graph of $y = \cos x$. Then, graph $y = \cos(2x)$.

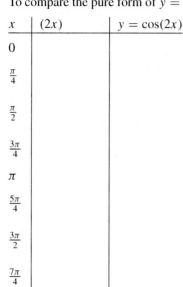

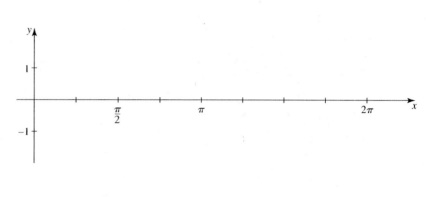

x	$(2x)$	$y = \cos(2x)$
0		
$\frac{\pi}{4}$		
$\frac{\pi}{2}$		
$\frac{3\pi}{4}$		
π		
$\frac{5\pi}{4}$		
$\frac{3\pi}{2}$		
$\frac{7\pi}{4}$		
2π		

a) Are both graphs sinusoidal? _____

b) Do they have the same amplitude? _____

c) What is the period of $y = \cos x$? _____ $y = \cos(2x)$? _____

d) What is **the effect of multiplying the arc by a value**? _____

e) Does one cycle of $y = \cos(2x)$ consist of four identically shaped arc sections? _____

f) What are the x-intercepts of $y = \cos x$? _____ $y = \cos(2x)$? _____

2. *Find a general formula for the period and x-intercepts.*

For $y = \cos(Bx)$ or $y = \sin(Bx)$, the period $P = $ _____

The x-intercepts for $y = \cos(Bx)$ are _____.

The x-intercepts for $y = \sin(Bx)$ are _____.

Each of the four arc sections of one cycle occurs in $\dfrac{1}{4}$ of the _____ along the x-axis.

3. To sketch the graph of $y = -6 \sin\left(-\frac{1}{2}x\right)$ for a minimum of two periods, do the following:

   a) Use the negative identities to rewrite the equation in the form $y = A \sin(Bx)$, where $B > 0$.

   $y = $ _____

   b) Find the period and amplitude. $P = $ _____   Amp $= $ _____

   c) Mark off one period along the x-axis and divide this interval into four subintervals. Mark off the y-axis to accommodate the amplitude. Plot the critical points and connect them with the sine form of a sinusoidal wave.

   d) Repeat the pattern one more cycle.

   e) List the graphs x-intercepts. Find a formula for all the x-intercepts. _____

   f) Check your graph with a graphing utility.

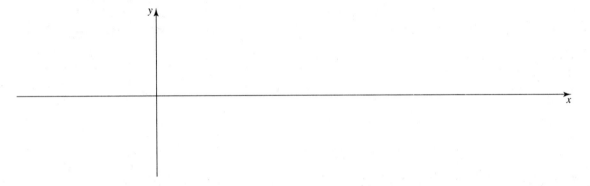

4. To compare the pure form of $y = \sin x$ with $y = \sin\left(x + \frac{\pi}{4}\right)$, dot in the graph of $y = \sin x$. Then, graph $y = \sin\left(x + \frac{\pi}{4}\right)$.

x	$x + \frac{\pi}{4}$	$y = \sin\left(x + \frac{\pi}{4}\right)$
0		
$\frac{\pi}{4}$		
$\frac{\pi}{2}$		
$\frac{3\pi}{4}$		
π		
$\frac{5\pi}{4}$		
$\frac{3\pi}{2}$		
$\frac{7\pi}{4}$		
2π		

Since $y = \sin\left(x + \frac{\pi}{4}\right) = \sin\left(x - \left(-\frac{\pi}{4}\right)\right)$, then for $y = \sin(x - C)$, what is **the effect of subtracting a value (C) from the arc?** Make a conjecture if $C > 0$ and complete the following statement.

For $\left.\begin{array}{l} y = \cos(x - C) \\ y = \sin(x - C) \end{array}\right\}$ if $C > 0$ _____, if $C < 0$ _____.

This is called a **phase shift** or a _____ **shift**.

5. To sketch the graph of $y = 3\cos(2x - \pi)$ for a minimum of two periods, do the following:

a) Rewrite the equation in the form $y = A\cos[B(x - C)]$. $y =$ _____

b) Find the period and amplitude. $P =$ _____   Amp = _____

c) Dot in the graph determined by the period and amplitude, $y = A\cos Bx$, and label the critical points.

d) Since the graph has a phase shift, shift each critical point the indicated value and direction. Connect the shifted critical points with a sinusoidal wave.

e) Repeat the pattern for another cycle.

f) Check your graph with a graphing utility.

6. To compare the pure form of $y = \cos x$ with $y = \cos x + 4$, dot in the graph of $y = \cos x$. Then, graph $y = \cos x + 4$.

x	$y = \cos x + 4$
0	
$\dfrac{\pi}{2}$	
π	
$\dfrac{3\pi}{2}$	
2π	

a) For $y = \cos x + D$, or $y = \sin x + D$, $D > 0$, what is **the effect of adding a value to a sinusoidal function?**

_____

What do you think would happen if $D < 0$? _____

This translation is called a _____ **shift**.

7. Identify the graph with an equation of the form $y = A \cos[B(x - C)] + D$, or $y = A \sin[B(x - C)] + D$. To help determine an equation, highlight the critical points. Check your answer with a graphing calculator. Is there more than one equation to describe each graph?

a) _____

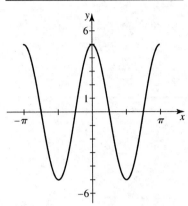

b) _____

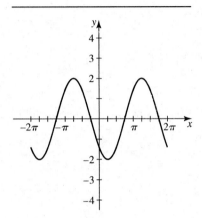

c) _____

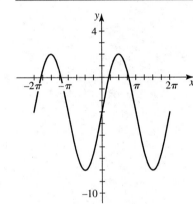

8. Is the statement true or false? If it is false, tell why or give an example that shows why it is false.

_____ a) The graph of $y = \sin 2x$ is the same as the graph of $y = \sin(2x)$.

_____ b) The graph of $y = \cos 2x$ is the same as the graph of $y = 2 \cos x$.

_____ c) The graph of $y = \cos\left(\dfrac{1}{2}x - \pi\right)$ is the same as the graph of $y = \cos\left[\dfrac{1}{2}(x - 2\pi)\right]$.

_____ d) The graph of $y = \sin(-5x)$ is the same as the graph of $y = -\sin 5x$.

_____ e) The graph of $y = \sin x + \pi$ is the same as the graph of $y = \sin(x + \pi)$.

_____ f) For most graphing utilities, parentheses around the arc are unnecessary.

Worksheet 2.3 Applications and Modeling with Sinusoidal Functions

The frequency F of an object moving in simple harmonic motion is the number of periods of the motion per unit of time. The period of the motion $P = \dfrac{2\pi}{B}$ represents the time t it takes to complete one period (units of time per period). Since the frequency is the number of periods per unit of time, the frequency F and period P are related by $F = \dfrac{1}{P} = \dfrac{B}{2\pi}$.

1.   If it takes a spring 4 seconds to complete one period, to go up and back down, what is the frequency?

   _____

2.   The simple harmonic motion of a spring with a weight attached to one end is given by $y = -6\cos\left(\dfrac{\pi}{2}x\right)$, where x is in seconds and y is in inches. The spring was stretched 6 in. out of its rest position at time $x = 0$, then released. Graph two cycles for $x \geq 0$.

   a) Since $A < 0$, what does it tell you about the initial displacement $(x = 0)$?

   _____

   b) What is the period of the spring? _____ What is the frequency? _____

   c) Why use the cosine function, as opposed to the sine function, to model this motion?

   _____

   _____

   _____

3. Consider the following data that describes the monthly average number of daylight hours for Houston, Texas.

Jan	Feb	Mar	April	May	June	July	Aug	Sept	Oct	Nov	Dec
10.1	10.5	11.3	12.3	13	14	14	13.5	12.5	11.8	10.8	10.3

a) Plot the data over a one year period and determine a sinusoidal function that would closely model this data.

b) Use a graphing calculator to create a scatter plot of the data. Then find a sine regression equation in the form $y = a \sin(bx + c) + d$ to model this data. Compare the regression equation with the one you found in part (a).

4. Do the following scatter plots appear to have sinusoidal functions model the data?

a) _____

b) _____

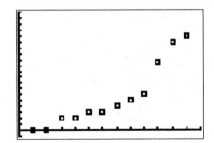

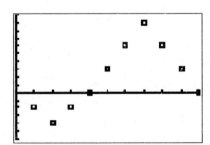

Worksheet 2.4   Graphs of Tangent, Cotangent, Secant and Cosecant Functions

1.   Graph at least one cycle of the following circular functions. Indicate the domain and range.

a) $y = \tan x$ Domain: _____   **b)** $y = \cot x$ Domain: _____

Range: _____   Range: _____

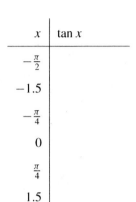

x	$\tan x$
$-\frac{\pi}{2}$	
-1.5	
$-\frac{\pi}{4}$	
0	
$\frac{\pi}{4}$	
1.5	
$\frac{\pi}{2}$	

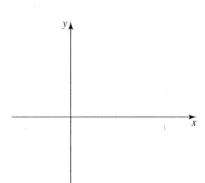

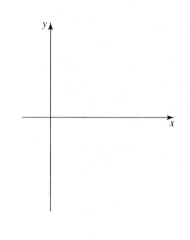

c) $y = \csc x$ Domain: _____   **d)** $y = \sec x$ Domain: _____

Range: _____   Range: _____

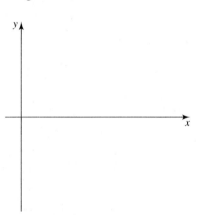

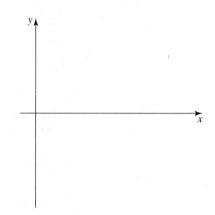

2.   **a)** What do we call the dotted vertical lines drawn where the function is not defined?

_____

b) How many identically shaped arcs are there for one cycle of the pure forms of $y = \tan x$ and $y = \cot x$?
_____ What are the differences in the arcs between these two functions?_____

_____

c) Are there four identically shaped arc sections for one cycle of the pure form of $y = \csc x$ and $y = \sec x$?

_____

d) How many U-shaped branches make up one cycle of $y = \sec x$ or $y = \csc x$? _____

e) Are any of these new graphs sinusoidal? _____ Do any have amplitude? _____

3. Recall the effects that A, B, and C have on the graphs of the pure forms. Then graph at least one cycle of the following. Make sure to indicate the period (P), range, and label the asymptotes. Check your graph with a graphing utility.

a) $y = \tan(2x)$

$P = $ _____

Range = _____

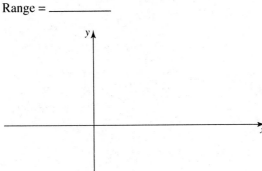

b) $y = \cot\left(x - \dfrac{\pi}{4}\right)$

$P = $ _____

Range = _____

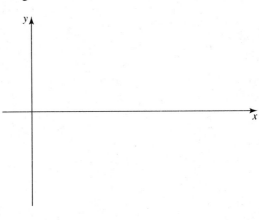

c) $y = -3\sec\left(\tfrac{1}{4}x\right)$

Guide Function: _____

$P = $ _____

Range: _____

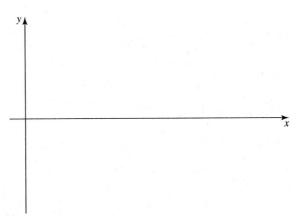

4. Find an equation of a circular function that represents the graph.

a) $y = $ _____

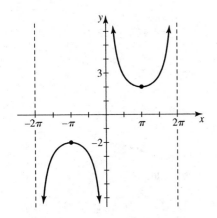

b) $y = $ _____

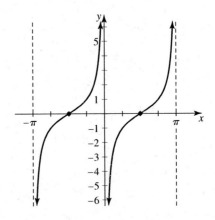

5. Find a second equation for 4(b). _____

Worksheet 2.5   Inverses of the Circular Functions

1–6 Rewrite each of the following without inverse notation. State the restricted interval for y. Then find the exact value for y.

1. $y = \arcsin\left(\dfrac{1}{2}\right)$ _____ $\leq y \leq$ _____

2. $y = \sin^{-1}\left(-\dfrac{1}{2}\right)$

3. $y = \arctan(1)$ _____ $< y <$ _____

4. $y = \tan^{-1}\left(-\sqrt{3}\right)$

5. $y = \arccos(1)$ _____ $\leq y \leq$ _____

6. $y = \cos^{-1}\left(-\dfrac{1}{\sqrt{2}}\right)$

7.   List the inverse functions that have similar ranges to that indicated on the unit circle.

a) _____

b) _____

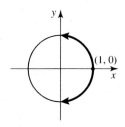

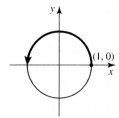

8–17 Simplify each expression without using a calculator.

8. $\arccos\left(\dfrac{1}{2}\right)$

9. $\tan^{-1}(0)$

10. $\csc^{-1}\left(\sqrt{2}\right)$

11. $\operatorname{arcsec}\left(-\dfrac{2}{\sqrt{3}}\right)$

12. $\sin^{-1}\left(-\dfrac{\sqrt{3}}{2}\right)$

13. $\text{arccot}\left(\sqrt{3}\right)$

---

14. $\arccos(\sin 0)$

15. $\text{arccsc}\left(\tan\dfrac{5\pi}{4}\right)$

---

16. $\sin\left(\cos^{-1}\dfrac{3}{5}\right)$

17. $\tan\left(\arcsin\dfrac{1}{4}\right)$

18–21 Find an approximation rounded to four decimal places for each expression.

18. $\arcsin(0.887501)$

19. $\tan^{-1}\left(-\dfrac{13}{12}\right)$

20. $\text{arcsec}\,(5.06)$

21. $\cos^{-1}(\sin 55.76)$

22. Solve for x: $18\sin 4x + 3 = 12$

23. What happens when you use your calculator

to find $\sin^{-1}\left(\dfrac{15}{7}\right)$?

Explain why there is no real solution for $\sin^{-1}\left(\dfrac{15}{7}\right)$.

24. a) Graph $y = \sin x$ on $\left[-\dfrac{\pi}{2}, \dfrac{\pi}{2}\right]$ and label the critical points.

   b) Graph $y = \sin^{-1} x$. (Hint: Interchange the x and y coordinates of the critical points from part (a). Your graph should be a reflection of $y = \sin x$ about the line $x = y$.)

a)

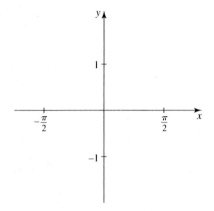

b)

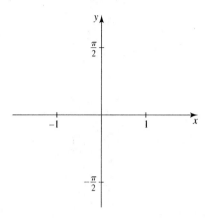

25. True or False?

_____ **a)** $\sin^{-1} x = \dfrac{1}{\sin x}$

_____ **b)** $\sec^{-1}\left(\dfrac{5}{3}\right) = \cos^{-1}\left(\dfrac{3}{5}\right)$

_____ **c)** The graph to the right is arccos $x = y$.

_____ **d)** A function must be one-to-one to have an inverse function.

_____ **e)** The definition of an inverse circular function includes the range.

_____ **f)** All calculators have keys for arcsec x, arccsc x, and arccot x.

_____ **g)** There is a real number answer for $\sin^{-1} 2$.

_____ **h)** The restricted domain for $y = \cos x$ $(0 \le x \le \pi)$ becomes the range of $y = \cos^{-1} x$ $(0 \le y \le \pi)$.

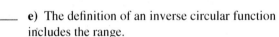

26. What is the equation of the inverse circular function that is graphed below?

$y = $ _____

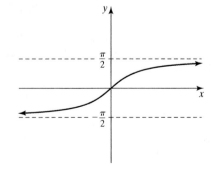

Chapter 3

The Trigonometric Functions

Worksheet 3.1 Angles and Their Measure

1–4 Convert the radian measure to degrees (or nearest degree). Draw the angle in standard position and determine the quadrant the angle is in.

1. $\dfrac{\pi}{4}$
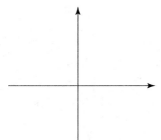

2. $\dfrac{5\pi}{6}$
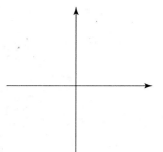

3. $\dfrac{31\pi}{16}$
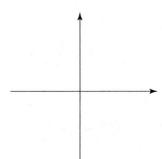

4. $-\dfrac{2\pi}{3}$
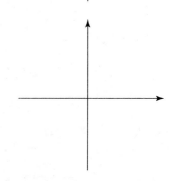

5–8 Draw the angle in standard position and state the quadrant the angle is in. Then convert the degree measure to radians. Leave the answer in terms of π.

5. $135°$
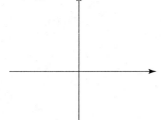

6. $-180°$
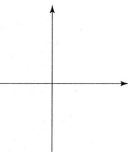

7. $55°$
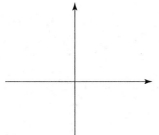

8. $-390°$

9–10   **a)** Find the smallest positive coterminal angle with the same measurement unit.
       b) Use this smallest positive coterminal angle to write a formula for all its coterminal angles.

9. $\dfrac{15\pi}{4}$ **10.** $-832°$

    a) _____   **a)** _____

    b) _____   **b)** _____

11. Find the length of the arc s, where $s = r\theta$, and θ is in radians.

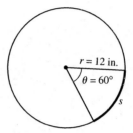

12. Fill in the blanks to make a true statement.

    Linear Velocity is: $v = \dfrac{s}{\rule{1cm}{0.4pt}} = \dfrac{\rule{1cm}{0.4pt} \cdot \theta}{\rule{1cm}{0.4pt} \quad \rule{1cm}{0.4pt}}$, where θ is in _____, and

    Angular Velocity is: $\omega = \dfrac{\rule{1cm}{0.4pt}}{t}$.

13. It takes 6 seconds for a point moving at constant velocity on a circle of radius 10 feet to go from point A to point B as it sweeps out an angle of 120°.

    a) Find the angular velocity of the point.   **b)** Find the linear velocity.

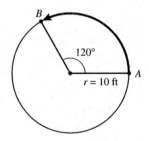

         $\omega = $ _____ $v = $ _____

14. True or False?

_____ **a)** $\pi = 180$

_____ **b)** On the unit circle, $s = \theta$.

_____ **c)** $\cos 13° = \sin 77°$

Worksheet 3.2 Trigonometric Functions

1. Complete the following definition of the trigonometric functions.

    If (x, y) is any point other than the origin on the terminal side of a standard position angle θ, and if $r = \sqrt{x^2 + y^2}$, the trigonometric functions of θ are defined as:

    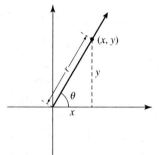

    $\cos \theta = \underline{\;\;\dfrac{x}{r}\;\;}$ $\qquad\qquad$ $\sec \theta = \underline{\hspace{2cm}}$

    $\sin \theta = \underline{\hspace{2cm}}$ $\qquad\qquad$ $\csc \theta = \underline{\hspace{2cm}}$

    $\tan \theta = \underline{\hspace{2cm}}$ $\qquad\qquad$ $\cot \theta = \underline{\hspace{2cm}}$

2. Find the six trigonometric function values for an angle in standard position if $(-12, -5)$ is on the terminal side of the angle. Draw the angle.

    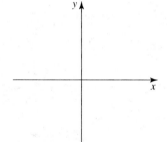

    $\cos \theta = \underline{\hspace{2cm}}$ $\qquad\qquad$ $\sec \theta = \underline{\hspace{2cm}}$

    $\sin \theta = \underline{\hspace{2cm}}$ $\qquad\qquad$ $\csc \theta = \underline{\hspace{2cm}}$

    $\tan \theta = \underline{\hspace{2cm}}$ $\qquad\qquad$ $\cot \theta = \underline{\hspace{2cm}}$

3. Find the quadrant that contains the terminal side of angle θ if $\tan \theta < 0$ and $\sec \theta > 0$.

    _____

4. Find the exact trigonometric values.

    a) If $\sin \alpha = -\dfrac{1}{2}$, α in QIV, find $\cos \alpha$ and $\tan \alpha$. $\qquad$ **b)** If $\cot \alpha = 2$, $180° < \alpha < 270°$, find $\cos \alpha$, $\sin \alpha$.

5. Complete the following table.

θ	$\theta°$	$\cos\theta$	$\sin\theta$	$\tan\theta$
0				
$\dfrac{\pi}{6}$				
$\dfrac{\pi}{4}$				
$\dfrac{\pi}{3}$				
$\dfrac{\pi}{2}$				
π				
$\dfrac{3\pi}{2}$				
2π				

6. Find the exact functional value.

    a) $\cos(-135°)$ **b)** $\csc 120°$ **c)** $\tan\dfrac{11\pi}{6}$

    d) $\arcsin\left(\dfrac{1}{2}\right)$, in degrees   **e)** $\tan^{-1}(-1)$, in radians   **f)** $\arccos\left(-\dfrac{\sqrt{3}}{2}\right)$, in degrees

7. Find an approximation for each of the following to four decimal places. Be careful to be in the correct mode.

    a) $\sin 35.6°$ **b)** $\cot(-121°10')$ **c)** $\sec\dfrac{\pi}{17}$

8. Find an approximate value to the nearest tenth of a degree.

    a) $\cos^{-1}(-0.752298)$ **b)** arccsc 12

9. Find the exact value for $\sin\left(\arccos\dfrac{12}{13}\right)$.

Worksheet 3.3   Right Triangles

1. Use α (alpha), β (beta), b and c to label the remaining angles and sides of the right triangle, where γ (gamma) $= 90°$.

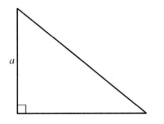

$$\alpha + \beta = \underline{\hspace{2cm}}°$$

$$a^2 + b^2 = \underline{\hspace{2cm}}$$

a) Which side is adjacent to α? _____   **b)** Which side is across from β? _____

c) Use the triangle above to complete the ratios with the appropriate names of sides (opposite, adjacent, or hypotenuse), then with the appropriate letters of the sides.

$\sin \alpha = \underline{\hspace{3cm}}$ $\sin \beta = \underline{\hspace{3cm}}$

$\cos \alpha = \underline{\hspace{3cm}}$ $\cos \beta = \underline{\hspace{3cm}}$

$\tan \alpha = \underline{\hspace{3cm}}$ $\tan \beta = \underline{\hspace{3cm}}$

2. **i)** Set up the trigonometric ratio to find x, where possible.
    ii) Use the trigonometric ratio to find x to the nearest tenth of a degree for angles, and nearest hundredth of a unit for sides.

a)

b)

c)

_____   _____   _____

d)

e)

_____   _____

3. Solve the right triangle ($\gamma = 90°$).

a) $a = 5, c = 7$

a		α	
b		β	
c		$\gamma = 90°$	

b) $\beta = 15°, a = 9.3$

a		α	
b		β	
c		$\gamma = 90°$	

4. Romeo and Juliet are looking for each other. From a height of 25 feet, Juliet spots the top of Romeo's head at a 35° angle of depression. Romeo is 5 feet 6 inches tall.

a) What angle of elevation should he use to see Juliet? _____

b) How far is he (to the nearest foot) from the castle?

5. A ship heads out on a course of bearing S 42° E and travels for 20 miles.

a) At that point, how far east is he from his starting position?

b) What is the bearing necessary to return him to his starting position?

Worksheet 3.4   Law of Sines

1. **a)** Complete the Law of Sines: $\dfrac{\sin \alpha}{\ \ } = \dfrac{}{b} = \dfrac{}{\ \ }$

   b) What given information about a triangle allows you to use the Law of Sines?

   _____

2–5 State the information you are given (i.e., AAS, SSA) and solve the triangle.

_____   **2.** $\alpha = 43°$, $\beta = 57°$, $a = 4.56$

$a =$	$\alpha =$
b	$\beta =$
c	$\gamma =$

_____   **3.** $a = 15$, $b = 25$, $\alpha = 67°$

$a =$	$\alpha =$
$b =$	β
c	$\gamma =$

_____   **4.** $c = 25$, $b = 10$, $\gamma = 42°$

a	α	a	α
$b =$	β	$b =$	β
$c =$	$\gamma =$	$c =$	$\gamma =$

_____ **5.** $a = 8, b = 7, \beta = 51°42'$

Solution 1		Solution 2	
$a =$	α	$a =$	α
$b =$	$\beta =$	$b =$	$\beta =$
c	γ	c	γ

6. Two fire trucks that are 4 miles apart are asked to respond to the same house fire. The bearing from truck A to the fire is 35°, while the bearing from truck B to the fire is 335°. Find the distance, to the nearest tenth of a mile, between the fire and each fire truck if truck A is directly west of truck B.

Worksheet 3.5   Law of Cosines

1. a) Complete the Law of Cosines.

$$c^2 = a^2 + b^2 - 2 \underline{\hspace{2cm}}$$

$$\underline{\hspace{2cm}} = a^2 + c^2 - 2ac \cos \underline{\hspace{2cm}}$$

$$a^2 = \underline{\hspace{2cm}} + \underline{\hspace{2cm}} - 2bc \cos \alpha$$

   b) What information about a triangle allows you to use the Law of Cosines?

   _____

2–3 State the information you are given (i.e., SSS, SAS) and solve the triangle.

_____ **2.** $a = 24, c = 32, \beta = 115°$

$a =$	α
b	$\beta =$
$c =$	γ

_____ **3.** $a = 18, b = 25, c = 12$

$a =$	α
$b =$	β
$c =$	γ

4. A surveyor is attempting to find the distance between two points R and B. The wetlands and trees are between these points and obstruct the surveyors view. So he determines that the distance RA is 156 feet, the distance AB is 190 feet, and angle RAB is $83°36'$. Find the distance between R and B.

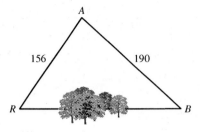

5. Fill in the blank to make a true statement.

a) We can solve a triangle if we are given the measurements of three of its parts, where one of these parts must be a _____.

b) If we know the measures of two _____ of a triangle, we immediately know the third.

c) If we are given two angles, neither of which is a right angle, and the included side of a triangle, we use the _____ to solve the triangle.

d) If we are given two sides and the included angle of a triangle, we use the _____ to solve the triangle. If the angle is a right angle, we use _____ to solve the triangle.

e) The ambiguous case is the result of being given two _____ and the _____.

f) If we are given three sides of a triangle, we use the _____ to solve the triangle.

g) To use trigonometric ratios the triangle must have a _____ angle.

h) Information about the parts of a triangle can lead to one solution, _____ or _____ solutions.

Chapter 4

Identities

Worksheet 4.1 Proving Identities

Complete the following basic identities.

1. $\cos^2 x + \sin^2 x =$ _____

2. $\tan x = \dfrac{\quad\quad}{\quad\quad}$

3. $\sec x = \dfrac{1}{\quad\quad}$, $\cos x = \dfrac{1}{\quad\quad}$

4. $\csc x = \dfrac{1}{\quad\quad}$, $\sin x = \dfrac{1}{\quad\quad}$,

5. $\cot x = \dfrac{1}{\quad\quad}$, $\tan x = \dfrac{1}{\quad\quad}$

6. $\cos(-x) =$ _____

7. $\sin(-x) =$ _____

8. $\tan(-x) =$ _____

9. Obtain four equivalent forms of the Pythagorean identity by subtracting $\cos^2 x$, $\sin^2 x$; and dividing by $\cos^2 x$, and $\sin^2 x$.

   $$\cos^2 x + \sin^2 x = 1 \longleftrightarrow \sin^2 x = 1 -$$

   a) _____

   b) _____

   c) _____

   d) _____

10. Simplify the following expressions.

    a) $\sec(-x)\cos x$

    b) $\cot\alpha\cos\alpha + \sin\alpha$

Prove the following identities.

11. $\tan x(\cos x + \cot x) = \sin x + 1$

12. $1 + \cos x = \dfrac{\sin^2 x}{1 - \cos x}$

13. $\tan^2 \beta = \dfrac{1 + \tan^2 \beta}{\csc^2 \beta}$

14. $\dfrac{1}{1 + \sin t} + \dfrac{1}{1 - \sin t} = 2 \sec^2 t$

15. Use a graphing utility to determine if the statement could be an identity. If so, prove it. If it cannot be an identity, find a counterexample by showing that the statement is not true for *one* value for which it is defined.

$$\tan x + \sin x = \sec x \csc x$$

Worksheet 4.2   Sum and Difference Identities for Cosine

1. Complete the following identities:

   a) $\cos(A + B) =$ _____

   b) $\cos(A - B) =$ _____

2. Find the exact value of $\cos 15°$.

3. Find the exact value of $\cos 13° \cos 32° - \sin 13° \sin 32°$.

4. Find the exact value of $\cos(A - B)$ if $\sin A = \dfrac{5}{13}$, $\cos B = -\dfrac{3}{5}$ and A, B are in QII.

$\cos A =$	$\cos B =$
$\sin A =$	$\sin B =$

5. Using the cosine sum or difference identity, rewrite each equation in a simpler form. Then determine which equation represents the graph below.

a) $y = \cos 6x \cos 4x - \sin 6x \sin 4x$ **b)** $y = \cos 3x \cos x + \sin 3x \sin x$

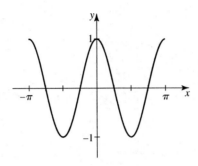

6. Prove the identity $\cos(90° + x) = -\sin x$.

7. Are the following statements true or false? Support your answers using the cosine sum or difference identity.

a) $\cos 7° \cos 38° - \sin 7° \sin 38° = \dfrac{\sqrt{2}}{2}$

b) $\cos \dfrac{\pi}{9} \cos \dfrac{5\pi}{9} + \sin \dfrac{\pi}{9} \sin \dfrac{5\pi}{9} = -\dfrac{1}{2}$

c) $\cos 100° \cos 80° + \sin 100° \sin 80° = -1$

Worksheet 4.3   Sum and Difference Identities for Sine and Tangent

1. Complete the following identities.

   a) $\sin(A + B) =$ _____

   b) $\sin(A - B) =$ _____

   c) $\tan(A + B) =$

   _____

   d) $\tan(A - B) =$

   _____

2. Find the exact functional value.

   a) $\sin \dfrac{\pi}{12}$ **b)** $\tan 75°$

   c) $\sin 78° \cos 18° - \cos 78° \sin 18°$ **d)** $\dfrac{\tan \dfrac{2\pi}{9} + \tan \dfrac{\pi}{9}}{1 - \tan \dfrac{2\pi}{9} \tan \dfrac{\pi}{9}}$

3. If $\cos A = \dfrac{1}{2}$, $\sin B = -\dfrac{3}{5}$ where A and B are in QIV, find:

a) $\sin(A + B)$

b) $\cos(A + B)$

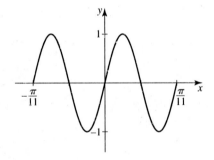

$\cos A =$	$\cos B =$
$\sin A =$	$\sin B =$

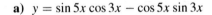

c) The quadrant for $(A + B)$

d) $\tan(A + B)$

4. Use the sum or difference identity of the sine to rewrite each equation in a simpler form. Then determine which equation represents the graph below.

a) $y = \sin 5x \cos 3x - \cos 5x \sin 3x$

b) $y = \sin 12x \cos 10x + \sin 12x \cos 10x$

c) $y = \sin 12x \cos 10x + \cos 12x \sin 10\,x$

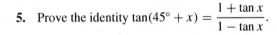

5. Prove the identity $\tan(45° + x) = \dfrac{1 + \tan x}{1 - \tan x}$.

Worksheet 4.4   Double-Angle Identities

1. Derive the double angle identities for sine, cosine and tangent.

   a) $\sin 2A = \sin(A + A) =$ _____

   _____

   b) $\cos 2A =$ _____

   _____

   _____

   _____

   c) $\tan 2A =$

   _____

2. The double angle identities allow you to rewrite functions of double angles as functions of a _____ angle.

3. If $\cos A = -\dfrac{5}{13}$, and A is in QII, find:

   a) $\sin 2A$ **b)** $\cos 2A$

   c) $\tan 2A$ **d)** The quadrant for $2A$

4. If $\cos 2x = -\dfrac{3}{4}$, and $2x$ is in QII $(90° < 2x < 180°)$, find $\cos x$.

5. Determine if the statements are true or false. If the statement is false, explain why.

a) $\sin 10x = 2\sin 5x \cos 5x$

b) $\cos 2x = 1 - 2\cos^2 x$

c) $\cos^2 4x - \sin^2 4x = \cos 8x$

d) $6\sin\dfrac{x}{2}\cos\dfrac{x}{2} = 3\sin x$

6. Which equation(s) represent the graph below?

a) $y = \cos 2x$

b) $y = \cos 3x \cos x + \sin 3x \sin x$

c) $y = \cos^2 x - \sin^2 x$

d) $y = 1 - 2\sin^2 x$

e) $y = \sin 2\left(x + \dfrac{\pi}{4}\right)$

f) $y = \sin 8x \cos 6x - \cos 8x \sin 6x$

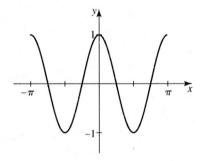

7. Prove the identity $\cos 2x + \sin^2 x = \cos^2 x$.

Worksheet 4.5   Half-Angle Identities

1. Solve the identities for the indicated function of a single angle A.

$\cos 2A = 1 - 2\sin^2 A$, solve for $\sin A$ $\cos 2A = 2\cos^2 A - 1$, solve for $\cos A$

2. Let $A = \dfrac{x}{2}$ and complete the *half-angle identities*

   a) $\sin \dfrac{x}{2} =$ _____

   b) $\cos \dfrac{x}{2} =$ _____

   c) $\tan \dfrac{x}{2} =$ _____

3. Use the half-angle identities to find the exact functional value.

   a) $\sin 15°$ b) $\tan 112.5°$

4. If $\sin A = \dfrac{7}{25}$, A is in QII, $\cos B = 1$, find the exact value.

a) $\sin \dfrac{A}{2}$

b) $\tan \dfrac{A}{2}$

cos A	cos B
sin A	sin B

c) $\cos 2A$

d) $\sin(A - B)$

5. Prove the following identity.

$$2 \sin^2 \dfrac{x}{2} + (\cos 2x \cos x + \sin 2x \sin x) = 1$$

Chapter 5

Trigonometric Equations

Worksheet 5.1 Solving Conditional Equations I

1–2 Solve each equation for exact values of x when **a)** $0 \leq x < 2\pi$ and **b)** $x \in \mathbb{R}$.

1. $\sin x = \dfrac{\sqrt{2}}{2}$

2. $\tan x = \sqrt{3}$

a) _____

a) _____

b) _____

b) _____

3–4 Solve each equation for x when **a)** $0° \leq x < 360°$ and **b)** $x \in A$.

3. $\sec x = -\dfrac{2\sqrt{3}}{3}$

4. $\csc x$ undefined

a) _____

a) _____

b) _____

b) _____

5–6 Solve each equation for **a)** $0° \leq x < 360°$ and **b)** $x \in A$. Approximate the solutions to the nearest tenth of a degree.

5. $\cos x = \dfrac{3}{4}$

6. $\sin x = -\dfrac{5}{13}$

a) ———————————————

b) ———————————————

———————————————

a) ———————————————

b) ———————————————

———————————————

Worksheet 5.2   Solving Trigonometric Conditional Equations II

1–4 Identify the following equations as having first-degree (linear) or second-degree (quadratic) form. Then solve the equations for exact values.

_____ **1. a)** $4u + 3 = 2u + 1$ **b)** $4\sin x + 3 = 2\sin x + 1, \quad 0 \le x < 2\pi$

_____ **2. a)** $2u^2 - 5u = -3$ **b)** $2\cos^2 x - 5\cos x = -3, \quad 0 \le x < 2\pi$

_____ **3. a)** $uv = \sqrt{3}\, v$ **b)** $\tan x \sin x = \sqrt{3}\sin x, \quad 0 \le x < 2\pi$

_____ **4. a)** $4u^2 = 3$ **b)** $4\cos^2 x = 3, \quad 0° \le x < 360°$

5–6 Solve the equations and approximate solutions to the nearest tenth of a degree where necessary.

5. a) $u^2 - 2 = 4u$ **b)** $\sin^2 x - 2 = 4\sin x, 0° \le x < 360°$

6. $3\tan^4 x = \tan^2 x, 0° \le x < 360°$

7. Find all solutions for x, $x \in \mathbb{R}$, in equation 1(b).

8. Use a graphing utility to find the solution(s) to the equation

$$\tan^2 x = \sin 2x, 0 \le x < 2\pi.$$

Worksheet 5.3   More Trigonometric Equations, Multiple-Angle Equations

1–4 Solve the equations for exact values of x, $0° \leq x < 360°$.

1. $5 \sin x - 2 \cos^2 x = 1$

2. $\cos x - 1 = \sin x$

3. $\sin x + \csc x = 2$

4. $\cos 2x + \sin^2 x = \dfrac{1}{4}$

5–6 Solve the following equations for exact values of x, $0 \leq x < 2\pi$.

5. $\tan 3x = 1$

6. $\sin 5x \cos 3x - \cos 5x \sin 3x = -\dfrac{1}{2}$

---

7. Find all solutions of x approximated to the nearest tenth of a degree.

   a) $2 \tan x + \cot x = 4$

---

8. Does $2 + 2 \tan^2 x = \sec x$ have a solution for x, $0 \leq x < 2\pi$?
Use a graphing utility to support your answer.

---

9. What are the strategies used in solving equations that *require* you to check solutions?

Worksheet 5.4 Parametric Equations

1–2 For the parametric equations do the following:

a) Eliminate the parameter to determine the rectangular equation.

b) Set up a table to determine the location of points on the curve for values of t.

c) Graph the motion and indicate the orientation. Label the start and end positions.

1. $x = \sin t$, $y = \cos t$

$$0 \leq t \leq 2\pi$$

t	$x = \sin t$	$y = \cos t$

Rectangular equation: _____

2. $x = 3\cos t$, $y = 4\sin t$, $0 \leq t \leq 2\pi$

t	$x = 3\cos t$	$y = 4\sin t$

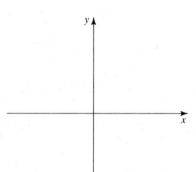

Rectangular equation: _____

3. $x = 2 - 2t$, $y = 4t$, $0 \leq t \leq 2$

t	$x = 2 - 2t$	$y = 4t$

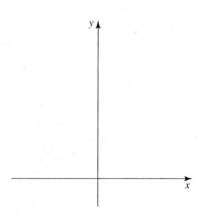

Rectangular equation: _____

4. Determine the value of t on the graph of the given parametric equations
$x = 2t, \quad y = 4t^2 + 1, \quad 0 \le t \le 10$.

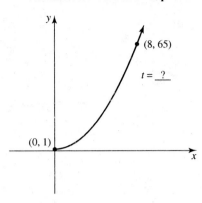

5.   a) Find two sets of parametric equations for $x + y = 1$.

(1)   (2)

b) What are the differences between the two sets?   (Do they describe a different path on the line, a different orientation, different motion, or different start and end points?)

6. If a projectile is fired with initial velocity v_o in the direction of angle α with the horizontal, then the motion (neglecting air resistance) is given by

$$x = (v_o \cos \alpha)t$$

$$y = -16t^2 + (v_o \sin \alpha)t$$

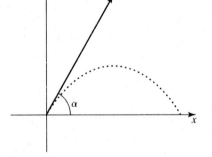

where t is measured in seconds, x and y are measured in feet.
Find the equations for
$\alpha = 60°$ and $v_o = 64$ feet per second (fps)

and sketch the motion by doing one of the following:
a) Complete a table and plot the points (x, y).

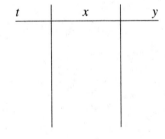

t	x	y

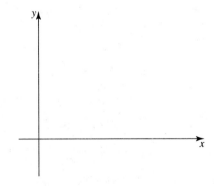

_or_ **b)**   Use a graphing utility in parametric mode.
(Determine a good viewing window.)

Chapter 6

Vectors, Polar Equations, and Complex Numbers

Worksheet 6.1   Geometric Vectors and Applications

1. For vectors **u**, **v** and **w** fill in the blanks to make a true statement.

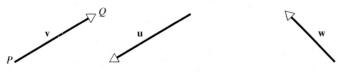

The initial point of **v** is _____, and Q is called the _____ point. Using the initial and ter-

minal point, the vector **v** can also be denoted as _____. Any vector has _____ and

direction. Two vectors are equivalent if they have the same _____ and _____.

If **u** has the same magnitude as **v** but opposite direction, we then write _____ = _____.

2. By sketching vectors equivalent to **v** and **w** (above), sketch the scalar multiple.

   a) 2**v**   **b)**   −3**w**

3. By sketching vectors equivalent to **v** and **w** (above) use the indicated method to find the following.

   a) **v** + **w** (triangle)   **b)**   2**v** − 3**w** (parallelogram)

4. Two forces of 8 and 12 pounds with an angle of 75° between them act on a point. Find the magnitude of the resultant to the nearest tenth of a pound, and the angle the resultant makes with the 12 pound force to the nearest tenth of a degree.

5. An airplane is headed 123° with an air speed of 310 mph with a wind of 40 mph on a bearing of 200°. Find the ground speed to the nearest mph, and the true course of the airplane to the nearest degree.

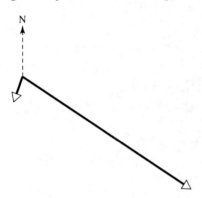

6. John is considering lifting weights at FITLIFE GYM. The 120 pound weight is lying on the bench which is on an incline of 45°. To the nearest tenth of a pound, what force is necessary to keep the weight from rolling down the bench?

Worksheet 6.2 Algebraic Vectors

1. Consider vectors $\mathbf{v} = 2\mathbf{i} + 6\mathbf{j}$ and $\mathbf{w} = -3\mathbf{i} + 2\mathbf{j}$.

    a) Draw each vector in standard position.

    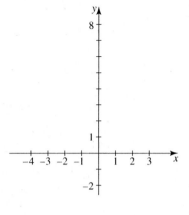

    b) Sketch the resultant and find the $\mathbf{i}$, $\mathbf{j}$ form of $\mathbf{v} + \mathbf{w}$.

    c) Find $\mathbf{w} - 2\mathbf{v}$.   **d)** Find $|\mathbf{w} - 2\mathbf{v}|$.

2. If $|\mathbf{u}| = 8$ and the direction angle θ of $\mathbf{u}$ is $30°$, find the horizontal and vertical components and then the component form of $\mathbf{u}$.

    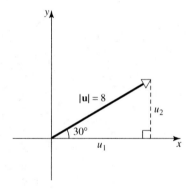

3. Complete the following definition of **Dot Product (Inner Product, Scalar Product).**
    The **dot product** $\mathbf{v} \cdot \mathbf{w}$ of vectors $\mathbf{v} = v_1\mathbf{i} + v_2\mathbf{j}$ and $\mathbf{w} = w_1\mathbf{i} + w_2\mathbf{j}$ is defined to be

    $\mathbf{v} \cdot \mathbf{w} =$ _____. The result of the dot product is a _____
    – ***not*** a vector.

4. Find the dot product of $\mathbf{v} = 2\mathbf{i} + 6\mathbf{j}$ and $\mathbf{w} = -3\mathbf{i} + 2\mathbf{j}$.

5. *Another form* of the dot product is

$$\mathbf{v} \cdot \mathbf{w} = |\mathbf{v}||\mathbf{w}| \cos \theta,$$

where θ is the angle between $\mathbf{v}$ and $\mathbf{w}$. Use this form to find, to the nearest tenth of a degree, the angle θ between the vectors $\mathbf{v} = 2\mathbf{i} + 6\mathbf{j}$ and $\mathbf{w} = -3\mathbf{i} + 2\mathbf{j}$.

6. Find the component of $\mathbf{v}$ along $\mathbf{w}$ $\left(\text{comp}_\mathbf{w} \mathbf{v} = \dfrac{\mathbf{v} \cdot \mathbf{w}}{|\mathbf{w}|}\right)$ if $\mathbf{v} = 4\mathbf{i} + 6\mathbf{j}$, and $\mathbf{w} = 5\mathbf{i} - \mathbf{j}$ and demonstrate your answer graphically.

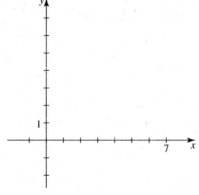

7. Find the equivalent standard position vector for $\overrightarrow{PQ}$.

$$\overrightarrow{PQ} = \underline{\hspace{2cm}} \mathbf{i} + \underline{\hspace{2cm}} \mathbf{j}$$

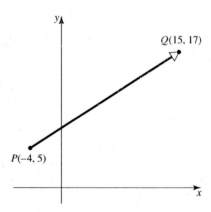

8. Find the work done ($W = \mathbf{F} \cdot \mathbf{D}$), to the nearest ft · lb, by pulling a 42 pound box across the floor for 20 feet using a rope on an angle of 50° with the floor.

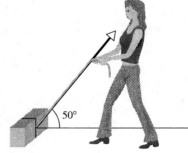

Worksheet 6.3   Polar Coordinates

1. Graph the polar coordinates and find two other sets of polar coordinates for the point.

    a) $\left(4, \dfrac{\pi}{3}\right)$ **b)** $(-3, 120°)$

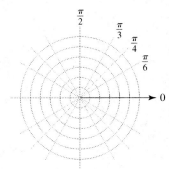   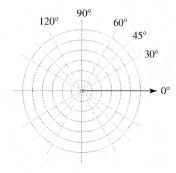

2. Find the rectangular coordinates for the given polar coordinates.

    a) $\left(4, \dfrac{\pi}{3}\right)$ **b)** $(-3, 120°)$

3. Find polar coordinates for the rectangular coordinates $(-1, -1)$.

4. Complete the chart by converting the equation to the missing form.

Polar equation	Rectangular equation
	$x^2 + y^2 = 9$
$r = 2\sec\theta$	

5. Graph $r = \cos\theta$.

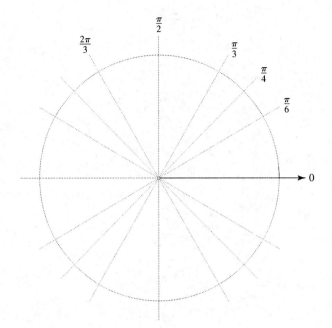

6. Graph the following with a graphing utility in polar mode.

    a) $r = 2$

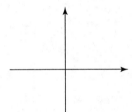

    b) $r = -\cos\theta$

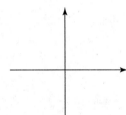

    c) $r = \sin\theta$

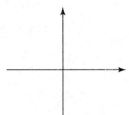

    d) $r = \sec\theta$

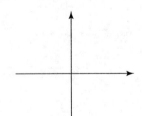

    e) $r = 1 + \cos\theta$

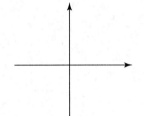

    f) $r = 1 + \sin\theta$

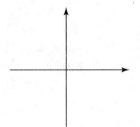

g) $r = 1 - \sin\theta$

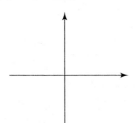

h) $r = 1 + 2\cos\theta$

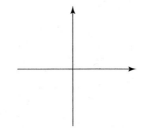

i) $r = 2 + \cos\theta$

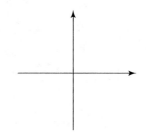

j) $r = \cos 2\theta$

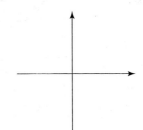

k) $r = \sin 3\theta$

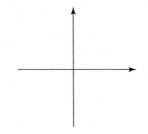

Worksheet 6.4   Complex Numbers

1. Fill in the blanks to make true statements.
    The number that is the square root of -1 is called _____, or $\sqrt{-1} =$ _____.

    A number of the form $a + bi$ is called a _____ number, where $i^2 =$ _____, $a, b \in \mathbb{R}$.

2. Perform the indicated operations with the complex numbers. Leave your answer in $a + bi$ form.

    a) $(9 - 11i) - (4 - 6i)$

    b) $(5 - 2i)(7 + 3i)$

    c) $\sqrt{-6}\,\sqrt{-24}$

    d) $\sqrt{-3}\left(9 + \sqrt{12}\right)$

    e) $\dfrac{3i}{(2 - i)}$

    f) i^{27}

3. **a)** Graph the complex number $6 - 3i$ in the complex plane.

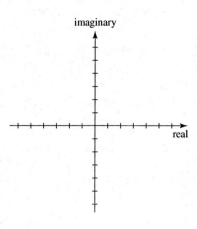

b) Find $|6 - 3i|$, the modulus of $6 - 3i$.

Worksheet 6.5 Trigonometric Form For Complex Numbers

1. Fill in the blanks to make true statements.

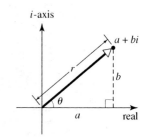

Angle θ is called the _____ of the complex number $a + bi$.

For complex numbers $a + bi$ with modulus $r\,(r \geq 0)$ and argument θ, the **trigonometric form** is given by

$$a + bi = (r\text{_____}) + (\text{_____}\sin\theta)i.$$

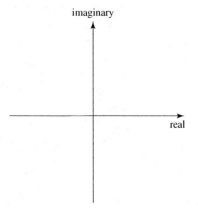

2. Graph $1 + i$ and express it in trigonometric form.

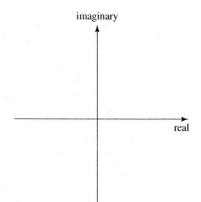

3. Graph the complex number whose trigonometric form is $6(\cos 150° + i \sin 150°)$ and express it in $a + bi$ form.

4. Perform the indicated operations and leave the answer in $a + bi$ form.

a) $5(\cos 12° + i \sin 12°) \cdot 3(\cos 213° + i \sin 213°)$

b) $\dfrac{20(\cos 157° + i \sin 157°)}{4(\cos 37° + i \sin 37°)}$

c) $\left(\sqrt{2} - i\sqrt{2}\right)^4$ using DeMoivre's Theorem

5. Find the two square roots of $16(\cos 120° + i \sin 120°)$ and leave the answers in trigonometric form.

Appendix Exercises

Appendix Exercises

A.1 Real Number System

1–6 State the property of the real numbers demonstrated by the statement.

1. $6 + 7 = 7 + 6$

2. $5(x + 2) = 5x + 10$

3. $9 + (2 + y) = (9 + 2) + y$

4. $12 \cdot 2 = 2 \cdot 12$

5. $(81 - t)2 = 162 - 2t$

6. $2 \cdot (5 \cdot 7) = (2 \cdot 5) \cdot 7$

7–16 Simplify the expressions.

7. $4^2 \div 2 + 3(5 - 4)$

8. $1 - \left(\dfrac{1}{2}\right)^2$

9. $\sqrt{8^2 + 6^2}$

10. $\left|\dfrac{-3}{2}\right| - \dfrac{6(4 - 5)}{5}$

11. $\dfrac{1 + \dfrac{1}{2}}{2}$

12. $8^2 + 5^2 - 2 \cdot 8 \cdot 5 \cdot \dfrac{1}{2}$

13. $\dfrac{9^2 - 4^2 - 6^2}{-2(4)(6)}$

14. $-33.9 \div 10 + |0.61 - 8|$

15. $2\left(-\dfrac{12}{13}\right)\left(\dfrac{5}{13}\right)$

16. $\dfrac{1 - \dfrac{3}{5}}{\dfrac{1}{2}}$

17–18 Find the distance d between the two points on the real number line.

17. $25, -17$

18. $-9.5, -2.7$

A.2 Exponents and Radicals

1–6 Simplify the expressions and eliminate any negative exponent(s).

1. $(-2)^0 - 100^0$

2. $3^4 3^{-2} + \dfrac{3^2}{2^{-2}}$

3. $\left(\dfrac{1}{7}\right)^{-3} \left(\dfrac{7}{5}\right)^{-2}$

4. $\dfrac{4x^3 y^7}{16x y^{-2}}$

5. $\left(\dfrac{a^2 b^{-3}}{x^{-1} b^4}\right)^2 \left(\dfrac{a^{-3} b}{x^3}\right)$

6. $\dfrac{(a^3 b^2)^4 (ab^4)^{-2}}{a^2 b}$

7–14 Simplify each radical expression. Assume all variables represent positive numbers.

7. $\sqrt{\dfrac{4}{9}}$

8. $\sqrt{2}\sqrt{6}$

9. $3\sqrt{8} - \sqrt{32}$

10. $\dfrac{1}{\sqrt{3}}$

11. $\sqrt[3]{56}$

12. $\dfrac{1}{\left(1 + \sqrt{2}\right)}$

13. $\dfrac{\sqrt{3} + 1}{\sqrt{3} - 1}$

14. $\sqrt{\dfrac{2}{3}}$

15. $\sqrt[4]{x^5 y^8}$

16. $\sqrt[3]{a^2 b}\ \sqrt[3]{ab^5}$

17–20 Write each expression in radical form. Then, simplify the radical expression.

17. $x^{\frac{3}{2}}$

18. $a^{-\frac{3}{2}}$

19. $z^{-\frac{1}{5}}$

20. $5y^{\frac{3}{4}}$

21–26 Simplify the expression and eliminate any negative exponent(s). Assume all variables represent positive numbers.

21. $\left(\dfrac{25}{16}\right)^{-\frac{1}{2}}$

22. $(-32)^{\frac{3}{5}}$

23. $\left(\dfrac{1 + \dfrac{4}{5}}{2}\right)^{\frac{1}{2}}$

24. $\left(\dfrac{1 - \dfrac{8}{9}}{9}\right)^{-\frac{1}{2}}$

25. $\left(\dfrac{x^6 y}{y^4}\right)^{\frac{1}{2}}$

26. $(4b)^{\frac{1}{2}} (8b^3)^{\frac{2}{3}}$

A.3 Algebraic Expressions

1–8 Simplify each expression.

1. $x^5 + 3x - 5 + 8x^5 - 4x^2 - 3x + 10$

2. $(4a - 2b + c) - (a - 3b + 2c)$

3. $\left(-3x^2y^3z\right)\left(-x^4z^2\right)$

4. $-3s(5s - 6)$

5. $2x^2(x^2 - 3x - 2)$

6. $(t + 2)(t - 4)$

7. $(a + b)^2$

8. $(2x - 5)^2$

9–16 Factor each expression.

9. $9x + 36$

10. $25x^2 - 36y^2$

11. $4x^2 - 8x + 2$

12. $3x^2 - 3$

13. $k^2 - 4k + 3$

14. $3y^2 - 2y - 1$

15. $uv - v^2$

16. $ax + bx - ay - by$

17–24 Simplify each rational expression.

17. $\dfrac{x^2 - 1}{x - 1}$

18. $\dfrac{2\sqrt{2} - 4x}{2}$

19. $\dfrac{4}{4 - \sqrt{2}}$

20. $\sqrt{\dfrac{1 + \frac{1}{2}}{2}}$

21. $\dfrac{x^2 - 5x - 14}{7 - x}$

22. $\dfrac{1}{1 - a} + \dfrac{1}{1 + a}$

23. $-\sqrt{\dfrac{1 - \frac{\sqrt{3}}{2}}{2}}$

24. $\dfrac{x + \frac{1}{\sqrt{3}}}{1 - (x)\left(\frac{1}{\sqrt{3}}\right)}$

A.4 Solving Equations

1–22 Solve the following equations.

1. $3x + 2 = 4(x - 6)$

2. $ab = a$

3. $4x^2 = 1$

4. $25y^2 = 9$

5. $10x^2 - 13x = -3$

6. $c^2 = 5^2 + 6^2 - 2(5)(6)\left(\dfrac{1}{2}\right)$

7. $\dfrac{x}{5} = \dfrac{3}{7}$

8. $\dfrac{21}{4} = \dfrac{8}{x}$

9. $4 + 3x = \dfrac{14}{2x}$

10. $10^2 = 5^2 + x^2 - 10x$

11. $x^2 - 2 = 1$

12. $25 = -16t^2 + 40t$

13. $2xy - \sqrt{3}y = 0$

14. $4y^2 + 33y = 27$

15. $3x - \dfrac{1}{x} = 1$

16. $\sqrt{\dfrac{1+x}{2}} + x = 0$

17. $\sqrt{\dfrac{1-t}{2}} = \sqrt{\dfrac{1}{2} - t}$

18. $1 - 2r^2 = 1 - 2r$

19. $x + \dfrac{1}{x} + 2 = 0$

20. $4x^2 = 4x$

21. $\dfrac{1}{x} + \dfrac{1}{x-3} = \dfrac{9}{x^2 - 3x}$

22. $\dfrac{3x}{x} = 3$

A.5 The Coordinate Plane

1–6 Plot the points and state the quadrant that they are in.

1. $(6, -5)$

2. $(9, 2)$

3. $(-2, -7)$

4. $(0, 2)$

5. $(-3, 1)$

6. $(-8, 0)$

7–14 Graph the equation in the xy-coordinate plane and indicate any intercepts.

7. $2x + y = 9$

8. $y = \dfrac{1}{2}x + 6$

9. $y = 4x^2 - 2$

10. $x^2 + y^2 = 1$

11. $16x^2 + 9y^2 = 144$

12. $y = -x^2 + 5$

13. $4x^2 + 4y^2 = 16$

14. $x^2 + 25y^2 = 25$

15–18 Find the distance between P and Q.

15. $P(5, -4),\ Q(8, 0)$

16. $P\left(\sqrt{2}, 5\right),\ Q\left(3\sqrt{2}, 4\right)$

17. $P\left(\dfrac{\sqrt{3}}{2}, \dfrac{1}{2}\right),\ Q(0, 1)$

18. $P(3, 8),\ Q(-2, 13)$

A.6 Relations and Functions

1–4 If $f(x) = -4.9x^2 + 18x + 2$, find the following.

1. $f(0)$

2. $f(2)$

3. $f(a)$

4. $f(a + b)$

5–8 Determine whether the graphs represent functions.

5.

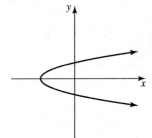

6.

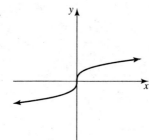

7.

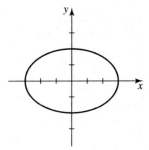

8.

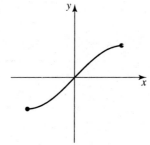

9–12 Determine by their graphs whether the functions are one-to-one functions.

9.

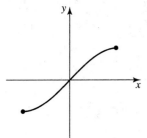

10.

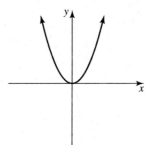

11.

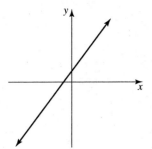

12.

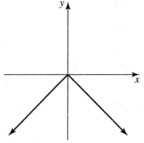

13–14 Find the inverse of the one-to-one function.

13. $f(x) = 3x + 4$

14. $g(x) = \dfrac{1}{2x}$

15–16 Find the graph of the inverse of the one-to-one function.

15.

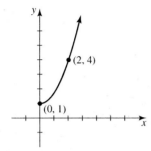

16.

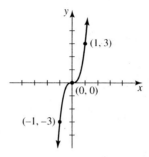

17–20 Determine whether the graphs are symmetric with respect to the y-axis, x-axis, and the origin.

17.

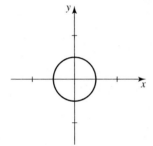

18.

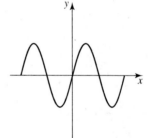

19.

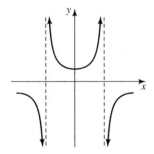

20.

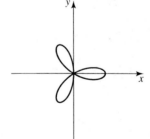

Selected Solutions to
Text Exercises

Chapter 1   Trigonometry Student's Solutions Manual

Exercise Set 1.2, p. 13

1. A portion of the real (a) <u>number line</u> was wrapped around the (b) <u>unit</u> circle to create an arc whose length and (c) <u>direction</u> can be represented by any real number t. Arcs, with initial point (d) <u>(1, 0)</u>, that are wrapped (e) <u>counterclockwise</u> are considered to be positive, and those that are wrapped clockwise are considered to be (f) <u>negative</u>.

3. The functional value sine t is defined to be the (a) <u>y-coordinate</u> at the terminal point of an arc (b) <u>t</u> whose initial point is (1, 0) on the unit circle. The largest value for sin t is (c) <u>1</u> and the smallest value for sin t is (d) <u>−1</u>.

5. The Pythagorean identity is ((a)<u>cos t</u>)^2 + (sin t)^2 = 1, or cos^2 t + (b)<u>sin^2 t</u> = 1.

7. *For reference, see page 6 of the text.*

7. **a.** 0   **b.** $\dfrac{\pi}{6}$ **c.** $\dfrac{\pi}{4}$ **d.** $\dfrac{\pi}{3}$

     e. $\dfrac{\pi}{2}$ **f.** π **g.** $\dfrac{3\pi}{2}$

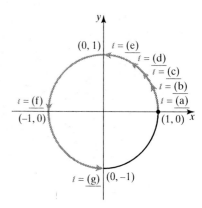

9. Using the common denominator 6, the terminal point of the arc is in QIII since $\dfrac{6\pi}{6} < \dfrac{7\pi}{6} < \dfrac{9\pi}{6}, \Rightarrow \pi < \dfrac{7\pi}{6} < \dfrac{3\pi}{2}$.

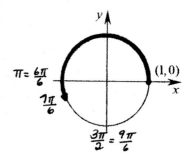

11. Using the common denominator 6, and $\dfrac{4\pi}{3} = \dfrac{8\pi}{6}$, the terminal point of the arc is in QIII since $\dfrac{6\pi}{6} < \dfrac{8\pi}{6} < \dfrac{9\pi}{6}, \Rightarrow \pi < \dfrac{4\pi}{3} < \dfrac{3\pi}{2}$.

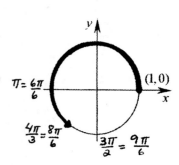

13. Using the common denominator 4, the terminal point of the arc is in QIV

since $\dfrac{6\pi}{4} < \dfrac{7\pi}{4} < \dfrac{8\pi}{4}, \Rightarrow \dfrac{3\pi}{2} < \dfrac{7\pi}{4} < 2\pi$.

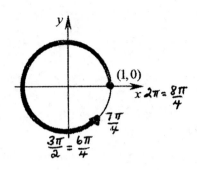

15. Since $\dfrac{17\pi}{6}$ is larger than one wrap, $\left(2\pi = \dfrac{12\pi}{6}\right)$, we subtract multiples

of 2π until we obtain an arc within one wrap: $\dfrac{17\pi}{6} - \dfrac{12\pi}{6} = \dfrac{5\pi}{6}$. Using

the common denominator 6, the terminal point of the arc is in QII since

$\dfrac{3\pi}{6} < \dfrac{5\pi}{6} < \dfrac{6\pi}{6}, \Rightarrow \dfrac{\pi}{2} < \dfrac{5\pi}{6} < \pi$.

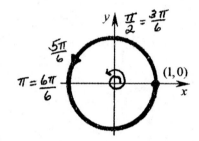

17. Using the common denominator 6, and $-\dfrac{5\pi}{3} = -\dfrac{10\pi}{6}$ the terminal point of

the arc is in QI since $-\dfrac{12\pi}{6} < -\dfrac{10\pi}{6} < -\dfrac{9\pi}{6}, \Rightarrow -2\pi < -\dfrac{5\pi}{3} < -\dfrac{3\pi}{2}$.

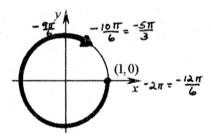

19. Using the common denominator 4, the terminal point of the arc is in QII

since $-\dfrac{6\pi}{4} < -\dfrac{5\pi}{4} < -\dfrac{4\pi}{4}, \Rightarrow -\dfrac{3\pi}{2} < -\dfrac{5\pi}{4} < -\pi$.

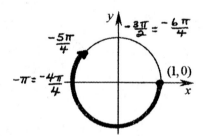

21. Since $-\dfrac{15\pi}{4}$ is larger than one wrap, $\left(-2\pi = -\dfrac{8\pi}{4}\right)$, we subtract multi-

ples of -2π until we obtain an arc within one wrap: $-\dfrac{15\pi}{4} + \dfrac{8\pi}{4} = -\dfrac{7\pi}{4}$.

Using the common denominator 4, the terminal point of the arc is in QI

since $-\dfrac{8\pi}{4} < -\dfrac{7\pi}{4} < -\dfrac{6\pi}{4}, \Rightarrow -2\pi < -\dfrac{7\pi}{4} < -\dfrac{3\pi}{2}$.

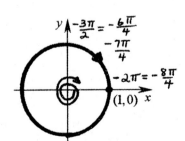

23. Since 2 is not in terms of π, we use $\pi \approx 3.14$ to locate the terminal point of the arc in QII since $1.57 < 2 < 3.14,\ \Rightarrow \dfrac{\pi}{2} < 2 < \pi$.

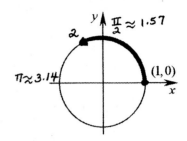

25. Since 7.1 is not in terms of π, we use $\pi \approx 3.14$. The arc is also more than one wrap, $2\pi \approx 6.28$, so we subtract multiples of 2π until we obtain an arc within one wrap: $7.1 - 2\pi \approx 7.1 - 6.28 = 0.82$. The terminal point of the arc is in QI since $0 < 0.82 < 1.57,\ \Rightarrow 0 < 0.82 < \dfrac{\pi}{2}$.

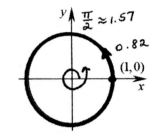

27. Since -1.82 is not in terms of π, we use $-\pi \approx -3.14$ to locate the terminal point of the arc in QIII since $-3.14 < -1.82 < -1.57$,

$$\Rightarrow -\pi < -1.82 < -\frac{\pi}{2}.$$

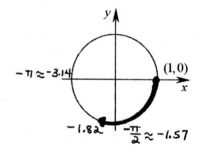

29. Since -6.5 is not in terms of π, we use $-\pi \approx -3.14$. The are is also more than one wrap, $-2\pi \approx -6.28$, so we subtract multiples of -2π until we obtain an arc within one wrap: $-6.5 + 2\pi \approx -6.5 + 6.28 = -0.22$. The terminal point of the arc is in QIV since $-1.57 < -0.22 < 0$,

$$\Rightarrow -\frac{\pi}{2} < -0.22 < 0.$$

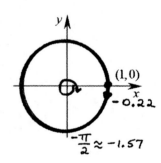

31. For $\cos t > 0$ and $\sin t > 0$, we have $(\cos t, \sin t) = (+, +)$, which is in QI.

33. For $\sin t < 0$ and $\cos t > 0$, we have $(\cos t, \sin t) = (+, -)$, which is in QIV.

35, 37, 39, 41, and 43. *Given one functional value (either* sin *t or* cos *t) and the quadrant that contains the arc, we use the Pythagorean identity*

$$\cos^2 t + \sin^2 t = 1, \quad or \quad (\cos\ t)^2 + (\sin\ t)^2 = 1,$$

to find the other functional value.

35. $\sin t = \dfrac{5}{13}, \cos t > 0$

$$(\cos t)^2 + (\sin t)^2 = 1$$

$$(\cos t)^2 + \left(\frac{5}{13}\right)^2 = 1$$

$$(\cos t)^2 + \frac{25}{169} = 1$$

$$(\cos t)^2 = 1 - \frac{25}{169} = \frac{169}{169} - \frac{25}{169} = \frac{144}{169}$$

$$\cos t = \pm\sqrt{\frac{144}{169}} = \pm\frac{12}{13}$$

Since $\cos t > 0$, $\cos t = \dfrac{12}{13}$.

37. $\cos t = -\dfrac{\sqrt{2}}{2}, \sin t < 0$

$$(\cos t)^2 + (\sin t)^2 = 1$$

$$\left(-\frac{\sqrt{2}}{2}\right)^2 + (\sin t)^2 = 1$$

$$\frac{2}{4} + (\sin t)^2 = 1$$

$$(\sin t)^2 = 1 - \frac{2}{4} = \frac{2}{2} - \frac{1}{2} = \frac{1}{2}$$

$$\sin t = \pm\sqrt{\frac{1}{2}} = \pm\frac{1}{\sqrt{2}}$$

Since $\sin t < 0$, $\sin t = -\dfrac{1}{\sqrt{2}} = -\dfrac{\sqrt{2}}{2}$.

39. **a.** Since $\dfrac{\pi}{2} < t < \pi$, the quadrant that contains t is QII.

b. $(\cos t)^2 + (\sin t)^2 = 1$

$$\left(-\frac{8}{17}\right)^2 + (\sin t)^2 = 1$$

$$\frac{64}{289} + (\sin t)^2 = 1$$

$$(\sin t)^2 = 1 - \frac{64}{289} = \frac{289}{289} - \frac{64}{289} = \frac{225}{289}$$

$$\sin t = \pm\sqrt{\frac{225}{289}} = \pm\frac{15}{17}$$

Since t is in QII, $\sin t > 0$, so $\sin t = \dfrac{15}{17}$.

c. $\dfrac{1}{\cos t} = \dfrac{1}{\left(-\dfrac{8}{17}\right)} = -\dfrac{17}{8}$

d. $\dfrac{1}{\sin t} = \dfrac{1}{\left(\dfrac{15}{17}\right)} = \dfrac{17}{15}$

e. $\dfrac{\sin t}{\cos t} = \dfrac{\left(\dfrac{15}{17}\right)}{\left(-\dfrac{8}{17}\right)} = \left(\dfrac{15}{\cancel{17}}\right)\left(-\dfrac{\cancel{17}}{8}\right) = -\dfrac{15}{8}$

f. $\dfrac{\cos t}{\sin t} = \dfrac{\left(-\dfrac{8}{17}\right)}{\left(\dfrac{15}{17}\right)} = \left(-\dfrac{8}{\cancel{17}}\right)\left(\dfrac{\cancel{17}}{15}\right) = -\dfrac{8}{15}$

41. a. Since $\sin t = -\dfrac{\sqrt{3}}{2}$, or $\sin t < 0$, and $\cos t > 0$, the quadrant that contains t is QIV.

b.
$$(\cos t)^2 + (\sin t)^2 = 1$$
$$(\cos t)^2 + \left(-\dfrac{\sqrt{3}}{2}\right)^2 = 1$$
$$(\cos t)^2 + \dfrac{3}{4} = 1$$
$$(\cos t)^2 = 1 - \dfrac{3}{4} = \dfrac{4-3}{4} = \dfrac{1}{4}$$
$$\cos t = \pm\sqrt{\dfrac{1}{4}} = \pm\dfrac{1}{2}$$

Since $\cos t > 0$, $\cos t = \dfrac{1}{2}$.

c. $\dfrac{1}{\cos t} = \dfrac{1}{\left(\dfrac{1}{2}\right)} = 1 \cdot \dfrac{2}{1} = 2$

d. $\dfrac{1}{\sin t} = \dfrac{1}{\left(-\dfrac{\sqrt{3}}{2}\right)} = -\dfrac{2}{\sqrt{3}} = \left(-\dfrac{2}{\sqrt{3}}\right)\left(\dfrac{\sqrt{3}}{\sqrt{3}}\right) = -\dfrac{2\sqrt{3}}{3}$

e. $\dfrac{\sin t}{\cos t} = \dfrac{\left(-\dfrac{\sqrt{3}}{2}\right)}{\left(\dfrac{1}{2}\right)} = \left(-\dfrac{\sqrt{3}}{\cancel{2}}\right)\left(\dfrac{\cancel{2}}{1}\right) = -\sqrt{3}$

f. $\dfrac{\cos t}{\sin t} = \dfrac{\left(\dfrac{1}{2}\right)}{\left(-\dfrac{\sqrt{3}}{2}\right)} = \left(\dfrac{1}{\cancel{2}}\right)\left(-\dfrac{\cancel{2}}{\sqrt{3}}\right) = -\dfrac{1}{\sqrt{3}} = -\dfrac{\sqrt{3}}{3}$

43.
$$(\cos t)^2 + (\sin t)^2 = 1$$
$$(x)^2 + (\sin t)^2 = 1$$
$$(\sin t)^2 = 1 - x^2$$
$$\sin t = \pm\sqrt{1 - x^2}$$
Since $\sin t < 0$, $\sin t = -\sqrt{1 - x^2}$.

Exercise Set 1.3, p. 23

1. **a.** Since $\cos t = \dfrac{\sqrt{2}}{2}$, $t = \dfrac{\pi}{4}$.

b. $\sin t = \sin \dfrac{\pi}{4} = \dfrac{\sqrt{2}}{2}$

3. **a.** $\sin t = \sin \dfrac{3\pi}{2} = -1$

b. $\cos t = \cos \dfrac{3\pi}{2} = 0$

5.

x	$\cos x$
0	1
$\dfrac{\pi}{4}$	$\dfrac{1}{\sqrt{2}} = \dfrac{\sqrt{2}}{2}$
π	-1
$\dfrac{\pi}{3}$	$\dfrac{1}{2}$
$\dfrac{3\pi}{2}$	0
$\dfrac{\pi}{2}$	0
$\dfrac{\pi}{6}$	$\dfrac{\sqrt{3}}{2}$
2π	1

7. $\cos^2 \dfrac{\pi}{6} = \left(\cos \dfrac{\pi}{6} \right)^2 = \left(\dfrac{\sqrt{3}}{2} \right)^2 = \dfrac{3}{4}$

9. $\dfrac{\sin \left(\dfrac{2\pi}{4} - \dfrac{\pi}{4} \right)}{\cos 0 - \cos \pi} = \dfrac{\sin \dfrac{\pi}{4}}{\cos 0 - \cos \pi} = \dfrac{\left(\dfrac{\sqrt{2}}{2} \right)}{1 - (-1)} = \dfrac{\left(\dfrac{\sqrt{2}}{2} \right)}{2} = \dfrac{\sqrt{2}}{4}$

11. $3 \sin \dfrac{\pi}{2} - \sin \dfrac{\pi}{3} = 3(1) - \dfrac{\sqrt{3}}{2} = \dfrac{6}{2} - \dfrac{\sqrt{3}}{2} = \dfrac{6 - \sqrt{3}}{2}$

13. $\left(\cos \dfrac{\pi}{3} \right)^2 + \sin^2 \dfrac{\pi}{3} =$

$\left(\cos \dfrac{\pi}{3} \right)^2 + \left(\sin \dfrac{\pi}{3} \right)^2 = \left(\dfrac{1}{2} \right)^2 + \left(\dfrac{\sqrt{3}}{2} \right)^2 = \dfrac{1}{4} + \dfrac{3}{4} = \dfrac{4}{4} = 1$

15. $\dfrac{\sin \dfrac{\pi}{6}}{\cos \dfrac{\pi}{6}} = \dfrac{\left(\dfrac{1}{2} \right)}{\left(\dfrac{\sqrt{3}}{2} \right)} = \dfrac{1}{\cancel{2}} \cdot \dfrac{\cancel{2}}{\sqrt{3}} = \dfrac{1}{\sqrt{3}} = \dfrac{\sqrt{3}}{3}$

17. $\dfrac{\cos^2 2\pi + \sin \dfrac{\pi}{3}}{\cos \dfrac{3\pi}{2} + \sin 0} =$

$\dfrac{(\cos 2\pi)^2 + \sin \dfrac{\pi}{3}}{\cos \dfrac{3\pi}{2} + \sin 0} = \dfrac{(1)^2 + \left(\dfrac{\sqrt{3}}{2} \right)}{0 + 0} \rightarrow \text{undefined}$

19. $\cos^2 \dfrac{\pi}{4} - \sin \dfrac{3\pi}{2} =$

$$\left(\cos \dfrac{\pi}{4} \right)^2 - \sin \dfrac{3\pi}{2} = \left(\dfrac{1}{\sqrt{2}} \right)^2 - (-1)$$

$$= \dfrac{1}{2} + \dfrac{2}{2} = \dfrac{3}{2}$$

21. $\dfrac{\sin \dfrac{\pi}{6} + \cos \dfrac{\pi}{3}}{\sin^2 \dfrac{\pi}{4} + \sin \pi} =$

$$\dfrac{\sin \dfrac{\pi}{6} + \cos \dfrac{\pi}{3}}{\left(\sin \dfrac{\pi}{4} \right)^2 + \sin \pi} = \dfrac{\dfrac{1}{2} + \dfrac{1}{2}}{\left(\dfrac{1}{\sqrt{2}} \right)^2 + 0} = \dfrac{1}{\left(\dfrac{1}{2} \right)} = 2$$

23. $\sin \left(\dfrac{\pi}{2} + \dfrac{\pi}{2} \right) \overset{?}{=} \sin \dfrac{\pi}{2} \cos \dfrac{\pi}{2} + \cos \dfrac{\pi}{2} \sin \dfrac{\pi}{2}$

$$\sin(\pi) \overset{?}{=} 1(0) + 0(1)$$

$$0 = 0 \quad \text{True}$$

25.

$$\dfrac{\cos \dfrac{\pi}{3}}{\sin \dfrac{\pi}{3}} \overset{?}{=} \sqrt{3}$$

$$\dfrac{\left(\dfrac{1}{2} \right)}{\left(\dfrac{\sqrt{3}}{2} \right)} \overset{?}{=} \sqrt{3}$$

$$\left(\dfrac{1}{2} \right) \left(\dfrac{2}{\sqrt{3}} \right) \overset{?}{=} \sqrt{3}$$

$$\dfrac{1}{\sqrt{3}} \neq \sqrt{3} \quad \text{False}$$

27. $\cos \dfrac{\pi}{6} \overset{?}{=} \sin \dfrac{\pi}{3}$

$$\dfrac{\sqrt{3}}{2} = \dfrac{\sqrt{3}}{2} \quad \text{True}$$

29. $\cos^2 \dfrac{\pi}{4} + \sin^2 0 \overset{?}{=} 1$

$$\left(\dfrac{1}{\sqrt{2}} \right)^2 + 0 \overset{?}{=} 1$$

$$\dfrac{1}{2} + 0 \overset{?}{=} 1$$

$$\dfrac{1}{2} \neq 1 \quad \text{False}$$

31. $\sin 1.2$

$\sin(1.2)$ $\boxed{\text{ENTER}}$ ≈ 0.9320

33. $\cos(\pi + 0.14)$ $\boxed{\text{ENTER}}$ ≈ -0.9902

35. $\sin \dfrac{11\pi}{13}$

$\sin(11\pi \div 13)$ $\boxed{\text{ENTER}}$ ≈ 0.4647

37. $\sin 2(4.3)$

$\sin(2(4.3))$ $\boxed{\text{ENTER}}$ ≈ 0.7344

39. $\dfrac{1}{\sin 0.287}$

$1 \div \sin(0.287)$ $\boxed{\text{ENTER}}$ ≈ 3.5326

41. $\dfrac{\cos 1.56 - \sin 1.1}{\sin 0.1}$

$(\cos(1.56) - \sin(1.1)) \div \sin(0.1)$ $\boxed{\text{ENTER}}$ ≈ -8.8188

Exercise Set 1.4, p. 36

1.

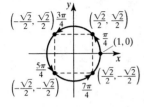

3.

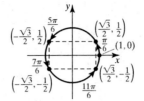

5. Since $\cos x = \dfrac{1}{2}$ and $\sin x = -\dfrac{\sqrt{3}}{2}$, $\hat{x} = \dfrac{\pi}{3}$. We want the arc in the negative direction in QIV with reference arc $\hat{x} = \dfrac{\pi}{3}$.

So, $x = 0 - \dfrac{\pi}{3} = -\dfrac{\pi}{3}$.

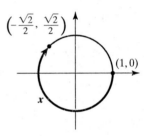

7. Since $\cos x = -\dfrac{\sqrt{2}}{2}$ and $\sin x = \dfrac{\sqrt{2}}{2}$, $\hat{x} = \dfrac{\pi}{4}$. We want the arc in the negative direction in QII that has reference arc $\hat{x} = \dfrac{\pi}{4}$.

So, $x = -\pi - \dfrac{\pi}{4} = -\dfrac{5\pi}{4}$.

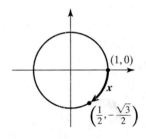

9.

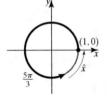

$$\hat{x} = 2\pi - \frac{5\pi}{3} = \frac{6\pi}{3} - \frac{5\pi}{3} = \frac{\pi}{3}$$

11.

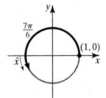

$$\hat{x} = \frac{7\pi}{6} - \pi = \frac{\pi}{6}$$

13.

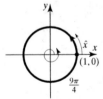

least positive coterminal arc: $\dfrac{9\pi}{4} - 2\pi = \dfrac{\pi}{4}$

$$\hat{x} = \frac{\pi}{4}$$

15.

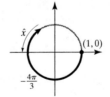

least positive coterminal arc: $-\dfrac{4\pi}{3} + 2\pi = \dfrac{2\pi}{3}$

$$\hat{x} = \pi - \frac{2\pi}{3} = \frac{\pi}{3}$$

17.

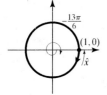

least positive coterminal arc:

$$-\frac{13\pi}{6} + 4\pi = \frac{11\pi}{6}$$

$$\hat{x} = 2\pi - \frac{11\pi}{6} = \frac{\pi}{6}$$

19.

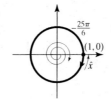

least positive coterminal arc:

$$-\frac{25\pi}{6} + 6\pi = \frac{11\pi}{6}$$

$$\hat{x} = 2\pi - \frac{11\pi}{6} = \frac{\pi}{6}$$

21. sin x > 0

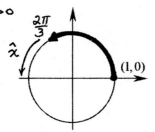

$$\hat{x} = \frac{\pi}{3}, \sin\frac{2\pi}{3} = \sin\frac{\pi}{3} = \frac{\sqrt{3}}{2}$$

23.

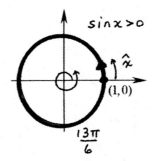

$$\hat{x} = \frac{\pi}{6}, \cos\frac{7\pi}{6} = -\cos\frac{\pi}{6} = -\frac{\sqrt{3}}{2}$$

25.

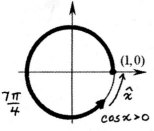

$$\hat{x} = \frac{\pi}{4}, \cos\frac{7\pi}{4} = \cos\frac{\pi}{4} = \frac{\sqrt{2}}{2}$$

27.

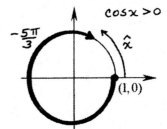

$$\hat{x} = \frac{\pi}{6}, \sin\frac{13\pi}{6} = \sin\frac{\pi}{6} = \frac{1}{2}$$

29.

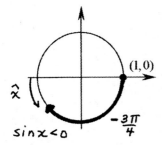

$$\hat{x} = \frac{\pi}{4}, \sin\left(-\frac{3\pi}{4}\right) = -\sin\frac{\pi}{4} = -\frac{\sqrt{2}}{2}$$

31.

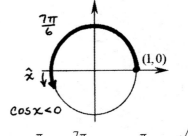

$$\hat{x} = \frac{\pi}{3}, \cos\left(-\frac{5\pi}{3}\right) = \cos\frac{\pi}{3} = \frac{1}{2}$$

33.

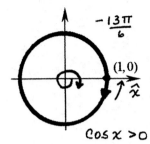

$$\hat{x} = \frac{\pi}{6}, \cos\left(-\frac{13\pi}{6}\right) = \cos\frac{\pi}{6} = \frac{\sqrt{3}}{2}$$

35. $\dfrac{\cos^2 \pi}{\sin\dfrac{5\pi}{4}} =$

$$\frac{(\cos \pi)^2}{\sin\dfrac{5\pi}{4}} = \frac{(-1)^2}{\left(-\dfrac{1}{\sqrt{2}}\right)} = -\sqrt{2}$$

37. $\cos 21.23$

$\cos(21.23)\boxed{\text{ENTER}} \approx -0.7240$

39. $15\cos(-0.98)\boxed{\text{ENTER}} \approx 8.3553$

41. $\sin\dfrac{\pi}{11}$

$\sin(\pi \div 11)\boxed{\text{ENTER}} \approx 0.2817$

43. $\sin\left(-\dfrac{5\pi}{6}\right) + \cos\left(\dfrac{7\pi}{4}\right) = -\dfrac{1}{2} + \dfrac{\sqrt{2}}{2} = \dfrac{\sqrt{2}-1}{2}$

45. $\dfrac{-5}{\cos 2.763215 + 13\sin 0}$

$-5 \div (\cos(2.763215) + 13\sin 0)\boxed{\text{ENTER}} \approx 5.3806$

47. False; we are not able to find the exact functional values of an arc like $\dfrac{\pi}{11}$ because it is not a multiple of a common arc.

49. True

51. False; using a calculator we see the values are not equal, rather they are opposites.

$$\sin 59.1 \approx 0.5566$$
$$\sin(-59.1) \approx -0.5566$$

53. True

55. False; $2x \neq 2t$.

$\cos^2 \square + \sin^2 \square = 1$ when $\square$ is replaced with the same expression. The cosine and sine values at the terminal point of the same arc $\square$ satisfy the Pythagorian identity.

57. False; $\cos\dfrac{\pi}{3} = \dfrac{1}{2}$.

59. True

61. True

63. Since $\cos x > 0$ and $\sin x < 0$, arc x is in QIV, and $\hat{x} = \dfrac{\pi}{3}$.

So, $x = 2\pi - \dfrac{\pi}{3} = \dfrac{5\pi}{3}$.

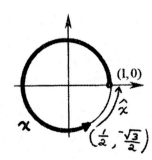

65. Since $\sin x = -1$ and $\cos x = 0$, $x = \dfrac{3\pi}{2}$.

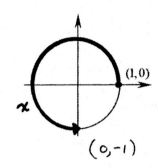

67. Since $\sin x = -\dfrac{\sqrt{2}}{2}$ then $\hat{x} = \dfrac{\pi}{4}$. For $-\dfrac{\pi}{2} \le x \le \dfrac{\pi}{2}$, x is in a negative direction, so $x = -\dfrac{\pi}{4}$.

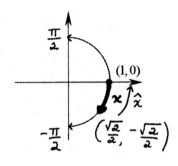

69. Since $\cos x = -\dfrac{\sqrt{3}}{2}$, then $\hat{x} = \dfrac{\pi}{6}$. For $0 \le x \le \pi$, x is in QII, so,

$x = \pi - \dfrac{\pi}{6} = \dfrac{5\pi}{6}$.

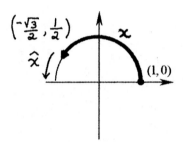

Exercise Set 1.5, p. 48

1. $\tan 0 = 0$, $\tan \dfrac{\pi}{6} = \dfrac{1}{\sqrt{3}} = \dfrac{\sqrt{3}}{3}$, $\tan \dfrac{\pi}{4} = 1$, $\tan \dfrac{\pi}{3} = \sqrt{3}$, $\tan \dfrac{\pi}{2} \to$ undefined

3. $\sec 0 = \dfrac{1}{\cos 0} = 1$, $\sec \dfrac{\pi}{6} = \dfrac{1}{\cos \dfrac{\pi}{6}} = \dfrac{2}{\sqrt{3}} = \dfrac{2\sqrt{3}}{3}$, $\sec \dfrac{\pi}{3} = \dfrac{1}{\cos \dfrac{\pi}{3}} = \dfrac{1}{\left(\dfrac{1}{2}\right)} = 2$,

$\sec \dfrac{3\pi}{4} = \dfrac{1}{\cos \dfrac{3\pi}{4}} = \dfrac{1}{-\cos \dfrac{\pi}{4}} = \dfrac{1}{\left(-\dfrac{1}{\sqrt{2}}\right)} = -\sqrt{2}$

$\sec \pi = \dfrac{1}{\cos \pi} = \dfrac{1}{-1} = -1$, $\sec \dfrac{3\pi}{2} = \dfrac{1}{\cos \dfrac{3\pi}{2}} = \dfrac{1}{0} \to$ undefined

$\sec \left(-\dfrac{\pi}{4}\right) = \dfrac{1}{\cos \left(-\dfrac{\pi}{4}\right)} = \dfrac{1}{\cos \dfrac{\pi}{4}} = \dfrac{1}{\left(\dfrac{1}{\sqrt{2}}\right)} = \sqrt{2}$

5. If $\sec x = \sqrt{2}$, then $\cos x = \dfrac{1}{\sqrt{2}}$. For $0 < x < \dfrac{\pi}{2}$, x is in QI, so $x = \dfrac{\pi}{4}$.

7. If $\cot x = \sqrt{3}$, then $\tan x = \dfrac{1}{\sqrt{3}}$, and x is in QI. So, $x = \dfrac{\pi}{6}$.

9. Since $\cos x > 0$ in QI, QIV and $\tan x < 0$ in QII, QIV, the quadrant that satisfies both conditions is QIV.

11. Since $\tan x > 0$ in QI, QIII and $\sec x > 0$ ($\cos x > 0$) in QI, QIV, the quadrant that satisfies both conditions is QI.

13. Since $\cot x > 0$ ($\tan x > 0$) in QI, QIII and $\csc x < 0$ ($\sin x < 0$) in QIII, QIV, the quadrant that satisfies both conditions is QIII.

15. Since $\sin x > 0$ in QI, QII and $\sec x < 0$ ($\cos x < 0$) in QII, QIII, the quadrant that satisfies both conditions is QII.

17.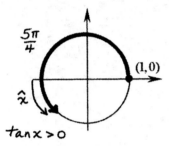

$$\hat{x} = \dfrac{\pi}{4}$$

$$\tan \dfrac{5\pi}{4} = \tan \dfrac{\pi}{4} = 1$$

19.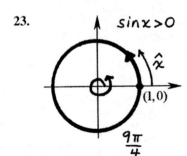

$$\hat{x} = \dfrac{\pi}{6}$$

$$\sec \dfrac{5\pi}{6} = \dfrac{1}{\cos \dfrac{5\pi}{6}} = \dfrac{1}{-\cos \dfrac{\pi}{6}} = \dfrac{1}{\left(-\dfrac{\sqrt{3}}{2}\right)} = -\dfrac{2}{\sqrt{3}} = -\dfrac{2\sqrt{3}}{3}$$

21. $\csc \dfrac{\pi}{6} = \dfrac{1}{\sin \dfrac{\pi}{6}} = \dfrac{1}{\left(\dfrac{1}{2}\right)} = 2$

23.

$$\hat{x} = \dfrac{\pi}{4}$$

$$\csc \dfrac{9\pi}{4} = \dfrac{1}{\sin \dfrac{9\pi}{4}} = \dfrac{1}{\sin \dfrac{\pi}{4}} = \dfrac{1}{\left(\dfrac{1}{\sqrt{2}}\right)} = \sqrt{2}$$

25.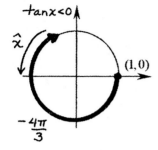

$\hat{x} = \dfrac{\pi}{3}$

$\cot\left(-\dfrac{4\pi}{3}\right) = \dfrac{1}{\tan\left(-\dfrac{4\pi}{3}\right)} = \dfrac{1}{-\tan\dfrac{\pi}{3}}$

$\qquad\qquad = \dfrac{1}{-\sqrt{3}} = -\dfrac{\sqrt{3}}{3}$

27.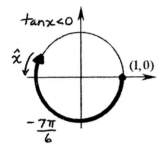

$\hat{x} = \dfrac{\pi}{6}$

$\tan\left(-\dfrac{7\pi}{6}\right) = -\tan\dfrac{\pi}{6} = -\dfrac{\sqrt{3}}{3}$

29.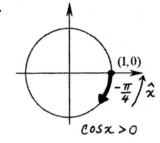

$\hat{x} = \dfrac{\pi}{4}$

$\sec\left(-\dfrac{\pi}{4}\right) = \dfrac{1}{\cos\left(-\dfrac{\pi}{4}\right)} = \dfrac{1}{\cos\dfrac{\pi}{4}} = \dfrac{1}{\left(\dfrac{1}{\sqrt{2}}\right)} = \sqrt{2}$

31.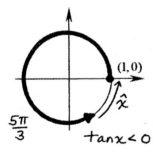

$\hat{x} = \dfrac{\pi}{3}$

$\tan\dfrac{5\pi}{3} = -\tan\dfrac{\pi}{3} = -\sqrt{3}$

33.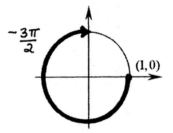

$\sec\left(-\dfrac{3\pi}{2}\right) = \dfrac{1}{\cos\left(-\dfrac{3\pi}{2}\right)} = \dfrac{1}{0} \rightarrow \text{undefined}$

35.

$\hat{x} = \dfrac{\pi}{3}$

$\csc\left(-\dfrac{2\pi}{3}\right) = \dfrac{1}{\sin\left(-\dfrac{2\pi}{3}\right)} = \dfrac{1}{-\sin\dfrac{\pi}{3}} = \dfrac{1}{\left(-\dfrac{\sqrt{3}}{2}\right)} = -\dfrac{2}{\sqrt{3}} = -\dfrac{2\sqrt{3}}{3}$

37. $\csc^2 \dfrac{7\pi}{6} + (\sec 0)\left(\cos \dfrac{\pi}{6}\right)$

$= \left(\csc \dfrac{7\pi}{6}\right)^2 + (\sec 0)\left(\csc \dfrac{\pi}{6}\right)$

$= \left(\dfrac{1}{\sin \dfrac{7\pi}{6}}\right)^2 + \left(\dfrac{1}{\cos 0}\right)\left(\dfrac{1}{\sin \dfrac{\pi}{6}}\right)$

$= \left(\dfrac{1}{\left(-\dfrac{1}{2}\right)}\right)^2 + \left(\dfrac{1}{1}\right)\left(\dfrac{1}{\left(\dfrac{1}{2}\right)}\right)$

$= \dfrac{1}{\left(\dfrac{1}{4}\right)} + \dfrac{1}{\left(\dfrac{1}{2}\right)}$

$= 4 + 2 = 6$

39. $\dfrac{\sin \dfrac{\pi}{2} + \tan \dfrac{2\pi}{3}}{\sec \dfrac{5\pi}{3}}$

$= \dfrac{1 + \left(-\sqrt{3}\right)}{\left(\dfrac{1}{\cos \dfrac{5\pi}{3}}\right)}$

$= \dfrac{1 - \sqrt{3}}{\left(\dfrac{1}{\left(\dfrac{1}{2}\right)}\right)}$

$= \dfrac{1 - \sqrt{3}}{2}$

41. $\tan \dfrac{7\pi}{9}$

$\tan(7\pi \div 9)\boxed{\text{ENTER}} \approx -0.8391$

43. $\csc \left(\dfrac{5}{9} + \dfrac{2}{3}\right)$

$1 \div \sin(5 \div 9 + 2 \div 3)\boxed{\text{ENTER}} \approx 1.0640$

45. $\sec 89.09$

$1 \div \cos(89.09)\boxed{\text{ENTER}} \approx 2.3212$

47. $\tan^2 1.56689$

$(\tan(1.56689)) \wedge 2 \boxed{\text{ENTER}} \approx 65{,}532.7566$

49. $15 \csc 5 + 2.2 \cot 1$

$15 \div \sin(5) + 2.2 \div \tan(1)\boxed{\text{ENTER}} \approx -14.2299$

51. $\cot \dfrac{\pi}{5} - \dfrac{3 \sin(-9)}{\tan 33}$

$1 \div \tan(\pi \div 5) - 3 \sin(-9) \div \tan(33)\boxed{\text{ENTER}} \approx 1.3600$

53, 55, and 57. *We use the Pythagorean identity to find either* $\sin x$ *or* $\cos x$ *and then the reciprocal definitions to find the required value.*

53. $(\cos x)^2 + (\sin x)^2 = 1$

$(\cos x)^2 + \left(-\dfrac{5}{13}\right)^2 = 1$

$(\cos x)^2 = 1 - \dfrac{25}{169} = \dfrac{144}{169}$

$\cos x = -\sqrt{\dfrac{144}{169}} = -\dfrac{12}{13},$ since $\cos x < 0$

So, $\tan x = \dfrac{\sin x}{\cos x} = \dfrac{\left(-\dfrac{5}{13}\right)}{\left(-\dfrac{12}{13}\right)} = \left(-\dfrac{5}{\cancel{13}}\right)\left(-\dfrac{\cancel{13}}{12}\right) = \dfrac{5}{12}.$

55. **a.** $(\cos x)^2 + (\sin x)^2 = 1$

$$\left(-\frac{7}{25}\right)^2 + (\sin x)^2 = 1$$

$$(\sin x)^2 = 1 - \frac{49}{625} = \frac{576}{625}$$

$$\sin x = \sqrt{\frac{576}{625}} = \frac{24}{25}, \text{ since } \sin x > 0.$$

b. $\sec x = \dfrac{1}{\cos x} = -\dfrac{25}{7}$

c. $\tan x = \dfrac{\sin x}{\cos x} = \dfrac{\left(\dfrac{24}{25}\right)}{\left(-\dfrac{7}{25}\right)} = -\dfrac{24}{7}$

d. $\csc x = \dfrac{1}{\sin x} = \dfrac{25}{24}$

e. $\cot x = \dfrac{1}{\tan x} = -\dfrac{7}{24}$

57. $(\cos x)^2 + (\sin x)^2 = 1$

$$\left(-\frac{5}{\sqrt{26}}\right)^2 + (\sin x)^2 = 1$$

$$(\sin x)^2 = 1 - \frac{25}{26} = \frac{1}{26}$$

$$\sin x = -\sqrt{\frac{1}{26}} = -\frac{1}{\sqrt{26}}, \text{ since } x \text{ is in QIII.}$$

So $\cot x = \dfrac{\cos x}{\sin x} = \dfrac{\left(-\dfrac{5}{\sqrt{26}}\right)}{\left(-\dfrac{1}{\sqrt{26}}\right)} = 5.$

59. False; $\tan x = \dfrac{\sin x}{\cos x}.$

61. True

63. True

65. False; $\tan \pi = \dfrac{\sin \pi}{\cos \pi} = \dfrac{0}{-1} = 0.$

67. False; $\cos x = \dfrac{1}{\sec x}.$

69. True

71. $\cot x \overset{?}{=} \cos x \cdot \csc x$

$$= \cos x \cdot \frac{1}{\sin x}$$

$$= \frac{\cos x}{\sin x}$$

$\cot x = \cot x$ This is an identity.

73. $\sec^2 x \overset{?}{=} \dfrac{\cos^2 x + \sin^2 x}{\cos^2 x}$

$$= \frac{1}{\cos^2 x}$$

$\sec^2 x = \sec^2 x$ This is an identity.

75. Since $\tan x = 1$, $\cos x = -\dfrac{1}{\sqrt{2}}$, we recognize $\hat{x} = \dfrac{\pi}{4}$. And since

$\tan x > 0$, $\cos x < 0$, x is in QIII where $0 < x < 2\pi$.

So $x = \pi + \hat{x}$

$$x = \pi + \frac{\pi}{4} = \frac{5\pi}{4}.$$

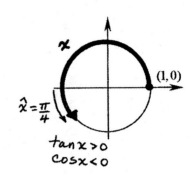

77. Since $\cos x = -\dfrac{1}{2}$, we recognize $\hat{x} = \dfrac{\pi}{3}$. And since x is in QII $\left(\dfrac{\pi}{2} < x < \pi\right)$,

$$x = \pi - \hat{x}$$
$$x = \pi - \frac{\pi}{3} = \frac{2\pi}{3}.$$

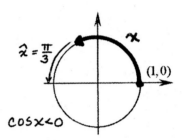

79. If $\csc x = -1$, then $\sin x = -1$. For $0 < x < 2\pi$, $x = \dfrac{3\pi}{2}$.

81. For $k = -2$: $x \neq \dfrac{\pi}{2} + (-2)\pi$ or $x \neq -\dfrac{3\pi}{2}$.

For $k = -1$: $x \neq \dfrac{\pi}{2} + (-1)\pi$ or $x \neq -\dfrac{\pi}{2}$.

For $k = 0$: $x \neq \dfrac{\pi}{2}$.

For $k = 1$: $x \neq \dfrac{\pi}{2} + (1)\pi$ or $x \neq \dfrac{3\pi}{2}$.

For $k = 2$: $x \neq \dfrac{\pi}{2} + (2)\pi$ or $x \neq \dfrac{5\pi}{2}$.

Exercise Set 1.6, p. 61

1. sine, cosine, cosecant, secant   **3.** True

5. True   **7.** True

9. False; $\sin 3x = \sin(3x)$.   **11.** True

13. $\sin \dfrac{2\pi}{3} = \dfrac{\sqrt{3}}{2}$; iii, $\sin \dfrac{8\pi}{3} = \dfrac{\sqrt{3}}{2}$; vii, $-\sin\left(-\dfrac{2\pi}{3}\right) = \sin \dfrac{2\pi}{3}$

15. $\cos \dfrac{7\pi}{6} = -\dfrac{\sqrt{3}}{2}$; iv, v, vi

17. a. If $\cos x = \dfrac{1}{2}$, then $\hat{x} = \dfrac{\pi}{3}$.

Since $\cos x > 0$ in QI, QIV: $x = \dfrac{\pi}{3}$, $x = 2\pi - \dfrac{\pi}{3} = \dfrac{5\pi}{3}$ where $0 \le x < 2\pi$;

$x = \dfrac{\pi}{3} + k \cdot 2\pi$, $x = \dfrac{5\pi}{3} + k \cdot 2\pi$ (for all x).

b. If $\sin x = -\dfrac{\sqrt{2}}{2}$, then $\hat{x} = \dfrac{\pi}{4}$.

Since $\sin x < 0$ in QIII, QIV: $x = \pi + \dfrac{\pi}{4} = \dfrac{5\pi}{4}$, $x = 2\pi - \dfrac{\pi}{4} = \dfrac{7\pi}{4}$ where $0 \le x < 2\pi$;

$x = \dfrac{5\pi}{4} + k \cdot 2\pi$, $x = \dfrac{7\pi}{4} + k \cdot 2\pi$ (for all x).

c. If $\tan x = 1$, then $\hat{x} = \dfrac{\pi}{4}$.

Since $\tan x > 0$ in QI, QIII: $x = \dfrac{\pi}{4}$, $x = \dfrac{\pi}{4} + \pi = \dfrac{5\pi}{4}$ where $0 \le x < 2\pi$;

$x = \dfrac{\pi}{4} + k \cdot \pi$ (for all x).

19, 21. *Displacement is approximated to the nearest tenth of an inch (where necessary).*

19. $d\left(\dfrac{1}{2}\right) = 4\cos\left(\pi\left(\dfrac{1}{2}\right)\right)$

$= 4\cos\left(\dfrac{\pi}{2}\right) = 4 \cdot 0 = 0$

The displacement is 0 in.

21. $d\left(\dfrac{3}{2}\right) = 4\cos\left(\pi\left(\dfrac{3}{2}\right)\right)$

$= 4\cos\left(\dfrac{3\pi}{2}\right) = 4 \cdot 0 = 0$

The displacement is 0 in.

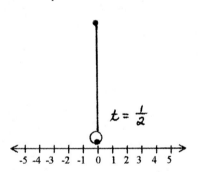

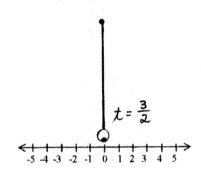

23 and 25. *Displacement is approximated to the nearest tenth of a centimeter.*

23. $d(0.002) = 15\cos(5(0.002))$

$= 15\cos(0.01) \approx 15.0$

The displacement is 15.0 cm.

25. $d(2) = 15\cos(5(2))$

$= 15\cos 10 \approx -12.6$

The displacement is -12.6 cm.

27 and 29. *Voltage is approximated to the nearest tenth of a volt.*

27. $E(0.005) = 170\sin(376(0.005))$
$$= 170\sin(1.88) \approx 161.9$$
The voltage is 161.9 volts.

29. $E\left(\dfrac{1}{4}\right) = 170\sin\left(376\left(\dfrac{1}{4}\right)\right)$
$$= 170\sin(94) \approx -41.7$$
The voltage is -41.7 volts.

31 and 33. *Pressure is approximated to the nearest thousandth of a pound per square foot (psf).*

31. $P(0.01) = 0.001\sin\left(1882\pi(0.01) + \dfrac{\pi}{4}\right)$
$$\approx 0.001\sin(59.9102)$$
$$\approx -0.00021843$$
The pressure is 0 psf.

33. $P(4) = 0.001\sin\left(1882\pi(4) + \dfrac{\pi}{4}\right)$
$$\approx 0.001\sin(23{,}650.69489)$$
$$\approx 0.0007071067$$
The pressure is 0.001 psf.

35. Since $\cos(\pi t)$ is never larger than 1 or smaller than -1, the displacement for $d(t) = -5.2\cos(\pi t) : -5.2\cos(\pi t)$ will never be smaller than -5.2 in. or larger than 5.2 in.

37.

	QII	QI	
	$S : \sin x, \dfrac{1}{\sin x}$	$A :$ all functions	
	are positive	are positive	
	$T : \tan x, \dfrac{1}{\tan x}$	$C : \cos x, \dfrac{1}{\cos x}$	
	are positive	are positive	
	QIII	QIV	

Chapter 1 Review Exercises, p. 66

1. **a.** x **b.** terminal   **c.** t **d.** $(1, 0)$ **e.** unit   **f.** length

2. 1   **3.** -1 **4.** **a.** positive   **b.** clockwise

5. $\cos^2 t + \sin^2 t = 1$ **6.** $\mathbb{R}$

7. **a.**

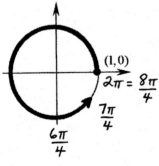

QIV, since $\dfrac{6\pi}{4} \leq \dfrac{7\pi}{4} \leq 2\pi$

b.

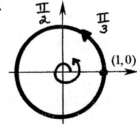

QI, since $\dfrac{7\pi}{3} - 2\pi = \dfrac{\pi}{3}$ and $0 \leq \dfrac{\pi}{3} \leq \dfrac{\pi}{2}$

c.

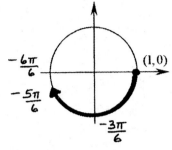

QIII, since $-\dfrac{6\pi}{6} \le -\dfrac{5\pi}{6} \le -\dfrac{3\pi}{6}$

d.

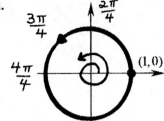

QII, since $\dfrac{11\pi}{4} - 2\pi = \dfrac{3\pi}{4}$ and $\dfrac{2\pi}{4} \le \dfrac{3\pi}{4} \le \dfrac{4\pi}{4}$

e.

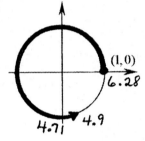

QIV, since $4.71 \le 4.9 \le 6.28$

f.

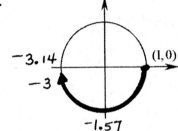

QIII, since $-3.14 \le -3 \le -1.57$

g.

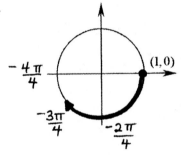

QIII, since $-\dfrac{4\pi}{4} \le -\dfrac{3\pi}{4} \le -\dfrac{2\pi}{4}$

h.

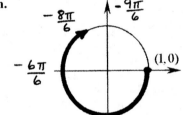

QII, since $-\dfrac{4\pi}{3} = -\dfrac{8\pi}{6}$, and $-\dfrac{9\pi}{6} \le -\dfrac{8\pi}{6} \le -\dfrac{6\pi}{6}$

8. a. $\sin t < 0$ in QIII and QIV; $\cos t > 0$ in QI and QIV. The quadrant that satisfies both conditions is QIV.
  b. $\cos t < 0$ and $\sin t < 0$; both are negative in QIII.

9–10. *Use the Pythagorean identity to find either* $\sin x$ *or* $\cos x$.

9. a. Since $\sin t > 0$, $\cos t < 0$, t is in QII.

  b. $(\cos t)^2 + \left(\dfrac{\sqrt{3}}{2}\right)^2 = 1$

  $(\cos t)^2 = 1 - \dfrac{3}{4} = \dfrac{1}{4}$

  $\cos t = -\sqrt{\dfrac{1}{4}} = -\dfrac{1}{2}$, since $\cos t < 0$

(Note: We should recognize that when $\sin t = \dfrac{\sqrt{3}}{2}$, then $\cos t = \pm\dfrac{1}{2}$, depending on the quadrant for

$t \left(\hat{t} = \dfrac{\pi}{3}\right)$.)

c. $\dfrac{1}{\sin t} = \dfrac{2}{\sqrt{3}} = \dfrac{2\sqrt{3}}{3}$

d. $\dfrac{1}{\cos t} = -2$

e. $\dfrac{\sin t}{\cos t} = \dfrac{\left(\dfrac{\sqrt{3}}{2}\right)}{\left(-\dfrac{1}{2}\right)} = -\sqrt{3}$

f. $\dfrac{\cos t}{\sin t} = -\dfrac{1}{\sqrt{3}} = -\dfrac{\sqrt{3}}{3}$

10. a. Since $\cos t > 0$, $\sin t < 0$, t is in QIV.

b. $\cos^2 t + \sin^2 t = 1$

$\left(\dfrac{3}{5}\right)^2 + (\sin t)^2 = 1$

$(\sin t)^2 = 1 - \dfrac{9}{25} = \dfrac{16}{25}$

$\sin t = -\sqrt{\dfrac{16}{25}} = -\dfrac{4}{5}$, since $\sin t < 0$.

c. $\dfrac{1}{\sin t} = -\dfrac{5}{4}$

d. $\dfrac{1}{\cos t} = \dfrac{5}{3}$

e. $\dfrac{\sin t}{\cos t} = \dfrac{\left(-\dfrac{4}{5}\right)}{\left(\dfrac{3}{5}\right)} = -\dfrac{4}{3}$

f. $\dfrac{\cos t}{\sin t} = -\dfrac{3}{4}$

11. a. $\cos t = \cos \pi = -1$
$\sin t = \sin \pi = 0$

b. $t = \dfrac{\pi}{3}$

$\sin t = \sin \dfrac{\pi}{3} = \dfrac{\sqrt{3}}{2}$

c. $t = \dfrac{\pi}{4}$

$\cos t = \cos \dfrac{\pi}{4} = \dfrac{\sqrt{2}}{2}$

12. a. $\sin \dfrac{\pi}{3} + \cos 0$

$= \dfrac{\sqrt{3}}{2} + 1$

$= \dfrac{\sqrt{3} + 2}{2}$

b. $2\cos^2 \dfrac{\pi}{6} + \left(\sin \dfrac{\pi}{4}\right)^2$

$= 2\left(\cos \dfrac{\pi}{6}\right)^2 + \left(\sin \dfrac{\pi}{4}\right)^2$

$= 2\left(\dfrac{\sqrt{3}}{2}\right)^2 + \left(\dfrac{1}{\sqrt{2}}\right)^2$

$= 2 \cdot \dfrac{3}{4} + \dfrac{1}{2}$

$= \dfrac{3}{2} + \dfrac{1}{2} = 2$

c. $\cos^2 \dfrac{\pi}{6} - \sin^2 \dfrac{\pi}{6}$

$= \left(\cos \dfrac{\pi}{6}\right)^2 - \left(\sin \dfrac{\pi}{6}\right)^2$

$= \left(\dfrac{\sqrt{3}}{2}\right)^2 - \left(\dfrac{1}{2}\right)^2$

$= \dfrac{3}{4} - \dfrac{1}{4} = \dfrac{1}{2}$

d. $4 \sin \dfrac{\pi}{3} \cdot \cos \dfrac{\pi}{3}$

$= 4 \cdot \dfrac{\sqrt{3}}{2} \cdot \dfrac{1}{2}$

$= \sqrt{3}$

e. $\dfrac{\cos \dfrac{\pi}{2} + \sin \dfrac{\pi}{6}}{-2 \cos^2 \pi}$

$= \dfrac{\cos \dfrac{\pi}{2} + \sin \dfrac{\pi}{6}}{-2(\cos \pi)^2}$

$= \dfrac{0 + \dfrac{1}{2}}{-2(-1)^2} = \dfrac{\left(\dfrac{1}{2}\right)}{\left(-\dfrac{2}{1}\right)}$

$= \left(\dfrac{1}{2}\right)\left(-\dfrac{1}{2}\right) = -\dfrac{1}{4}$

f. $\dfrac{\sin^2 \left(\dfrac{\pi}{4} + \dfrac{\pi}{4}\right)}{\sin \dfrac{\pi}{4}}$

$= \dfrac{\left(\sin \left(\dfrac{\pi}{4} + \dfrac{\pi}{4}\right)\right)^2}{\sin \dfrac{\pi}{4}}$

$= \dfrac{\left(\sin \dfrac{\pi}{2}\right)^2}{\sin \dfrac{\pi}{4}}$

$= \dfrac{1}{\left(\dfrac{1}{\sqrt{2}}\right)} = \sqrt{2}$

13. a. $2 \cos \dfrac{\pi}{4} + \sin \dfrac{\pi}{8}$

$2 \cos(\pi \div 4) + \sin(\pi \div 8)\boxed{\text{ENTER}} \approx 1.7969$

b. $4 \cos 2(1.423 + 0.12)$

$4 \cos(2(1.423 + 0.12))\boxed{\text{ENTER}} \approx -3.9938$

c. $\sin \dfrac{5\pi}{9} + \dfrac{1}{\cos 1}$

$\sin(5\pi \div 9) + 1 \div \cos(1)\boxed{\text{ENTER}} \approx 2.8356$

d. $\dfrac{\cos \dfrac{2}{3}}{\sin \dfrac{1}{5}}$

$\cos(2 \div 3) \div \sin(1 \div 5)\boxed{\text{ENTER}} \approx 3.9558$

e. $\dfrac{1}{\sin^2 0.0001}$

$1 \div (\sin(0.0001)) \wedge 2\boxed{\text{ENTER}} \approx 100{,}000{,}000.3333$

14. **a.** $\cos \dfrac{\pi}{4} \overset{?}{=} \sin \dfrac{\pi}{4}$

$\dfrac{1}{\sqrt{2}} = \dfrac{1}{\sqrt{2}}$ True

b. $\dfrac{1}{\sin \dfrac{3\pi}{2}} \overset{?}{=} 0$

$\dfrac{1}{(-1)} \neq 0$ False

c. $\dfrac{\sin \dfrac{\pi}{6}}{\cos \dfrac{\pi}{3}} \overset{?}{=} 1$

$\dfrac{\left(\dfrac{1}{2}\right)}{\left(\dfrac{1}{2}\right)} = 1$ True

d. $\sin\left(\dfrac{\pi}{2} - \dfrac{\pi}{4}\right) \overset{?}{=} \sin \dfrac{\pi}{2} \cos \dfrac{\pi}{4} - \cos \dfrac{\pi}{2} \sin \dfrac{\pi}{4}$

$\sin\left(\dfrac{\pi}{4}\right) \overset{?}{=} (1)\left(\dfrac{1}{\sqrt{2}}\right) - (0)\left(\dfrac{1}{\sqrt{2}}\right)$

$\dfrac{1}{\sqrt{2}} = \dfrac{1}{\sqrt{2}}$ True

e. $\cos^2 \dfrac{\pi}{2} \overset{?}{=} 1 - \sin^2 \dfrac{\pi}{2}$

$(0)^2 \overset{?}{=} 1 - (1)^2$

$0 = 0$ True

f. $\sin\left(\dfrac{\pi}{2} + \dfrac{\pi}{2}\right) \overset{?}{=} \sin \dfrac{\pi}{2} + \sin \dfrac{\pi}{2}$

$\sin(\pi) \overset{?}{=} 1 + 1$

$0 \neq 2$ False

g. $\cos^2\left(\dfrac{\pi}{6}\right) + \sin^2\left(\dfrac{\pi}{6}\right) = 1$

True (Pythagorean identity)

h. $\cos\left(\dfrac{\pi}{4} + \dfrac{\pi}{4}\right) \overset{?}{=} \cos \dfrac{\pi}{4} + \cos \dfrac{\pi}{4}$

$\cos\left(\dfrac{\pi}{2}\right) \overset{?}{=} \dfrac{1}{\sqrt{2}} + \dfrac{1}{\sqrt{2}}$

$0 \neq \dfrac{2}{\sqrt{2}}$ False

i. $\sin\left(2 \cdot \dfrac{\pi}{2}\right) \overset{?}{=} 2 \sin \dfrac{\pi}{2}$

$\sin(\pi) \overset{?}{=} 2(1)$

$0 \neq 2$ False

j. $\sec \dfrac{\pi}{2} \overset{?}{=} 0$

$\dfrac{1}{\cos \dfrac{\pi}{2}} \overset{?}{=} 0$

$\dfrac{1}{0} \neq 0$ False

15. **a.** $\hat{x} = 2\pi - \dfrac{5\pi}{3} = \dfrac{\pi}{3}$

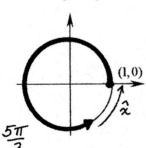

b. $\hat{x} = \dfrac{9\pi}{4} - 2\pi = \dfrac{\pi}{4}$

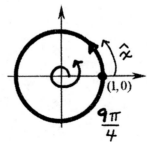

c. Since $-\dfrac{7\pi}{6}$ is coterminal with $\dfrac{5\pi}{6}$, $\hat{x} = \pi - \dfrac{5\pi}{6} = \dfrac{\pi}{6}$.

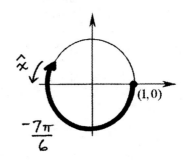

d. Since $-\dfrac{3\pi}{4}$ is coterminal with $\dfrac{5\pi}{4}$, $\hat{x} = \dfrac{5\pi}{4} - \pi = \dfrac{\pi}{4}$.

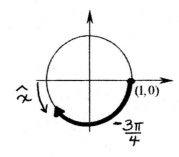

16. **a–d.** *Refer to Exercise 15 for finding the reference arc and location of the arc.*

a. $\sin\dfrac{5\pi}{3} = -\sin\dfrac{\pi}{3} = -\dfrac{\sqrt{3}}{2}$

b. $\cos\dfrac{9\pi}{4} = \cos\dfrac{\pi}{4} = \dfrac{\sqrt{2}}{2}$

c. $\cos\left(-\dfrac{7\pi}{6}\right) = -\cos\dfrac{\pi}{6} = -\dfrac{\sqrt{3}}{2}$

d. $\sin\left(-\dfrac{3\pi}{4}\right) = -\sin\dfrac{\pi}{4} = -\dfrac{\sqrt{2}}{2}$

17. **a.** $\dfrac{\sin\dfrac{7\pi}{4}}{\cos\left(-\dfrac{3\pi}{4}\right)} = \dfrac{\left(-\dfrac{1}{\sqrt{2}}\right)}{\left(-\dfrac{1}{\sqrt{2}}\right)} = 1$

b. $\cos^2 2.4 + \sin^2 2.4 = 1$ (Pythagorean identity)

c. $\cos(\pi + 2) \cdot \sin(2(-6.2)) \approx 0.0689$

d. $\cos\pi + \sin\dfrac{3\pi}{2} + \cancel{\sin 4.2} - \cancel{\sin 4.2} = (-1) + (-1) = -2$

18. **a.** We recognize $\hat{x} = \dfrac{\pi}{6}$, and since $\cos x < 0$ and $\sin x < 0$,

x is in QIII. If x is within one counterclockwise wrap,

$x = \pi + \dfrac{\pi}{6} = \dfrac{7\pi}{6}$.

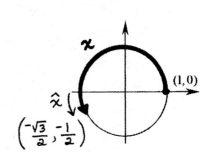

b. We recognize $\hat{x} = \dfrac{\pi}{4}$, and since $\cos x < 0$ and $\sin x > 0$,

x is in QII. So, $x = \pi - \dfrac{\pi}{4} = \dfrac{3\pi}{4}$.

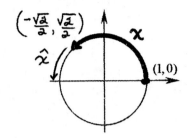

c. If $\cos x = 0$ and $\sin x = -1$, then $x = \dfrac{3\pi}{2}$.

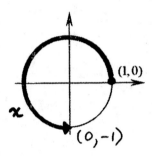

d. We recognize $\hat{x} = \dfrac{\pi}{3}$, and since $\cos x > 0$ and $\sin x > 0$,

x is in QI. So, $x = \dfrac{\pi}{3}$.

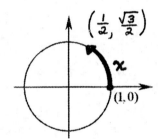

19.   **a.** $\hat{x} = \dfrac{\pi}{6}$, and since x is in QII, $x = \pi - \dfrac{\pi}{6} = \dfrac{5\pi}{6}$.

$$\csc x = \frac{1}{\sin x} = \frac{1}{\sin \dfrac{5\pi}{6}} = \frac{1}{\sin \dfrac{\pi}{6}} = 2$$

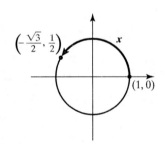

b. $\hat{x} = \dfrac{\pi}{3}$, and since x is in QIV in a negative direction, $x = -\dfrac{\pi}{3}$.

$$\tan x = \tan\left(-\frac{\pi}{3}\right) = -\sqrt{3}$$

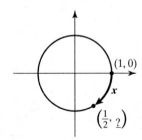

c. Since $\tan x = 1$, $\hat{x} = \dfrac{\pi}{4}$

For x in QIII, $x = \pi + \dfrac{\pi}{4} = \dfrac{5\pi}{4}$.

$\sec x = \dfrac{1}{\cos \dfrac{5\pi}{4}} = \dfrac{1}{-\cos \dfrac{\pi}{4}} = -\sqrt{2}$

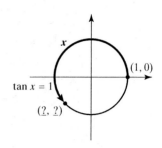

20. **a.** If $\tan x < 0$ (QII, QIV) and $\sec x > 0$ (QI, QIV), then x is in QIV.
    b. If $\cot x > 0$ (QI, QIII) and $\sin x < 0$ (QIII, QIV), then x is in QIII.
    c. If $\sec x > 0$ (QI, QIV) and $\cos x < 0$ (QII, QIII), then x cannot be in any quadrant.
    d. If $\csc x < 0$ (QIII, QIV) and $\sec x > 0$ (QI, QIV), then x is in QIV.
    e. If $\cot x > 0$ (QI, QIII) and $\sec x > 0$ (QI, QIV), then x is in QI.
    f. If $\csc x > 0$ (QI, QII) and $\cos x < 0$ (QII, QIII), then x is in QII.
    g. If $\cot x > 0$ (QI, QIII) and $\tan x > 0$ (QI, QIII), then x is in QI or QIII.

21. **a.** $\tan \dfrac{2\pi}{3} = -\tan \dfrac{\pi}{3} = -\sqrt{3}$

    b. $\csc \dfrac{5\pi}{4} = \dfrac{1}{\sin \dfrac{5\pi}{4}} = \dfrac{1}{-\sin \dfrac{\pi}{4}} = -\sqrt{2}$

    c. $\sec \dfrac{19\pi}{6} = \dfrac{1}{\cos \dfrac{19\pi}{6}} = \dfrac{1}{-\cos \dfrac{\pi}{6}} = -\dfrac{2}{\sqrt{3}} = -\dfrac{2\sqrt{3}}{3}$

    d. $\cot \dfrac{5\pi}{3} = -\dfrac{1}{\tan \dfrac{5\pi}{3}} = \dfrac{1}{-\tan \dfrac{\pi}{3}} = -\dfrac{1}{\sqrt{3}} = -\dfrac{\sqrt{3}}{3}$

    e. $\tan^2\left(-\dfrac{11\pi}{6}\right)$

    $= \left(\tan\left(-\dfrac{11\pi}{6}\right)\right)^2 = \left(\tan \dfrac{\pi}{6}\right)^2 = \left(\dfrac{1}{\sqrt{3}}\right)^2 = \dfrac{1}{3}$

    f. $\sec\left(-\dfrac{3\pi}{2}\right) = \dfrac{1}{\cos\left(-\dfrac{3\pi}{2}\right)} = \dfrac{1}{\cos \dfrac{\pi}{2}} = \dfrac{1}{0} \rightarrow$ undefined

    g. $\csc^2\left(-\dfrac{7\pi}{6}\right)$

    $= \left(\csc\left(-\dfrac{7\pi}{6}\right)\right)^2 = \left(\dfrac{1}{\sin\left(-\dfrac{7\pi}{6}\right)}\right)^2 = \left(\dfrac{1}{\sin \dfrac{\pi}{6}}\right)^2 = \left(\dfrac{1}{\left(\dfrac{1}{2}\right)}\right)^2 = (2)^2 = 4$

    h. $\cot 0 = \dfrac{\cos 0}{\sin 0} = \dfrac{1}{0} \rightarrow$ undefined

    i. $\dfrac{\sec 5\pi + \csc \dfrac{2\pi}{3}}{\tan \dfrac{11\pi}{4}} = \dfrac{(-1) + \left(\dfrac{2\sqrt{3}}{3}\right)}{(-1)} = \dfrac{\left(\dfrac{-3 + 2\sqrt{3}}{3}\right)}{(-1)} = \dfrac{3 - 2\sqrt{3}}{3}$

22.   **a.** $3\cot 5.1 + \sec\left(-\dfrac{7\pi}{5}\right)$

$3 \div \tan(5.1) + 1 \div \cos(-7\pi \div 5)\,\boxed{\text{ENTER}} \approx -4.4609$

b. $\dfrac{\csc 5}{\cot(-9.1)}$

$(1 \div \sin(5)) \div (1 \div \tan(-9.1))\,\boxed{\text{ENTER}} \approx -0.3511$

c. $\cot(-7.62) + \tan\left(\dfrac{5}{3}\right)$

$1 \div \tan(-7.62) + \tan(5 \div 3)\,\boxed{\text{ENTER}} \approx -10.6371$

d. $\dfrac{\sec 1.5}{\tan \dfrac{\pi}{12}}$

$(1 \div \cos(1.5)) \div \tan(\pi \div 12)\,\boxed{\text{ENTER}} \approx 52.7594$

23.   **a.** $\cos^2 x + \sin^2 x = 1$

$(\cos x)^2 + \left(\dfrac{8}{17}\right)^2 = 1$

$(\cos x)^2 = 1 - \dfrac{64}{289} = \dfrac{225}{289}$

$\cos x = -\sqrt{\dfrac{225}{289}} = -\dfrac{15}{17}$, since $\cos x < 0$

$\tan x = \dfrac{\left(\dfrac{8}{17}\right)}{\left(-\dfrac{15}{17}\right)} = -\dfrac{8}{15}$

b. If $\cos x = \dfrac{\sqrt{2}}{2}$, then $\hat{x} = \dfrac{\pi}{4}$, and since x is in QIV $\left(\dfrac{3\pi}{2} < x < 2\pi\right)$, $\sin x < 0$. So, $\sin x = -\sin\dfrac{\pi}{4} = -\dfrac{\sqrt{2}}{2}$.
Also, $\cot x = -\cot\dfrac{\pi}{4} = -1$, since $\cot x < 0$ in QIV.

(Or you can use the Pythagorean identity first to find $\sin x$.)

c. $\left(-\dfrac{12}{13}\right)^2 + (\sin x)^2 = 1$

$(\sin x)^2 = 1 - \dfrac{144}{169} = \dfrac{25}{169}$

$\sin x = -\sqrt{\dfrac{25}{169}} = -\dfrac{5}{13}$, since x in QIII where $\sin x < 0$

$\csc x = \dfrac{1}{\sin x} = -\dfrac{13}{5}$

$\sec x = \dfrac{1}{\cos x} = -\dfrac{13}{12}$

d. $(\cos x)^2 + \left(-\dfrac{2}{3}\right)^2 = 1$

$$(\cos x)^2 = 1 - \dfrac{4}{9} = \dfrac{5}{9}$$

$$\cos x = \sqrt{\dfrac{5}{9}} = \dfrac{\sqrt{5}}{3}, \text{ since } x \text{ is in QIV}$$

$$\tan x = \dfrac{\left(-\dfrac{2}{3}\right)}{\left(\dfrac{\sqrt{5}}{3}\right)} = -\dfrac{2}{\sqrt{5}} = -\dfrac{2\sqrt{5}}{5}$$

24.   **a.** $x = \dfrac{\pi}{3}$ **b.** $x = \dfrac{\pi}{4}$ **c.** $x = \dfrac{\pi}{6}$

25.   **a.** $x = \dfrac{3\pi}{4}$ **b.** $x = -\dfrac{\pi}{6}$ **c.** $x = -\dfrac{\pi}{4}$

26.   **a.** $\tan x \overset{?}{=} \left(\dfrac{\sin x}{\cos x}\right)^2 \cdot \dfrac{1}{\sin x} \cdot \cos x$

$\qquad \overset{?}{=} \dfrac{(\sin x)^2}{(\cos x)^2} \cdot \dfrac{1}{\sin x} \cdot \dfrac{\cos x}{1}$

$\qquad \overset{?}{=} \dfrac{\sin x}{\cos x}$

$\qquad = \tan x$ This is an identity.

b. $1 \overset{?}{=} \dfrac{\sin^2 x}{\cos^2 x} \cdot \cos^2 x + \dfrac{\cos^2 x}{\sin^2 x} \cdot \sin^2 x$

$\qquad \overset{?}{=} \sin^2 x + \cos^2 x$

$\qquad = 1$ This is an identity.

c. $\sec x \overset{?}{=} \dfrac{\cos x}{\sin x} \cdot \sin x \cdot \dfrac{1}{\sin x} \cdot \dfrac{1}{\cos x}$

$\qquad \overset{?}{=} \dfrac{1}{\sin x}$

$\sec x \neq \csc x$ This is not an identity.

d. $\cot x \overset{?}{=} \dfrac{1}{(\cos x)^2} \cdot \dfrac{\cos x}{1} \cdot \dfrac{\sin x}{1}$

$\qquad \overset{?}{=} \dfrac{\sin x}{\cos x}$

$\cot x \neq \tan x$ This is not an identity.

e. $1 \overset{?}{=} 2\sin^2 x + \dfrac{\cos^2 x}{\sin^2 x} \cdot \sin^2 x - \sin^2 x$

$\qquad \overset{?}{=} 2\sin^2 x + \cos^2 x - \sin^2 x$

$\qquad \overset{?}{=} \sin^2 x + \cos^2 x$

$\qquad = 1$ This is an identity.

27.   **a.** True

   b. False; if $x = \dfrac{\pi}{2}$, $\sin\left(\dfrac{\pi}{2} + \pi\right) = -1$, which is not equal to $\sin\left(\dfrac{\pi}{2}\right) = 1$.

   c. True   **d.** False; $\csc(-x) = -\csc x$.

   e. True   **f.** True

28. a.

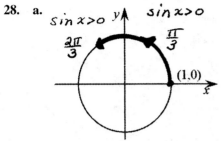

$$x = \frac{\pi}{3}, x = \frac{2\pi}{3}; \text{ since the period of } \sin x \text{ is } 2\pi, x = \frac{\pi}{3} + k \cdot 2\pi, x = \frac{2\pi}{3} + k \cdot 2\pi$$

b.

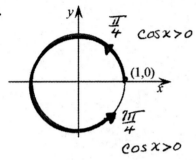

$$\sec x = \sqrt{2} \rightarrow \cos x = \frac{1}{\sqrt{2}} \rightarrow \hat{x} = \frac{\pi}{4}$$

$$x = \frac{\pi}{4}, x = \frac{7\pi}{4}; \text{ since the period of } \cos x \text{ is } 2\pi, x = \frac{\pi}{4} + k \cdot 2\pi, x = \frac{7\pi}{4} + k \cdot 2\pi$$

c.

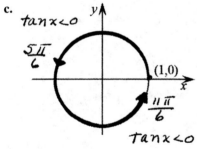

$$\hat{x} = \frac{\pi}{6},$$

$$x = \frac{5\pi}{6}, x = \frac{11\pi}{6}; \text{ since the period of } \tan x \text{ is } \pi, x = \frac{5\pi}{6} + k \cdot \pi$$

29. $d\left(\frac{1}{5}\right) = 12\cos\left(2\pi\left(\frac{1}{5}\right)\right)$, for $t = \frac{1}{5}$

$$\approx 12\cos(1.256637061)$$

$$\approx 3.7082$$

The displacement is 3.7082 cm.

30. $d(3.5) = 1.3\cos(5.2(3.5))$, for $t = 3.5$

$$= 1.3\cos(18.2)$$

$$\approx 1.0353$$

The displacement is 1.0353 in.

31. **a.** The arc $\dfrac{4\pi}{11}$ is not a common arc, so we do not know its exact functional values.

     b. $\sec(4\pi/11) = 1 \div \cos(4\pi \div 11)\ \boxed{\text{ENTER}} \approx 2.4072$
Elka's answer is correct.

     c. Tom input $1 \div \sin(4\pi \div 11) \approx 1.0993$ which finds the $\csc\left(\dfrac{4\pi}{11}\right)$. So Tom used the wrong definition of $\sec x$.

Chapter 1 Test, p. 71

1. **a.** y-coordinate   **b.** unit   **c.** direction   **d.** $\underline{\cos^2 x + \sin^2 x = 1}$

     e. $\mathbb{R}$ **f.** $-1 \le \sin x \le 1$ **g.** 2π **h.** $x \ne \dfrac{\pi}{2} + k \cdot \pi, x \in \mathbb{R}$

     i. $\mathbb{R}$ **j.** π

2.

x	$\sin x$	$\tan x$	$\sec x$
0	0	0	1
$\dfrac{\pi}{6}$	$\dfrac{1}{2}$	$\dfrac{1}{\sqrt{3}}$ or $\dfrac{\sqrt{3}}{3}$	$\dfrac{2}{\sqrt{3}}$ or $\dfrac{2\sqrt{3}}{3}$
$\dfrac{\pi}{4}$	$\dfrac{1}{\sqrt{2}}$ or $\dfrac{\sqrt{2}}{2}$	1	$\sqrt{2}$
$\dfrac{\pi}{3}$	$\dfrac{\sqrt{3}}{2}$	$\sqrt{3}$	2
$\dfrac{\pi}{2}$	1	undefined	undefined
π	0	0	-1
$\dfrac{3\pi}{2}$	-1	undefined	undefined

3. **a.** If $\cos x < 0$ (QII, QIII) and $\sin x > 0$ (QI, QII), then x is in QII.
     b. If $\csc x < 0$ (QIII, QIV) and $\tan x < 0$ (QII, QIV), then x is in QIV.

4. **a.**

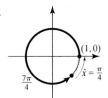

b.

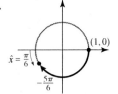

$$\sin \frac{7\pi}{4} = -\sin \frac{\pi}{4} = -\frac{1}{\sqrt{2}} = -\frac{\sqrt{2}}{2}$$

$$\sec\left(-\frac{5\pi}{6}\right) = \frac{1}{\cos\left(-\dfrac{5\pi}{6}\right)} = \frac{1}{-\cos\dfrac{\pi}{6}} = -\frac{2}{\sqrt{3}} = -\frac{2\sqrt{3}}{3}$$

5.

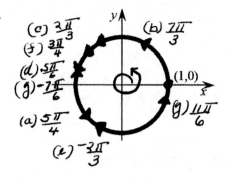

a. $\dfrac{5\pi}{4}$ is in QIII, and $\hat{x} = \dfrac{\pi}{4}$.

$$\cos \dfrac{5\pi}{4} = -\cos \dfrac{\pi}{4} = -\dfrac{\sqrt{2}}{2}$$

b. $\sin^2 \dfrac{7\pi}{3}$

$$= \left(\sin \dfrac{7\pi}{3}\right)^2 = \left(\sin \dfrac{\pi}{3}\right)^2 = \left(\dfrac{\sqrt{3}}{2}\right)^2 = \dfrac{3}{4}$$

c. $\tan \dfrac{2\pi}{3} = -\tan \dfrac{\pi}{3} = -\sqrt{3}$

d. $\csc \dfrac{5\pi}{6} = \dfrac{1}{\sin \dfrac{5\pi}{6}} = \dfrac{1}{\sin \dfrac{\pi}{6}} = \dfrac{1}{\left(\dfrac{1}{2}\right)} = 2$

e. $\cos \left(-\dfrac{2\pi}{3}\right) = -\cos \dfrac{\pi}{3} = -\dfrac{1}{2}$

f. $\left(\csc \dfrac{3\pi}{4}\right)^2 + \sec \pi =$

$$\left(-\sqrt{2}\right)^2 + (-1) = 2 - 1 = 1$$

g. $\cot \left(\dfrac{11\pi}{6}\right) + \cos \left(-\dfrac{7\pi}{6}\right)$

$$= \left(-\sqrt{3}\right) + \left(-\dfrac{\sqrt{3}}{2}\right)$$

$$= -\dfrac{3\sqrt{3}}{2}$$

6. a. If $\cos x = -\dfrac{\sqrt{2}}{2}$, $\hat{x} = \dfrac{\pi}{4}$ and x is in QIII $\left(\pi \le x \le \dfrac{3\pi}{2}\right)$.

So $\sin x = -\sin \dfrac{\pi}{4}$

$$= -\dfrac{\sqrt{2}}{2}, \text{ since } \sin x < 0 \text{ in QIII.}$$

b. $\tan x = \tan \dfrac{\pi}{4} = 1$, since $\tan x > 0$ in QIII.

c. $\sec x = \dfrac{1}{\cos x} = \dfrac{1}{\left(-\dfrac{\sqrt{2}}{2}\right)} = -\sqrt{2}$

7. a. Since $\sin t > 0$ and $\cos t < 0$, t is in QII.

b.
$$\cos^2 t + \sin^2 t = 1$$
$$(\cos t)^2 + \left(\frac{3}{4}\right)^2 = 1$$
$$(\cos t)^2 = 1 - \frac{9}{16} = \frac{7}{16}$$
$$\cos t = -\sqrt{\frac{7}{16}} = -\frac{\sqrt{7}}{4}, \text{ since } \cos t < 0$$

c. $\tan t = \dfrac{\sin t}{\cos t} = \dfrac{\left(\dfrac{3}{4}\right)}{\left(-\dfrac{\sqrt{7}}{4}\right)} = -\dfrac{3}{\sqrt{7}} = -\dfrac{3\sqrt{7}}{7}$

8. a. Since $\cos x > 0$ and $\sin x < 0$, x is in QIV.

b. From $\cos x = \dfrac{1}{2}$, we recognize that $\hat{x} = \dfrac{\pi}{3}$, and since x is in QIV, where $0 \le x \le 2\pi$, $x = 2\pi - \dfrac{\pi}{3} = \dfrac{5\pi}{3}$.

9. a. $\cos^2 35.08$

$(\cos(35.08)) \wedge 2 \boxed{\text{ENTER}} \approx 0.7510$

b. $\tan(-4.76\pi)$

$\tan(-4.76\pi) \boxed{\text{ENTER}} \approx 0.9391$

c. $\csc 3\left(\dfrac{\pi}{7} + \dfrac{\pi}{9}\right)$

$1 \div \sin(3(\pi \div 7 + \pi \div 9)) \boxed{\text{ENTER}} \approx 1.4702$

d. $\cot 5 + \sec 2$

$1 \div \tan(5) + 1 \div \cos(2) \boxed{\text{ENTER}} \approx -2.6988$

e. $\dfrac{5\cos 8.9 - \tan 4.5}{\sin 9}$

$(5\cos(8.9) - \tan(4.5)) \div \sin(9) \boxed{\text{ENTER}} \approx -21.7523$

10. a.
$$\cot x \overset{?}{=} \frac{1}{\sin x} \cdot \cos x$$
$$\overset{?}{=} \frac{\cos x}{\sin x}$$
$$\cot x = \cot x \quad \text{True}$$

b. False; if $\cos x = 0$, $\sin x = 1$ or $\sin x = -1$.

c. True

d. False; $\tan^2 x = (\tan x)^2 \ne \tan(x \cdot x)$.

e. False; the period of the cosecant function is 2π.

f. False; $\cos(-x) = \cos x$.

g. True

h. True

i. False; $1 = \cos^2 x + \sin^2 x$.

If $x = \dfrac{\pi}{4}$, $1 \ne \cos\dfrac{\pi}{4} + \sin\dfrac{\pi}{4}$

$\qquad\qquad 1 \ne \sqrt{2}$.

j. False; $\cos 2\pi \ne 2\cos\pi$

$\qquad\qquad 1 \ne 2(-1)$.

11. **a.** If $\cos x = \dfrac{\sqrt{3}}{2}$, $\hat{x} = \dfrac{\pi}{6}$. Since $\cos x > 0$ in QI, QIV, then $x = \dfrac{\pi}{6}$, $x = 2\pi - \dfrac{\pi}{6} = \dfrac{11\pi}{6}$, where $0 \le x \le 2\pi$.

$x = \dfrac{\pi}{6} + k \cdot 2\pi$, $x = \dfrac{11\pi}{6} + k \cdot 2\pi$ (for all x)

b. If $\tan x = -\sqrt{3}$, $\hat{x} = \dfrac{\pi}{3}$. Since $\tan x < 0$ in QII and QIV, then $x = \pi - \dfrac{\pi}{3} = \dfrac{2\pi}{3}$, $x = 2\pi - \dfrac{\pi}{3} = \dfrac{5\pi}{3}$, where $0 \le x \le 2\pi$.

$x = \dfrac{2\pi}{3} + k \cdot \pi$ (for all x)

12. $d(0.2) = 7\cos(2\pi(0.2))$, for $t = 0.2$

$\approx 7\cos(1.256637061)$

≈ 2.1631

The displacement is 2.1631 cm.

Chapter 2   Trigonometry Student's Solutions Manual

Exercise Set 2.1, p. 85

1.   a.

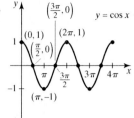

b.

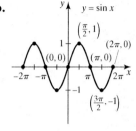

3. *Since A = 6, we have a vertical stretch.*
amplitude $= |A| = 6$
Plot the critical points for $y = 6 \cos x$ on $0 \le x \le 2\pi$:

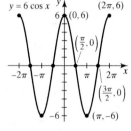

- The x-intercepts are the same as $y = \cos x$.
- The maximum and minimum y-coordinates of the critical points are 6 and -6, respectively.

Connect the critical points with four identical arc sections in the cosine form of a sinusoidal wave. Repeat the pattern for one more cycle.

range: $|y| \le 6$, x-intercepts: $-\dfrac{3\pi}{2}, -\dfrac{\pi}{2}, \dfrac{\pi}{2}, \dfrac{3\pi}{2}$ or $x = \dfrac{\pi}{2} + k\pi$

5. *Since A = $-\pi$, we have a vertical stretch and a reflection across the x-axis.*
amplitude $= |A| = \pi$
Plot the critical points for $y = -\pi \sin x$ on $0 \le x \le 2\pi$:

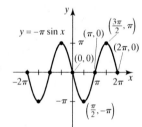

- The x-intercepts are the same as $y = \sin x$.
- The maximum and minimum y-coordinates of the critical points are π and $-\pi$, respectively.

Connect the critical points with four identical arc sections in the sine form of a sinusoidal wave. Repeat the pattern for one more cycle.

range: $|y| \le \pi$, x-intercepts: $-2\pi, -\pi, 0, \pi, 2\pi$ or $x = k\pi$

7. *Since A = 7, we have a vertical stretch.*
amplitude $= |A| = 7$
Plot the critical points for $y = 7 \sin x$ on $0 \le x \le 2\pi$:

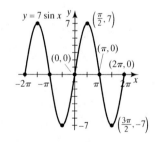

- The x-intercepts are the same as $y = \sin x$.
- The maximum and minimum y-coordinates of the critical points are 7 and -7, respectively.

Connect the critical points with four identical arc sections in the sine form of a sinusoidal wave. Repeat the pattern for one more cycle.

range: $|y| \le 7$, x-intercepts: $-2\pi, -\pi, 0, \pi, 2\pi$ or $x = k\pi$

9. *Since A = −0.4, we have a vertical shrink and a reflection across the x-axis.*
amplitude = | A | = 0.4
Plot the critical points for $y = -0.4 \cos x$ on $0 \le x \le 2\pi$:

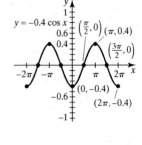

- The x-intercepts are the same as $y = \cos x$.
- The maximum and minimum y-coordinates of the critical points are 0.4 and −0.4, respectively.

Connect the critical points with four identical arc sections in the cosine form of a sinusoidal wave. Repeat the pattern for one more cycle.

range: $| y | \le 0.4$, x-intercepts: $-\dfrac{3\pi}{2}, -\dfrac{\pi}{2}, \dfrac{\pi}{2}, \dfrac{3\pi}{2}$ or $x = \dfrac{\pi}{2} + k\pi$

11. *Since $A = \dfrac{3}{2}$, we have a vertical stretch.*

amplitude = $| A | = \dfrac{3}{2}$

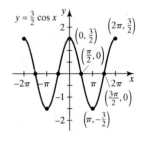

Plot the critical points for $y = \dfrac{3}{2} \cos x$ on $0 \le x \le 2\pi$:

- The x-intercepts are the same as $y = \cos x$.
- The maximum and minimum y-coordinates of the critical points are $\dfrac{3}{2}$ and $-\dfrac{3}{2}$, respectively.

Connect the critical points with four identical arc sections in the cosine form of a sinusoidal wave. Repeat the pattern for one more cycle.

range: $| y | \le \dfrac{3}{2}$, x-intercepts: $-\dfrac{3\pi}{2}, -\dfrac{\pi}{2}, \dfrac{\pi}{2}, \dfrac{3\pi}{2}$ or $x = \dfrac{\pi}{2} + k\pi$

13. The amplitude is 2 and the sine graph has been reflected across the x-axis, so $y = -2 \sin x$.

15. The amplitude is 3 in the cosine form, $y = 3 \cos x$.

17. The amplitude is 0.3 in the sine form, so $y = 0.3 \sin x$.

19. No, the period or cycle should be 2π.

21. No, the graph should be arc shaped.

23. No, the x-intercept is incorrect. There should be four equal arcs, and the period should be 2π.

25. **a.** The distance along the x-axis from -4π to 6π is $| 6\pi - (-4\pi) | = 10\pi$. Since each cycle is 2π, there are five complete cycles.

 b. The distance along the x-axis from -3π to 2π is $| 2\pi - (-3\pi) | = 5\pi$. Since each cycle is 2π, there are two complete cycles.

27. We can use the negative identity $\cos(-x) = \cos x$ to verify that the cosine function is even.

29. **a.** Since $A = 3$, there is a vertical stretch, with maximum and minimum y-coordinates at 3 and −3, respectively.

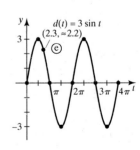

 b. By inspection, we see $d(t)$ (or y) is zero when $t = 0, \pi, 2\pi, 3\pi, 4\pi$.

 c. The maximum displacement is 3 in.

 d. The maximum displacement is equal to the amplitude.

 e. $d(2.3) = 3 \sin(2.3) \approx 2.2$ in. (see graph in part (a))

31. **a.** The arc on the unit circle is $\dfrac{\pi}{2}$, and the cosine value is 0. The point on the cosine graph that corresponds to $\left(\dfrac{\pi}{2}, 0\right)$ is *B*.

b. The arc on the unit circle is $\dfrac{\pi}{2}$, and the sine value is 1. The point on the sine graph that corresponds to $\left(\dfrac{\pi}{2}, 1\right)$ is *F*.

33. True   **35.** True   **37.** True

39. False; the graph is symmetric with respect to the origin.

Exercise Set 2.2, p. 104

For **1–21:** $\text{Period} = \dfrac{\text{pure period}}{|B|} = \dfrac{2\pi}{|B|}$

1. $A = 1,\ B = \dfrac{1}{2}$

amplitude: $|A| = 1$

period: $\dfrac{2\pi}{\left(\frac{1}{2}\right)} = 4\pi$

Start at the origin, mark off one period, and divide it into four subintervals. Using the sine form, plot the critical points.
By inspection the *x*-intercepts are at $x = -4\pi,\ -2\pi,\ 0,\ 2\pi$ or $x = k \cdot 2\pi$.

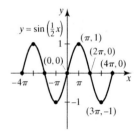

3. Using negative identities, $y = \cos(-4x) \rightarrow y = \cos(4x)$, so $A = 1,\ B = 4$.

amplitude: $|A| = 1$

period: $\dfrac{2\pi}{4} = \dfrac{\pi}{2}$

Start at the origin, mark off one period, and divide it into four subintervals. Using the cosine form, plot the critical points.
x-intercepts: $-\dfrac{3\pi}{8},\ -\dfrac{\pi}{8},\ \dfrac{\pi}{8},\ \dfrac{3\pi}{8}$ or $x = \dfrac{\pi}{8} + k \cdot \dfrac{\pi}{4}$

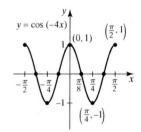

5. Using negative identities, $y = \sin\left(-\dfrac{1}{3}x\right) \rightarrow y = -\sin\left(\dfrac{1}{3}x\right)$, so

$A = -1,\ B = \dfrac{1}{3}$.

amplitude: $|A| = 1$

period: $\dfrac{2\pi}{\left(\frac{1}{3}\right)} = 2\pi \cdot \dfrac{3}{1} = 6\pi$

Start at the origin, mark off one period, and divide it into four subintervals. Using the sine form reflected across the *x*-axis, plot the critical points.
x-intercepts: $-6\pi,\ -3\pi,\ 0,\ 3\pi,\ 6\pi$ or $x = k \cdot 3\pi$

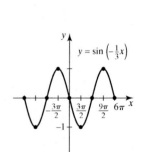

7. $A = 3, B = \dfrac{1}{4}$

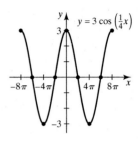

amplitude: $|A| = 3$

period: $\dfrac{2\pi}{\left(\dfrac{1}{4}\right)} = 8\pi$

Start at the origin, mark off one period, and divide it into four subintervals. Using the cosine form, plot the critical points.

x-intercepts: $-6\pi, -2\pi, 2\pi, 6\pi$ or $x = 2\pi + k \cdot 4\pi$

9. $A = -4, B = 2$

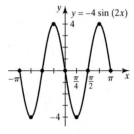

amplitude: $|A| = 4$

period: $\dfrac{2\pi}{2} = \pi$

Start at the origin, mark off one period, and divide it into four subintervals. Using the sine form reflected across the x-axis, plot the critical points.

x-intercepts: $-\pi, -\dfrac{\pi}{2}, 0, \dfrac{\pi}{2}, \pi$ or $x = k \cdot \dfrac{\pi}{2}$

11. $A = 0.5, B = \pi$

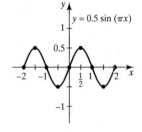

amplitude: $|A| = 0.5$

period: $\dfrac{2\pi}{\pi} = 2$

Start at the origin, mark off one period, and divide it into four subintervals. Using the sine form, plot the critical points.

x-intercepts: $-2, -1, 0, 1, 2$ or $x = k$

13. $A = -2, B = \dfrac{\pi}{4}$

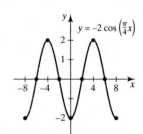

Since $A < 0$, the graph reflects across the x-axis.

amplitude: $|A| = 2$

period: $\dfrac{2\pi}{\left(\dfrac{\pi}{4}\right)} = 8$

Start at the origin, mark off one period, and divide it into four subintervals. Using the cosine form, plot the critical points.

x-intercepts: $-6, -2, 2, 6$ or $x = 2 + k \cdot 4$

15. amplitude: 2
period: 2π } Dot in $y = 2\cos x$.

phase shift: right π
range: $|y| \le 2$

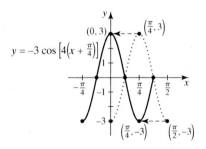

$y = 2\cos(x - \pi)$

17. amplitude: 4
period: 4π } Dot in $y = 4\sin\left(\dfrac{1}{2}x\right)$.

phase shift: left $\dfrac{\pi}{2}$
range: $|y| \le 4$

$y = 4\sin\left[\frac{1}{2}\left(x + \frac{\pi}{2}\right)\right]$

19. amplitude: 3
period: $\dfrac{\pi}{2}$ } Dot in $y = -3\cos(4x)$.

phase shift: left $\dfrac{\pi}{4}$
range: $|y| \le 3$

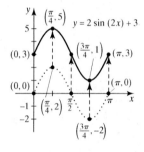

$y = -3\cos\left[4\left(x + \frac{\pi}{4}\right)\right]$

21. amplitude: 2
period: π } Dot in $y = 2\sin(2x)$.

vertical shift: up 3
range: $1 \le y \le 5$

$y = 2\sin(2x) + 3$

23. The graph can represent $y = \sin x$ reflected across the x-axis (g), or the graph can represent $y = \cos x$ shifted left $\dfrac{\pi}{2}$ (b).

25. The graph can represent $y = \cos x$ reflected across the x-axis (h), or the graph can represent $y = \sin x$ shifted right $\dfrac{\pi}{2}$ (d).

27, 29, 31. *There are many possible answers.*

27. By inspection, amplitude $= 2$, $P = \pi = \dfrac{2\pi}{|B|} \rightarrow B = 2$.

Since the graph has the cosine form, $y = 2\cos(2x)$.

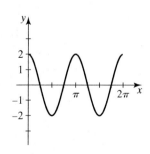

29. The amplitude $= \left| \dfrac{5 - 1}{2} \right| = 2$, so $A = 2$. And since $P = 2\pi$, $B = 1$.

Since the sine form has been shifted up three, $y = 2 \sin x + 3$.

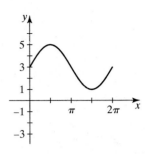

31. By inspection, amplitude $= 4$, $P = 4\pi = \dfrac{2\pi}{|B|} \to B = \dfrac{1}{2}$.

Since the cosine form has been reflected across the x-axis, $y = -4 \cos\left(\dfrac{1}{2}x \right)$.

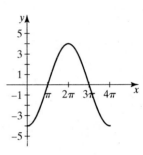

33, 35, 37. *Make sure that $B > 0$, and that the values of C stay within the restrictions: $-\pi < C < 0$ and $0 < C < \pi$ (which means that all graphs must be the result of a phase shift).*

33. $y = \sin\left[2\left(x + \dfrac{\pi}{4} \right) \right]$, or $y = \sin\left[2\left(x - \dfrac{3\pi}{4} \right) \right]$ **35.** $y = \cos\left[\dfrac{1}{2}\left(x - \dfrac{\pi}{2} \right) \right]$, or $y = \sin\left[\dfrac{1}{2}\left(x + \dfrac{\pi}{2} \right) \right]$

37. $y = \sin\left(x - \dfrac{\pi}{2} \right)$ **39.** $y = -6\sin\left(\dfrac{1}{2}x \right)$, $y = 6\cos\left[\dfrac{1}{2}(x + \pi) \right]$

41. Rewrite as $y = \dfrac{1}{4}\sin\left[4\left(x - \dfrac{1}{2} \right) \right]$. amplitude $= |A| = \dfrac{1}{4}$, $P = \dfrac{2\pi}{4} = \dfrac{\pi}{2}$, phase shift: right $\dfrac{1}{2}$, range: $|y| \leq \dfrac{1}{4}$

43. amplitude: 2.3, $P = 12\pi$, vertical shift: up π, range: $-2.3 + \pi \leq y \leq 2.3 + \pi$

45. **a.** $y = \sin x + 2$ shifts the graph of $y = \sin x$ up 2 units; $y = \sin(x + 2)$ shifts the graph of $y = \sin x$ left 2 units.

b. $y = \sin(2x)$ has an amplitude of 1 and a period of π; $y = 2\sin x$ has an amplitude of 2 and a period of 2π.

c. $y = \dfrac{1}{2}\sin 2x$ has an amplitude of $\dfrac{1}{2}$ and a period of π; $y = \sin x$ has an amplitude of 1 and a period of 2π.

d. $y = \sin\left(x + \dfrac{\pi}{2} \right)$ shifts $y = \sin x$ left $\dfrac{\pi}{2}$ units; $y = \sin x + \sin\dfrac{\pi}{2}$ is the same as $y = \sin x + 1$, which shifts $y = \sin x$ up 1 unit.

Exercise Set 2.3, p. 115

1. **a.** maximum $= 88.7$, minimum $= 80.1$ **b.** amplitude $= \left| \dfrac{88.7 - 80.1}{2} \right| = 4.3$

3. **a.** maximum $= 74.5$, minimum $= 58.5$ **b.** amplitude $= \left| \dfrac{74.5 - 58.5}{2} \right| = 8$

5. Yes

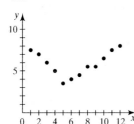

7. No

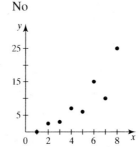

9. Yes

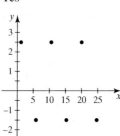

11, 13. *Note: For the sine or cosine form, the consecutive maximum and minimum critical points occur one-half period apart (or max to max points are a period apart).*

11. amplitude $= \left| \dfrac{21 - 10.5}{2} \right| = 5.25$ We let $A = 5.25$.

As a result of the repetition of maximum (or minimum) critical points occurring 15 units apart along the x-axis, the period is 15.

$$P = 15 = \frac{2\pi}{|B|} \rightarrow B = \frac{2\pi}{15}$$

With period 15, each arc occurs in a length of $\dfrac{15}{4} = 3.75$ units along the x-axis. Using the sine form, and knowing a maximum critical point occurs at $x = 2$, the phase shift is $2 - 3.75 = -1.75$ (left). So $C = -1.75$.
If $A = 5.25$ and the minimum y-coordinate is 10.5, the shift up is

$$D = 10.5 + 5.25 = 15.75.$$

Therefore, $y = 5.25 \sin \left[\dfrac{2\pi}{15}(x + 1.75) \right] + 15.75$.

13. amplitude $= \left| \dfrac{90 - 71}{2} \right| = 9.5$ We let $A = 9.5$.

As a result of the minimum y-coordinate occurring at $x = 2$, and the maximum y-coordinate at $x = 8$, we use the period 12.

$$P = 12 = \frac{2\pi}{|B|} \rightarrow B = \frac{\pi}{6}$$

With period 12, each arc occurs in a length of $\dfrac{12}{4} = 3$ units along the x-axis. Using the sine form and knowing a maximum critical value occurs at $x = 8$, the phase shift is $8 - 3 = 5$ units right. So $C = 5$.
If $A = 9.5$ and the minimum y-coordinate is 71, the shift up is

$$D = 71 + 9.5 = 80.5.$$

Therefore, $y = 9.5 \sin \left[\dfrac{\pi}{6}(x - 5) \right] + 80.5$.

15 and 17. *Sine regression values may vary due to the calculator model or manufacturer. The following values are from a TI-83 Plus, using only one period of values.*

15. $a \approx 5.1767, \quad b \approx 0.3748,$
$c \approx 1.4498, \quad d \approx 16.1445$

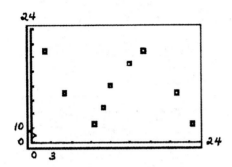

$y = 5.1767 \sin(0.3748x + 1.4498) + 16.1445$

17. **a.** Let $x = 0$ represent 12 midnight: $a \approx 1.4346, b \approx 0.5664, c \approx -1.8332, d \approx 5.3372$
So $y = 1.4346 \sin(0.5664x - 1.8332) + 5.3372$, where y represents the water depth in feet.
   b. At 5AM, $x = 5$ and the water depth is:

$$y = 1.4346 \sin(0.5664(5) - 1.8332) + 5.3372$$
$$= 6.5 \text{ ft (to the nearest half-foot)}$$

At 4PM, $x = 16$ and depth ≈ 6.5 ft.
   c. At 9PM, $x = 21$ and depth ≈ 4.5 ft, which means the depth is not enough to bring the boat in since it needs a depth of 5 ft.

19. **a.** Since P_1 has a frequency of 10, with cosine form, $F = 10 = \dfrac{1}{P} \rightarrow P = \dfrac{1}{10} = \dfrac{2\pi}{|B|} \rightarrow B = 20\pi$.

$$P_1 : y = \cos(20\pi x)$$

Since P_2 has a frequency of 12, with reflected cosine form, $F = 12 = \dfrac{1}{P} \rightarrow P = \dfrac{1}{12} = \dfrac{2\pi}{|B|} \rightarrow B = 24\pi$.

$$P_2 : y = -\cos(24\pi x)$$

   b. No
   c. By inspection, period $= \dfrac{1}{2}$, which means the frequency is 2.

Exercise Set 2.4, p. 129

Function	Domain	Range	Period	Asymptotes	x-intercepts	y-intercepts	Graph
1. $y = \sin x$	$x \in \mathbb{R}$	$|y| \le 1$	2π	—	$x = k\pi$	$(0, 0)$	

Function	Domain	Range	Period	Asymptotes	x-intercepts	y-intercepts	Graph
3. $y = \tan x$	$x \neq \dfrac{\pi}{2} + k\pi$	$y \in \mathbb{R}$	π	$x = \dfrac{\pi}{2} + k\pi$	$x = k\pi$	$(0, 0)$	
5. $y = \sec x$	$x \neq \dfrac{\pi}{2} + k\pi$	$|y| \geq 1$	2π	$x = \dfrac{\pi}{2} + k\pi$	—	$(0, 1)$	

7. $y = \sin x$, $y = \tan x$

9. $y = \tan x$, $y = \cot x$, $y = \csc x$, $y = \sin x$

11. all

13. $y = \tan x$, $y = \cot x$, $y = \sec x$, $y = \csc x$

For **15, 17, 19, 21, 23, 25, 27**, $P = \dfrac{\text{pure period}}{|B|}$.

15. Step 1. $B = \dfrac{1}{2}$, so $P = \dfrac{\pi}{\left(\dfrac{1}{2}\right)} = 2\pi$.

Step 2. asymptotes: $x = \dfrac{\dfrac{\pi}{2} + k\pi}{\left(\dfrac{1}{2}\right)} = \pi + k \cdot 2\pi$ For $k = -1, 0$ we get $x = -\pi, \pi$.

Step 3. x-intercepts: $x = \dfrac{k\pi}{\left(\dfrac{1}{2}\right)} = k \cdot 2\pi$ For $k = 0$ we get $x = 0$.

Steps 4–6.

x	y
$-\dfrac{\pi}{2}$	-1
$\dfrac{\pi}{2}$	1

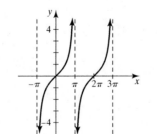

$y = \tan\left(\dfrac{1}{2}x\right)$

17. Rewrite as $y = \tan\left(x - \left(-\frac{\pi}{2}\right)\right)$.

Step 1. $B = 1$, so $P = \pi$

Step 2. Asymptotes for $y = \tan x$ are $x = -\frac{\pi}{2}$ and $x = \frac{\pi}{2}$.

Since $C = -\frac{\pi}{2}$, the graph of $y = \tan x$ shifts left $\frac{\pi}{2}$. The asymptotes for $y = \tan\left(x - \left(-\frac{\pi}{2}\right)\right)$ are

$$x = -\frac{\pi}{2} + \left(-\frac{\pi}{2}\right) = -\pi, \ x = \frac{\pi}{2} + \left(-\frac{\pi}{2}\right) = 0, \text{ or } x = k\pi.$$

Step 3. x-intercept: $x = -\frac{\pi}{2}, \frac{\pi}{2}$ (one-half the distance between the asymptotes) or $x = \frac{\pi}{2} + k\pi$.

Steps 4–6.

x	y
$-\dfrac{3\pi}{4}$	-1
$-\dfrac{\pi}{4}$	1

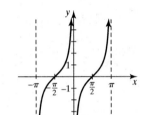

$$y = \tan\left(x + \frac{\pi}{2}\right)$$

19. Since $A = -2$, we have a reflection across the x-axis.

Step 1. $B = 2$, so $P = \frac{\pi}{2}$

Step 2. Asymptotes: $x = \frac{k \cdot \pi}{2}$

For $k = 0, 1$ we get $x = 0$, and $x = \frac{\pi}{2}$.

Step 3. x-intercepts: $\dfrac{\frac{\pi}{2} + k\pi}{2} = \frac{\pi}{4} + k \cdot \frac{\pi}{2}$

For $k = 0$ we get $x = \frac{\pi}{4}$ (one-half the distance between the asymptotes).

Steps 4–6.

x	y
$\dfrac{\pi}{8}$	-2
$\dfrac{3\pi}{8}$	2

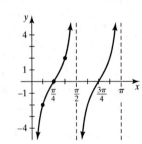

$$y = -2\cot(2x)$$

21. For $y = -\cot x + 1$, since $A < 1$, we have a reflection; $D = 1$ indicates a vertical shift of $y = -\cot x$ up 1.

    Step 1. $P = \pi$

    Step 2. Asymptotes: $x = k\pi$

    Step 3. Since the graph shifts up 1 and the x-intercepts are where $y = 0$, then $0 = -\cot x + 1 \rightarrow \cot x = 1$, so
    $$x = \frac{\pi}{4}, \frac{5\pi}{4}, \ldots \text{ or } x = \frac{\pi}{4} + k\pi.$$

    Step 4–6.

x	$-\cot x$	$-\cot x + 1$
$\dfrac{\pi}{4}$	-1	0
$\dfrac{3\pi}{4}$	1	2

    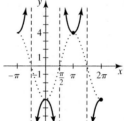

    $y = -\cot x + 1$

23. Step 1. Dot in the graph of the guide function $y = -4\cos x$.

    Step 2. At each x-intercept, plot the asymptotes.

    Step 3. Draw the four arc sections in the form of two separate U-shaped branches between the asymptotes.

    $P = 2\pi$, range: $|y| \geq 4$

    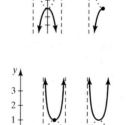

    $y = -4\sec x$

25. Step 1. Dot in $y = \sin(-2x) = -\sin(2x)$ as the guide function.

    Step 2. Plot the asymptotes at each x-intercept.

    Step 3. Draw the four arc sections in the form of two U-shaped branches between the asymptotes.

    $P = \pi$, range: $|y| \geq 1$

    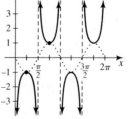

    $y = \csc(-2x)$

27. Step 1. Dot in $y = 4\cos\left(x + \dfrac{\pi}{2}\right)$ as the guide function.

    Step 2. Plot the asymptotes at each x-intercept.

    Step 3. Draw the four arc sections in the form of two U-shaped branches between the asymptotes.

    $P = 2\pi$, range: $|y| \geq 4$

    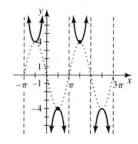

    $y = 4\sec\left(x + \dfrac{\pi}{2}\right)$

29. **c.** Use $y = \cos\left(\frac{1}{2}x\right) + 2$ as a guide function. Since $B = \frac{1}{2}$, $P = 4\pi$, and since $D = 2$, there is a vertical shift up 2.

31. **a.** Since $B = 2$, $P = \frac{\pi}{2}$ in cotangent form.

33. The graph does not represent a function since it does not pass the vertical line test. The graph should not cross its asymptotes.

35. One branch is missing. The cycle is incomplete.

37. **a, c;**

Since $y = \tan x$ has period π, then $y = -\tan x = -\tan(x + \pi)$ (a).

Also $y = \cot x$ shifted right $\frac{\pi}{2}$, is the same as $y = -\tan x$ (c).

Exercise Set 2.5, p. 143

1. $y = \arcsin \frac{\sqrt{3}}{2} \longleftrightarrow \sin y = \frac{\sqrt{3}}{2}, \quad -\frac{\pi}{2} \le y \le \frac{\pi}{2}$

Since $\hat{y} = \frac{\pi}{3}$, the only arc with this sine value in the restricted range is $y = \frac{\pi}{3}$.

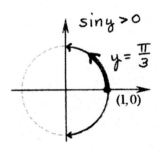

3. $y = \cos^{-1} 1 \longleftrightarrow \cos y = 1, \; 0 \le y \le \pi$
The only arc with this cosine value in the restricted range is $y = 0$.

5. $y = \text{arccsc}\,(-\sqrt{2}) \longleftrightarrow \csc y = -\sqrt{2}, \quad -\frac{\pi}{2} \le y < 0, \; 0 < y \le \frac{\pi}{2}$

$\longleftrightarrow \sin y = -\frac{1}{\sqrt{2}}$

Since $\hat{y} = \frac{\pi}{4}$, the only arc in the restricted range with this sine value $y = -\frac{\pi}{4}$.

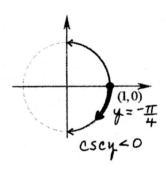

7. $\tan^{-1} 1 \longleftrightarrow \tan y = 1, \quad -\frac{\pi}{2} < y < \frac{\pi}{2}$

$\hat{y} = \frac{\pi}{4}$, so $y = \frac{\pi}{4}$

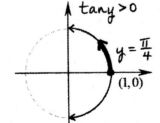

9. $\arccos \frac{1}{2} \longleftrightarrow \cos y = \frac{1}{2}, \; 0 \le y \le \pi$

$\hat{y} = \frac{\pi}{3}$, so $y = \frac{\pi}{3}$

11. $\arcsin 0 \longleftrightarrow \sin y = 0,\ -\dfrac{\pi}{2} \le y \le \dfrac{\pi}{2}$ so $y = 0$

13. $\sec^{-1}(-1) \longleftrightarrow \sec y = -1,\ 0 \le y < \dfrac{\pi}{2},\ \dfrac{\pi}{2} < y \le \pi$

$\longleftrightarrow \cos y = -1$ so, $y = \pi$

15. $\cot^{-1} 1 \longleftrightarrow \cot y = 1,\ 0 < y < \pi$

$\longleftrightarrow \tan y = 1$, so $y = \dfrac{\pi}{4}$

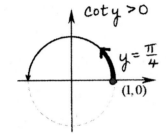

17. $\arctan(-\sqrt{3}) \longleftrightarrow \tan y = -\sqrt{3},\ -\dfrac{\pi}{2} < y < \dfrac{\pi}{2}$

$\hat{y} = \dfrac{\pi}{3}$, so $y = -\dfrac{\pi}{3}$

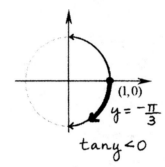

19. $\cos^{-1}\left(-\dfrac{\sqrt{3}}{2}\right) \longleftrightarrow \cos y = -\dfrac{\sqrt{3}}{2},\ 0 \le y \le \pi$

$\hat{y} = \dfrac{\pi}{6}$, so $y = \dfrac{5\pi}{6}$

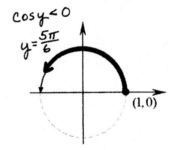

21, 23, 25, 27, 29, 31, 33. *Your calculator should be in radian mode.*

21. $\arccos\left(-\dfrac{2}{3}\right)$

$\cos^{-1}(-2 \div 3)\ \boxed{\text{ENTER}} \approx 2.3005$

23. $\tan^{-1}\dfrac{4}{3}$

$\tan^{-1}(4 \div 3)\ \boxed{\text{ENTER}} \approx 0.9273$

25. $\sec^{-1}(-1.23)$

$\cos^{-1}(1 \div -1.23)\ \boxed{\text{ENTER}} \approx 2.5201$

27. $\text{arccsc}\ \dfrac{13}{5}$

$\cos^{-1}(5 \div 13)\ \boxed{\text{ENTER}} \approx 0.3948$

29. $\arcsin 0.6445$

$\sin^{-1}(0.6445)\ \boxed{\text{ENTER}} \approx 0.7004$

31. $\tan^{-1}(-5.967)$

$\tan^{-1}(-5.967)\ \boxed{\text{ENTER}} \approx -1.4048$

33. $\cos^{-1}\sqrt{\dfrac{2}{33}}$

$\cos^{-1}\left(\sqrt{(2 \div 33)}\right)\ \boxed{\text{ENTER}} \approx 1.3221$

35. $\sin\left(\cos^{-1}\dfrac{1}{2}\right) = \sin\left(\dfrac{\pi}{3}\right) = \dfrac{\sqrt{3}}{2}$

37. $\cos\left(\cos^{-1} 1\right) = \cos(0) = 1$

39. $\tan\left(\arctan\sqrt{3}\right) = \tan\left(\dfrac{\pi}{3}\right) = \sqrt{3}$

41. $\cos(\arcsin 1) = \cos\left(\dfrac{\pi}{2}\right) = 0$

43. $\csc\left(\cos^{-1}\left(-\dfrac{\sqrt{3}}{2}\right)\right) = \csc\left(\dfrac{5\pi}{6}\right) = \dfrac{1}{\sin\left(\dfrac{5\pi}{6}\right)} = 2$

45. $\cos\left(\arcsin\left(-\dfrac{\sqrt{2}}{2}\right)\right) = \cos\left(-\dfrac{\pi}{4}\right) = \dfrac{\sqrt{2}}{2}$

47. $\cot\left(\cos^{-1}\left(-\dfrac{1}{2}\right)\right) = \cot\left(\dfrac{2\pi}{3}\right) = \dfrac{1}{\tan\left(\dfrac{2\pi}{3}\right)} = \dfrac{1}{-\sqrt{3}} = -\dfrac{\sqrt{3}}{3}$

49. $\sin^{-1}\left(\cos\dfrac{7\pi}{6}\right) = \sin^{-1}\left(-\dfrac{\sqrt{3}}{2}\right) = -\dfrac{\pi}{3}$

51. $\arctan\left(\cos\dfrac{\pi}{2}\right) = \arctan(0) = 0$

53. $\sin^{-1}\left(\cos\left(-\dfrac{\pi}{3}\right)\right) = \sin^{-1}\left(\dfrac{1}{2}\right) = \dfrac{\pi}{6}$

55. $\operatorname{arcsec}\left(\tan\dfrac{3\pi}{4}\right) = \operatorname{arcsec}(-1) = \arccos(-1) = \pi$

57. $\sin\left(\cos^{-1}\dfrac{12}{13}\right)$ Let $y = \cos^{-1}\dfrac{12}{13} \longleftrightarrow \cos y = \dfrac{12}{13},\ 0 \le y \le \pi$

So we want $\sin y$, where $\cos y = \dfrac{12}{13}$. Use the Pythagorean identity.

$$\left(\dfrac{12}{13}\right)^2 + (\sin y)^2 = 1$$
$$(\sin y)^2 = 1 - \dfrac{144}{169} = \dfrac{25}{169}$$
$$\sin y = \dfrac{5}{13},\ \text{since } \sin y > 0 \text{ for } 0 \le y \le \pi$$

59. $\cos\left(\sin^{-1}\dfrac{8}{17}\right)$ Let $y = \sin^{-1}\dfrac{8}{17} \longleftrightarrow \sin y = \dfrac{8}{17},\ -\dfrac{\pi}{2} \le y \le \dfrac{\pi}{2}$

So we want $\cos y$, where $\sin y = \dfrac{8}{17}$. Use the Pythagorean identity.

$$(\cos y)^2 + \left(\dfrac{8}{17}\right)^2 = 1$$
$$(\cos y)^2 = 1 - \dfrac{64}{289} = \dfrac{225}{289}$$
$$\cos y = \dfrac{15}{17},\ \text{since } \cos y > 0 \text{ for } -\dfrac{\pi}{2} \le y \le \dfrac{\pi}{2}$$

61. $\tan(\sin^{-1} 0.2657)$

   $\tan(\sin^{-1}(0.2657))$ $\boxed{\text{ENTER}}$ ≈ 0.2756

63. $\sin(\cos^{-1} 0.4675)$

   $\sin(\cos^{-1}(0.4675))$ $\boxed{\text{ENTER}}$ ≈ 0.8840

65. $\arctan(\sin 3.95)$

   $\tan^{-1}(\sin(3.95))$ $\boxed{\text{ENTER}}$ ≈ -0.6261

67. $\csc\left(\arcsin\left(-\dfrac{5}{9}\right)\right)$

   $1 \div \sin(\sin^{-1}(-5 \div 9))$ $\boxed{\text{ENTER}}$ $= -\dfrac{9}{5} = -1.8000$

69. $\sec^{-1}\left(\tan \dfrac{\sqrt{7}}{2}\right)$

   $\cos^{-1}\left(1 \div \tan\left(\sqrt{(7)} \div 2\right)\right)$ $\boxed{\text{ENTER}}$ ≈ 1.3149

71. **a.** $y = \tan x$, **ii.** $y = \arctan x$ **b.** $y = \sin x$, **i.** $y = \arcsin x$ **c.** $y = \cos x$, **iii.** $y = \arccos x$

73. $5\sin(6x) = -5$

   $\sin(6x) = -1$ Multiply each side by $\dfrac{1}{5}$.

   $6x = \sin^{-1}(-1)$ Use the definition of inverse sine function.

   $6x = -\dfrac{\pi}{2}$ $\sin^{-1}(-1) = -\dfrac{\pi}{2}$

   $x = -\dfrac{\pi}{12}$ Multiply each side by $\dfrac{1}{6}$.

75. $4\tan(9x) = 7$

   $\tan(9x) = \dfrac{7}{4}$ Multiply each side by $\dfrac{1}{4}$.

   $9x = \tan^{-1}\left(\dfrac{7}{4}\right)$ Use the definition of inverse tangent function.

   $x = \dfrac{1}{9}\tan^{-1}\left(\dfrac{7}{4}\right)$ Multiply each side by $\dfrac{1}{9}$.

   ≈ 0.1169 (Find a calculator approximation.)

77. $\sin^{-1} x$ is the inverse function of $\sin x$, whereas $(\sin x)^{-1}$ is the reciprocal function of $\sin x$. Another name for $\sin^{-1} x$ is $\arcsin x$, and another name for $(\sin x)^{-1}$ is $\csc x$.

Chapter 2 Review Exercises, p. 151

1. amplitude = 2

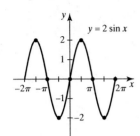

2. amplitude = 3

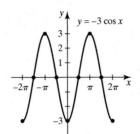

3. amplitude = 0.7

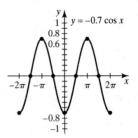

4. amplitude = $\dfrac{1}{2}$

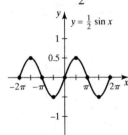

5. amplitude = $\dfrac{3}{2}$

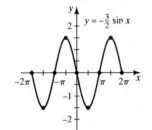

6. amplitude = 2π

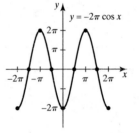

7. Since $A = 4$ and $B = \dfrac{1}{2}$,

amplitude: 4

period: $\dfrac{2\pi}{\left(\dfrac{1}{2}\right)} = 4\pi$

range: $|y| \le 4$

x-intercepts: $x = \pi + k \cdot 2\pi$

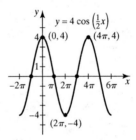

8. Since $A = 1.5$ and $B = 2$,

amplitude: 1.5

period: $\dfrac{2\pi}{2} = \pi$

range: $|y| \le 1.5$, x-intercepts: $x = k \cdot \dfrac{\pi}{2}$

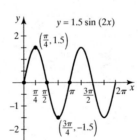

9. Rewrite: $y = -3\sin\left(-\dfrac{1}{4}x\right)$

as $y = 3\sin\left(\dfrac{1}{4}x\right)$

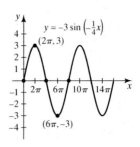

$\rightarrow A = 3,\ B = \dfrac{1}{4}$

amplitude: 3

period: $\dfrac{2\pi}{\left(\dfrac{1}{4}\right)} = 8\pi$

range: $|y| \le 3$, x-intercept: $x = k \cdot 4\pi$

10. Rewrite: $y = -2\cos\left(-\dfrac{1}{2}x\right)$

as $y = -2\cos\left(\dfrac{1}{2}x\right)$

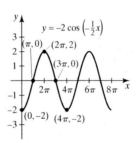

$\rightarrow A = -2,\ B = \dfrac{1}{2}$

amplitude: 2

period: $\dfrac{2\pi}{\left(\dfrac{1}{2}\right)} = 4\pi$

range: $|y| \le 2$, x-intercept: $x = \pi + k \cdot 2\pi$

11. Rewrite: $y = -\cos(-\pi x)$

as $y = -\cos(\pi x)$

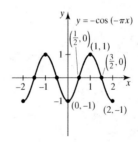

$\rightarrow A = -1,\ B = \pi$

amplitude: 1

period: $\dfrac{2\pi}{\pi} = 2$

range: $|y| \le 1$, x-intercept: $x = \dfrac{1}{2} + k$

12. Rewrite: $y = 5 \sin \left(-\dfrac{2\pi}{5} x\right)$

as $y = -5 \sin \left(\dfrac{2\pi}{5} x\right)$

$\rightarrow A = -5, \; B = \dfrac{2\pi}{5}$

amplitude: 5

period: $\dfrac{2\pi}{\left(\dfrac{2\pi}{5}\right)} = 5,$

range: $|y| \le 5$, x-intercept: $x = k \cdot \dfrac{5}{2}$

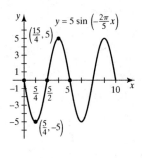

13. Since $A = 1$, $B = 1$, and $C = \dfrac{\pi}{2}$,

period: 2π, phase shift: right $\dfrac{\pi}{2}$

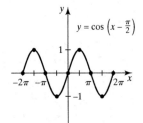

14. Since $A = -1$, $B = 1$, and $C = -\dfrac{\pi}{2}$,

period: 2π, phase shift: left $\dfrac{\pi}{2}$

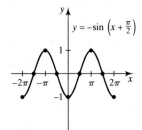

15. Since $A = -4$, $B = \dfrac{1}{2}$, and $C = -\pi$,

period: 4π, phase shift: left π

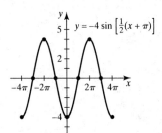

16. Since $A = 2.5$, $B = 2$, and $C = \dfrac{\pi}{4}$,

period: π, phase shift: right $\dfrac{\pi}{4}$

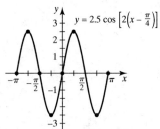

17. Since $A = 2$, $B = \dfrac{1}{3}$, $C = 0$, and $D = 4$,

period: 6π, vertical shift: up 4

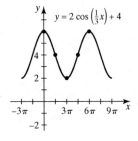

18. Since $A = \dfrac{1}{2}$, $B = 2$, $C = 0$, and $D = -\dfrac{1}{2}$,

period: π, vertical shift: down $\dfrac{1}{2}$

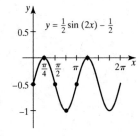

19. $y = 5 \sin x$ **20.** $y = -4 \cos x$

21. $y = 0.6 \cos x$ **22.** $y = -\dfrac{1}{2} \sin x$

23–24. *There are many possible answers. Answers different from the ones given can be checked with a graphing utility.*

23. amplitude $= 4$

period $= \pi = \dfrac{2\pi}{|B|} \rightarrow B = 2$

If we consider the sine form shifted right $\dfrac{\pi}{2}$:

$$y = 4 \sin \left[2 \left(x - \frac{\pi}{2} \right) \right]$$

or shifted left $\dfrac{\pi}{2}$:

$$y = 4 \sin \left[2 \left(x + \frac{\pi}{2} \right) \right].$$

If we consider the cosine form shifted left $\dfrac{\pi}{4}$:

$$y = 4 \cos \left[2 \left(x + \frac{\pi}{4} \right) \right]$$

or reflected and shifted right $\dfrac{\pi}{4}$:

$$y = -4 \cos \left[2 \left(x - \frac{\pi}{4} \right) \right].$$

24. amplitude $= 1$

period $= \pi = \dfrac{2\pi}{|B|} \rightarrow B = 2$

If we consider the sine form shifted left $\dfrac{\pi}{8}$:

$$y = \sin \left[2 \left(x + \frac{\pi}{8} \right) \right]$$

or shifted right $\dfrac{7\pi}{8}$:

$$y = \sin \left[2 \left(x - \frac{7\pi}{8} \right) \right].$$

If we consider the cosine form shifted right $\dfrac{\pi}{8}$:

$$y = \cos \left[2 \left(x - \frac{\pi}{8} \right) \right]$$

or shifted left $\dfrac{7\pi}{8}$:

$$y = \cos \left[2 \left(x + \frac{7\pi}{8} \right) \right]$$

or reflected and shifted left $\dfrac{3\pi}{8}$:

$$y = -\cos \left[2 \left(x + \frac{3\pi}{8} \right) \right]$$

25. See answers for Exercise 23 or check your answer with a graphing utility.

26. See answers for Exercise 24 or check your answer with a graphing utility.

27. **a.** $A = 4$, $B = \pi \rightarrow$ amplitude $= |A| = 4$, and $P = \dfrac{2\pi}{\pi} = 2$

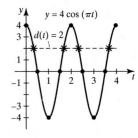

b. Each time the point is in the rest position, or when $d(t) = 0$, it is at an t-intercept. By inspection this occurs when

$$t = \frac{1}{2}, \frac{3}{2}, \frac{5}{2}, \frac{7}{2}.$$

c. See the graph in part (a) for the times when the displacement is 2 inches from the rest position. (Here displacement is positive, so the positions are above the rest position.)

28. **a.** $A = 4.5$ $P = \dfrac{2\pi}{\left(\dfrac{1}{2}\right)} = 4\pi$

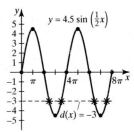

b. See the graph in part (a). Here the displacement is negative, so the positions are below the rest position.

29. **a.** Amplitude $= \left| \dfrac{14.75 - 9.5}{2} \right| = 2\dfrac{5}{8}$. We let $A = 2\dfrac{5}{8}$.

As a result of the maximum y-coordinate occurring at $x = 6$ and the minimum y-coordinate occurring at $x = 12$, we use the period 12.

$$P = 12 = \frac{2\pi}{|B|} \rightarrow B = \frac{\pi}{6}$$

With period 12, each arc occurs in a length of 3 along the x-axis. Using the sine form and knowing the maximum occurs at $x = 6$, the phase shift is $6 - 3 = 3$ units right. So $C = 3$.

If $A = 2\dfrac{5}{8}$ and the minimum y-coordinate is $9\dfrac{1}{2}$,

$$D = 9\frac{1}{2} + 2\frac{5}{8} = 12\frac{1}{8}.$$

Therefore,

$$y = 2\frac{5}{8} \sin\left[\frac{\pi}{6}(x - 3)\right] + 12\frac{1}{8}.$$

b.

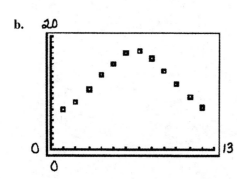

c. For $y = a \sin(bx + c) + d$:

$$a \approx 2.6327, \qquad b \approx 0.5073,$$
$$c \approx -1.4729, \quad c \approx 12.1466$$

30. a. Amplitude $= \left| \dfrac{17.5 - 7}{2} \right| = 5\dfrac{1}{4}$. We let $A = 5\dfrac{1}{4}$. Since this table reflects yearly occurences, we let

$$P = 12 = \frac{2\pi}{|B|} \to B = \frac{\pi}{6}.$$

With period 12, each arc occurs in a length of 3 along the x-axis. Using the sine form and knowing the maximum occurs at $x = 7$, the phase shift is $7 - 3 = 4$ units right.
So $C = 4$.

If $A = 5\dfrac{1}{4}$ and the minimum y-coordinate is 7,

$$D = 7 + 5\frac{1}{4} = 12\frac{1}{4}.$$

Therefore,

$$y = 5\frac{1}{4} \sin\left[\frac{\pi}{6}(x - 4)\right] + 12\frac{1}{4}.$$

b.

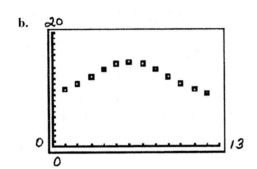

c. For $y = a\sin(bx + c) + d$:

$$a \approx 5.1516, \qquad b \approx 0.5094,$$
$$c \approx -1.8199, \quad d \approx 12.1474$$

31. Step 1. $B = \dfrac{1}{3}$, so $P = \dfrac{\pi}{\left(\dfrac{1}{3}\right)} = 3\pi$

Step 2. asymptotes: $x = \dfrac{k\pi}{\left(\dfrac{1}{3}\right)} = k \cdot 3\pi$

For $k = 0, 1$ we get $x = 0,\ 3\pi$.

Step 3. x-intercepts: $x = \dfrac{\dfrac{\pi}{2} + k\pi}{\left(\dfrac{1}{3}\right)} = \dfrac{3\pi}{2} + k \cdot 3\pi$

For $k = 0$ we get $x = \dfrac{3\pi}{2}$ (one-half the distance between the asymptotes) or $x = \dfrac{3\pi}{2} + k \cdot 3\pi$
(one period apart).

Steps 4–6.

x	y
$\dfrac{3\pi}{4}$	3
$\dfrac{9\pi}{4}$	-3

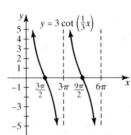

range: $\mathbb{R}$

32. Step 1. $B = 2$, so $P = \dfrac{\pi}{2}$

Step 2. asymptotes: $x = \dfrac{\dfrac{\pi}{2} + k\pi}{2} = \dfrac{\pi}{4} + k \cdot \dfrac{\pi}{2}$

   For $k = -1, 0$ we get $x = -\dfrac{\pi}{4}, \dfrac{\pi}{4}$.

Step 3. x-intercepts: $x = \dfrac{k \cdot \pi}{2} = k \cdot \dfrac{\pi}{2}$

   For $k = 0$ we get $x = 0$ (one-half the distance between the asymptotes) or $x = 0 + k \cdot \dfrac{\pi}{2} = k \cdot \dfrac{\pi}{2}$ (one period apart).

Steps 4–6. Since $A < 0$, the graph will reflect across the x-axis.

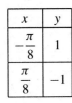

x	y
$-\dfrac{\pi}{8}$	1
$\dfrac{\pi}{8}$	-1

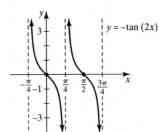

range: $\mathbb{R}$

33. Step 1. $B = \dfrac{1}{4}$, so $P = \dfrac{\pi}{\left(\dfrac{1}{4}\right)} = 4\pi$

Step 2. asymptote for $y = \tan \dfrac{1}{4}x$ are $x = \dfrac{\dfrac{\pi}{2} + k\pi}{\left(\dfrac{1}{4}\right)} = 2\pi + k \cdot 4\pi$

   For $k = -1, 0$ we get $x = -2\pi, 2\pi$. Since $C = \pi$, we shift each asymptote right π for $y = \tan\left[\dfrac{1}{4}(x - \pi)\right]$ and get

$$x = -2\pi + \pi = -\pi, \; x = 2\pi + \pi = 3\pi, \quad \text{or} \quad x = -\pi + k \cdot 4\pi.$$

Step 3. x-intercept: $x = \pi + k \cdot 4\pi$ (one-half the distance between the asymptotes and a period apart).

Steps 4–6.

x	y
0	-1
2π	1

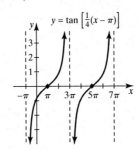

range: $\mathbb{R}$

34. Step 1. $B = \dfrac{1}{2}$, so $P = \dfrac{\pi}{\left(\dfrac{1}{2}\right)} = 2\pi$

Step 2. asymptote for $y = \cot\left(\dfrac{1}{2}x\right)$ are $x = \dfrac{k\pi}{\left(\dfrac{1}{2}\right)} = k \cdot 2\pi$. For $k = 0, 1$ we get $x = 0, 2\pi$. Since $C = -\pi$,

we shift each asymptote left π for $y = \cot\left[\dfrac{1}{2}(x + \pi)\right]$ and get

$$x = 0 - \pi = -\pi, \ x = 2\pi - \pi = \pi, \quad \text{or} \quad x = \pi + k \cdot 2\pi.$$

Step 3. x-intercept: $x = 0 + k \cdot 2\pi$ (one-half the distance between the asymptotes and a period apart).

Steps 4–6.

x	y
$-\dfrac{\pi}{2}$	1
$\dfrac{\pi}{2}$	-1

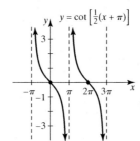

range: $\mathbb{R}$

35. Step 1. Dot in $y = -\dfrac{1}{2}\sin\left(\dfrac{1}{2}x\right)$ as the guide function.

Step 2. Plot the asymptotes at each x-intercept.

Step 3. Draw the four arcs in the form of two U-shaped branches between the asymptotes.

The period is 4π, and the range is $|y| \geq \dfrac{1}{2}$.

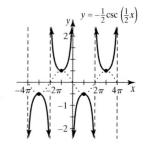

36. Step 1. Dot in $y = \cos\left[2\left(x + \dfrac{\pi}{2}\right)\right]$ as a guide function.

Step 2. Plot the asymptotes at each x-intercept.

Step 3. Draw the four arcs in the form of two U-shaped branches between the asymptotes.

The period is π, and the range is $|y| \geq 3$.

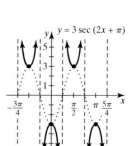

37. Step 1. Dot in the guide function $y = \cos(2x)$.

Step 2. Plot the asymptote at each x-intercept.

Step 3. Dot in the four arcs in the form of two U-shaped branches between the asymptotes.

Step 4. Since $D = 4$, shift each branch up 4.

The period is π, and the range is $y \geq 5$ or $y \leq 3$.

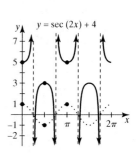

38. Step 1. Dot in the guide function $y = 2\sin x$.

Step 2. Plot the asymptotes at each x-intercept.

Step 3. Dot in the four arc sections in the form of two U-shaped branches between the asymptotes.

Step 4. Since $D = -2$, shift each branch down 2.

The period is 2π, and the range is $y \geq 0$ or $y \leq -4$.

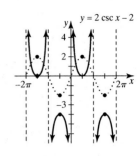

39–42. *Many answers are possible.*

39. Using the tangent form that has been reflected with period 2π, we get

$$A = -1,\ B = \frac{1}{2}\left(\text{since } P = 2\pi = \frac{\pi}{|B|}\right).$$

So $y = -\tan\left(\frac{1}{2}x\right)$. Or, using the cotangent form with period 2π shifted left π, we get $y = \cot\left[\frac{1}{2}(x+\pi)\right]$.

40. Dotting in the guide function, we get $y = 3\sin(2x)$ (since $A = 3$ and period $P = \pi = \frac{2\pi}{B} \rightarrow B = 2$).
So $y = 3\csc(2x)$.

41. Dotting in the guide function, we get $y = 2\cos\left(\frac{1}{4}x\right)$

$$\left(\text{since } A = 2,\ P = 8\pi = \frac{2\pi}{|B|} \rightarrow B = \frac{1}{4}\right).$$

So $y = 2\sec\left(\frac{1}{4}x\right)$.

42. Using the cotangent form with period π shifted left $\frac{\pi}{4}$, we get

$$y = \cot\left(x + \frac{\pi}{4}\right).$$

43. $y = \arcsin\left(\frac{\sqrt{2}}{2}\right) \longleftrightarrow \sin y = \frac{\sqrt{2}}{2}$, where $-\frac{\pi}{2} \leq y \leq \frac{\pi}{2}$

So $y = \frac{\pi}{4}$, or $\arcsin\frac{\sqrt{2}}{2} = \frac{\pi}{4}$.

44. $y = \arccos(-1) \longleftrightarrow \cos y = -1$, where $0 \leq y \leq \pi$
So $y = \pi$, or $\arccos(-1) = \pi$.

45. $y = \tan^{-1}(-\sqrt{3}) \longleftrightarrow \tan y = -\sqrt{3}$, where $-\frac{\pi}{2} < y < \frac{\pi}{2}$

So $y = -\frac{\pi}{3}$, or $\tan^{-1}(-\sqrt{3}) = -\frac{\pi}{3}$.

46. $y = \csc^{-1}\left(-\frac{2}{\sqrt{3}}\right) \longleftrightarrow \csc y = \frac{-2}{\sqrt{3}},\ -\frac{\pi}{2} \leq y < 0,\ 0 < y \leq \frac{\pi}{2}$

$$\longleftrightarrow \sin y = \frac{-\sqrt{3}}{2}.$$

So $y = -\frac{\pi}{3}$, or $\csc^{-1}\left(-\frac{2}{\sqrt{3}}\right) = -\frac{\pi}{3}$.

47. $y = \sec^{-1}\left(-\sqrt{2}\right) \longleftrightarrow \sec y = -\sqrt{2},\ 0 \le y < \dfrac{\pi}{2},\ \text{or } \dfrac{\pi}{2} < y \le \pi$

$\longleftrightarrow \cos y = -\dfrac{1}{\sqrt{2}}.$

So $y = \dfrac{3\pi}{4}$, or $\sec^{-1}\left(-\sqrt{2}\right) = \dfrac{3\pi}{4}.$

48. $y = \cot^{-1}(0) \longleftrightarrow \cot y = 0,\ 0 < y < \pi$

So $y = \dfrac{\pi}{2}$ $\left(y = \dfrac{\pi}{2} - \tan^{-1}(0) = \dfrac{\pi}{2} - 0 = \dfrac{\pi}{2}\right)$, or $\cot^{-1}(0) = \dfrac{\pi}{2}.$

49. $\cos(\arctan 1) = \cos\left(\dfrac{\pi}{4}\right) = \dfrac{\sqrt{2}}{2}$

50. $\arcsin\left(\cos\dfrac{\pi}{3}\right) = \arcsin\left(\dfrac{1}{2}\right) = \dfrac{\pi}{6}$

51. $\csc\left(\cos^{-1}\left(-\dfrac{\sqrt{2}}{2}\right)\right) = \csc\left(\dfrac{3\pi}{4}\right) = \dfrac{1}{\sin\left(\dfrac{3\pi}{4}\right)} = \sqrt{2}$

52. $\cot\left(\sin^{-1}(-1)\right) = \cot\left(-\dfrac{\pi}{2}\right) = 0$

53. $\arcsin(\sec\pi) = \arcsin(-1) = -\dfrac{\pi}{2}$

54. $\cos^{-1}\left(\sin\dfrac{11\pi}{6}\right) = \cos^{-1}\left(-\dfrac{1}{2}\right) = \dfrac{2\pi}{3}$

55. $\sin\left(\cos^{-1}\dfrac{5}{13}\right) = \sin y$, where $y = \cos^{-1}\dfrac{5}{13}$. So $\cos y = \dfrac{5}{13}, 0 \le y \le \pi$, and we want $\sin y$. Use the Pythagorean identity:

$$(\cos y)^2 + (\sin y)^2 = 1$$
$$\left(\dfrac{5}{13}\right)^2 + (\sin y)^2 = 1$$
$$(\sin y)^2 = 1 - \dfrac{25}{169} = \dfrac{144}{169}$$
$$\sin y = \dfrac{12}{13}, \text{ since } \sin y > 0 \text{ for } 0 \le y \le \pi.$$

So, $\sin\left(\cos^{-1}\dfrac{5}{13}\right) = \dfrac{12}{13}.$

56. $\tan\left(\sin^{-1}\dfrac{8}{17}\right) = \tan y$, where $y = \sin^{-1}\dfrac{8}{17}$. So $\sin y = \dfrac{8}{17}, \dfrac{-\pi}{2} \le y \le \dfrac{\pi}{2}$, and we want $\tan y$. Use the Pythagorean identity:

$$(\cos y)^2 + (\sin y)^2 = 1$$
$$(\cos y)^2 + \left(\dfrac{8}{17}\right)^2 = 1$$
$$(\cos y)^2 = 1 - \dfrac{64}{289} = \dfrac{225}{289}$$
$$\cos y = \dfrac{15}{17}, \text{ since } \cos y > 0 \text{ for } -\dfrac{\pi}{2} \le y \le \dfrac{\pi}{2}.$$

So, $\tan\left(\sin^{-1}\dfrac{8}{17}\right) = \tan y = \dfrac{\sin y}{\cos y} = \dfrac{\left(\dfrac{8}{17}\right)}{\left(\dfrac{15}{17}\right)} = \dfrac{8}{15}.$

57–62. *Use a calculator in radian mode.*

57. $\cos^{-1}(\sin 55) \approx 3.1195$

58. $\cos(\tan^{-1}(-3.76)) \approx 0.2570$

59. $\cos(\csc^{-1} 7)$
$\cos(\sin^{-1}(1 \div 7)) \approx 0.9897$

60. $\sec^{-1}\left(\dfrac{22}{7}\right)$

$\cos^{-1}(7 \div 22) \approx 1.2470$

61. $\tan^{-1}\left(\sin \sqrt{(2.6)}\right) \approx 0.7850$

62. $\arcsin (\cot 2.4\pi)$
$\sin^{-1}(1 \div \tan(2.4\pi)) \approx 0.3309$

63. $y = \arcsin x$

64. $y = \arctan x$

65. $0.5 = 4\sin(2x)$

$4\sin(2x) = 0.5$

$\sin(2x) = \dfrac{0.5}{4}$ Multiply each side by $\dfrac{1}{4}$.

$2x = \sin^{-1}(0.125)$ Use the definition of arcsine.

$x = \dfrac{1}{2}\sin^{-1}(0.125)$ Multiply each side by $\dfrac{1}{2}$.

≈ 0.0627 Find the calculator approximation.

66. $3.2\cos\left(\dfrac{1}{2}x\right) = 0.9$

$\cos\left(\dfrac{1}{2}x\right) = \dfrac{0.9}{3.2}$ Divide each side by 3.2.

$\dfrac{1}{2}x = \cos^{-1}\left(\dfrac{0.9}{3.2}\right)$ Use the definition of arccosine.

$x = 2\cos^{-1}\left(\dfrac{0.9}{3.2}\right)$ Multiply each side by 2.

≈ 2.5714 Find the calculator approximation.

67. $-6\tan(4x) = 2y$

$\tan(4x) = -\dfrac{2y}{6} = -\dfrac{y}{3}$ Divide each side by -6.

$4x = \tan^{-1}\left(-\dfrac{y}{3}\right)$ Use the definition of arctangent.

$x = \dfrac{1}{4}\tan^{-1}\left(-\dfrac{y}{3}\right)$ Multiply each side by $\dfrac{1}{4}$.

68. $\pi \sin(-4x) = y$

$\sin(-4x) = \dfrac{y}{\pi}$ Divide each side by π.

$-4x = \sin^{-1}\left(\dfrac{y}{\pi}\right)$ Use the definition of arcsine.

$x = -\dfrac{1}{4}\sin^{-1}\left(\dfrac{y}{\pi}\right)$ Divide each side by -4.

69. False; the graph of $y = \sec x$ is not sinusoidal, for example.

70. False; the period is $\dfrac{\pi}{\left(\dfrac{1}{2}\right)} = 2\pi$.

71. False; for $y = 3 \sin x$, the amplitude is 3 and the period is 2π, whereas $y = \sin 3x$ has amplitude 1 and period $\dfrac{2\pi}{3}$.

72. True
73. True (since $\cos y \neq -100$)

74. False; amplitude $= \left| \dfrac{y\,\max - y\,\min}{2} \right|$.

75. False; the graph of $y = \cos(-x)$ is the same as $y = \cos x$ as a result of the negative identities.

76. True
77. True $\left(\text{since } \csc y = \dfrac{5}{3} \text{ is equivalent to } \sin y = \dfrac{3}{5}\right)$

78. False; $\cos^{-1} x$ is the inverse function of $\cos x$, whereas $\dfrac{1}{\cos x}$ is the reciprocal of $\cos x$.

79. True
80. False; $\arccos\left(-\dfrac{1}{2}\right) = \dfrac{2\pi}{3}$.

81. False; $\sin^{-1}(-1) = -\dfrac{\pi}{2}$. $\left(\dfrac{3\pi}{2} \text{ is not in the range } -\dfrac{\pi}{2} \leq y \leq \dfrac{\pi}{2}\right)$

82. False; there are several equations to represent one graph. (See Exercises 25 and 26.)

83. True
84. False; the guide is $y = 4 \sin(2x)$.

85. Jo is correct. If you use the guide Jack suggests, you will not be able to locate the asymptote since $y = \cos(2x) + 4$ has no x-intercepts.

Chapter 2 Test, p. 155

1. Rewrite $y = 5 \sin\left(-\dfrac{1}{2}x\right)$ as $y = -5 \sin\left(\dfrac{1}{2}x\right)$.

period: $\dfrac{2\pi}{\left(\dfrac{1}{2}\right)} = 4\pi$, amplitude: $|A| = 5$, x-intercept: $x = k \cdot 2\pi$

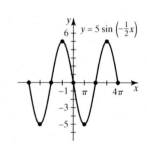

2. amplitude $= 1$

period: $\dfrac{2\pi}{2} = \pi$, phase shift: right $\dfrac{\pi}{2}$, x-intercepts: $x = \dfrac{\pi}{4} + k \cdot \dfrac{\pi}{2}$

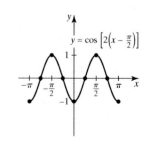

3. period: $\dfrac{\pi}{\left(\dfrac{1}{2}\right)} = 2\pi$, asymptotes: $x = \dfrac{\dfrac{\pi}{2} + k \cdot \pi}{\left(\dfrac{1}{2}\right)} = \pi + k \cdot 2\pi$, range: $\mathbb{R}$

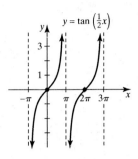

4. period: 2π, asymptotes: $x = \dfrac{\pi}{2} + k \cdot \pi$, range: $|y| \geq 3$

    (Use $y = 3\cos x$ as a guide.)

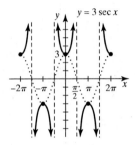

5. amplitude $= 2$

    period: $= \dfrac{2\pi}{\pi} = 2$, x-intercepts: $x = \dfrac{3}{2} + k \cdot 2$, range: $0 \leq y \leq 4$

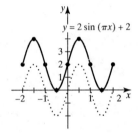

6. range: $|y| \geq 5$, asymptotes: $x = \dfrac{\pi}{2} + k\pi$

    (Use $y = 5\sin\left(x - \dfrac{\pi}{2}\right)$ as a guide.)

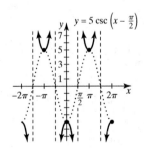

7. *There are many possible answers.*

7. **a.** Using the reflected form of cosine, with period 2π and amplitude 2, we get

    $$y = -2\cos x.$$

    b. Using the tangent form with period $\dfrac{\pi}{2}$, we get

    $$y = \tan(2x).$$

c. Dotting in the guide, we get $y = 4\cos\left(\dfrac{1}{2}x\right)$ (since the amplitude is 4 and the period is 4π).

So, $y = 4\sec\left(\dfrac{1}{2}x\right)$.

d. The graph is the sine form, with amplitude 1 and period 2π, with a shift left $\dfrac{\pi}{4}$.

So, $y = \sin\left(x + \dfrac{\pi}{4}\right)$.

8. Using the same amplitude and period, we consider phase shifts of the cosine or sine form. If we do so, a few possible answers are:

$$y = 2\sin\left(x - \dfrac{\pi}{2}\right), \qquad y = 2\cos(x - \pi)$$

$$y = 2\sin\left(x - \dfrac{3\pi}{2}\right), \qquad y = -2\cos\left(x + \dfrac{\pi}{2}\right)$$

(Check other answers with a graphing utility.)

9. a. amplitude: 5, period: $\dfrac{2\pi}{\left(\dfrac{\pi}{2}\right)} = 4$

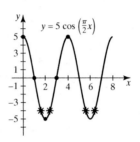

b. 5 cm

c. See the graph in part (a).

10. *Make sure your answers are in the range of the respective inverse function.*

10. a. $\arccos\dfrac{1}{2} = \dfrac{\pi}{3}$ $\left(\text{since } \cos\dfrac{\pi}{3} = \dfrac{1}{2}\right)$ **b.** $\arctan 0 = 0$ (since $\tan 0 = 0$)

c. $\sin^{-1}\dfrac{\sqrt{2}}{2} = \dfrac{\pi}{4}$ $\left(\text{since } \sin\dfrac{\pi}{4} = \dfrac{\sqrt{2}}{2}\right)$ **d.** $\text{arccsc } 2 \rightarrow \arcsin\dfrac{1}{2} = \dfrac{\pi}{6}$ $\left(\text{since } \sin\dfrac{\pi}{6} = \dfrac{1}{2}\right)$

e. $\sec^{-1}\left(-\sqrt{2}\right) \rightarrow \cos^{-1}\left(-\dfrac{1}{\sqrt{2}}\right) = \dfrac{3\pi}{4}$ $\left(\text{since } \cos\dfrac{3\pi}{4} = -\dfrac{1}{\sqrt{2}}\right)$

f. $\arctan(-1) = -\dfrac{\pi}{4}$ $\left(\text{since } \tan\left(-\dfrac{\pi}{4}\right) = -1\right)$ **g.** $\arccos(-1) = \pi$ (since $\cos\pi = -1$)

h. $\cot^{-1}\left(\dfrac{1}{\sqrt{3}}\right) = \dfrac{\pi}{3}$ $\left(\text{since } \cot\dfrac{\pi}{3} = \dfrac{1}{\sqrt{3}}\right)$ or $\dfrac{\pi}{2} - \tan^{-1}\left(\dfrac{1}{\sqrt{3}}\right) = \dfrac{\pi}{3}$ $\left(\text{since } \tan\dfrac{\pi}{6} = \dfrac{1}{\sqrt{3}}\right)$

i. $\sin\left(\arccos\dfrac{3}{5}\right) = \sin y$, where $\arccos\dfrac{3}{5} = y$ for $0 \le y \le \pi$.

So we want $\sin y$, where $\cos y = \dfrac{3}{5}$. Use the Pythagorean identity:

$$(\cos y)^2 + (\sin y)^2 = 1$$

$$\left(\dfrac{3}{5}\right)^2 + (\sin y)^2 = 1$$

$$(\sin y)^2 = 1 - \dfrac{9}{25} = \dfrac{16}{25}$$

$$\sin y = \dfrac{4}{5}, \text{ since } y > 0 \text{ for } 0 \le y \le \pi.$$

Therefore, $\sin\left(\arccos\dfrac{3}{5}\right) = \sin y = \dfrac{4}{5}$.

j. $\sec^{-1}(\cos\pi) = \sec^{-1}(-1)$

$\qquad\qquad\quad = \cos^{-1}(-1) = \pi \ \ (\text{since } \cos\pi = -1)$

11. a. $\tan^{-1} 13.4$

$\qquad \tan^{-1}(13.4) \approx 1.4963$

b. $\arccos(-0.89)$

$\qquad \cos^{-1}(-0.89) \approx 2.6681$

c. $\sec^{-1}\left(-\dfrac{13}{7}\right)$

$\qquad \cos^{-1}(-7 \div 13) \approx 2.1394$

d. $\sin^{-1} 0.56$

$\qquad \sin^{-1}(0.56) \approx 0.5944$

e. $\tan(\arctan(-3.67))$

$\qquad \tan(\tan^{-1}(-3.67)) = -3.6700$

f. $\cos(\text{arccot } 4.65)$

$\qquad \cos\left(\dfrac{\pi}{2} - \tan^{-1}(4.65)\right) \approx 0.9776$

12. a. $6\sin 8x = 3$

$\sin 8x = \dfrac{1}{2}$	Multiply each side by $\dfrac{1}{6}$.
$8x = \sin^{-1}\left(\dfrac{1}{2}\right)$	Use the definition of arcsine.
$8x = \dfrac{\pi}{6}$	$\sin\dfrac{\pi}{6} = \dfrac{1}{2}$
$x = \dfrac{\pi}{48}$	Multiply each side by $\dfrac{1}{8}$.
≈ 0.0654	Find the calculator approximation.

b. $4\tan 2x = y$

$\tan 2x = \dfrac{y}{4}$	Multiply each side by $\dfrac{1}{4}$.
$2x = \tan^{-1}\left(\dfrac{y}{4}\right)$	Use the definition of arctangent.
$x = \dfrac{1}{2}\tan^{-1}\left(\dfrac{y}{4}\right)$	Multiply each side by $\dfrac{1}{2}$.

13. a. $y = \tan^{-1} x$ **b.** $y = \cos^{-1} x$

14. a. False; the graph of $y = \tan x$ is not a sine wave, for example.

    b. True   **c.** True

    d. False; the graph of $y = A \tan(-Bx)$ is the same as $y = -A \tan(Bx)$.

    e. False; the graph of $y = \sin(2x)$ has amplitude 1 and period π, whereas $y = 2\sin x$ has amplitude 2 and period 2π.

    f. True   **g.** True

    h. False; the graph of $y = \sin\left(x + \dfrac{\pi}{2}\right)$ shifts $y = \sin x$ left $\dfrac{\pi}{2}$, while $y = \sin x + \sin \dfrac{\pi}{2} = \sin x + 1$ shifts the graph of $y = \sin x$ up 1.

    i. True ($\sin x \neq 25.6$)

15. a. The minimum y-coordinate (number of daylight hours) appears to be 6. This occurs between $x = 2$ and $x = 3$, or in February.
    b. From April to December there will be at least 8 hours of daylight.
    c. The maximum y-coordinate appears to be 18. This occurs between $x = 8$ and $x = 9$, or during August.

Chapter 3   *Trigonometry Student's Solutions Manual*

Exercise Set 3.1, p. 169

1. θ radians $= \theta \cdot \left(\dfrac{180}{\pi} \right)$ degrees   (R→D)

3.

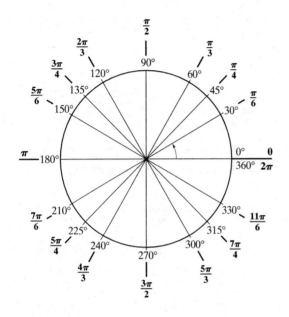 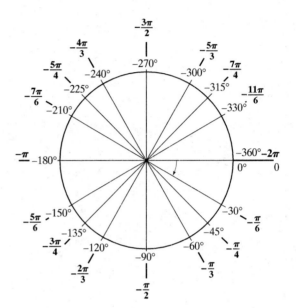

3. Values are found from 0° counterclockwise.

$$D \to R: 0° = 0$$

$$R \to D: \frac{\pi}{6} \left(\frac{180°}{\pi} \right) = 30°,$$

$$D \to R: 45 \left(\frac{\pi}{180} \right) = \frac{\pi}{4},$$

$$D \to R: 60 \left(\frac{\pi}{180} \right) = \frac{\pi}{3},$$

$$R \to D: \frac{\pi}{2} \left(\frac{180°}{\pi} \right) = 90°,$$

$$R \to D: \frac{2\pi}{3} \left(\frac{180°}{\pi} \right) = 120°, \text{ (and so on)}$$

$$\frac{3\pi}{4}, \frac{5\pi}{6}, 180°, 210°, 225°, \frac{4\pi}{3}, \frac{3\pi}{2}, \frac{5\pi}{3}, 315°, 330°$$

5, 7, 9, 11, 13, 15. $R \rightarrow D$. *The angle is drawn in standard position.*

5. $\dfrac{\pi}{4} \left(\dfrac{180°}{\pi} \right) = 45°$

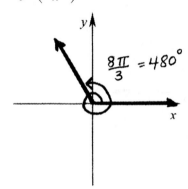

7. $\dfrac{5\pi}{6} \left(\dfrac{180°}{\pi} \right) = 150°$

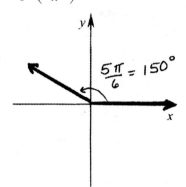

9. $\dfrac{8\pi}{3} \left(\dfrac{180°}{\pi} \right) = 480°$

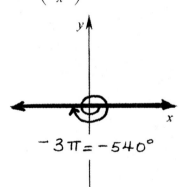

11. $-\dfrac{7\pi}{6} \left(\dfrac{180°}{\pi} \right) = -210°$

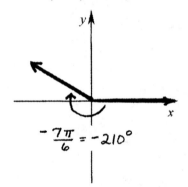

13. $-3\pi \left(\dfrac{180°}{\pi} \right) = -540°$

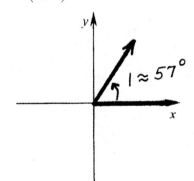

15. $1 \left(\dfrac{180°}{\pi} \right) \approx 57°$

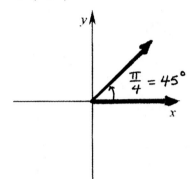

17, 19, 21, 23. $D \to R$ *Convert from degrees to radians.*

17. $75 \left(\dfrac{\pi}{180} \right) = \dfrac{5\pi}{12}$

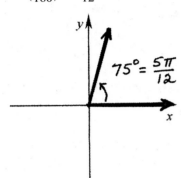

19. $225 \left(\dfrac{\pi}{180} \right) = \dfrac{5\pi}{4}$

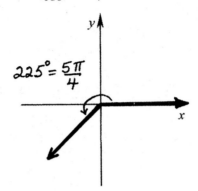

21. $-12 \left(\dfrac{\pi}{180} \right) = -\dfrac{\pi}{15}$

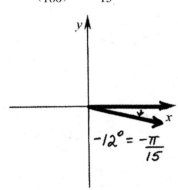

23. $-120 \left(\dfrac{\pi}{180} \right) = -\dfrac{2\pi}{3}$

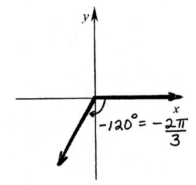

25 and 27. *Convert from degrees to radians.*

25. $16 \left(\dfrac{\pi}{180} \right) \approx 0.28$

27. $238°30' = 238.5 \left(\dfrac{\pi}{180} \right) \approx 4.16$

29, 31, 33, 35. *To find the smallest positive coterminal angle, we add or subtract multiples of 2π or $360°$ to obtain a positive angle within one revolution.*

29. **a.** $\dfrac{8\pi}{3} - \dfrac{6\pi}{3} = \dfrac{2\pi}{3}$ **b.** $\dfrac{2\pi}{3} + k \cdot 2\pi$

31. **a.** $412° - 360° = 52°$ **b.** $52° + k \cdot 360°$

33. **a.** $-5.21 + 2\pi \approx 1.07$ **b.** $1.07 + k \cdot 2\pi$

35. **a.** $-710°30' : -710.5° + 720° \approx 10°$ **b.** $10° + k \cdot 360°$

37, 39, 41. *The formula for arc length is* $s = r \cdot \theta$, *where* θ *is in radians.*

37. $s = r \cdot \theta = 5$ in. $\left(\dfrac{7\pi}{6} \right) \approx 18.33$ in.

39. $s = r \cdot \theta = 3$ cm$(3.5) = 10.5$ cm

41. Since $\theta = 120°$, we convert θ to radians. $\theta = 120° = \dfrac{2\pi}{3}$

$$s = 16 \text{ m} \left(\frac{2\pi}{3} \right) \approx 33.51 \text{ m}$$

43.
$$s = r \cdot \theta$$
$$12 \text{ in.} = r(1.5)$$
$$r = \frac{12 \text{ in.}}{1.5} = 8 \text{ in.}$$

45. a. $s = r \cdot \theta$, if $r = 1$:
$$\frac{\pi}{4} = 1 \cdot \theta \rightarrow \theta = \frac{\pi}{4}$$

b. $s = r \cdot \theta$, if $r = 1$:
$$\frac{\pi}{3} = 1 \cdot \theta \rightarrow \theta = \frac{\pi}{3}$$

c. $\pi = 1 \cdot \theta \rightarrow \theta = \pi$

d. $\dfrac{\pi}{2} = 1 \cdot \theta \rightarrow \theta = \dfrac{\pi}{2}$

47. Since $v = \dfrac{s}{t} = \dfrac{r\theta}{t} = r \cdot \dfrac{\theta}{t}$ and $\omega = \dfrac{\theta}{t}$, then $v = r \cdot \omega$ or $\dfrac{v}{r} = \omega$.

49. Since $\theta = 30°$, we convert it to radians, $\theta = \dfrac{\pi}{6}$, and use the formula for linear velocity:

$$v = \frac{s}{t} = \frac{r \cdot \theta}{t} = \frac{(3 \text{ ft})\left(\dfrac{\pi}{6} \right)}{2 \text{ hrs}} = \frac{\pi}{4} \text{ ft/hr} \approx 0.79 \text{ ft/hr}$$

51. $\omega = \dfrac{\theta}{t} = \dfrac{\left(\dfrac{\pi}{2} \right)}{10 \text{ sec}} = \dfrac{\pi}{20}$ rad/sec ≈ 0.16 rad/sec

53. $v = r \cdot \omega$ (See Exercise 47.)
$$= 4 \text{ ft} \left(\frac{2 \text{ rad}}{\text{min}} \right) = 8 \text{ ft/min}$$

55. $v = \dfrac{s}{t}$

$$35 \text{ ft/sec} = \frac{s}{4 \text{ sec}}$$

$$s = \left(\frac{35 \text{ ft}}{1 \text{ sec}} \right) (4 \text{ sec}) \quad \text{Multiply each side by 4 sec.}$$

$$s = 140 \text{ ft} \qquad\qquad \text{Simplify.}$$

57. $v = \dfrac{s}{t}$

$s = v \cdot t$ \qquad\qquad Multiply each side by t.

$s = (r \cdot \omega)t$ \qquad\quad $v = r \cdot \omega$ (See Exercise 47.)

$$s = \left(2.6 \text{ ft} \cdot \frac{6 \text{ rad}}{1 \text{ sec}} \right) (4 \text{ sec})$$

$$s = 62.4 \text{ ft}$$

59. False; $\pi = 180°$. (You can't leave off the degree symbol for angles measured in degrees.)

61. True

63. False; θ needs to be measured in radians.

65. Angular speed of 2500 rpm means

$\omega = 2500$ rpm $= 2500(2\pi$ rad) per minute

$\omega = 5000\pi$ radians per minute

$\omega \approx 15{,}707.96$ radians per minute.

67. It takes Earth 365 days to travel one revolution, so the angular velocity for one day is $\omega = \dfrac{\theta}{t} = \dfrac{2\pi}{365 \text{ days}}$.

To find the distance Earth travels in one day, we find the arc length for one day:

$$s = r \cdot \omega \cdot t = r \cdot \frac{\theta}{t} \cdot t$$
$$s = 93{,}000{,}000 \text{ miles} \left(\frac{2\pi}{365 \text{ days}} \right) (1 \text{ day})$$
$$s \approx 1{,}600{,}921 \text{ mi}$$

In one day Earth travels 1,600,921 miles. (No wonder you're tired at the end of one day!)

69. Since $v = \dfrac{s}{t}$, and using s from Exercise 68, we get

$$v = \frac{11{,}206{,}448 \text{ mi}}{1 \text{ week}} = 11{,}206{,}448 \text{ mi/wk.}$$

71. Since $s = r \cdot \theta$, and $\theta = \left(\dfrac{1}{60} \right)^{\circ} = \dfrac{\pi}{60(180)}$ rad, 1 nautical mile $= (4000$ statute miles$) \left(\dfrac{\pi}{60(180)} \right)$.

So 1 nautical mile ≈ 1.16 miles (statute).

73. If $\omega = 300$ rpm $= 300(2\pi)$ rad per minute, then

$$v = r \cdot \omega$$
$$= 1.25 \text{ in.} \left(\frac{600\pi \text{ rad}}{1 \text{ min}} \right)$$
$$v \approx 2356 \text{ in./min.}$$

75. a. $A = \dfrac{\theta}{2} \cdot r^2$

$\quad = \dfrac{2}{2}(7 \text{ in.})^2$

$\quad = 49$ sq in.

b. $A = \dfrac{\theta}{2} \cdot r^2$

$\quad = \dfrac{\left(\dfrac{\pi}{2} \right)}{2}(4 \text{ ft})^2$

$\quad = 4\pi$ sq ft

c. $\theta = 30° = \dfrac{\pi}{6}$

$\quad A = \dfrac{\left(\dfrac{\pi}{6} \right)}{2}(10 \text{ cm})^2$

$\quad = \dfrac{25\pi}{3}$ sq cm

Exercise Set 3.2, p. 182

1. If $(x, y) = (8, 15)$ then $x = 8$, $y = 15$.

$$r = \sqrt{x^2 + y^2}$$
$$r = \sqrt{(8)^2 + (15)^2} = 17$$

Using the definitions of the trigonometric functions, we get

$$\cos \theta = \frac{x}{r} = \frac{8}{17},$$
$$\sin \theta = \frac{y}{r} = \frac{15}{17},$$
$$\tan \theta = \frac{y}{x} = \frac{15}{8}.$$

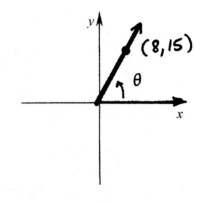

3. $(x, y) = (2, -2) \rightarrow x = 2$, $y = -2$

$$r = \sqrt{x^2 + y^2}$$
$$r = \sqrt{(2)^2 + (-2)^2}$$
$$= 2\sqrt{2}$$

Using the definitions of the trigonometric function, we get

$$\cos \theta = \frac{x}{r} = \frac{2}{2\sqrt{2}} = \frac{1}{\sqrt{2}} \text{ or } \frac{\sqrt{2}}{2},$$
$$\sin \theta = \frac{y}{r} = \frac{-2}{2\sqrt{2}} = -\frac{\sqrt{2}}{2},$$
$$\tan \theta = \frac{y}{x} = \frac{-2}{2} = -1.$$

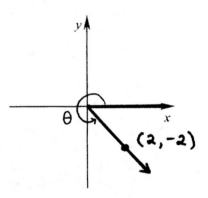

5. $(x, y) = (-4, 3) \rightarrow x = -4$, $y = 3$

$$r = \sqrt{x^2 + y^2}$$
$$= \sqrt{(-4)^2 + (3)^2} = 5$$

So: $\cos \theta = \frac{x}{r} = -\frac{4}{5},$

$$\sin \theta = \frac{y}{r} = \frac{3}{5},$$
$$\tan \theta = \frac{y}{x} = \frac{3}{-4} = -\frac{3}{4}$$

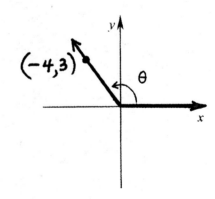

7. $(x, y) = (-\sqrt{3}, -1) \to x = -\sqrt{3}, y = -1$

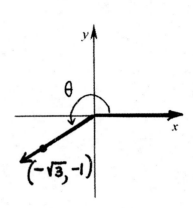

$$r = \sqrt{x^2 + y^2}$$

$$r = \sqrt{(-\sqrt{3})^2 + (-1)^2} = \sqrt{3 + 1} = 2$$

So: $\cos\theta = \dfrac{x}{r} = -\dfrac{\sqrt{3}}{2}$,

$\sin\theta = \dfrac{y}{r} = -\dfrac{1}{2}$,

$\tan\theta = \dfrac{y}{x} = \dfrac{-1}{-\sqrt{3}} = \dfrac{\sqrt{3}}{3}$

9. $(x, y) = (-5, 0) \to x = -5, y = 0$

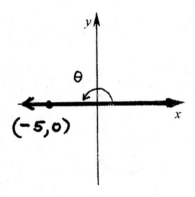

$$r = \sqrt{x^2 + y^2}$$

$$r = \sqrt{(-5)^2 + 0^2} = 5$$

So: $\cos\theta = \dfrac{x}{r} = \dfrac{-5}{5} = -1$,

$\sin\theta = \dfrac{y}{r} = \dfrac{0}{5} = 0$,

$\tan\theta = \dfrac{y}{x} = \dfrac{0}{-5} = 0$

11. $\sin\alpha < 0$ in QIII, QIV and $\sec\alpha > 0$ in QI, QIV: The quadrant that satisfies both is QIV.

13. $\csc\alpha > 0$ in QI, QII ($\sin\alpha > 0$) and $\cos\alpha < 0$ in QII, QIII: The quadrant that satisfies both is QII.

15. $\cos\beta = \dfrac{1}{4} = \dfrac{x}{r}$ and β in QIV where $(x, y) = (+, -) \to x = 1, r = 4$

$$r = \sqrt{x^2 + y^2}$$
$$4 = \sqrt{(1)^2 + y^2}$$
$$16 = 1 + y^2$$
$$y^2 = 15$$
$$y = -\sqrt{15}, \text{ since } \beta \text{ is in QIV}$$

Using the definition of the trigonometric ratios, we get:

$\cos\beta = \dfrac{x}{r}$	$\sin\beta = \dfrac{y}{r}$	$\tan\beta = \dfrac{y}{x}$	$\sec\beta = \dfrac{r}{x}$	$\csc\beta = \dfrac{r}{y}$	$\cot\beta = \dfrac{x}{y}$
$\dfrac{1}{4}$	$-\dfrac{\sqrt{15}}{4}$	$-\sqrt{15}$	4	$\dfrac{4\sqrt{15}}{15}$	$-\dfrac{\sqrt{15}}{15}$

17. $\sec\beta = 1.5 = \dfrac{3}{2} = \dfrac{r}{x}$ and β in QI where $(x, y) = (+, +) \rightarrow x = 2, r = 3$

$$r = \sqrt{x^2 + y^2}$$
$$3 = \sqrt{(2)^2 + y^2}$$
$$9 = 4 + y^2$$
$$y^2 = 5$$
$$y = \sqrt{5}, \text{ since } \beta \text{ in QI}$$

Using the definition of the trigonometric ratios, we get:

$\cos\beta = \dfrac{x}{r}$	$\sin\beta = \dfrac{y}{r}$	$\tan\beta = \dfrac{y}{x}$	$\sec\beta = \dfrac{r}{x}$	$\csc\beta = \dfrac{r}{y}$	$\cot\beta = \dfrac{x}{y}$
$\dfrac{2}{3}$	$\dfrac{\sqrt{5}}{3}$	$\dfrac{\sqrt{5}}{2}$	$\dfrac{3}{2}$	$\dfrac{3\sqrt{5}}{5}$	$\dfrac{2\sqrt{5}}{5}$

19. $\csc\beta = -\dfrac{4}{1} = \dfrac{r}{y} \rightarrow r = 4, y = -1$, and $\cos\beta < 0 \rightarrow x < 0$

$$r = \sqrt{x^2 + y^2}$$
$$4 = \sqrt{x^2 + (-1)^2}$$
$$16 = x^2 + 1$$
$$x^2 = 15$$
$$x = -\sqrt{15}, \text{ since } x < 0$$

Using the definition of the trigonometric ratios, we get:

$\cos\beta = \dfrac{x}{r}$	$\sin\beta = \dfrac{y}{r}$	$\tan\beta = \dfrac{y}{x}$	$\sec\beta = \dfrac{r}{x}$	$\csc\beta = \dfrac{r}{y}$	$\cot\beta = \dfrac{x}{y}$
$-\dfrac{\sqrt{15}}{4}$	$-\dfrac{1}{4}$	$\dfrac{\sqrt{15}}{15}$	$-\dfrac{4\sqrt{15}}{15}$	-4	$\sqrt{15}$

21. $\tan\beta = -\dfrac{1}{2} = \dfrac{y}{x}$ and β in QII where $(x, y) = (-, +), \rightarrow x = -2, y = 1$

$$r = \sqrt{x^2 + y^2}$$
$$r = \sqrt{(-2)^2 + (1)^2}$$
$$= \sqrt{5}$$

Using the definition of the trigonometric ratios, we get:

$\cos\beta = \dfrac{x}{r}$	$\sin\beta = \dfrac{y}{r}$	$\tan\beta = \dfrac{y}{x}$	$\sec\beta = \dfrac{r}{x}$	$\csc\beta = \dfrac{r}{y}$	$\cot\beta = \dfrac{x}{y}$
$-\dfrac{2\sqrt{5}}{5}$	$\dfrac{\sqrt{5}}{5}$	$-\dfrac{1}{2}$	$-\dfrac{\sqrt{5}}{2}$	$\sqrt{5}$	-2

23. $\sin 120° = \sin 60° = \dfrac{\sqrt{3}}{2}$

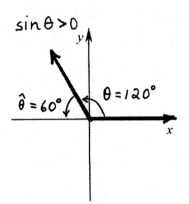

25. $\csc 330° = \dfrac{1}{\sin 330°} = \dfrac{1}{-\sin 30°} = \dfrac{1}{\left(-\dfrac{1}{2}\right)} = -2$

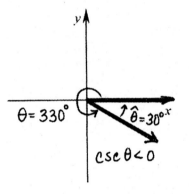

27. $\sec^2 900° = (\sec 900°)^2 = \left(\dfrac{1}{\cos 900°}\right)^2 = \left(\dfrac{1}{\cos 180°}\right)^2 = \left(\dfrac{1}{-1}\right)^2 = 1$

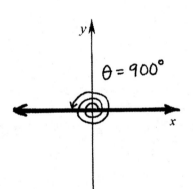

29. $\cot \dfrac{7\pi}{4} = \dfrac{1}{\left(\tan \dfrac{7\pi}{4}\right)} = \dfrac{1}{-\tan \dfrac{\pi}{4}} = \dfrac{1}{-1} = -1$

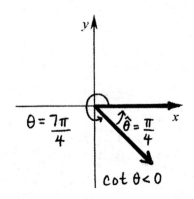

31. $\cos\left(-\dfrac{\pi}{2}\right) = 0$

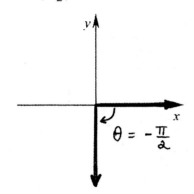

33. $\tan(-150°) = \tan 30° = \dfrac{\sqrt{3}}{3}$

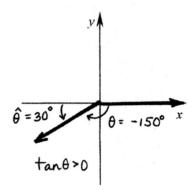

35. $\tan\left(-\dfrac{5\pi}{2}\right)$ is undefined since $\tan\theta = \dfrac{y}{x}$, and $x = 0$ for any

point on the terminal side of θ.

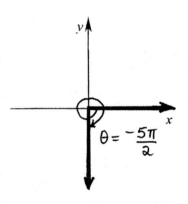

37, 39, 41, 43, 45, 47. *To find angles in degrees, set your calculator to degree mode. Otherwise, use radian mode.*

37. $\tan 25°$
$\tan(25°) \approx 0.4663$

39. $\sin\dfrac{5\pi}{9}$
$\sin(5\pi \div 9) \approx 0.9848$

41. $\cos 53°24'$
$\cos(53 + 24 \div 60)° \approx 0.5962$

43. $\sec\left(-125\dfrac{3}{4}^{°}\right)$
$1 \div \cos(-125.75)° \approx -1.7116$

45. $\cot 9.25$
$1 \div \tan(9.25) \approx -5.6632$

47. $\sin(\cos^{-1} 0.55)$
$\sin(\cos^{-1}(0.55)) \approx 0.8352$

49. $\alpha = \arccos\dfrac{\sqrt{3}}{2} \longleftrightarrow \cos\alpha = \dfrac{\sqrt{3}}{2}, 0° \le \alpha \le 180°$
$\phantom{\alpha = \arccos\dfrac{\sqrt{3}}{2}} \longleftrightarrow \alpha = 30°$

51. $\alpha = \sin^{-1}\left(-\dfrac{1}{2}\right) \longleftrightarrow \sin\alpha = -\dfrac{1}{2}, -90° \le \alpha \le 90°$
$\hat{\alpha} = 30°$, so $\alpha = -30°$

53. $\alpha = \cot^{-1} 0 \longleftrightarrow \cot \alpha = 0, \ 0° < \alpha < 180°$

$$\alpha = 90° - \tan^{-1}(0)$$
$$\alpha = 90° - 0°$$
$$\alpha = 90°$$

55, 57, 59. *Set your calculator to degree mode.*

55. $\theta = \cos^{-1} 0.225$
$\cos^{-1}(0.225) \approx 77.0°$

57. $\theta = \sin^{-1}(-0.456)$
$\sin^{-1}(-0.456) \approx -27.1°$

59. $\theta = \arctan(-0.4577)$
$\tan^{-1}(-0.4577) \approx -24.6°$

61. $\cos\left(\arcsin \dfrac{1}{4}\right) = \cos\theta$, where

$$\theta = \arcsin \frac{1}{4}, \ -\frac{\pi}{2} \le \theta \le \frac{\pi}{2}$$
$$\longleftrightarrow \sin\theta = \frac{1}{4}$$

We want $\cos\theta$ knowing $\sin\theta = \dfrac{1}{4}$. So, we use the Pythagorean identity (or trigonometric ratios).

$$(\cos\theta)^2 + (\sin\theta)^2 = 1$$
$$(\cos\theta)^2 + \left(\frac{1}{4}\right)^2 = 1$$
$$(\cos\theta)^2 = 1 - \frac{1}{16} = \frac{15}{16}$$
$$\cos\theta = \frac{\sqrt{15}}{4}, \text{ since } \cos\theta > 0 \text{ for } -\frac{\pi}{2} \le \theta \le \frac{\pi}{2}$$

So, $\cos\left(\arcsin \dfrac{1}{4}\right) = \cos\theta = \dfrac{\sqrt{15}}{4}$.

63. $\tan\left(\cos^{-1} \dfrac{3}{5}\right) = \tan\theta$, where $\qquad \theta = \cos^{-1} \dfrac{3}{5}, 0 \le \theta \le \pi$

$$\longleftrightarrow \cos\theta = \frac{3}{5}$$

We want $\tan\theta$ knowing that $\cos\theta = \dfrac{3}{5}$. We can proceed using the Pythagorean identity or the trigonometric functions. Using the trigonometric functions, we get

$$\cos\theta = \frac{3}{5} = \frac{x}{r} \rightarrow r = 5, x = 3.$$

To find $\tan\theta = \dfrac{y}{x}$,
we need y.

$$r = \sqrt{x^2 + y^2}$$
$$5 = \sqrt{(3)^2 + y^2}$$
$$y^2 = 16$$
$$y = 4, \text{ since } y > 0 \text{ for } 0 \le \theta \le \pi$$

So, $\tan\left(\cos^{-1} \dfrac{3}{5}\right) = \tan\theta = \dfrac{y}{x} = \dfrac{4}{3}$.

65. $\csc\left(\tan^{-1}\dfrac{5}{12}\right) = \csc\theta$, where

$$\theta = \tan^{-1}\frac{5}{12}, \; -\frac{\pi}{2} < \theta < \frac{\pi}{2}$$

$$\longleftrightarrow \tan\theta = \frac{5}{12}$$

$$\tan\theta = \frac{5}{12} = \frac{y}{x} \to x = 12, \; y = 5$$

To find $\csc\theta$, we need r: $r = \sqrt{x^2 + y^2}$

$$r = \sqrt{(12)^2 + (5)^2}$$

$$r = 13$$

So, $\csc\left(\tan^{-1}\dfrac{5}{12}\right) = \csc\theta = \dfrac{1}{\sin\theta} = \dfrac{r}{y} = \dfrac{13}{5}.$

67. $\cos\left(\arcsin\dfrac{x}{2}\right) = \cos\theta$, where

$$\theta = \arcsin\frac{x}{2}, \; -\frac{\pi}{2} \le \theta \le \frac{\pi}{2}$$

$$\longleftrightarrow \sin\theta = \frac{x}{2} \; \left(\text{Note: } -1 \le \frac{x}{2} \le 1, \text{ or } -2 \le x \le 2\right)$$

$$(\cos\theta)^2 + (\sin\theta)^2 = 1$$

$$(\cos\theta)^2 + \left(\frac{x}{2}\right)^2 = 1$$

$$(\cos\theta)^2 = 1 - \frac{x^2}{4} = \frac{4 - x^2}{4}$$

$$\cos\theta = \frac{\sqrt{4 - x^2}}{2}, \text{ since } \cos\theta > 0 \text{ for } -\frac{\pi}{2} \le \theta \le \frac{\pi}{2}$$

So, $\cos\left(\arcsin\dfrac{x}{2}\right) = \cos\theta = \dfrac{\sqrt{4 - x^2}}{2}.$

Exercise Set 3.3, p. 195

1. $\cos 30° = \sin(90° - 30°) = \sin 60°$

3. $\sec 83.7° = \csc(90° - 83.7°) = \csc 6.3°$

5. $\tan 13°17' = \cot(90° - 13°17')$
$\quad\quad = \cot(89°60' - 13°17') = \cot 76°43'$

7.   **a.** y **b.** x **c.** $\dfrac{x}{z}$ **d.** $\dfrac{x}{y}$ **e.** T

9. $\cos 70° = \dfrac{\text{adj}}{\text{hyp}} = \dfrac{3}{x}$ **11.** $\sin x = \dfrac{\text{opp}}{\text{hyp}} = \dfrac{6}{10} = \dfrac{3}{5}$

13. There is not enough information. (We need one side's length.)

15, 17. *We need all sides to find* $\sin\alpha$, $\cos\alpha$, *and* $\tan\alpha$, *so we use* $a^2 + b^2 = c^2$ *(Pythagorean Theorem) to find the missing side.*

15. $c^2 = a^2 + b^2$

$\qquad = 4^2 + 3^2$

$\quad c = \sqrt{25}$

$\qquad = 5$

$$\sin\alpha = \frac{\text{opp}}{\text{hyp}} = \frac{4}{5}, \qquad \cos\alpha = \frac{\text{adj}}{\text{hyp}} = \frac{3}{5}, \qquad \tan\alpha = \frac{\text{opp}}{\text{adj}} = \frac{4}{3}$$

17. $a^2 + b^2 = c^2$

$\quad 1^2 + b^2 = 2^2$

$\qquad\quad b = \sqrt{3}$

$$\sin\alpha = \frac{\text{opp}}{\text{hyp}} = \frac{1}{2}, \qquad \cos\alpha = \frac{\text{adj}}{\text{hyp}} = \frac{\sqrt{3}}{2}, \qquad \tan\alpha = \frac{\text{opp}}{\text{adj}} = \frac{1}{\sqrt{3}} = \frac{\sqrt{3}}{3}$$

19. Since $\alpha + \beta = 90°$ in a right triangle ($\gamma = 90°$),

$$\alpha + 43.6° = 90°$$
$$\alpha = 46.4°.$$

21. $\alpha = 31°6'$, $b = 8$,
Since we are looking for the hypotenuse c and know α and its adjacent side, we use:

$$\cos\alpha = \frac{\text{adj}}{\text{hyp}} = \frac{b}{c}$$

$$\cos 31°6' = \frac{8}{c}$$

$$c = \frac{8}{\cos 31°6'} = \frac{8}{\cos 31.1°} \approx 9.34$$

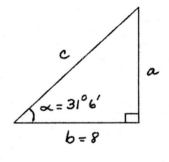

23. $a = 3$, $b = 9$
To find c, we use the Pythagorean Theorem:

$$a^2 + b^2 = c^2$$
$$3^2 + 9^2 = c^2$$
$$c = \sqrt{90} = 3\sqrt{10} \approx 9.49$$

25. $\alpha = 63°30'$, $a = 6.2$
Since we want b, the adjacent side of α, and know α and a, the opposite side of α, we use:

$$\tan\alpha = \frac{\text{opp}}{\text{adj}} = \frac{a}{b}$$

$$\tan 63.5° = \frac{6.2}{b}$$

$$b = \frac{6.2}{\tan 63.5°} \approx 3.09$$

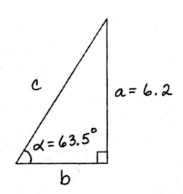

27. $b = 2, c = 6$

Since we want β and are given its opposite side b and the hypotenuse c, we use:

$$\sin \beta = \frac{\text{opp}}{\text{hyp}} = \frac{b}{c}$$

$$\sin \beta = \frac{2}{6}$$

$$\beta = \sin^{-1}\left(\frac{1}{3}\right) \approx 19.5°$$

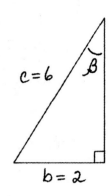

29.

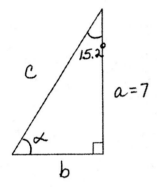

$$\alpha + \beta = 90°$$
$$\alpha = 90° - 15.2°$$
$$\alpha = 74.8°$$

Next we find c and b:

$$\cos \beta = \frac{a}{c}$$

$$\cos 15.2° = \frac{7}{c}$$

$$c = \frac{7}{\cos 15.2°} \approx 7.25$$

$$\tan \beta = \frac{b}{a}$$

$$\tan 15.2° = \frac{b}{7}$$

$$b = 7 \tan 15.2° \approx 1.90$$

$a = 7$	$\alpha = 74.8°$
$b \approx 1.90$	$\beta = 15.2°$
$c \approx 7.25$	$\gamma = 90°$

31.

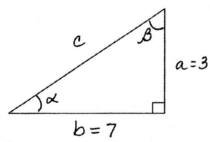

$$\tan \alpha = \frac{\text{opp}}{\text{adj}} = \frac{a}{b}$$

$$\tan \alpha = \frac{3}{7}$$

$$\alpha = \tan^{-1}\left(\frac{3}{7}\right)$$

$$\alpha \approx 23.20$$

$a = 3$	$\alpha \approx 23.2°$
$b = 7$	$\beta \approx 66.8°$
$c = \sqrt{58}$	$\gamma = 90°$
≈ 7.62	

To find β:

$$\alpha + \beta = 90°$$
$$\beta = 90° - \alpha$$
$$\beta \approx 90° - 23.2°$$
$$\beta \approx 66.8°$$

To find c:

$$a^2 + b^2 = c^2$$
$$c = \sqrt{3^2 + 7^2}$$
$$c = \sqrt{58} \approx 7.62$$

33.

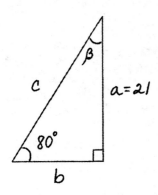

$$\alpha + \beta = 90°$$
$$\beta = 90° - 80°$$
$$\beta = 10°$$

$a = 21$	$\alpha = 80°$
$b \approx 3.70$	$\beta = 10°$
$c \approx 21.32$	$\gamma = 90°$

To find c: $\sin \alpha = \dfrac{\text{opp}}{\text{hyp}} = \dfrac{a}{c}$ To find b: $\tan \alpha = \dfrac{\text{opp}}{\text{adj}} = \dfrac{a}{b}$

$$\sin 80° = \frac{21}{c}$$

$$\tan 80° = \frac{21}{b}$$

$$c = \frac{21}{\sin 80°} \approx 21.32$$

$$b = \frac{21}{\tan 80°} \approx 3.70$$

35.

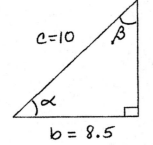

$$a^2 + b^2 = c^2$$
$$a^2 = 10^2 - 8.5^2$$
$$a = \sqrt{27.75}$$
$$a \approx 5.27$$

$a = \sqrt{27.75}$	
$a \approx 5.27$	$\alpha \approx 31.8°$
$b = 8.5$	$\beta \approx 58.2°$
$c = 10$	$\gamma = 90°$

To find β: $\sin \beta = \dfrac{\text{opp}}{\text{hyp}} = \dfrac{b}{c}$ To find α: $\alpha + \beta = 90°$

$$\sin \beta = \frac{8.5}{10}$$

$$\alpha \approx 90° - 58.2°$$

$$\beta = \sin^{-1}\left(\frac{8.5}{10}\right) \approx 58.2°$$

$$\alpha \approx 31.8°$$

37.

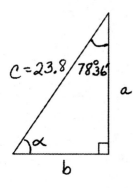

$$\alpha + \beta = 90°$$
$$\alpha = 90° - 78°36'$$
$$\alpha = 11°24'$$

$a \approx 4.70$	$\alpha = 11°24'$
$b \approx 23.33$	$\beta = 78°36'$
$c = 23.8$	$\gamma = 90°$

To find a: $\sin \alpha = \dfrac{\text{opp}}{\text{hyp}} = \dfrac{a}{c}$ To find b: $\cos \alpha = \dfrac{\text{adj}}{\text{hyp}} = \dfrac{b}{c}$

$$\sin 11.4° = \dfrac{a}{23.8}$$

$$a = 23.8 \sin 11.4° \approx 4.70$$

$$\cos 11.4° = \dfrac{b}{23.8}$$

$$b = 23.8 \cos 11.4° \approx 23.33$$

39. Each trigonometric ratio contains two sides, which would mean each equation would have two unknown values since we don't know any side. For example, if $\sin 30° = \dfrac{a}{c}$, then we are unable to solve for either a or c.

41.   **a.** No, we could consider either a or b as adjacent sides to γ.

     b. If $\gamma = 90°$, $\tan \gamma = \tan 90°$, which is undefined.

     c. If $\gamma = 90°$, then:

$$\cos \gamma = \dfrac{\text{adj}}{\text{hyp}}$$

$$\cos 90° = \dfrac{\text{adj}}{\text{hyp}}$$

$$0 = \dfrac{\text{adj}}{\text{hyp}}$$

     This implies the adjacent side is 0, which means we have no triangle!

43.   **a.** Angles 1, 3, 8, and 11 are angles of elevation since one side of each is horizontal, and the other side is above the horizontal.

     b. Angles 4, 5, 9, and 10 are angles of depression since one side of each is horizontal and the other is below the horizontal.

     c. Neither side of the angle is horizontal.

45. Since we know $\alpha = 53°$ and adjacent side $b = 25$, and since we want the opposite side a, we use the tangent ratio:

$$\tan \alpha = \dfrac{\text{opp}}{\text{adj}} = \dfrac{a}{b}$$

$$\tan 53° = \dfrac{a}{25}$$

$$a = 25 \tan 53° \approx 33.1761$$

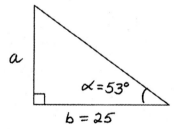

So the height of the tree, to the nearest foot, is 33 ft.

47. $\sin \alpha = \dfrac{\text{opp}}{\text{hyp}} = \dfrac{a}{c}$

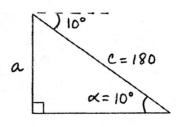

$\sin 10° = \dfrac{a}{180}$

$a = 180 \sin 10° \approx 31.2567$

The depth of the submarine, to the nearest tenth of a meter, is 31.3 m below sea level.

49. $\tan \alpha = \dfrac{\text{opp}}{\text{adj}} = \dfrac{a}{b}$

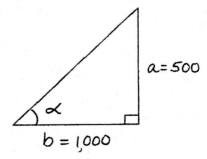

$\tan \alpha = \dfrac{500}{1000}$

$\alpha = \tan^{-1}\left(\dfrac{500}{1000}\right) \approx 26.5651°$

The video camera should be placed on a 26.6° angle of elevation.

51. *Angles of an equilateral triangle are 60°.*

51. $\sin \alpha = \dfrac{\text{opp}}{\text{hyp}} = \dfrac{h}{c}$

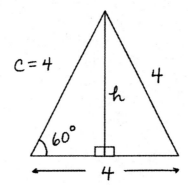

$\sin 60° = \dfrac{h}{4}$

$h = 4 \sin 60°$

$\quad = 4\left(\dfrac{\sqrt{3}}{2}\right)$

$\quad = 2\sqrt{3}$

The altitude is $2\sqrt{3}$ in.

For area: $A = \dfrac{1}{2}$ (base)(altitude)

$\qquad A = \dfrac{1}{2}(4 \text{ in.})\left(2\sqrt{3} \text{ in.}\right)$

$\qquad A = 4\sqrt{3}$ sq in. ≈ 6.93 sq in.

53. $\tan 35° = \dfrac{a}{14}$

$a = 14 \tan 35°$, using the upper triangle

and $\tan 22° = \dfrac{b}{14}$

$b = 14 \tan 22°$, using the lower triangle.

So, $h = a + b = 14 \tan 35° + 14 \tan 22°$

$h \approx 15.4593$

To the nearest foot, the height of the statue is 15 ft.

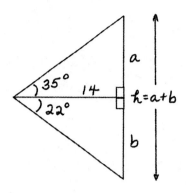

55. a. $\angle 1$ **b.** $\angle 4$

57. Let x represent the miles east.

a. $\sin 42° = \dfrac{x}{3}$

$x = 3 \sin 42° \approx 2.0074$, using the lower triangle

Karen is approximately 2.01 mi east of Gary.

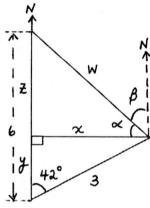

b. To find β and w, we first find y.

$\cos 42° = \dfrac{y}{3}$

$y = 3 \cos 42°$, using the lower triangle

and $z = 6 - y = 6 - 3 \cos 42°$

To find α: $\tan \alpha = \dfrac{z}{x} = \dfrac{(6 - 3 \cos 42°)}{(3 \sin 42°)}$ (x is from part (a)), using the upper triangle

$\tan \alpha \approx 1.8783$

$\alpha \approx \tan^{-1}(1.8783)$

$\alpha \approx 61.9698°$

To find the bearing, we need β:

$\beta = 90° - \alpha \approx 28°$

To find Gary, Karen should use a bearing of N28°W.

Since $x = 3 \sin 42° \approx 2.01$ m,

$z = 6 - 3 \cos 42° \approx 3.77$ m

and $w^2 = x^2 + z^2$

$w \approx \sqrt{(2.01)^2 + (3.77)^2}$

$w \approx 4.2723$

To find Gary, Karen should walk 4.27 mi on a bearing of N28°W.

59. (1) $\tan 40° = \dfrac{h}{x + 20}$, using the large right triangle

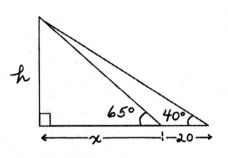

(2) $\tan 65° = \dfrac{h}{x}$ using the smaller (left) right triangle

Solving the second equation for x, we get

$$x = \frac{h}{\tan 65°}.$$

Substituting x into the first equation, we get:

$$\tan 40° = \frac{h}{\left(\dfrac{h}{\tan 65°}\right) + 20}$$

$$\tan 40° \left(\frac{h}{\tan 65°} + 20\right) = h$$

$$h\left(\frac{\tan 40°}{\tan 65°}\right) + 20\tan 40° = h$$

$$20\tan 40° = h - h\left(\frac{\tan 40°}{\tan 65°}\right)$$

$$20\tan 40° = h\left(\frac{\tan 65° - \tan 40°}{\tan 65°}\right)$$

$$h = \frac{20\tan 40° \tan 65°}{\tan 65° - \tan 40°}$$

So, $h \approx 27.57$.

61. Using the strategy of Exercise 59, we get:

$$h = \frac{120\tan 72.8° \tan 60.5°}{\tan 72.8° - \tan 60.5°}$$

$h \approx 468.35$ ft

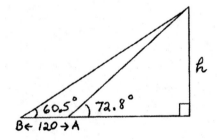

63. Let c be the hypotenuse in the parking lot.

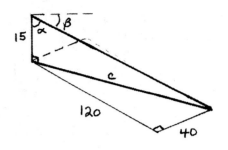

$$120^2 + 40^2 = c^2$$
$$c = \sqrt{16000} = 40\sqrt{10},$$

Also, $\qquad \tan\alpha = \dfrac{c}{15} = \dfrac{40\sqrt{10}}{15}$

$$\alpha = \tan^{-1}\left(\frac{40\sqrt{10}}{15}\right) \approx 83.2°$$

The angle of depression of the camera is β:

$$\beta = 90 - \alpha \approx 90° - 83.2°$$
$$\beta \approx 6.8°$$

The camera should be placed at a 6.8° angle of depression.

65. a. 65°

b. Between two points the angle of depression is equal to the angle of elevation.

Exercise Set 3.4, p. 214

1. AAS; law of sines

3. SSA; law of sines (ambiguous case)

5. SAS; not law of sines

7. SSS; not law of sines

9. AAS; we use the law of sines.
Since we know $\beta = 14°$ and $\gamma = 62°$, we find $\alpha = 180° - \beta - \gamma = 180° - 14° - 62° = 104°$.

To find b: $\qquad \dfrac{b}{\sin\beta} = \dfrac{a}{\sin\alpha}$

$$\frac{b}{\sin 14°} = \frac{7}{\sin 104°}$$

$$b = \frac{7\sin 14°}{\sin 104°}$$

$$b \approx 1.75$$

To find c: $\qquad \dfrac{c}{\sin\gamma} = \dfrac{a}{\sin\alpha}$

$$\frac{c}{\sin 62°} = \frac{7}{\sin 104°}$$

$$c = \frac{7\sin 62°}{\sin 104°}$$

$$c \approx 6.37$$

$a = 7$	$\alpha = 104°$
$b \approx 1.75$	$\beta = 14°$
$c \approx 6.37$	$\gamma = 62°$

11. AAS; we use the law of sines.

Since we know $\beta = 100°$, $\alpha = 15.6°$, we find $\gamma = 180° - \beta - \alpha = 180° - 100° - 15.6° = 64.4°$.

To find b: $\qquad \dfrac{b}{\sin \beta} = \dfrac{a}{\sin \alpha}$ To find c: $\qquad \dfrac{c}{\sin \gamma} = \dfrac{a}{\sin \alpha}$

$$\dfrac{b}{\sin 100°} = \dfrac{6}{\sin 15.6°} \qquad\qquad\qquad \dfrac{c}{\sin 64.4°} = \dfrac{6}{\sin 15.6°}$$

$$b \approx 21.97 \qquad\qquad\qquad\qquad c \approx 20.12$$

$a = 6$	$\alpha = 15.6°$
$b \approx 21.97$	$\beta = 100°$
$c \approx 20.12$	$\gamma = 64.4°$

13. SSA (ambiguous case)

We first determine how many triangles are possible, where $\beta = 30°$, $b = 9$, $c = 7$, by finding γ using the law of sines:

$$\dfrac{\sin \gamma}{c} = \dfrac{\sin \beta}{b}$$

$$\dfrac{\sin \gamma}{7} = \dfrac{\sin 30°}{9}$$

$$\sin \gamma \approx 0.3888$$

$$\gamma \approx \sin^{-1}(0.3888)$$

$\gamma \approx 22.9°$ or $\gamma' = 180° - 22.9° = 167.1°$ (Since $\gamma' + \beta > 180°$, we have only one triangle.)

Next we find α: $\qquad \alpha = 180° - \beta - \gamma \approx 180° - 30° - 22.9°$

$$\alpha \approx 127.1°$$

To find a: $\qquad \dfrac{a}{\sin \alpha} = \dfrac{b}{\sin \beta}$

$$\dfrac{a}{\sin 127.1°} = \dfrac{9}{\sin 30°}$$

$$a \approx 14.36$$

$a \approx 14.36$	$\alpha \approx 127.1°$
$b = 9$	$\beta = 30°$
$c = 7$	$\gamma \approx 22.9°$

15. SSA (ambiguous case)

We first determine how many triangles are possible, where $b = 16.8$, $\gamma = 110°$, $c = 19$, by finding β using the law of sines.

$$\dfrac{\sin \beta}{b} = \dfrac{\sin \gamma}{c}$$

$$\dfrac{\sin \beta}{16.8} = \dfrac{\sin 110°}{19}$$

$$\sin \beta \approx 0.8309$$

$$\beta \approx \sin^{-1}(0.8309)$$

$\beta \approx 56.2°$ or $\beta' \approx 180° - 56.2° = 123.8°$ (Since $\beta' + \gamma > 180°$, we have only one triangle.)

Next we find α: $\alpha = 180° - \beta - \gamma \approx 180° - 56.2° - 110° = 13.8°$.

To find a: $\qquad \dfrac{a}{\sin \alpha} = \dfrac{c}{\sin \gamma}$

$$\dfrac{a}{\sin 13.8°} = \dfrac{19}{\sin 110°}$$

$$a \approx 4.82$$

$a \approx 4.82$	$\alpha \approx 13.8°$
$b = 16.8$	$\beta \approx 56.2°$
$c = 19$	$\gamma = 110°$

17. SSA (ambiguous case)
Use the law of sines.

To find α: $\qquad \dfrac{\sin \alpha}{a} = \dfrac{\sin \beta}{b}$

$$\dfrac{\sin \alpha}{10} = \dfrac{\sin 45°}{5.9}$$

$$\sin \alpha \approx 1.1984$$

There is no solution since $\sin \alpha$ cannot be greater than 1 ($\sin \alpha \not> 1$).

19. SSA (ambiguous case)
Use the law of sines.

To find β: $\qquad \dfrac{\sin \beta}{b} = \dfrac{\sin \gamma}{c}$

$$\dfrac{\sin \beta}{7} = \dfrac{\sin 37°}{5}$$

$$\sin \beta \approx 0.8425$$

$$\beta \approx \sin^{-1}(0.8425)$$

$$\beta \approx 57.4° \quad \text{or} \quad \beta' \approx 180° - 57.4° = 122.6° \text{ (Since } \beta' + \gamma = 159.6° < 180°, \text{ we}$$
$$\text{have a second triangle solution.)}$$

We complete each solution.

<table>
<tr><td align="center">Solution 1</td><td align="center">Solution 2</td></tr>
</table>

Solution 1	Solution 2
$\alpha = 180° - \beta - \gamma \approx 180° - 57.4° - 37°$	$\alpha' = 180° - \beta' - \gamma \approx 180° - 122.6° - 37°$
$\alpha \approx 85.6°$	$\alpha' \approx 20.4°$

To find a: $\qquad \dfrac{a}{\sin \alpha} = \dfrac{c}{\sin \alpha}$

$$\dfrac{a}{\sin 85.6°} = \dfrac{5}{\sin 37°}$$

$$a \approx 8.28$$

To find a': $\qquad \dfrac{a'}{\sin \alpha'} = \dfrac{c}{\sin \gamma}$

$$\dfrac{a'}{\sin 20.4°} = \dfrac{5}{\sin 37°}$$

$$a' \approx 2.90$$

$a \approx 8.28$	$\alpha \approx 85.6°$
$b = 7$	$\beta \approx 57.4°$
$c = 5$	$\gamma = 37°$

$a' \approx 2.90$	$\alpha' \approx 20.4°$
$b = 7$	$\beta' \approx 122.6°$
$c = 5$	$\gamma = 37°$

21. SSA (ambiguous case)
Use the law of sines.

To find γ: $\dfrac{\sin \gamma}{c} = \dfrac{\sin \alpha}{a}$

$$\dfrac{\sin \gamma}{3.2} = \dfrac{\sin 30°}{1.6}$$

$$\sin \gamma = 1$$

$\gamma = 90°$ (Since $\gamma' = 180° - \gamma = 90°$, we have only one triangle.)

Since we have a right triangle, we can use the Pythagorean Theorem to find b.

$$a^2 + b^2 = c^2$$

$$b = \sqrt{(3.2)^2 - (1.6)^2} = \sqrt{7.68}$$

$$b \approx 2.77$$

$a = 1.6$	$\alpha = 30°$
$b \approx 2.77$	$\beta = 60°$
$c = 3.2$	$\gamma = 90°$

23. Since the angle across from side 24.8 is $180° - 54° - 54° = 72°$, we use the law of sines to find x.

$$\dfrac{x}{\sin 54°} = \dfrac{24.8}{\sin 72°}$$

$$x = \dfrac{24.8 \sin 54°}{\sin 72°}$$

$$x \approx 21.10 \text{ in.}$$

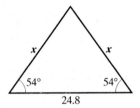

25. Since we have a right triangle, we use the sine ratio

$\sin 48° = \dfrac{\text{opp}}{\text{hyp}} = \dfrac{h}{25}$, and solve for h:

$$h = 25 \sin 48° \approx 18.58.$$

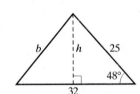

To find the area: $A = \dfrac{1}{2}$ (base)(height)

$$\approx \dfrac{1}{2}(32)(18.5786)$$

So, $A \approx 297$ sq units.

27. Since $\sin \beta = \dfrac{h}{c}$, for the right triangle on the left,

$$h = c \sin \beta,$$

and the area of the triangle is

$$A = \frac{1}{2} \text{(base)(height)},$$

$$A = \frac{1}{2}a \cdot h = \frac{1}{2}ac \sin \beta.$$

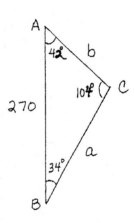

If we multiply each ratio in the law of sines by abc, we notice:

$$abc \left[\frac{\sin \alpha}{a} \right] = abc \left[\frac{\sin \beta}{b} \right] = abc \left[\frac{\sin \gamma}{c} \right]$$

$$bc \sin \alpha = ac \sin \beta = ab \sin \gamma$$

Substituting these equalities in our area formula, we get

$$A = \frac{1}{2}ac \sin \beta = bc \sin \alpha = ab \sin \gamma.$$

29. Use the law of sines.

$$\frac{a}{\sin 42°} = \frac{270}{\sin 104°}$$

$$a \approx 186.20$$

$$\frac{b}{\sin 34°} = \frac{270}{\sin 104°}$$

$$b \approx 155.60$$

The rescheduled trip is $a + b \approx 186.20 + 155.60$, or 342 mi (to the nearest mile).

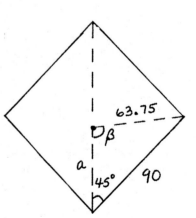

31. SSA (ambiguous case)
Use the law of sines.

$$\frac{\sin \beta}{90} = \frac{\sin 45°}{63.75}$$

$$\sin \beta \approx 0.9983$$

$$\beta \approx 86.6° \quad \text{or} \quad \beta' \approx 180° - 86.6° = 93.4°$$

Of the choices, β' is correct since the pitcher's mound is closer to home plate.
To find a: $\alpha \approx 180° - 93.4° - 45° = 41.6°$

$$\frac{a}{\sin \alpha} = \frac{c}{\sin \gamma}$$

$$\frac{a}{\sin 41.6°} = \frac{63.75}{\sin 45°}$$

$$a \approx 59.86$$

or $\qquad a \approx 60$ ft (to the nearest half-foot)

33. If the man is traveling at a rate of $\dfrac{5 \text{ ft}}{\text{sec}}$, after $1\frac{1}{2}$ minutes (90 sec) he has

traveled a distance = rate · time

$$= \frac{5 \text{ ft}}{\text{sec}} \cdot 90 \text{ sec} = 450 \text{ ft.}$$

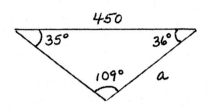

Using the law of sines, we get:

$$\frac{a}{\sin 35°} = \frac{450}{\sin 109°}$$

$$a \approx 272.98 \text{ ft}$$

35. If we let γ be the angle across from the 18-ft side, then we have SSA (ambiguous case) where:

$$\frac{\sin \gamma}{18} = \frac{\sin 45°}{14}$$

$$\sin \gamma = \frac{18 \sin 45°}{14} \approx 0.9091$$

Therefore, $\gamma \approx \sin^{-1}(0.9091) \approx 65.4°$ or $\gamma' \approx 180° - 65.4° = 114.6°$.

Since we have two triangle solutions ($45° + 114.6° < 180°$), we find the third angle θ, θ' of each solution:

Solution 1	Solution 2
$\theta \approx 180° - 45° - 65.4°$	$\theta' \approx 180° - 114.6° - 45°$
$\theta \approx 69.6°$	$\theta' \approx 20.4°$
So, $\dfrac{d}{\sin \theta} = \dfrac{14}{\sin 45°}$	So, $\dfrac{d'}{\sin \theta'} = \dfrac{14}{\sin 45°}$
$d = \dfrac{14 \sin 69.6°}{\sin 45°}$	$d' = \dfrac{14 \sin 20.4°}{\sin 45°}$
$d \approx 18.6$	$d' \approx 6.9$

Since the length of d can be at most 15 ft, we select Solution 2, in which d', the distance between the cameras, to the nearest half-foot, is 7 ft.

Exercise Set 3.5, p. 224

1. SAS; law of cosines

3. SSS; law of cosines

5. SSA; law of sines or law of cosines

7. AAS; law of sines

9. To find α, use the law of cosines.

$$a^2 = b^2 + c^2 - 2bc \cos \alpha$$

$$15^2 = 24^2 + 11^2 - 2(24)(11) \cos \alpha$$

$$\frac{15^2 - 24^2 - 11^2}{-2(24)(11)} = \cos \alpha$$

$$\alpha \approx \cos^{-1}(0.8939)$$

$$\alpha \approx 26.6°$$

Thus, $\gamma = 180° - \alpha - \beta \approx 19.2$.

To find β, use the law of cosines.

$$b^2 = a^2 + c^2 - 2ac \cos \beta$$

$$\frac{24^2 - 15^2 - 11^2}{-2(15)(11)} = \cos \beta$$

$$\beta \approx \cos^{-1}(-0.6970)$$

$$\beta \approx 134.2°$$

$a = 15$	$\alpha \approx 26.6°$
$b = 24$	$\beta \approx 134.2°$
$c = 11$	$\gamma \approx 19.2°$

11. To find c, use the law of cosines.

$$c^2 = a^2 + b^2 - 2ab \cos \gamma$$

$$c^2 = 6^2 + 9^2 - 2(6)(9) \cos 73°$$

$$c^2 \approx 85.4239$$

$$c \approx 9.24$$

Thus, $\beta = 180° - \alpha - \gamma \approx 68.6°$.

To find α, use the law of cosines.

$$a^2 = b^2 + c^2 - 2bc \cos \alpha$$

$$\frac{6^2 - 9^2 - 9.24^2}{-2(9)(9.24)} = \cos \alpha$$

$$\alpha \approx 38.4°$$

$a = 6$	$\alpha \approx 38.4°$
$b = 9$	$\beta \approx 68.6°$
$c \approx 9.24$	$\gamma = 73°$

13. Use the law of cosines.

$$b^2 = a^2 + c^2 - 2ac \cos \beta$$

$$b^2 = 16^2 + 9^2 - 2(16)(9) \cos(94.4°)$$

$$b \approx 18.95 \text{ ft}$$

Thus, $\gamma = 180° - \alpha - \beta \approx 28.3°$.

To find α, use the law of cosines.

$$a^2 = b^2 + c^2 - 2bc \cos \alpha$$

$$\frac{16^2 - 18.95^2 - 9^2}{-2(18.95)(9)} = \cos \alpha$$

$$\alpha \approx 57.3°$$

$a = 16$ ft	$\alpha \approx 57.3°$
$b \approx 18.95$ ft	$\beta = 94.4°$
$c = 9$ ft	$\gamma \approx 28.3°$

15. Use the law of cosines.

$$c^2 = a^2 + b^2 - 2ab \cos \gamma$$

$$c^2 = 7^2 + 5^2 - 2(7)(5) \cos 28.7°$$

$$c \approx 3.55 \text{ cm}$$

Thus, $\alpha = 180° - \beta - \gamma \approx 108.7°$.

To find β:

$$b^2 = a^2 + c^2 - 2ac \cos \beta$$

$$\frac{5^2 - 7^2 - 3.55^2}{-2(7)(3.55)} = \cos \beta$$

$$\beta \approx 42.6°$$

$a = 7$ cm	$\alpha \approx 108.7°$
$b = 5$ cm	$\beta \approx 42.6°$
$c \approx 3.55$ cm	$\gamma = 28.7°$

17. There is no solution since there is not enough information.

19. There is no solution since $a + c \not> b$.

21. Use the law of cosines.

$$a^2 = b^2 + c^2 - 2bc \cos \alpha$$

$$\frac{5^2 - 6^2 - 4^2}{-2(6)(4)} = \cos \alpha$$

$$\alpha \approx \mathbf{55.8°}$$

To find β:

$$b^2 = a^2 + c^2 - 2ac \cos \beta$$

$$\frac{6^2 - 5^2 - 4^2}{-2(5)(4)} = \cos \beta$$

$$\beta \approx 82.8°$$

Thus, $\gamma = 180° - \alpha - \beta \approx 41.4°$.

$a = 5$	$\alpha \approx 55.8°$
$b = 6$	$\beta \approx 82.8°$
$c = 4$	$\gamma \approx 41.4°$

23. $\gamma = 180° - \alpha - \beta$

   $= 180° - 82° - 34° = 64°$

We continue by using the law of sines.

To find a:

$$\frac{a}{\sin \alpha} = \frac{c}{\sin \gamma}$$

$$\frac{a}{\sin 82°} = \frac{9}{\sin 64°}$$

$$a \approx 9.92$$

To find b:

$$\frac{b}{\sin \beta} = \frac{c}{\sin \gamma}$$

$$\frac{b}{\sin 34°} = \frac{9}{\sin 64°}$$

$$b \approx 5.60$$

$a \approx 9.92$	$\alpha = 82°$
$b \approx 5.60$	$\beta = 34°$
$c = 9$	$\gamma = 64°$

25. Since the largest angle is across from the longest side, we find γ across from 15 by using the law of cosines.

$$15^2 = 9^2 + 12^2 - 2(9)(12) \cos \gamma$$

$$\frac{15^2 - 9^2 - 12^2}{-2(9)(12)} = \cos \gamma$$

$$\gamma = 90°$$

27. Since each plane travels for 2 hours, their distances are:

$$d = r \cdot t,$$

$$d = \frac{300 \text{ mi}}{1 \text{ hr}} \cdot 2 \text{ hrs} = 600 \text{ mi}$$

and

$$d = \frac{245 \text{ mi}}{1 \text{ hr}} \cdot 2 \text{ hrs} = 490 \text{ mi},$$

with an angle between their courses of $97° - 42° = 55°$. We use the law of cosines to find c.

$$c^2 = 600^2 + 490^2 - 2(600)(490) \cos 55°$$

$$c \approx 513 \text{ mi}$$

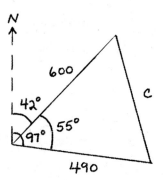

29. **a.** Use the law of cosines (and 220 mph $\left(\dfrac{1}{2}\text{ hr}\right) = 110$ mi).

$$a^2 = 330^2 + 110^2 - 2(330)(110)\cos 10°$$
$$a \approx 222.49 \text{ mi}$$

b. To find β we continue with the law of cosines.

$$b^2 = a^2 + c^2 - 2ac\cos\beta$$

$$\frac{330^2 - 110^2 - 222.49}{-2(110)(222.49)} = \cos\beta$$

$$\beta \approx 165.1°$$

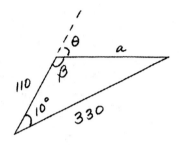

The correction angle, represented by θ, is:

$$\theta = 180° - \beta \approx 180° - 165.1°$$
$$\theta \approx 14.9°$$

To correct his course, the pilot should turn $14.9°$.

31. **a.** The angle α beween the sides $50'$ and $70'$ will be across from $60'$, and we use the law of cosines.

$$60^2 = 50^2 + 70^2 - 2(50)(70)\cos\alpha$$
$$\alpha \approx 57.1°$$

b. The area of the triangle is (see Exercise 27 in Section 3.4):

$$A = \frac{1}{2}bc\sin\alpha$$
$$A = \frac{1}{2}(50')(70')\sin 57.1217°$$
$$A \approx 1470 \text{ sq ft.}$$

33. Use the law of cosines.

$$30^2 = 56^2 + 46^2 - 2(56)(46)\cos\alpha$$
$$\alpha \approx 32.4°$$

Therefore, the King Line should turn $32.4°$.

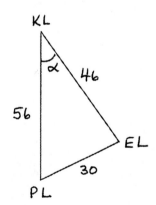

35. Use the law of cosines.

$$a^2 = 120^2 + 86.5^2 - 2(120)(86.5)\cos 120°$$

$$a = \sqrt{32262.25}$$

$$a \approx 180 \text{ ft}$$

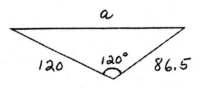

So, the width of the scoreboard is 180 ft.

37. a. Since $9^2 + 7^2 \neq 15^2$, we do not have a rectangle ($\alpha \neq 90°$).
So we draw two parallelograms with sides 7 and 9 with a diagonal 15.
To determine which diagram is correct, we find α using the law of cosines:

$$15^2 = 7^2 + 9^2 - 2(7)(9)\cos \alpha$$

$$\alpha \approx 138.9°,$$

which is an obtuse angle.
Therefore, Parallelogram 1 is the correct diagram. Since Parallelogram 1
has α as the obtuse angle, the other base angle of this parallelogram is the
supplement of α, or

$$180° - 138.9° = 41.1°.$$

b. Using the triangle formed using the second diagonal d and sides 7 and 9,
with 41.4° as the angle between these sides, we see by using the law of
cosines that:

$$d^2 = 7^2 + 9^2 - 2(7)(9)\cos 41.4°$$

$$d \approx \sqrt{35.486} \approx 5.96 \text{ m.}$$

So, our first diagonal of 15 m was the longer.

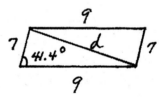

39. Using the law of cosines to solve the ambiguous case, we start by finding c.

$$a^2 = b^2 + c^2 - 2bc \cos \alpha$$

$$7^2 = 3^2 + c^2 - 2(3)c \cos 60°$$

$$0 = c^2 - 3c - 40$$

$$0 = (c - 8)(c + 5)$$

$$c = 8 \quad (c = -5 \text{ is not possible for the length of a side.})$$

Therefore, we have *one* triangle solution. We find β using the law of cosines:

$$b^2 = a^2 + c^2 - 2ac \cos \beta$$

$$\frac{3^2 - 7^2 - 8^2}{-2(7)(8)} = \cos \beta$$

$$\beta \approx 21.8°,$$

and
$$\gamma = 180° - \alpha - \beta$$
$$\approx 180° - 60° - 21.8°$$
$$\gamma \approx 98.2°$$

$a = 7$	$\alpha = 60°$
$b = 3$	$\beta \approx 21.8°$
$c = 8$	$\gamma \approx 98.2°$

41. Using the law of cosines to solve the ambiguous case, we start by finding a.

$$b^2 = a^2 + c^2 - 2ac\cos\beta$$
$$3^2 = a^2 + 4^2 - 2a(4)\cos 40°$$
$$0 = a^2 - 6.1284a + 7$$

Using the quadratic formula we get: $\quad a \approx 1.52, a' \approx 4.61$

We see we obtain two triangle solutions, and we use the law of cosines to complete each solution.

<table>
<tr><td>Solution 1</td><td>Solution 2</td></tr>
</table>

Solution 1

To find α:

$$a^2 = b^2 + c^2 - 2bc\cos\alpha$$
$$\frac{1.52^2 - 3^2 - 4^2}{-2(3)(4)} = \cos\alpha$$
$$\alpha \approx 19.0°$$
$$\gamma = 180° - \alpha - \beta \approx 121.0°$$

$a \approx 1.52$	$\alpha \approx 19.0°$
$b = 3$	$\beta = 40°$
$c = 4$	$\gamma \approx 121.0°$

Solution 2

To find α':

$$(a')^2 = b^2 + c^2 - 2bc\cos\alpha'$$
$$\frac{4.61^2 - 3^2 - 4^2}{-2(3)(4)} = \cos\alpha'$$
$$\alpha' \approx 81.0°$$
$$\gamma' = 180° - \alpha' - \beta \approx 59.0°$$

$a' \approx 4.61$	$\alpha' \approx 81.0°$
$b = 3$	$\beta = 40°$
$c = 4$	$\gamma' \approx 59.0°$

Chapter 3 Review Exercises, p. 230

1. R→D: $\dfrac{5\pi}{6}\left(\dfrac{180°}{\pi}\right) = 150°$

The angle is in QII.

2. R→D: $4\left(\dfrac{180°}{\pi}\right) \approx 229°$

The angle is in QIII.

3. D→R: $55\left(\dfrac{\pi}{180}\right) = \dfrac{11\pi}{36}$

4. D→R: $-140\left(\dfrac{\pi}{180}\right) = -\dfrac{7\pi}{9}$

5. a. We subtract multiples of 360° until we obtain a positive angle within one revolution:

$$993° - 720° = 273°$$

b. To find all the coterminal angles, we add multiples of 360° to get

$$273° + k \cdot 360°.$$

6. a. We subtract multiples of 2π until we obtain a positive angle within one revolution:

$$\frac{25\pi}{4} - \frac{24\pi}{4} = \frac{\pi}{4}$$

b. $\dfrac{\pi}{4} + k \cdot 2\pi$

7. To find arc length, we use the formula $s = r\theta$, where θ is in radians.
    Since $\theta = 120°$, D→R: $\theta = 120\left(\dfrac{\pi}{180}\right) = \dfrac{2\pi}{3}$. So, $s = 6$ ft $\left(\dfrac{2\pi}{3}\right) = 4\pi$ ft ≈ 12.6 ft.

8. The skater did 5 laps or $5(2\pi)$ radians on the circle of radius 10 ft in 15.6 seconds.

    Therefore, $\quad v = \dfrac{r \cdot \theta}{t} = \dfrac{10 \text{ ft}(10\pi)}{15.6 \text{ sec}} \approx 20.1$ ft/sec.

9. Since angular velocity is found using

    $$\omega = \frac{\theta}{t}, \text{ and } \theta \text{ can be measured in degrees,}$$

    $$\omega = \frac{900°}{2.7 \text{ sec}} \approx 333.3 \text{ deg/sec.}$$

10. Using the arc length formula

    $$s = r \cdot \theta, \text{ where } \theta \text{ is measured in rad,}$$

    $$18\text{m} = 12\text{m} \cdot \theta$$

    $$\theta = \frac{18\cancel{\text{m}}}{12\cancel{\text{m}}} = 1.5 \text{ rad.}$$

11. If the point on the terminal side of θ is

    $$(-15, 8) \to x = -15, y = 8.$$

    To use the trigonometric ratios to find $\cos\theta$ or $\sin\theta$, we need to find r.

    $$r = \sqrt{x^2 + y^2}$$
    $$r = \sqrt{(-15)^2 + 8^2}$$
    $$= 17$$

    So, $\cos\theta = \dfrac{x}{r} = -\dfrac{15}{17}$, $\sin\theta = \dfrac{y}{r} = \dfrac{8}{17}$, and $\tan\theta = \dfrac{y}{x} = -\dfrac{8}{15}$.

12. $(5, 12) \to x = 5, y = 12$

    To find r:
    $$r = \sqrt{x^2 + y^2}$$
    $$r = \sqrt{5^2 + 12^2}$$
    $$= 13$$

    So, $\cos\theta = \dfrac{x}{r} = \dfrac{5}{13}$, $\sin\theta = \dfrac{y}{r} = \dfrac{12}{13}$, and $\tan\theta = \dfrac{y}{x} = \dfrac{12}{5}$.

13. $(2\sqrt{3},\ -2) \to x = 2\sqrt{3},\ y = -2$

To find r:

$$r = \sqrt{x^2 + y^2}$$
$$r = \sqrt{(2\sqrt{3})^2 + (-2)^2}$$
$$= 4$$

So, $\cos\theta = \dfrac{x}{r} = \dfrac{2\sqrt{3}}{4} = \dfrac{\sqrt{3}}{2}$, $\sin\theta = \dfrac{y}{r} = \dfrac{-2}{4} = -\dfrac{1}{2}$, and $\tan\theta = \dfrac{y}{x} = \dfrac{-2}{2\sqrt{3}} = -\dfrac{\sqrt{3}}{3}$.

14. $(-5,\ -2) \to x = -5,\ y = -2$

To find r:

$$r = \sqrt{x^2 + y^2}$$
$$r = \sqrt{(-5)^2 + (-2)^2}$$
$$= \sqrt{29}$$

So, $\cos\theta = \dfrac{x}{r} = -\dfrac{5\sqrt{29}}{29}$, $\sin\theta = \dfrac{y}{r} = -\dfrac{2\sqrt{29}}{29}$, and $\tan\theta = \dfrac{y}{x} = \dfrac{2}{5}$.

15. **a.** $\sec\theta > 0$ (or $\cos\theta > 0$) in QI, QIV and $\cot\theta < 0$ (or $\tan\theta < 0$) in QII, QIV. So, the quadrant that satisfies both is QIV.
 b. $\sin\theta > 0$ in QI, QII and $\tan\theta < 0$ in QII, QIV. So, the quadrant that satisfies both is QII.

16. The point, radian, and degree values are listed from $(1, 0)$ counterclockwise:

$(1, 0),\ 0,\ \underline{0°};\ \left(\dfrac{\sqrt{3}}{2}, \dfrac{1}{2}\right),\ \dfrac{\pi}{6},\ \underline{30°};$

$\left(\dfrac{\sqrt{2}}{2}, \dfrac{\sqrt{2}}{2}\right),\ \dfrac{\pi}{4},\ \underline{45°};\ \left(\dfrac{1}{2}, \dfrac{\sqrt{3}}{2}\right),\ \dfrac{\pi}{3},\ \underline{60°};$

$(0, 1),\ \dfrac{\pi}{2},\ \underline{90°};\ \underline{(-1, 0)},\ \pi,\ \underline{180°};\ \underline{(0, -1)},\ -\dfrac{\pi}{2},\ -90°$

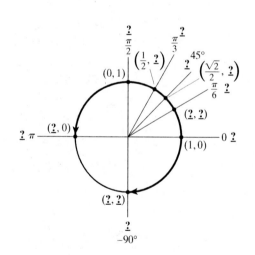

17. $\sin\dfrac{7\pi}{6} = -\sin\dfrac{\pi}{6} = -\dfrac{1}{2}$

18. $\cos\left(-\dfrac{5\pi}{3}\right) = \cos\dfrac{\pi}{3} = \dfrac{1}{2}$

19. $\tan\left(-\dfrac{\pi}{2}\right)$ is undefined.

20. $\cos^2 120° = (\cos 120°)^2 = (-\cos 60°)^2 = \left(-\dfrac{1}{2}\right)^2 = \dfrac{1}{4}$

21. $\sec 3\pi = \dfrac{1}{\cos 3\pi} = \dfrac{1}{\cos \pi} = \dfrac{1}{(-1)} = -1$

22. $\cot(-60°) = \dfrac{1}{\tan(-60°)} = \dfrac{1}{-\sqrt{3}} = -\dfrac{\sqrt{3}}{3}$

23. $\sin(-390°) = \sin(-30°) = -\sin 30° = -\dfrac{1}{2}$

24. $\cos 135° = -\cos 45° = -\dfrac{\sqrt{2}}{2}$

25. $\tan \dfrac{9\pi}{4} = \tan \dfrac{\pi}{4} = 1$

26. $\csc(-270°) = \dfrac{1}{\sin(-270°)} = \dfrac{1}{1} = 1$

27. $\sec^2(-45°) = (\sec(\ 45°))^2 = \left(\dfrac{1}{\cos(-45°)} \right)^2 = \left(\dfrac{1}{\left(\dfrac{1}{\sqrt{2}} \right)} \right)^2 = 2$

28. $\sin 180° = 0$

29. $\arccos\left(-\dfrac{1}{\sqrt{2}} \right) = 135°$ (since $\cos 135° = -\dfrac{1}{\sqrt{2}}$ and $0° \le 135° \le 180°$)

30. $\sin^{-1}(-1) = -90°$ (since $\sin(-90°) = -1$ and $-90° \le -90° \le 90°$)

31. $\tan^{-1} \sqrt{3} = 60°$ (since $\tan 60° = \sqrt{3}$ and $-90° < 60° < 90°$)

32. $\text{arcsec } 2 = \arccos \dfrac{1}{2} = 60°$ (since $\cos 60° = \dfrac{1}{2}$ and $0° \le 60° \le 180°$)

33. $\text{arccsc } \dfrac{1}{2} = \arcsin 2$ is not possble (since $\sin \theta \ne 2$).

34. $\tan^{-1} 0 = 0° = 0$ (since $\tan 0° = 0$ and $-90° < 0° < 90°$)

35. $\cot^{-1}\left(-\sqrt{3} \right) = 90° - \tan^{-1}\left(-\sqrt{3} \right)$
$= 90° - (-60°)$
$= 150°$ (since $\cot 150° = -\sqrt{3}$ and $0° < 150° < 180°$)

36. $\cos^{-1} \dfrac{\sqrt{3}}{2} = 30°$ (since $\cos 30° = \dfrac{\sqrt{3}}{2}$ and $0° \le 30° \le 180°$)

37. $\sin^{-1} \dfrac{1}{2} = 30°$ (since $\sin 30° = \dfrac{1}{2}$ and $-90° \le 30° \le 90°$)

38. $\tan^{-1}(-1) = -45°$ (since $\tan(-45°) = -1$ and $-90° < -45° < 90°$)

39. $\cos^{-1} 3$ is not possible (since $\cos \theta \ne 3$).

40. $\text{arccsc}\left(-\dfrac{1}{\sqrt{2}} \right) = \arcsin\left(-\sqrt{2} \right)$ is not possible (since $\sin \theta \ne -\sqrt{2}$).

41. $\tan\left(\arccos \dfrac{1}{5} \right) = \tan \theta$, where $\theta = \arccos \dfrac{1}{5}, 0° \le \theta \le 180°$. So, $\cos \theta = \dfrac{1}{5} = \dfrac{x}{r} \rightarrow x = 1, r = 5$.
We want $\tan \theta = \dfrac{y}{x}$ which means we need y, that we find by using $x^2 + y^2 = r^2$.

$$1^2 + y^2 = 5^2$$
$$y = \sqrt{24} = 2\sqrt{6} \ (y > 0 \text{ for } 0° \le \theta \le 180°)$$

So, $\tan \theta = \dfrac{y}{x} = \dfrac{2\sqrt{6}}{1} = 2\sqrt{6}$.

Therefore, $\tan\left(\arccos \dfrac{1}{5} \right) = \tan \theta = 2\sqrt{6}$.

42. $\sin\left(\tan^{-1}\dfrac{1}{4}\right) = \sin\theta$, where $\theta = \tan^{-1}\dfrac{1}{4}$, $-90° < \theta < 90°$.

So, $\tan\theta = \dfrac{1}{4} = \dfrac{y}{x} \rightarrow y = 1, x = 4$. To find $\sin\theta = \dfrac{y}{r}$, we need r.

$$r^2 = x^2 + y^2$$
$$r = \sqrt{4^2 + 1^2}$$
$$= \sqrt{17}$$

So, $\sin\theta = \dfrac{y}{r} = \dfrac{1}{\sqrt{17}} = \dfrac{\sqrt{17}}{17}$.

Therefore, $\sin\left(\tan^{-1}\dfrac{1}{4}\right) = \sin\theta = \dfrac{\sqrt{17}}{17}$.

43. $\sin 45° = \cos(90° - 45°) = \cos 45°$

44. $\tan 60° = \cot(90° - 60°) = \cot 30°$

45. $\sec 15°35' = \csc(90° - 15°35') = \csc 74°25'$

46. $\cos 72° = \sin(90° - 72°) = \sin 18°$

47–50. *Since each triangle is a right triangle ($\gamma = 90°$), we use the trigonometric ratios for a right triangle or the Pythagorean Theorem to solve.*

47. We first find β: $\alpha + \beta = 90°$

$$\beta = 90° - \alpha = 90° - 27° = 63°$$

Next we find c: $\sin\alpha = \dfrac{\text{opp}}{\text{hyp}} = \dfrac{a}{c}$

$$\sin 27° = \dfrac{5}{c}$$

$$c = \dfrac{5}{\sin 27°} \approx 11.01$$

For b: $\tan\alpha = \dfrac{\text{opp}}{\text{adj}} = \dfrac{a}{b}$

$$\tan 27° = \dfrac{5}{b}$$

$$b = \dfrac{5}{\tan 27°} \approx 9.81$$

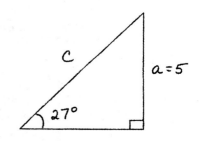

$a = 5$	$\alpha = 27°$
$b \approx 9.81$	$\beta = 63°$
$c \approx 11.01$	$\gamma = 90°$

48.   We first find α: $\alpha = 90° - \beta = 90° - 52° = 38°$

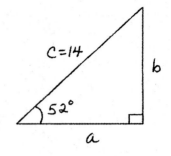

To find a: $\cos \beta = \dfrac{\text{adj}}{\text{hyp}} = \dfrac{a}{c}$

$\cos 52° = \dfrac{a}{14}$

$a = 14 \cos 52°$

$a \approx 8.62$

To find b: $\sin \beta = \dfrac{\text{opp}}{\text{hyp}} = \dfrac{b}{c}$

$\sin 52° = \dfrac{b}{14}$

$b = 14 \sin 52°$

$b \approx 11.03$

$a \approx 8.62$	$\alpha = 38°$
$b \approx 11.03$	$\beta = 52°$
$c = 14$	$\gamma = 90°$

49.   To find b, we use the Pythagorean Theorem:

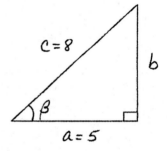

$$a^2 + b^2 = c^2$$
$$5^2 + b^2 = 8^2$$
$$b = \sqrt{39} \approx 6.24$$

Next we find α:

$\sin \alpha = \dfrac{\text{opp}}{\text{hyp}} = \dfrac{a}{c}$

$\sin \alpha = \dfrac{5}{8}$

$\alpha = \sin^{-1}\left(\dfrac{5}{8}\right)$

$\alpha \approx 38.7°$

and β:

$\beta = 90° - \alpha$

$\approx 90° - 38.7°$

$\beta \approx 51.3°$

$a = 5$	$\alpha \approx 38.7°$
$b \approx 6.24$	$\beta \approx 51.3°$
$c = 8$	$\gamma = 90°$

50. To find c, we use the Pythagorean Theorem:

$$c^2 = a^2 + b^2$$
$$c = \sqrt{93.1^2 + 49^2}$$
$$c \approx 105.21$$

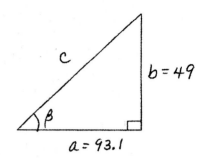

To find β: and α:

$$\tan \beta = \frac{\text{opp}}{\text{adj}} = \frac{b}{a}$$

$$\tan \beta = \frac{49}{93.1}$$

$$\beta = \tan^{-1}\left(\frac{49}{93.1}\right)$$

$$\beta \approx 27.8°$$

$$\alpha = 90° - \beta$$
$$\approx 90° - 27.8°$$
$$\alpha \approx 62.2°$$

$a = 93.1$	$\alpha \approx 62.2°$
$b = 49$	$\beta \approx 27.8°$
$c \approx 105.21$	$\gamma = 90°$

51. If we find the angle α, we will be able to determine the bearing. Since we have a right triangle, we use the tangent trigonometric ratio:

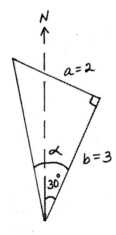

$$\tan \alpha = \frac{\text{opp}}{\text{adj}} = \frac{a}{b}$$

$$\tan \alpha = \frac{2}{3}$$

$$\alpha = \tan^{-1}\left(\frac{2}{3}\right)$$

$$\alpha \approx 33.7°$$

In our diagram, the angle between the original bearing of N30°E, and the current location indicates the pilot is on a bearing of N3.7°W from the central tower.

52. AAS; use the law of sines.

$$\alpha = 180° - \beta - \gamma = 68°$$

We solve for the sides.

b: $\dfrac{b}{\sin\beta} = \dfrac{a}{\sin\alpha}$ and c: $\dfrac{c}{\sin\gamma} = \dfrac{a}{\sin\alpha}$

$\dfrac{b}{\sin 12°} = \dfrac{10}{\sin 68°}$ $\dfrac{c}{\sin 100°} = \dfrac{10}{\sin 68°}$

$b \approx 2.24$ $c \approx 10.62$

$a = 10$	$\alpha = 68°$
$b \approx 2.24$	$\beta = 12°$
$c \approx 10.62$	$\gamma = 100°$

53. SSA (ambiguous case); use the law of sines. We start by determining how many triangle solutions we have by solving for α:

$$\frac{\sin\alpha}{a} = \frac{\sin\beta}{b}$$

$$\frac{\sin\alpha}{6} = \frac{\sin 110°}{5}$$

$$\sin\alpha = 1.27$$

There is no solution, since the sine function is never greater than 1 ($\sin\alpha \not> 1$).

54. SSA (ambiguous case); use the law of sines. We start by determining how many triangle solutions we have by solving for β:

$$\frac{\sin\beta}{b} = \frac{\sin\alpha}{a}$$

$$\frac{\sin\beta}{6} = \frac{\sin 10°}{3}$$

$$\sin\beta = \frac{6\sin 10°}{3} \approx 0.3473$$

$$\beta \approx \sin^{-1}(0.3473)$$

$\beta \approx 20.3°$ or $\beta' \approx 180 - 20.3° = 159.7°$ (We have a second triangle solution
since $\alpha + \beta' < 180°$.)

To complete each solution, we find the third angle and the remaining side.

Solution 1

$$\gamma = 180° - \alpha - \beta$$
$$\approx 180° - 10° - 20.3°$$
$$\gamma \approx 149.7°$$

Use the law of sines to find c:

$$\frac{c}{\sin \gamma} = \frac{a}{\sin \alpha}$$
$$\frac{c}{\sin 149.7°} = \frac{3}{\sin 10°}$$
$$c \approx 8.72$$

$a = 3$	$\alpha = 10°$
$b = 6$	$\beta \approx 20.3°$
$c \approx 8.72$	$\gamma \approx 149.7°$

Solution 2

$$\gamma' = 180° - \alpha - \beta'$$
$$\approx 180° - 10° - 159.7°$$
$$\gamma' \approx 10.3°$$

Use the law of sines to find c':

$$\frac{c'}{\sin \gamma'} = \frac{a}{\sin \alpha}$$
$$\frac{c'}{\sin 10.3°} = \frac{3}{\sin 10°}$$
$$c' \approx 3.09$$

$a = 3$	$\alpha = 10°$
$b = 6$	$\beta' \approx 159.7°$
$c' \approx 3.09$	$\gamma' \approx 10.3°$

55. SSA (ambiguous case); use the law of sines. We start by determining how many triangles are possible by solving for β.

$$\frac{\sin \beta}{b} = \frac{\sin \alpha}{a}$$
$$\frac{\sin \beta}{35} = \frac{\sin 122.5°}{50}$$
$$\sin \beta \approx 0.5904$$

$$\beta \approx 36.2° \quad \text{or} \quad \beta' \approx 180 - 36.2° = 143.8° \text{ (Since } \beta' + \alpha > 180°, \text{ we have only}$$
$$\text{one solution.)}$$

To find γ: $\gamma = 180 - \alpha - \beta \approx 21.3°$. We again use the law of sines to find c.

$$\frac{c}{\sin \gamma} = \frac{a}{\sin \alpha}$$
$$\frac{c}{\sin 21.3°} = \frac{50}{\sin 122.5°}$$
$$c \approx 21.54$$

$a = 50$	$\alpha = 122.5°$
$b = 35$	$\beta \approx 36.2°$
$c \approx 21.54$	$\gamma \approx 21.3°$

56.   AAS; we use the law of sines to find c in the left triangle.

$$\frac{c}{\sin 105°} = \frac{111}{\sin 5°}$$

$$c \approx 1230.1859$$

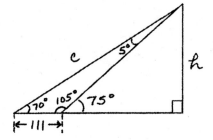

Next we use the large right triangle, whose hypotenuse is c, to find h:

$$\sin 70° = \frac{\text{opp}}{\text{hyp}} = \frac{h}{c}$$

$$\sin 70° = \frac{h}{1230.1859}$$

$$h \approx 1156 \text{ ft}$$

The height of the object on the CNN observation deck is 1156 ft.

57.   SSA (ambiguous case)
We start by finding the angle across from side 120, which we call α.

$$\frac{\sin \alpha}{120} = \frac{\sin 62°}{185}$$

$$\sin \alpha \approx 0.5727$$

$$\alpha \approx 34.9°$$

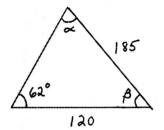

(or $\alpha' \approx 180° - 34.9 = 145.1°$ which is not possible since
$62° + 145.1° > 180°$)

We are interested in finding the angle that the tower makes with the ground, which is the third angle of this triangle, β:

$$\beta \approx 180° - 62° - 34.9° = 83.1°$$

Therefore, the tower makes an angle of 83.1° with the horizontal.

58. SAS; use the law of cosines.

$$b^2 = a^2 + c^2 - 2ac \cos \beta$$
$$b^2 = 3^2 + 2^2 - 2(3)(2) \cos 100°$$
$$b \approx 3.88$$

To find α:

$$a^2 = b^2 + c^2 - 2bc \cos \alpha$$

$$\frac{3^2 - 3.88^2 - 6^2}{-2(3.88)(6)} = \cos \alpha$$

$$\alpha \approx 49.5°$$

Therefore, $\gamma = 180° - \alpha - \beta \approx 30.5°$.

$a = 3$	$\alpha \approx 49.5°$
$b \approx 3.88$	$\beta = 100°$
$c = 2$	$\gamma \approx 30.5°$

59. Since $a + c \not> b$, there is no triangle solution.

60. SSS; use the law of cosines. First we find α:

$$a^2 = b^2 + c^2 - 2bc \cos \alpha$$

$$\frac{5^2 - 2^2 - 6^2}{-2(2)(6)} = \cos \alpha$$

$$\alpha \approx 51.3°$$

To find β:

$$b^2 = a^2 + c^2 - 2ac \cos \beta$$

$$\frac{2^2 - 5^2 - 6^2}{-2(5)(6)} = \cos \beta$$

$$\beta \approx 18.2°$$

Therefore, $\gamma = 180° - \alpha - \beta \approx 110.5°$.

$a = 5$	$\alpha \approx 51.3°$
$b = 2$	$\beta \approx 18.2°$
$c = 6$	$\gamma \approx 110.5°$

61. SAS; use the law of cosines. First we find c:

$$c^2 = a^2 + b^2 - 2ab \cos \gamma$$
$$c^2 = 2.3^2 + 1.2^2 - 2(2.3)(1.2) \cos 58.2°$$
$$c \approx 1.95$$

To find β:

$$b^2 = a^2 + c^2 - 2ac \cos \beta$$

$$\frac{1.2^2 - 2.3^2 - 1.95^2}{-2(2.3)(1.95)} = \cos \beta$$

$$\beta \approx 31.4°$$

Therefore, $\alpha = 180° - \beta - \gamma \approx 90.4°$.

$a = 2.3$	$\alpha \approx 90.4°$
$b = 1.2$	$\beta \approx 31.4°$
$c \approx 1.95$	$\gamma = 58.2°$

62. To find how far the boat is from Naples, we find a by using the law of cosines.

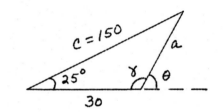

$$a^2 = b^2 + c^2 - 2bc \cos \alpha$$
$$a^2 = 150^2 + 30^2 - 2(150)(30) \cos 25°$$
$$a \approx 123.46$$

The boat is 123.46 mi from Naples.
To find θ, the angle the boat should turn, we first find γ.

$$c^2 = a^2 + b^2 - 2ab \cos \gamma$$

$$\frac{150^2 - 123.46^2 - 30^2}{-2(123.46)(30)} = \cos \gamma$$

$$\gamma \approx 149.1°$$

Since $\theta + \gamma = 180°$

$$\theta \approx 180° - 149.1°$$
$$\theta \approx 30.9°,$$

the boat should turn 30.9°.

63. **a.** law of cosines (SSS)   **b.** law of cosines (SAS)
   c. not possible, since of the three pieces of information, at least one must be a side.
   d. law of sines or law of cosines (SSA)
   e. trigonometric ratios for a right triangle, Pythagorean Theorem
   f. not possible; we need three pieces of information
   g. law of sines (AAS)

64. **a.** True
   b. False; you need one side included in the three pieces of information.
   c. False; SAS determines *one* triangle.   **d.** True
   e. False; they add to 180°.   **f.** True
   g. True   **h.** False; it applies only to a right triangle.
   i. True   **j.** True
   k. False; it applies only to a right triangle.

Chapter 3 Test, p. 233

1. a. R→D: $\dfrac{7\pi}{8}\left(\dfrac{180°}{\pi}\right) = 157.5°$ The angle is in QII.

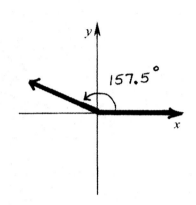

b. R→D: $1\left(\dfrac{180°}{\pi}\right) \approx 57.3°$ The angle is in QI.

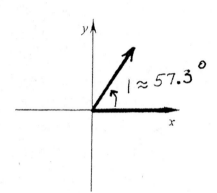

2. a. D→R: $-15\left(\dfrac{\pi}{180}\right) = -\dfrac{\pi}{12}$ **b.** D→R: $210\left(\dfrac{\pi}{180}\right) = \dfrac{7\pi}{6}$

3. a. Since the central angle is in degrees ($\alpha = 330°$) we convert to radians and then use the arc length formula (where $\alpha = \theta$). D→R: $\alpha = 330° = 330\left(\dfrac{\pi}{180}\right) = \dfrac{11\pi}{6}$.

$$s = r \cdot \alpha$$

$$s = 100 \text{ ft}\left(\dfrac{11\pi}{6}\right) \approx 576 \text{ ft}$$

b. $v = \dfrac{s}{t} = \dfrac{575.9587 \text{ ft}}{6 \text{ sec}} \approx 96 \text{ ft/sec}$ **c.** $\omega = \dfrac{\alpha}{t} = \dfrac{\left(\dfrac{11\pi}{6}\right)}{6} = \dfrac{11\pi}{36} \approx 1 \text{ rad/sec}$

4. $(3, -2) \to x = 3,\, y = -2$. To find functional values, we first find r:

$$r = \sqrt{x^2 + y^2}$$
$$r = \sqrt{(3)^2 + (-2)^2}$$
$$r = \sqrt{13}$$

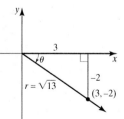

a. $\cos\theta = \dfrac{x}{r} = \dfrac{3\sqrt{3}}{13}$ **b.** $\sin\theta = \dfrac{y}{r} = -\dfrac{2\sqrt{13}}{13}$ **c.** $\cot\theta = \dfrac{x}{y} = -\dfrac{3}{2}$

5. If $\tan\alpha = -\dfrac{4}{3} = \dfrac{y}{x}$, and α is in QII,

    $\rightarrow x = -3$, $y = 4$.

    To find the functional values, we first find r:

    $$r = \sqrt{x^2 + y^2}$$
    $$r = \sqrt{(-3)^2 + (4)^2}$$
    $$r = 5$$

    a. $\cos\alpha = \dfrac{x}{r} = -\dfrac{3}{5}$

    b. $\csc\alpha = \dfrac{r}{y} = \dfrac{5}{4}$

6. **a.** $\cos(-120°) = -\cos 60° = -\dfrac{1}{2}$

    b. $\cot 150° = \dfrac{1}{\tan 150°} = \dfrac{1}{-\tan 30°} = -\sqrt{3}$

    c. $\tan\dfrac{7\pi}{3} = \tan\dfrac{\pi}{3} = \sqrt{3}$

    d. $\csc(-45°) = \dfrac{1}{\sin(-45°)} = -\sqrt{2}$

    e. $\sec(-\pi) = \dfrac{1}{\cos(-\pi)} = \dfrac{1}{-1} = -1$

    f. $\sin(-855°) = \sin(-135°) = -\sin 45° = -\dfrac{\sqrt{2}}{2}$

7. **a.** $\cos^{-1}(-1) = 180°$ (since $\cos 180° = -1$ and $0° \leq 180° \leq 180°$)

    b. $\csc^{-1} 2 = \sin^{-1}\left(\dfrac{1}{2}\right) = 30°$ (since $\sin 30° = \dfrac{1}{2}$, and $-90° \leq 30° \leq 90°$)

    c. $\arctan\sqrt{3} = 60°$ (since $\tan 60° = \sqrt{3}$, and $-90° \leq 60° \leq 90°$)

    d. $\arcsin 5.6$ is not possible (since $\sin\alpha$ can not be greater than 1, or $\sin\alpha \neq 5.6$).

8. **a.** $\cos 0.56$ (in radian mode)

    $\cos(0.56)$ $\boxed{\text{ENTER}}$ ≈ 0.8473

    b. $\tan 123°$ (in degree mode)

    $\tan(123)$ $\boxed{\text{ENTER}}$ ≈ -1.5399

    c. $\sec 20°$ (in degree mode)

    $1 \div \cos(20)$ $\boxed{\text{ENTER}}$ ≈ 1.0642

    d. $\cot(-2.89)$ (in radian mode)

    $1 \div \tan(-2.89)$ $\boxed{\text{ENTER}}$ ≈ 3.8905

    e. $\arcsin 0.9$ (in degree mode)

    $\sin^{-1}(0.9)$ $\boxed{\text{ENTER}}$ $\approx 64.2°$

    f. $\text{arcsec}(-3.5)$ (in radian mode)

    $\cos^{-1}(1 \div -3.5)$ $\boxed{\text{ENTER}}$ ≈ 1.8605

9. **a.** $\tan x = \dfrac{\text{opp}}{\text{adj}}$

    $\tan x = \dfrac{5}{11}$

    $x = \tan^{-1}\left(\dfrac{5}{11}\right) \approx 24.4°$

    b. $\sin 47° = \dfrac{\text{opp}}{\text{hyp}}$

    $\sin 47° = \dfrac{3}{x}$

    $x = \dfrac{3}{\sin 47°} \approx 4.10$

10. **a.** SSS; law of cosines

    b. AAS; law of sines

    c. There is not enough information, and we need at least one side.

    d. SAS; law of cosines

    e. right triangle $\rightarrow$ trigonometrc ratios or Pythagorean Theorem

11. **a.** Since one angle is 90°, we use trigonometrc ratios to find a.

$$\cos \beta = \frac{\text{adj}}{\text{hyp}} = \frac{a}{c}$$

$$\cos 42° = \frac{a}{12}$$

$$a = 12 \cos 42°$$

$$a \approx 8.92$$

   b. SSA (ambiguous case)
   We find β using the law of sines.

$$\frac{\sin \beta}{b} = \frac{\sin \alpha}{a}$$

$$\frac{\sin \beta}{4} = \frac{\sin 75°}{15}$$

$$\sin \beta \approx 0.2576$$

$$\beta \approx 14.9° \text{ (or } \beta' = 180° - \beta \approx 165.7°, \text{ which is}$$
$$\text{too large since } \alpha + \beta' > 180°)$$

12. The angle opposite the side 5045 is:
$$180° - 72° - 78° = 30°.$$

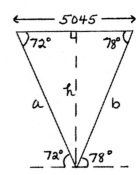

We find a using the large triangle and the law of sines (AAS).

$$\frac{a}{\sin 78°} = \frac{5045}{\sin 30°},$$

$$a = \frac{5045 \sin 78°}{\sin 30°} \approx 9869.5093$$

Using the right triangle on the left, we get:

$$\sin 72° = \frac{\text{opp}}{\text{hyp}} = \frac{h}{9869.5093}$$

$$h = 9869.5093 \sin 72° \approx 9386.46$$

So the height to the nearest tenth of a foot over the deepest point of the canyon is 9386.5 ft.

13. After $1\frac{1}{2}$ hrs, Anthony has gone a distance of

$$d = r \cdot t = \frac{36 \text{ mi}}{1 \text{ hr}} \cdot 1.5 \text{ hr} = 54 \text{ mi, and Rosalie has gone}$$

$$d = \frac{40 \text{ mi}}{1 \text{ hr}} \cdot 1.5 \text{ hr} = 60 \text{ mi.}$$

To determine the distance they are apart, we need to find a. Use the law of cosines (SAS) to find a:

$$a^2 = b^2 + c^2 - 2bc \cos \alpha$$

$$a^2 = 54^2 + 60^2 - 2(54)(60) \cos 42°$$

$$a \approx \sqrt{1700.4215}$$

$$a \approx 41.24$$

To the nearest mile, they are 41 mi apart.

14. Since the information presents the SSA situation (ambiguous case), we use the law of sines to find the angle across from the 4-ft side, which we will call α.

$$\frac{\sin \alpha}{4} = \frac{\sin 50}{3}$$

$$\sin \alpha = \frac{4 \sin 50}{3} \approx 1.0214$$

Since $\sin \alpha$ cannot be greater than 1 ($\sin \alpha \not> 1$) there is no triangle solution, which suggests that the 3-ft piece is not long enough.

15. **a.** $\alpha + \beta = 90°$. Since this is a right triangle, the acute angles are complementary.
    b. Using the trigonometric ratios of a right triangle, we get:

$$\cos \alpha = \frac{b}{c} = \frac{\text{adj}}{\text{hyp}}$$

$$\sin \beta = \frac{b}{c} = \frac{\text{opp}}{\text{hyp}}$$

Therefore, $\cos \alpha = \sin \beta$.
Since $\alpha + \beta = 90°$, from the definitions of the cofunctions,

$$\cos \alpha = \sin(90° - \alpha) = \sin \beta.$$

Chapter 4   Trigonometry Student's Solutions Manual

Exercise Set 4.1, p. 245

1. $\sin^2 x$; $1 - \cos^2 x = \underline{\sin^2 x}$

3. $\cot^2 x$; $\csc^2 x = 1 + \underline{\cot^2 x}$

5. $\cos^2 x$; $(1 - \sin x)(1 + \sin x) = 1 - \sin^2 x = \underline{\cos^2 x}$

7. $\tan^2 x$; $\sec^2 x - 1 = \underline{\tan^2 x}$

9. $\cos^2 x$; $\dfrac{1}{\sec^2 x} = \underline{\cos^2 x}$

11. $\pm\sqrt{1 - \sin^2 x}$; $\cos x = \underline{\pm\sqrt{1 - \sin^2 x}}$

13. Recall that $\cos(-x) = \cos x$.

$\sin x \sec(-x) \cos x$

$= \dfrac{\sin x}{1} \cdot \dfrac{1}{\cos(-x)} \cdot \dfrac{\cos x}{\sin x}$

$= 1$

15. Recall that $\sin(-x) = -\sin x$.

$\cos x \tan x + \sin x \csc x + \sin(-x)$

$= \dfrac{\cos x}{1} \cdot \dfrac{\sin x}{\cos x} + \dfrac{\sin x}{1} \cdot \dfrac{1}{\sin x} - \sin x$

$= \sin x + 1 - \sin x$

$= 1$

17. $(1 - \cos\alpha)(1 + \cos\alpha)$

$= 1 - \cos^2\alpha$

$= \sin^2\alpha$

19. $(\cos A + \sin A)^2$

$= \cos^2 A + 2\cos A \sin A + \sin^2 A$

$= 1 + 2\cos A \sin A$

21. $\dfrac{\sec\beta}{\tan\beta}$

$= \dfrac{\left(\dfrac{1}{\cos\beta}\right)}{\left(\dfrac{\sin\beta}{\cos\beta}\right)}$

$= \dfrac{1}{\cos\beta} \cdot \dfrac{\cos\beta}{\sin\beta}$

$= \dfrac{1}{\sin\beta}$

$= \csc\beta$

23. $\sin^3 x + \sin x \cos^2 x$

$= \sin x(\sin^2 x + \cos^2 x)$

$= \sin x$

25. $\cos^4 B - \sin^4 B$

$= (\cos^2 B)^2 - (\sin^2 B)^2$

$= (\cos^2 B + \sin^2 B)(\cos^2 B - \sin^2 B)$

$= \cos^2 B - \sin^2 B$

27. $\dfrac{1 - \sin^2 x}{1 - \sin x}$

$= \dfrac{(1 - \sin x)(1 + \sin x)}{1 - \sin x}$

$= 1 + \sin x$

29. $\cos A \tan A = \sin A$

$\cos A \cdot \dfrac{\sin A}{\cos A} = $

$\sin A = $

31. $\sin^2 x \sec x \csc x = \tan x$

$\sin^2 x \cdot \dfrac{1}{\cos x} \cdot \dfrac{1}{\sin x} = $

$\dfrac{\sin x}{\cos x} = $

$\tan x = $

33.
$$\sec t - \cos t = \tan t \sin t$$
$$\frac{1}{\cos t} - \frac{\cos t}{1} \cdot \frac{\cos t}{\cos t} =$$
$$\frac{1 - \cos^2 t}{\cos t} =$$
$$\frac{\sin^2 t}{\cos t} =$$
$$\frac{\sin t}{\cos t} \cdot \frac{\sin t}{1} =$$
$$\tan t \sin t =$$

35.
$$1 + \cot x = \frac{\cos x + \sin x}{\sin x}$$
$$= \frac{\cos x}{\sin x} + \frac{\sin x}{\sin x}$$
$$= \cot x + 1$$

37.
$$\cos^2 x - \sin^2 x = 2\cos^2 x - 1$$
$$\cos^2 x - (1 - \cos^2 x) =$$
$$2\cos^2 x - 1 =$$

39.
$$\tan^2 \beta - \sin^2 \beta = \tan^2 \beta \sin^2 \beta$$
$$\frac{\sin^2 \beta}{\cos^2 \beta} - \sin^2 \beta \cdot \frac{\cos^2 \beta}{\cos^2 \beta} =$$
$$\frac{\sin^2 \beta - \sin^2 \beta \cos^2 \beta}{\cos^2 \beta} =$$
$$\frac{\sin^2 \beta (1 - \cos^2 \beta)}{\cos^2 \beta} =$$
$$\frac{\sin^2 \beta}{\cos^2 \beta} \cdot \sin^2 \beta =$$
$$\tan^2 \beta \sin^2 \beta =$$

41.
$$\frac{\sin^4 x - \cos^4 x}{\sin^2 x - \cos^2} = 1$$
$$\frac{(\sin^2 x - \cos^2 x)(\sin^2 x + \cos^2 x)}{\sin^2 x - \cos^2 x} =$$
$$\sin^2 x + \cos^2 x =$$
$$1 =$$

43.
$$\frac{1}{1 + \cos A} = \csc^2 A - \csc A \cot A$$
$$= \frac{1}{\sin^2 A} - \frac{1}{\sin A} \cdot \frac{\cos A}{\sin A}$$
$$= \frac{1 - \cos A}{\sin^2 A}$$
$$= \frac{1 - \cos A}{1 - \cos^2 A}$$
$$= \frac{1 - \cos A}{(1 + \cos A)(1 - \cos A)}$$
$$= \frac{1}{1 + \cos A}$$

45.
$$\frac{1-\cos\alpha}{\sin\alpha} + \frac{\sin\alpha}{1-\cos\alpha} = 2\csc\alpha$$

$$\frac{(1-\cos\alpha)}{(1-\cos\alpha)}\cdot\frac{(1-\cos\alpha)}{\sin\alpha} + \frac{\sin\alpha}{(1-\cos\alpha)}\cdot\frac{\sin\alpha}{\sin\alpha} =$$

$$\frac{1-2\cos\alpha+\cos^2\alpha}{(1-\cos\alpha)\sin\alpha} + \frac{\sin^2\alpha}{(1-\cos\alpha)\sin\alpha} =$$

$$\frac{2-2\cos\alpha}{(1-\cos\alpha)\sin\alpha} =$$

$$\frac{2(1-\cos\alpha)}{(1-\cos\alpha)\sin\alpha} =$$

$$\frac{2}{\sin\alpha} =$$

$$2\csc\alpha =$$

47. $\sec^2\theta\csc^2\theta = \sec^2\theta + \csc^2\theta$

$$= \frac{1}{\cos^2\theta}\cdot\frac{\sin^2\theta}{\sin^2\theta} + \frac{1}{\sin^2\theta}\cdot\frac{\cos^2\theta}{\cos^2\theta}$$

$$= \frac{\sin^2\theta + \cos^2\theta}{\cos^2\theta\sin^2\theta}$$

$$= \frac{1}{\cos^2\theta\sin^2\theta}$$

$$= \frac{1}{\cos^2\theta}\cdot\frac{1}{\sin^2\theta}$$

$$= \sec^2\theta\csc^2\theta$$

49.
$$(\sin x + \cos x)^2 - 1 = 2\sin x\cos x$$
$$\sin^2 x + 2\sin x\cos x + \cos^2 x - 1 =$$
$$2\sin x\cos x + (\sin^2 x + \cos^2 x) - 1 =$$
$$2\sin x\cos x =$$

51.
$$\frac{\csc^2 x - \cot^2 x}{\sec^2 x} = \cos^2 x$$

$$\frac{(1+\cot^2 x) - \cot^2 x}{\sec^2 x} =$$

$$\frac{1}{\sec^2 x} =$$

$$\cos^2 x =$$

53.
$$2\cos^2 B - 1 = 1 - 2\sin^2 B$$
$$2(1 - \sin^2 B) - 1 =$$
$$2 - 2\sin^2 B - 1 =$$
$$1 - 2\sin^2 B =$$

55. $\sec(-A)\cot(-A)\sin(-A) = 1$

$$\dfrac{1}{\cos(-A)} \cdot \dfrac{\cos(-A)}{\sin(-A)} \cdot \sin(-A) = $$

$$1 = $$

57. The left side contains $\tan x$ that has a restriction on the variable. Since $\tan x = \dfrac{\sin x}{\cos x}$ is defined only when $\cos x \neq 0$, the identity is true for $x \neq \dfrac{\pi}{2} + k\pi,\, x \in \mathbb{R}$.

59. The left side contains $\sin x$ in the denominator, so it is defined only when $\sin x \neq 0$. Therefore, the identity is true for $x \neq k\pi,\, x \in \mathbb{R}$.

61. Krystn has an equivalent form of the correct answer.

$$-\tan x + \dfrac{\sin x}{\cos x - 1}$$

$$= \dfrac{-\sin x}{\cos x}\left(\dfrac{\cos x - 1}{\cos x - 1}\right) + \left(\dfrac{\sin x}{\cos x - 1}\right)\left(\dfrac{\cos x}{\cos x}\right)$$

$$= \dfrac{-\sin x \cos x + \sin x + \sin x \cos x}{\cos x(\cos x - 1)}$$

$$= \dfrac{\sin x}{\cos x(\cos x - 1)}$$

$$= \tan x \left(\dfrac{1}{\cos x - 1}\right)$$

Exercise Set 4.2, p. 254

1. $\cos 15° = \cos(45° - 30°)$

$= \cos 45° \cos 30° + \sin 45° \sin 30°$

$= \dfrac{\sqrt{2}}{2} \cdot \dfrac{\sqrt{3}}{2} + \dfrac{\sqrt{2}}{2} \cdot \dfrac{1}{2}$

$= \dfrac{\sqrt{6} + \sqrt{2}}{4}$

3. $\cos 195° = \cos(150° + 45°)$

$= \cos 150° \cos 45° - \sin 150° \sin 45°$

$= \left(-\dfrac{\sqrt{3}}{2}\right) \cdot \dfrac{\sqrt{2}}{2} - \dfrac{1}{2} \cdot \dfrac{\sqrt{2}}{2}$

$= -\dfrac{\sqrt{6} + \sqrt{2}}{4}$

5 and 7. *Problems can also be done after converting radians to degrees (e.g., $\dfrac{7\pi}{12} = 105°$).*

5. $\cos\left(\dfrac{7\pi}{12}\right) = \cos\left(\dfrac{3\pi}{12} + \dfrac{4\pi}{12}\right)$

$= \cos\left(\dfrac{\pi}{4} + \dfrac{\pi}{3}\right)$

$= \cos\dfrac{\pi}{4}\cos\dfrac{\pi}{3} - \sin\dfrac{\pi}{4}\sin\dfrac{\pi}{3}$

$= \dfrac{\sqrt{2}}{2} \cdot \dfrac{1}{2} - \dfrac{\sqrt{2}}{2} \cdot \dfrac{\sqrt{3}}{2}$

$= \dfrac{\sqrt{2} - \sqrt{6}}{4}$

7. $\sec\left(-\dfrac{\pi}{12}\right) = \dfrac{1}{\cos\left(-\dfrac{\pi}{12}\right)} = \dfrac{1}{\cos\dfrac{\pi}{12}}$

Since $\dfrac{\pi}{12} = 15°$, and Exercise 1 found

$\cos 15° = \dfrac{\sqrt{6}+\sqrt{2}}{4}$, then

$\sec\left(-\dfrac{\pi}{12}\right) = \dfrac{1}{\left(\dfrac{\sqrt{6}+\sqrt{2}}{4}\right)} = \dfrac{4}{\left(\sqrt{6}+\sqrt{2}\right)} \cdot \dfrac{\left(\sqrt{6}-\sqrt{2}\right)}{\left(\sqrt{6}-\sqrt{2}\right)} = \dfrac{4\left(\sqrt{6}-\sqrt{2}\right)}{4}$

$= \sqrt{6} - \sqrt{2}.$

9, 11, 13, and 15. *Use the cosine sum or difference identity to get the following form.*

9. $\cos(190° - 10°) = \cos(180°) = -1$

11. $\cos(27° + 63°) = \cos(90°) = 0$

13. $\cos\left(\dfrac{5\pi}{6} - \dfrac{\pi}{12}\right) = \cos\left(\dfrac{10\pi}{12} - \dfrac{\pi}{12}\right) = \cos\dfrac{3\pi}{4} = -\dfrac{\sqrt{2}}{2}$

15. $\cos\left(25\dfrac{1}{2}° + 4\dfrac{1}{2}°\right) = \cos(30°) = \dfrac{\sqrt{3}}{2}$

17, 19, 21, 23, and 25. *Use the cosine sum or difference identity and rewrite the left side of the statement to get the following form.*

17. $\cos(80° - 35°) = \cos 45° = \dfrac{\sqrt{2}}{2}$, True

19. $\cos\left(\dfrac{5\pi}{8} + \dfrac{3\pi}{8}\right) = \cos \pi = -1$, True

21. $\cos(112° - 8°) = \cos(104°) \neq -\dfrac{\sqrt{3}}{2}$, False

23. $\cos(9x + 8x) = \cos(17x) \neq \cos x$, False

25. $\dfrac{1}{\cos\left(\dfrac{x}{2} - 3x\right)} = \dfrac{1}{\cos\left(-\dfrac{5x}{2}\right)} = \dfrac{1}{\cos\left(\dfrac{5x}{2}\right)} = \sec\left(\dfrac{5x}{2}\right)$, True

27 and 29. *First rewrite the equations in Column A:*

a. $y = \cos 2x \cos x + \sin 2x \sin x$
$= \cos(2x - x) = \cos x$

b. $y = \cos 2x \cos x - \sin 2x \sin x$
$= \cos(2x + x) = \cos 3x$

c. $y = \cos \dfrac{1}{2}x \cos \dfrac{1}{2}x - \sin \dfrac{1}{2}x \sin \dfrac{1}{2}x$

$= \cos \left(\dfrac{1}{2}x + \dfrac{1}{2}x \right) = \cos x$

d. $y = \cos x \cos \dfrac{1}{2}x + \sin x \sin \dfrac{1}{2}x$

$= \cos \left(x - \dfrac{1}{2}x \right) = \cos \dfrac{1}{2}x$

e. $y = \cos 5x \cos x + \sin 5x \sin x$
$= \cos(5x - x) = \cos 4x$

f. $y = \cos 10x \cos 6x + \sin 10x \sin 6x$
$= \cos(10x - 6x) = \cos 4x$

g. $y = \cos 11\dfrac{1}{2}x \cos 11x + \sin 11\dfrac{1}{2}x \sin x$

$= \cos \left(11\dfrac{1}{2}x - 11x \right) = \cos \dfrac{1}{2}x$

27. The graph has cosine form with amplitude 1, period $= 4\pi = \dfrac{2\pi}{B}$ so $B = \dfrac{1}{2}$.

The graph can be represented by $y = \cos \left(\dfrac{1}{2}x \right)$, which is equivalent to:

$$\text{(d) } y = \cos \left(x - \dfrac{1}{2}x \right) = \cos \left(\dfrac{1}{2}x \right)$$

$$\text{and (g) } y = \cos \left(11\dfrac{1}{2}x - 11x \right) = \cos \left(\dfrac{1}{2}x \right).$$

29. The graph is the cosine form with $A = 1$, period $= \dfrac{\pi}{2} = \dfrac{2\pi}{|B|}$, so $B = 4$. It can be represented by $y = \cos(4x)$, which is equivalent to:

$$\text{(e) } y = \cos(5x - x) = \cos(4x)$$
$$\text{and (f) } y = \cos(10x - 6x) = \cos(4x).$$

31. $\cos(x - 270°) = \cos x \cos 270° + \sin x \sin 270°$
$= (\cos x)(0) + (\sin x)(-1)$
$= -\sin x$

33. $\cos \left(x - \dfrac{\pi}{2} \right) = \cos x \cos \dfrac{\pi}{2} + \sin x \sin \dfrac{\pi}{2}$
$= (\cos x)(0) + (\sin x)(1)$
$= \sin x$

35. $\cos(180° - x) = \cos 180° \cos x + \sin 180° \sin x$
$= -1 \cdot \cos x + 0 \cdot \sin x$
$= -\cos x$

37. $\cos \left(\dfrac{3\pi}{2} + x \right) = \cos \dfrac{3\pi}{2} \cos x - \sin \dfrac{3\pi}{2} \sin x$
$= 0 \cdot \cos x - (-1) \cdot \sin x$
$= \sin x$

39. Since A and B are in QIII, if $\cos A = -\dfrac{1}{2}$, then $\sin A = -\dfrac{\sqrt{3}}{2}$, and if $\sin B = -\dfrac{1}{2}$, then $\cos B = -\dfrac{\sqrt{3}}{2}$.

QIII	QIII
$\cos A = -\dfrac{1}{2}$	$\cos B = -\dfrac{\sqrt{3}}{2}$
$\sin A = -\dfrac{\sqrt{3}}{2}$	$\sin B = -\dfrac{1}{2}$

(These are common angle functional values, so we didn't need to use the Pythagorean identity to find $\sin A$ or $\cos B$.) We substitute these values into the following identities:

$$\cos(A + B) = \cos A \cos B - \sin A \sin B$$
$$= \left(-\frac{1}{2}\right)\left(-\frac{\sqrt{3}}{2}\right) - \left(-\frac{\sqrt{3}}{2}\right)\left(-\frac{1}{2}\right)$$
$$= 0$$
$$\cos(A - B) = \left(-\frac{1}{2}\right)\left(-\frac{\sqrt{3}}{2}\right) + \left(-\frac{\sqrt{3}}{2}\right)\left(-\frac{1}{2}\right)$$
$$= \frac{\sqrt{3} + \sqrt{3}}{4} = \frac{2\sqrt{3}}{4} = \frac{\sqrt{3}}{2}$$

41. Since we know $\cos A = -\dfrac{4}{5}$, where $90° < A < 180°$, we can find $\sin A$ by using the Pythagorean identity.

$$\cos^2 A + \sin^2 A = 1$$
$$\left(-\frac{4}{5}\right)^2 + \sin^2 A = 1$$
$$\sin^2 A = 1 - \frac{16}{25} = \frac{9}{25}$$
$$\sin A = \frac{3}{5}, \ A \text{ in QII}$$

Next we find $\sin B$ where $\cos B = \dfrac{12}{13}$, and $270° < B < 360°$.

$$\cos^2 B + \sin^2 B = 1$$
$$\sin^2 B = 1 - \frac{144}{169} = \frac{25}{169}$$
$$\sin B = -\frac{5}{13}, \ B \text{ in QIV}$$

QII	QIV
$\cos A = -\dfrac{4}{5}$	$\cos B = \dfrac{12}{13}$
$\sin A = \dfrac{3}{5}$	$\sin B = -\dfrac{5}{13}$

We substitute these values into the following identities:

$$\cos(A + B) = \cos A \cos B - \sin A \sin B$$
$$= \left(-\frac{4}{5}\right) \cdot \frac{12}{13} - \frac{3}{5} \cdot \left(-\frac{5}{13}\right) = -\frac{48}{65} + \frac{15}{65} = -\frac{33}{65}$$
$$\cos(A - B) = \left(-\frac{4}{5}\right) \cdot \frac{12}{13} + \frac{3}{5} \cdot \left(-\frac{5}{13}\right) = -\frac{48}{65} - \frac{15}{65} = -\frac{63}{65}$$

43. Since we know $A = \dfrac{1}{\sqrt{10}}$, and $0 \le A \le \dfrac{\pi}{2}$, we can find $\cos A$.

$$\cos^2 A + \sin^2 A = 1$$

$$\cos^2 A = 1 - \frac{1}{10} = \frac{9}{10}$$

$$\cos A = \frac{3}{\sqrt{10}}, \; A \text{ in QI}$$

QI	
$\cos A = \dfrac{3}{\sqrt{10}}$	$\cos B = -1$
$\sin A = \dfrac{1}{\sqrt{10}}$	$\sin B = 0$

Since $\cos B = -1$, $\sin B = 0$.

We substitute these values into the following identities:

$$\cos(A + B) = \cos A \cos B - \sin A \sin B$$

$$= \frac{3}{\sqrt{10}} \cdot (-1) - \frac{1}{\sqrt{10}} \cdot 0 = -\frac{3\sqrt{10}}{10}$$

$$\cos(A - B) = \frac{3}{\sqrt{10}} \cdot (-1) + \frac{1}{\sqrt{10}} \cdot 0 = -\frac{3\sqrt{10}}{10}$$

45. If $\sin A = -\dfrac{3}{5}$, and A in QIV, we can find $\cos A$.

$$\cos^2 A + \sin^2 A = 1$$

$$\cos^2 A = 1 - \frac{9}{25} = \frac{16}{25}$$

$$\cos A = \frac{4}{5}, \; A \text{ in QIV}$$

QIV	QI
$\cos A = \dfrac{4}{5}$	$\cos B = \dfrac{3}{5}$
$\sin A = -\dfrac{3}{5}$	$\sin B = \dfrac{4}{5}$

If $\tan B = \dfrac{4}{3} = \dfrac{\text{opp}(y)}{\text{adj}(x)}$ then we find the hypotenuse r.

$$r^2 = x^2 + y^2$$
$$r^2 = 3^2 + 4^2$$
$$r = \sqrt{25} = 5.$$

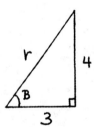

So, $\cos B = \dfrac{\text{adj}}{\text{hyp}} = \dfrac{3}{5}$ and $\sin B = \dfrac{\text{opp}}{\text{hyp}} = \dfrac{4}{5}$ (B is in QI).

We substitute these values into the following identities:

$$\cos(A + B) = \cos A \cos B - \sin A \sin B$$

$$= \left(\frac{4}{5}\right)\left(\frac{3}{5}\right) - \left(-\frac{3}{5}\right)\left(\frac{4}{5}\right)$$

$$= \frac{12}{25} + \frac{12}{25} = \frac{24}{25}$$

$$\cos(A - B) = \cos A \cos B + \sin A \sin B$$

$$= \left(\frac{4}{5}\right)\left(\frac{3}{5}\right) + \left(-\frac{3}{5}\right)\left(\frac{4}{5}\right) = 0$$

47. $\cos\left(\text{arcsec}\sqrt{2} + \arcsin\dfrac{1}{2}\right)$

$= \cos(A + B)$, where $A = \text{arcsec}\sqrt{2}$, $\;0° \le A \le 180°$

and $B = \arcsin\dfrac{1}{2}$, $\;-90° \le B \le 90°$

So, $\sec A = \sqrt{2}$ or $\cos A = \dfrac{1}{\sqrt{2}} \to A = 45°$,

and $\sin B = \dfrac{1}{2} \to B = 30°$.

Therefore: $\cos(A + B) = \cos(45° + 30°)$

$\qquad\qquad\qquad = \cos 45° \cos 30° - \sin 45° \sin 30°$

$\qquad\qquad\qquad = \dfrac{\sqrt{2}}{2} \cdot \dfrac{\sqrt{3}}{2} - \dfrac{\sqrt{2}}{2} \cdot \dfrac{1}{2}$

$\qquad\qquad\qquad = \dfrac{\sqrt{6} - \sqrt{2}}{4}$

49. $\cos\left(\tan^{-1} + \arccos\dfrac{1}{2}\right)$

$= \cos(A + B)$, where $A = \tan^{-1} 1$, $\;-90° < A < 90°$

and $B = \arccos\dfrac{1}{2}$, $\;0° \le B \le 180°$

So, $\tan A = 1 \to A = 45°$

and $\cos B = \dfrac{1}{2} \to B = 60°$.

Therefore: $\cos(A + B) = \cos(45° + 60°)$

$\qquad\qquad\qquad = \cos 45° \cos 60° - \sin 45° \sin 60°$

$\qquad\qquad\qquad = \dfrac{\sqrt{2}}{2} \cdot \dfrac{1}{2} - \dfrac{\sqrt{2}}{2} \cdot \dfrac{\sqrt{3}}{2}$

$\qquad\qquad\qquad = \dfrac{\sqrt{2} - \sqrt{6}}{4}$

51. $\cos\left[\cos^{-1}\left(-\dfrac{1}{2}\right) - \arcsin\left(-\dfrac{\sqrt{2}}{2}\right)\right]$

$= \cos(A - B),$ where $A = \cos^{-1}\left(-\dfrac{1}{2}\right),$ $0° \le A \le 180°$

and $B = \arcsin\left(-\dfrac{\sqrt{2}}{2}\right),$ $-90° \le B \le 90°$

So, $\cos A = -\dfrac{1}{2} \rightarrow A = 120°$

and $\sin B = -\dfrac{\sqrt{2}}{2} \rightarrow B = -45°.$

Therefore: $\cos(A - B) = \cos(120° - (-45°))$

$= \cos 120° \cos(-45°) + \sin 120° \sin(-45°)$

$= \left(-\dfrac{1}{2}\right) \cdot \dfrac{\sqrt{2}}{2} + \dfrac{\sqrt{3}}{2} \cdot \left(-\dfrac{\sqrt{2}}{2}\right)$

$= -\dfrac{-\sqrt{2} - \sqrt{6}}{4}$

53.   Use the cosine difference identity.

$$\cos(90° - \alpha) = \sin \alpha$$
$$\cos 90° \cdot \cos \alpha + \sin 90° \cdot \sin \alpha =$$
$$0 \cdot \cos \alpha + 1 \cdot \sin \alpha =$$
$$\sin \alpha =$$

55.   Use the cosine difference identity.

$$\cos(2\pi - A) = \cos A$$
$$\cos 2\pi \cdot \cos A + \sin 2\pi \cdot \sin A =$$
$$1 \cdot \cos A + 0 \cdot \sin A =$$
$$\cos A =$$

57.   For one possible counterexample,

let $A = \pi, B = \dfrac{\pi}{2}.$

$\cos\left(\pi + \dfrac{\pi}{2}\right) \ne \cos \pi + \cos \dfrac{\pi}{2}$

$\cos\left(\dfrac{3\pi}{2}\right) \ne (-1) + 0$

$0 \ne -1$

59.   Rewrite $2x = x + x$ and use the cosine sum identity.

$$\cos(2x) = \cos^2 x - \sin^2 x$$
$$\cos(x + x) =$$
$$\cos x \cos x - \sin x \sin x =$$
$$\cos^2 x - \sin^2 x =$$

Exercise Set 4.3, p. 263

1. $\sin 75° = \sin(45° + 30°)$

$= \sin 45° \cos 30° + \cos 45° \sin 30°$

$= \dfrac{\sqrt{2}}{2} \cdot \dfrac{\sqrt{3}}{2} + \dfrac{\sqrt{2}}{2} \cdot \dfrac{1}{2}$

$= \dfrac{\sqrt{6} + \sqrt{2}}{4}$

3. $\tan 195° = \tan(150° + 45°)$

$= \dfrac{\tan 150° + \tan 45°}{1 - \tan 150° \tan 45°}$

$= \dfrac{\left(-\dfrac{1}{\sqrt{3}}\right) + 1}{1 - \left(-\dfrac{1}{\sqrt{3}}\right)(1)} = \dfrac{\left(-\dfrac{1}{\sqrt{3}} + 1\right)}{\left(1 + \dfrac{1}{\sqrt{3}}\right)} \cdot \dfrac{\sqrt{3}}{\sqrt{3}}$

$= \dfrac{\left(\sqrt{3} - 1\right)}{\left(\sqrt{3} + 1\right)} \cdot \dfrac{\left(\sqrt{3} - 1\right)}{\left(\sqrt{3} - 1\right)} = \dfrac{3 - 2\sqrt{3} + 1}{3 - 1} = \dfrac{4 - 2\sqrt{3}}{2}$

$= \dfrac{2\left(2 - \sqrt{3}\right)}{2} = 2 - \sqrt{3}$

5. $\sin\left(-\dfrac{\pi}{12}\right) = \sin\left(\dfrac{3\pi}{12} - \dfrac{4\pi}{12}\right)$

$= \sin\left(\dfrac{\pi}{4} - \dfrac{\pi}{3}\right)$

$= \sin \dfrac{\pi}{4} \cos \dfrac{\pi}{3} - \cos \dfrac{\pi}{4} \sin \dfrac{\pi}{3}$

$= \dfrac{\sqrt{2}}{2} \cdot \dfrac{1}{2} - \dfrac{\sqrt{2}}{2} \cdot \dfrac{\sqrt{3}}{2}$

$= \dfrac{\sqrt{2} - \sqrt{6}}{4}$

7. $\tan \dfrac{5\pi}{12} = \tan\left(\dfrac{3\pi}{12} + \dfrac{2\pi}{12}\right)$

$= \tan\left(\dfrac{\pi}{4} + \dfrac{\pi}{6}\right)$

$= \dfrac{\tan \dfrac{\pi}{4} + \tan \dfrac{\pi}{6}}{1 - \tan \dfrac{\pi}{4}\tan \dfrac{\pi}{6}}$

$= \dfrac{1 + \dfrac{1}{\sqrt{3}}}{1 - 1\left(\dfrac{1}{\sqrt{3}}\right)} = \dfrac{\left(1 + \dfrac{1}{\sqrt{3}}\right)}{\left(1 - \dfrac{1}{\sqrt{3}}\right)} \cdot \dfrac{\sqrt{3}}{\sqrt{3}}$

$= \dfrac{\left(\sqrt{3}+1\right)\left(\sqrt{3}+1\right)}{\left(\sqrt{3}-1\right)\left(\sqrt{3}+1\right)} = \dfrac{3 + 2\sqrt{3} + 1}{3 - 1} = \dfrac{4 + 2\sqrt{3}}{2}$

$= \dfrac{2\left(2 + \sqrt{3}\right)}{2} = 2 + \sqrt{3}$

9. $\sin 140° \cos 40° + \cos 140° \sin 40°$

$= \sin(140° + 40°)$ Use the sine sum identity.

$= \sin 180°$

$= 0$

11. Use the sine difference identity.

$\sin \dfrac{7\pi}{8} \cos \dfrac{\pi}{8} - \cos \dfrac{7\pi}{8} \sin \dfrac{\pi}{8}$

$= \sin\left(\dfrac{7\pi}{8} - \dfrac{\pi}{8}\right)$

$= \sin \dfrac{3\pi}{4}$

$= \dfrac{\sqrt{2}}{2}$

13. Use the tangent sum identity.

$\dfrac{\tan 13° + \tan 32°}{1 - \tan 13° \tan 32°}$

$= \tan(13° + 32°)$

$= \tan 45°$

$= 1$

15. Use the tangent difference identity.

$\dfrac{\tan 233° - \tan 113°}{1 + \tan 233° \tan 113°}$

$= \tan(233° - 113°)$

$= \tan 120°$

$= -\sqrt{3}$

17. $\sin 102° \cos 72° - \cos 102° \sin 72°$

$= \sin(102° - 72°)$

$= \sin 30° = \dfrac{1}{2} \neq \dfrac{\sqrt{3}}{2},\ \ \text{False}$

19. $\dfrac{\tan 15° - \tan 45°}{1 + \tan 15° \tan 45°}$

$= \tan(15° - 45°)$

$= \tan(-30°) = -\dfrac{\sqrt{3}}{3},\ \ \text{True}$

21. $\sin 3x \cos 2x - \cos 3x \sin 2x$

$= \sin(3x - 2x) = \sin x,\ \ \text{True}$

23. $\dfrac{\tan 3x + \tan 2x}{1 - \tan 3x \tan 2x}$

$= \tan(3x + 2x)$

$= \tan(5x) \neq \tan x,\ \ \text{False}$

25. Using the sine form (with amplitude 1 and period $= 2\pi$), the graph can be represented by $y = \sin x$, which is equivalent to the following by using the sine sum identity:

$$(\text{f})\ y = \sin 2x \cos(-x) + \cos 2x \sin(-x)$$
$$= \sin(2x + (-x)) = \sin x$$

27. Using the tangent form, where $P = 2\pi = \dfrac{\pi}{|B|} \rightarrow B = \dfrac{1}{2}$, the graph can be represented by $y = \tan\left(\dfrac{1}{2}x\right)$, which is equivalent to the following using the tangent sum identity:

$$(\text{d})\ y = \dfrac{\tan \dfrac{1}{4}x + \tan \dfrac{1}{4}x}{1 - \tan \dfrac{1}{4}x \tan \dfrac{1}{4}x}$$

$$= \tan\left(\dfrac{1}{4}x + \dfrac{1}{4}x\right)$$

$$= \tan\left(\dfrac{1}{2}x\right)$$

29. $\sin(\pi - x) = \sin \pi \cos x - \cos \pi \sin x$

$= 0 \cdot \cos x - (-1)\sin x$

$= \sin x$

31. $\sin(x - 90°) = \sin x \cos 90° - \cos x \sin 90°$

$= (\sin x)(0) - (\cos x)(1)$

$= -\cos x$

33. $\tan(x + 180°) = \dfrac{\tan x + \tan 180°}{1 - \tan 180° \tan x}$

$= \dfrac{\tan x + 0}{1 - (0)\tan x}$

$= \tan x$

35. Since $\cos A = -\dfrac{4}{5}$ and A is in QII, we can find $\sin A$.

$$\cos^2 A + \sin^2 A = 1$$
$$\sin^2 A = 1 - \frac{16}{25} = \frac{9}{25}$$
$$\sin A = \frac{3}{5}, \; A \text{ in QII}$$

QII	QII
$\cos A = -\dfrac{4}{5}$	$\cos B = -\dfrac{12}{13}$
$\sin A = \dfrac{3}{5}$	$\sin B = \dfrac{5}{13}$

Since $\sin B = \dfrac{5}{13}$ and B is in QII, we can find $\cos B$.

$$\cos^2 B + \sin^2 B = 1$$
$$\cos^2 B = 1 - \frac{25}{169} = \frac{144}{169}$$
$$\cos B = -\frac{12}{13}, \; B \text{ in QII}$$

Therefore: $\sin(A + B) = \sin A \cos B + \cos A \sin B$

$$= \frac{3}{5} \cdot \left(-\frac{12}{13}\right) + \left(-\frac{4}{5}\right) \cdot \frac{5}{13}$$
$$= -\frac{56}{65}$$

37. Since $\sin A = -\dfrac{7}{25}$ and A is in QIV, we can find $\cos A$.

$$\cos^2 A + \sin^2 A = 1$$
$$\cos^2 A = 1 - \frac{49}{625} = \frac{576}{625}$$
$$\cos A = \frac{24}{25}, \; A \text{ in QIV}$$

QIV	QIV
$\cos A = \dfrac{24}{25}$	$\cos B = \dfrac{3}{5}$
$\sin A = -\dfrac{7}{25}$	$\sin B = -\dfrac{4}{5}$

Since $\cos B = \dfrac{3}{5}$ and B is in QIV, we can find $\sin B$.

$$\cos^2 B + \sin^2 B = 1$$
$$\sin^2 B = 1 - \frac{9}{25} = \frac{16}{25}$$
$$\sin B = -\frac{4}{5}, \; B \text{ in QIV}$$

Therefore: $\sin(A + B) = \sin A \cos B + \cos A \sin B$

$$= \left(-\frac{7}{25}\right) \cdot \frac{3}{5} + \frac{24}{25} \cdot \left(-\frac{4}{5}\right)$$
$$= -\frac{117}{125}$$

39. If $\sin A = -\dfrac{5}{13}$, and A is in QIII, we can find $\cos A$.

$$\cos^2 A + \sin^2 A = 1$$

$$\cos^2 A = 1 - \frac{25}{169} = \frac{144}{169}$$

$$\cos A = -\frac{12}{13}, \ A \text{ in QIII}$$

	QIII	QIV
$\cos A = -\dfrac{12}{13}$		$\cos B = \dfrac{3}{5}$
$\sin A = -\dfrac{5}{13}$		$\sin B = -\dfrac{4}{5}$
$\tan A = \dfrac{5}{12}$		$\tan B = -\dfrac{4}{3}$

If $\cos B = \dfrac{3}{5}$, then

$$\cos^2 B + \sin^2 B = 1$$

$$\sin^2 B = 1 - \frac{9}{25} = \frac{16}{25}$$

$$\sin B = -\frac{4}{5}, \ B \text{ is in QIV.}$$

a. $\sin(A - B) = \sin A \cos B - \cos A \sin B$

$$= \left(-\frac{5}{13}\right) \cdot \frac{3}{5} - \left(-\frac{12}{13}\right)\left(-\frac{4}{5}\right) = -\frac{63}{65}$$

b. $\tan(A + B) = \dfrac{\tan A + \tan B}{1 - \tan A \tan B} = \dfrac{\dfrac{5}{12} + \left(-\dfrac{4}{3}\right)}{1 - \left(\dfrac{5}{12}\right)\left(-\dfrac{4}{3}\right)} = -\dfrac{33}{56}$

c. $\cos(A + B) = \cos A \cos B - \sin A \sin B$

$$= \left(-\frac{12}{13}\right) \cdot \frac{3}{5} - \left(-\frac{5}{13}\right)\left(-\frac{4}{5}\right) = -\frac{56}{65}$$

d. Since part (b) tells us that $\tan(A + B) < 0$ and part (c) says $\cos(A + B) < 0$, the quadrant in which both tangent and cosine are negative is QII.

41. $\sin\left(\sin^{-1}\dfrac{\sqrt{2}}{2} - \cos^{-1}\dfrac{1}{2}\right)$

$= \sin(A - B)$, where $A = \sin^{-1}\dfrac{\sqrt{2}}{2}$, $-90° \le A \le 90°$,

and $B = \cos^{-1}\dfrac{1}{2}$, $0° \le B \le 180°$

So, $\sin A = \dfrac{\sqrt{2}}{2} \to A = 45°$

and $\cos B = \dfrac{1}{2} \to A = 60°$.

Therefore: $\sin(A - B) = \sin(45° - 60°)$

$= \sin 45° \cos 60° - \cos 45° \sin 60°$

$= \dfrac{\sqrt{2}}{2} \cdot \dfrac{1}{2} - \dfrac{\sqrt{2}}{2} \cdot \dfrac{\sqrt{3}}{2}$

$= \dfrac{\sqrt{2} - \sqrt{6}}{4}$

43. $\tan\left(\tan^{-1}\sqrt{3} + \csc^{-1}\sqrt{2}\right)$

$= \tan(A + B)$, where $A = \tan^{-1}\sqrt{3}$, $-90° < A < 90°$,

and $B = \csc^{-1}\sqrt{2}$

or $B = \sin^{-1}\left(\dfrac{1}{\sqrt{2}}\right)$, $-90° \le B < 0°, 0° < B \le 90°$

So, $\tan A = \sqrt{3} \to A = 60°$

and $\sin B = \dfrac{1}{\sqrt{2}} \to B = 45°$

Therefore: $\tan(A + B) = \tan(60° + 45°)$

$= \dfrac{\tan 60° + \tan 45°}{1 - \tan 60° \tan 45°}$

$= \dfrac{\sqrt{3} + 1}{1 - \left(\sqrt{3}\right)(1)} = \dfrac{\left(\sqrt{3} + 1\right)}{\left(1 - \sqrt{3}\right)} \cdot \dfrac{\left(1 + \sqrt{3}\right)}{\left(1 + \sqrt{3}\right)}$

$= \dfrac{3 + 2\sqrt{3} + 1}{1 - 3} = \dfrac{4 + 2\sqrt{3}}{-2}$

$= \dfrac{-2\left(-2 - \sqrt{3}\right)}{-2} = -2 - \sqrt{3}$

45. $\tan\left(\sec^{-1}\dfrac{3}{2}-\cos^{-1}\dfrac{2}{3}\right)$

$=\tan\left(\cos^{-1}\dfrac{2}{3}-\cos^{-1}\dfrac{2}{3}\right)$

$=\tan(0)=0$

47. $\tan(A+B)=\dfrac{\tan A+\tan B}{1-\tan A\tan B}$

$$3=\dfrac{\dfrac{1}{2}+\tan B}{1-\left(\dfrac{1}{2}\right)\tan B},\text{ for }\tan(A+B)=3\text{ and }\tan A=\dfrac{1}{2}$$

$$3\left(1-\dfrac{1}{2}\tan B\right)=\dfrac{1}{2}+\tan B$$

$$3-\dfrac{3}{2}\tan B=\dfrac{1}{2}+\tan B$$

$$\dfrac{5}{2}=\dfrac{5}{2}\tan B$$

$$1=\tan B$$

49.

$$\dfrac{\sin(A-B)}{\cos A\cos B}=\tan A-\tan B$$

$$\dfrac{\sin A\cos B-\cos A\sin B}{\cos A\cos B}=$$

$$\dfrac{\sin A\cos B}{\cos A\cos B}-\dfrac{\cos A\sin B}{\cos A\cos B}=$$

$$\dfrac{\sin A}{\cos A}-\dfrac{\sin B}{\cos B}=$$

$$\tan A-\tan B=$$

51.

$$\sin 2x=2\sin x\cos x$$

$$\sin(x+x)=$$

$$\sin x\cos x+\cos x\sin x=$$

$$2\sin x\cos x=$$

53. $\tan\left(\dfrac{\pi}{2}-x\right)=\cot x$

$$\dfrac{\sin\left(\dfrac{\pi}{2}-x\right)}{\cos\left(\dfrac{\pi}{2}-x\right)}=$$

$$\dfrac{\cos x}{\sin x}=$$

$$\cot x=$$

55. $\sin x+\cos x=\sqrt{2}\sin\left(x+\dfrac{\pi}{4}\right)$

$$=\sqrt{2}\left[\sin x\cos\dfrac{\pi}{4}+\cos x\sin\dfrac{\pi}{4}\right]$$

$$=\sqrt{2}\left[\sin x\cdot\dfrac{1}{\sqrt{2}}+\cos x\cdot\dfrac{1}{\sqrt{2}}\right]$$

$$=\sin x+\cos x$$

57. $\sin(A + B) = \sin A + \sin B$

To verify that this statement is not an identity, let $A = \dfrac{\pi}{2}$, $B = \dfrac{\pi}{2}$ (one possible counterexample).

$$\sin\left(\frac{\pi}{2} + \frac{\pi}{2}\right) \neq \sin\frac{\pi}{2} + \sin\frac{\pi}{2}$$

$$\sin(\pi) \neq \sin\frac{\pi}{2} + \sin\frac{\pi}{2}$$

$$0 \neq 1 + 1$$

$$0 \neq 2$$

59. Donald is using the cofunction identity $\sin 75° = \cos 15°$, since $75° + 15° = 90°$.

Exercise Set 4.4, p. 270

1, 3, 5, 7, 9, 11, 13, 15, 17, 19. *To find an equivalent form, we use and refer to one of the double-angle identities:*

(a) $\cos^2 A - \sin^2 A = \cos 2A$ (b) $1 - 2\sin^2 A = \cos 2A$ (c) $2\cos^2 A - 1 = \cos 2A$

(d) $2\sin A \cos A = \sin 2A$ (e) $\dfrac{2\tan A}{1 - \tan^2 A} = \tan 2A$

1. $\cos^2 x - \sin^2 x = \underline{\cos 2x}$, where $A = x$ in (a)

3. $2 - 4\sin^2 x = 2(1 - 2\sin^2 x) = \underline{2\cos 2x}$,
where $A = x$ in (b)

5. $6\sin 3x \cos 3x = 3(2\sin 3x \cos 3x)$ Let $A = 3x$ in (d).
$= 3\sin 2(3x) = \underline{3\sin 6x}$

7. $2\cos^2 8x - 1$ Let $A = 8x$ in (c).
$= \cos 2(8x) = \underline{\cos 16x}$

9. $\dfrac{2\tan x}{1 - \tan^2 x} = \underline{\tan 2x}$, where $A = x$ in (e)

11. $2\sin 15° \cos 15°$ Let $A = 15°$ in (d).
$= \sin 2(15°) = \sin 30° = \dfrac{1}{2}$

13. $1 - 2\sin^2 105°$ Let $A = 105°$ in (b).
$= \cos 2(105°) = \cos 210° = -\dfrac{\sqrt{3}}{2}$

15. $\dfrac{2\tan 75°}{1 - \tan^2 75°}$ Let $A = 75°$ in (e).
$= \tan 2(75°) = \tan 150° = -\dfrac{\sqrt{3}}{3}$

17. $6\cos^2\dfrac{\pi}{12} - 3 = 3\left(2\cos^2\dfrac{\pi}{12} - 1\right)$ Let $A = \dfrac{\pi}{12}$ in (c).

$= 3\left(\cos 2\left(\dfrac{\pi}{12}\right)\right) = 3\cos\dfrac{\pi}{6} = \dfrac{3\sqrt{3}}{2}$

19. $16\cos^2\dfrac{\pi}{8} - 16\sin^2\dfrac{\pi}{8}$ Let $A = \dfrac{\pi}{8}$ in (a).

$$= 16\left(\cos^2\dfrac{\pi}{8} - \sin^2\dfrac{\pi}{8}\right) = 16\left(\cos 2\left(\dfrac{\pi}{8}\right)\right) = 16\cos\dfrac{\pi}{4} = 8\sqrt{2}$$

21.   If $\cos A = \dfrac{3}{5}$ with A in QIV, we can find $\sin A$.

$$\cos^2 A + \sin^2 A = 1$$
$$\left(\dfrac{3}{5}\right)^2 + \sin^2 A = 1$$
$$\sin^2 A = 1 - \dfrac{9}{25} = \dfrac{16}{25}$$
$$\sin A = -\dfrac{4}{5}, A \text{ in QIV}$$

So, $\sin 2A = 2\sin A \cos A$

$$= 2\left(-\dfrac{4}{5}\right)\left(\dfrac{3}{5}\right)$$
$$= -\dfrac{24}{25}.$$

23.   Using the cosine double-angle formula that involves only $\sin x$, we get:

$$\cos 2x = 1 - 2\sin^2 x$$
$$= 1 - 2\left(\dfrac{24}{25}\right)^2, \text{ since } \sin x = \dfrac{24}{25}$$
$$= 1 - \dfrac{1152}{625}$$
$$= -\dfrac{527}{625}$$

25. $\tan 2A = \dfrac{2\tan A}{1 - \tan^2 A}$

$$= \dfrac{2\left(\dfrac{4}{3}\right)}{1 - \left(\dfrac{4}{3}\right)^2}, \text{ since } \tan A = \dfrac{4}{3}$$
$$= \dfrac{\left(\dfrac{8}{3}\right)}{\left(-\dfrac{7}{9}\right)}$$
$$= -\dfrac{24}{7}$$

27. $\cos 2B = 1 - 2\sin^2 B$

$\dfrac{5}{13} = 1 - 2\sin^2 B, \text{ since } \cos 2B = \dfrac{5}{13}$

$\dfrac{5}{13} - 1 = -2\sin^2 B$

$\dfrac{\left(-\dfrac{8}{13}\right)}{-2} = \sin^2 B$

$\sqrt{\dfrac{4}{13}} = \sin B, \qquad\qquad \dfrac{270°}{2} < \dfrac{2B}{2} < \dfrac{360°}{2} \to B \text{ in QII}$

So, $\sin B = \dfrac{2\sqrt{13}}{13}$.

29. Using the trigonometric ratios, if $\tan\theta = \dfrac{12}{5} = \dfrac{y}{x}$, for θ in QIII, then $x = -5$, $y = -12$, and $r = \sqrt{x^2 + y^2} = 13$.

$\cos 2\theta = 2\cos^2\theta - 1$

$= 2\left(-\dfrac{5}{13}\right)^2 - 1, \text{ since } \cos\theta = \dfrac{x}{r} = -\dfrac{5}{13}$

$= \dfrac{50}{169} - 1$

$= -\dfrac{119}{169}$

So, $\sec 2\theta = \dfrac{1}{\cos 2\theta} = -\dfrac{169}{119}$.

31. $\sin 2x = \dfrac{2\tan x}{1 + \tan^2 x}$

$= \dfrac{2\tan x}{\sec^2 x}$

$= \dfrac{\left(\dfrac{2\sin x}{\cos x}\right)}{\left(\dfrac{1}{\cos^2 x}\right)}$

$= \dfrac{2\sin x}{\cos x} \cdot \dfrac{\cos^2 x}{1}$

$= 2\sin x \cos x$

$= \sin 2x$

33. $\cot\theta = \dfrac{\sin 2\theta}{1 - \cos 2\theta}$

$= \dfrac{2\sin\theta\cos\theta}{1 - (1 - 2\sin^2\theta)}$

$= \dfrac{2\sin\theta\cos\theta}{2\sin^2\theta}$

$= \dfrac{\cos\theta}{\sin\theta}$

$= \cot\theta$

35. $\cos^2 A = \dfrac{1 + \cos 2A}{2}$

$\quad = \dfrac{1 + (2\cos^2 A - 1)}{2}$

$\quad = \dfrac{2\cos^2 A}{2}$

$\quad = \cos^2 A$

37. $1 = 2\sin^2 x + \cos 2x$

$\quad = 2\sin^2 x + (1 - 2\sin^2 x)$

$\quad = 1$

39.

$$\sin 3x = 3\sin x - 4\sin^3 x$$

$$\sin(2x + x) =$$

$$\sin 2x \cos x + \cos 2x \sin x =$$

$$(2\sin x \cos x)\cos x + (1 - 2\sin^2 x)\sin x =$$

$$2\sin x \cos^2 x + \sin x - 2\sin^3 x =$$

$$2\sin x(1 - \sin^2 x) + \sin x - 2\sin^3 x =$$

$$3\sin x - 4\sin^3 x =$$

41.

$$(\sin x - \cos x)^2 = 1 - \sin 2x$$

$$\sin^2 x - 2\sin x \cos x + \cos^2 x =$$

$$1 - 2\sin x \cos x =$$

$$1 - \sin 2x =$$

43. False; $\tan\left(\dfrac{\pi}{6} + \dfrac{\pi}{6}\right) \neq \tan\dfrac{\pi}{6} + \tan\dfrac{\pi}{6}$

$$\tan\left(\dfrac{\pi}{3}\right) \neq \dfrac{\sqrt{3}}{3} + \dfrac{\sqrt{3}}{3}$$

$$\sqrt{3} \neq \dfrac{2\sqrt{3}}{3}$$

45. False; $\cos(x - y) = \cos x \cos y + \sin x \sin y$.

47. True

49. False; $\dfrac{\sin 2x}{2} = \dfrac{2\sin x \cos x}{2} = \sin x \cos x$.

51. $\tan 2x = \dfrac{2\tan x}{1 - \tan^2 x}$

$\quad \tan(x + x) =$

$\quad \dfrac{\tan x + \tan x}{1 - \tan x \tan x} =$

$\quad \dfrac{2\tan x}{1 - \tan^2 x} =$

53. We know that $\tan\theta = \dfrac{4}{6} = \dfrac{2}{3}$, so we find $\tan 2\theta$:

$$\tan 2\theta = \frac{2\tan\theta}{1 - \tan^2\theta}$$

$$= \frac{2\left(\dfrac{2}{3}\right)}{1 - \left(\dfrac{2}{3}\right)^2}$$

$$= \frac{\left(\dfrac{4}{3}\right)}{\left(\dfrac{5}{9}\right)}$$

$$= \frac{36}{15}$$

From the diagram, if we let x be the height:

$$\tan 2\theta = \frac{x}{6}$$

$$\frac{36}{15} = \frac{x}{6}$$

$$x = 14.4$$

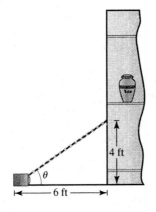 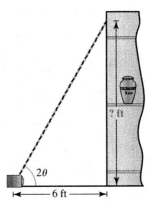

So, the height along the wall will be 14.4 ft.

Exercise Set 4.5, p. 280

1, 3, 5, 7, and 9. *Use the half-angle identities.*

1. $\cos 22\dfrac{1}{2}^{\circ} = \sqrt{\dfrac{1 + \cos 45^{\circ}}{2}}$ If $\dfrac{x}{2} = 22\dfrac{1}{2}^{\circ}$, then $x = 45^{\circ}$. Also, $22\dfrac{1}{2}^{\circ}$ is in QI.

$$= \sqrt{\dfrac{1 + \dfrac{\sqrt{2}}{2}}{2}}$$

$$= \frac{\sqrt{2 + \sqrt{2}}}{2}$$

3. $\sin 195° = -\sqrt{\dfrac{1 - \cos 390°}{2}}$ If $\dfrac{x}{2} = 195°$, then $x = 390°$. Also, 195° is in QIII.

$= -\sqrt{\dfrac{1 - \dfrac{\sqrt{3}}{2}}{2}}$ $\cos 390° = \cos 30° = \dfrac{\sqrt{3}}{2}$

$= -\dfrac{\sqrt{2 - \sqrt{3}}}{2}$

5. $\tan 165° = \dfrac{\sin 330°}{1 + \cos 330°}$

$= \dfrac{\left(-\dfrac{1}{2}\right) \cdot 2}{\left(1 + \dfrac{\sqrt{3}}{2}\right) \cdot 2}$

$= \dfrac{-1}{\left(2 + \sqrt{3}\right)} \dfrac{\left(2 - \sqrt{3}\right)}{\left(2 - \sqrt{3}\right)}$

$= -2 + \sqrt{3}$

or $\tan 165° = -\sqrt{\dfrac{1 - \cos 330°}{1 + \cos 330°}}$ Use another form of the identity.

$= -\sqrt{\dfrac{\left(1 - \dfrac{\sqrt{3}}{2}\right) \cdot 2}{\left(1 + \dfrac{\sqrt{3}}{2}\right) \cdot 2}}$

$= -\sqrt{\dfrac{\left(2 - \sqrt{3}\right)}{\left(2 + \sqrt{3}\right)} \dfrac{\left(2 - \sqrt{3}\right)}{\left(2 - \sqrt{3}\right)}}$

$= -\sqrt{7 - 4\sqrt{3}}$

7. $\cos \dfrac{\pi}{8} = \sqrt{\dfrac{1 + \cos \dfrac{\pi}{4}}{2}}$ **9.** $\sin^2 \dfrac{5\pi}{12} = \dfrac{1 - \cos \dfrac{5\pi}{6}}{2}$

$= \sqrt{\dfrac{1 + \dfrac{\sqrt{2}}{2}}{2}}$ $= \dfrac{1 + \dfrac{\sqrt{3}}{2}}{2}$

$= \dfrac{\sqrt{2 + \sqrt{2}}}{2}$ $= \dfrac{2 + \sqrt{3}}{4}$

11, 13, 15, 17, and 19. *Use one of the half-angle identities:*

a. $\pm\sqrt{\dfrac{1-\cos x}{2}} = \sin\dfrac{x}{2}$ b. $\pm\sqrt{\dfrac{1+\cos x}{2}} = \cos\dfrac{x}{2}$

c. $\pm\sqrt{\dfrac{1-\cos x}{1+\cos x}} = \dfrac{\sin x}{1+\cos x} = \dfrac{1-\cos x}{\sin x} = \tan\dfrac{x}{2}$

11. $\sqrt{\dfrac{1+\cos\dfrac{\pi}{7}}{2}} = \underline{\cos\dfrac{\pi}{14}}$, using (b) where $x = \dfrac{\pi}{7}$ and $\dfrac{x}{2} = \dfrac{\pi}{14}$.

13. $-\sqrt{\dfrac{1-\cos 488°}{2}} = \underline{\sin 244°}$, using (a) where $x = 488°$ and $\dfrac{x}{2} = 244°$.

15. $\pm\sqrt{\dfrac{1+\cos x}{2}} = \underline{\cos\dfrac{x}{2}}$, using (b).

17. $\sin^2 x = \dfrac{1-\cos 2x}{2}$, squaring both sides of (a).

19. $\dfrac{\sin 20°}{1+\cos 20°} = \underline{\tan 10°}$, using (c) where $x = 20°$ and $\dfrac{x}{2} = 10°$.

21. If $\cos x = -\dfrac{4}{5}$ and x is in QII, then $\sin x = \dfrac{3}{5}$ (using trigonometric ratios or the Pythagorean Theorem). Also, if x is in QII, then $\dfrac{90°}{2} \le \dfrac{x}{2} \le \dfrac{180°}{2}$, or $45° \le \dfrac{x}{2} \le 90°$. So, $\dfrac{x}{2}$ is in QI, where all functional values are positive.

a. $\cos\dfrac{x}{2} = \sqrt{\dfrac{1+\cos x}{2}}$ b. $\sin\dfrac{x}{2} = \sqrt{\dfrac{1-\cos x}{2}}$ c. $\tan\dfrac{x}{2} = \dfrac{\sin\dfrac{x}{2}}{\cos\dfrac{x}{2}}$

$= \sqrt{\dfrac{1-\dfrac{4}{5}}{2}}$ $= \sqrt{\dfrac{1+\dfrac{4}{5}}{2}}$ $= \dfrac{\left(\dfrac{3\sqrt{10}}{10}\right)}{\left(\dfrac{\sqrt{10}}{10}\right)}$

$= \dfrac{\sqrt{10}}{10}$ $= \dfrac{3\sqrt{10}}{10}$ $= 3$

23. If $\sin x = -\dfrac{1}{2}$ and x is in QIII, then $\cos x = -\dfrac{\sqrt{3}}{2}$ and $\dfrac{x}{2}$ is in QII.

a. $\cos \dfrac{x}{2} = -\sqrt{\dfrac{1 + \cos x}{2}}$

$= -\sqrt{\dfrac{1 - \dfrac{\sqrt{3}}{2}}{2}}$

$= -\dfrac{\sqrt{2 - \sqrt{3}}}{2}$

b. $\left(\sin \dfrac{x}{2}\right)^2 = \dfrac{1 - \cos x}{2}$

$= \dfrac{1 + \dfrac{\sqrt{3}}{2}}{2}$

$= \dfrac{2 + \sqrt{3}}{4}$

c. $\tan \dfrac{x}{2} = \dfrac{\sin x}{1 + \cos x}$

$= \dfrac{\left(-\dfrac{1}{2}\right)}{\left(1 - \dfrac{\sqrt{3}}{2}\right)}$

$= -2 - \sqrt{3}$

Or, using another form of the identity:

$\tan \dfrac{x}{2} = -\sqrt{\dfrac{1 - \cos x}{1 + \cos x}}$

$= -\sqrt{7 + 4\sqrt{3}}$

25. If $\tan A = 2$ and $\sin A > 0$, then A is in QI. Using trigonometric ratios, we get

$$\tan A = \dfrac{2}{1} = \dfrac{y}{x} \rightarrow x = 1, y = 2$$

and $r = \sqrt{x^2 + y^2} = \sqrt{5}$.

Thus, $\cos A = \dfrac{1}{\sqrt{5}} = \dfrac{\sqrt{5}}{5}$. Also, $\dfrac{A}{2}$ is in QI.

So, $\cos \dfrac{A}{2} = \sqrt{\dfrac{1 + \cos A}{2}}$

$= \sqrt{\dfrac{1 + \dfrac{\sqrt{5}}{5}}{2}}$

$= \dfrac{\sqrt{50 + 10\sqrt{5}}}{10}$.

27. $\sin \dfrac{B}{2} = \pm\sqrt{\dfrac{1 - \cos B}{2}}$

$\sin^2 \dfrac{B}{2} = \dfrac{1 - \cos B}{2}$ Square both sides.

$\left(\dfrac{\sqrt{3}}{3}\right)^2 = \dfrac{1 - \cos B}{2}$ $\sin \dfrac{B}{2} = \dfrac{\sqrt{3}}{3}$

$\dfrac{2}{3} = 1 - \cos B$ Multiply each side by 2.

$\cos B = \dfrac{1}{3}$ Subtract 1 from each side and then divide both sides by -1.

29. If $\sin A = \dfrac{3}{5}$, with $\dfrac{\pi}{2} < A < \pi$, then to find $\cos A$ we use the Pythagorean identity.

$$\cos^2 A + \sin^2 A = 1$$

$$\cos^2 A + \left(\frac{3}{5}\right)^2 = 1$$

$$\cos^2 A = 1 - \frac{9}{25} = \frac{16}{25}$$

$$\cos A = -\frac{4}{5}, \; A \text{ is in QII}$$

31. $\sin \dfrac{A}{2} = \sqrt{\dfrac{1 - \cos A}{2}}$

$$= \sqrt{\dfrac{1 + \dfrac{4}{5}}{2}} \quad \text{See Exercise 29.}$$

$$= \dfrac{3\sqrt{10}}{10}, \; \dfrac{A}{2} \text{ is in QI}$$

33. $\tan \dfrac{A}{2} = \dfrac{\sin A}{1 + \cos A}$

$$= \dfrac{\left(\dfrac{3}{5}\right)}{\left(1 - \dfrac{4}{5}\right)} = 3$$

35. $\cos 2A = \cos^2 A - \sin^2 A$

$$= \left(-\frac{4}{5}\right)^2 - \left(\frac{3}{5}\right)^2$$

$$= \frac{16}{25} - \frac{9}{25} = \frac{7}{25}$$

37. $\cos^2 \dfrac{B}{2} = \dfrac{1 + \cos B}{2}$

$$= \dfrac{1 + \dfrac{1}{2}}{2}$$

$$= \frac{3}{4}$$

39. $\sin(A - B) = \sin A \cos B - \cos A \sin B$

$$= \frac{3}{5} \cdot \frac{1}{2} - \left(-\frac{4}{5}\right) \cdot \frac{\sqrt{3}}{2}$$

$$= \frac{3 + 4\sqrt{3}}{10}$$

41. $\cos(A + B) = \cos A \cos B - \sin A \sin B$

$$= \left(-\frac{4}{5}\right) \cdot \frac{1}{2} - \frac{3}{5} \cdot \frac{\sqrt{3}}{2}$$

$$= \frac{-4 - 3\sqrt{3}}{10}$$

43. Since $\tan A = -\dfrac{3}{4}$, and $\tan B = \sqrt{3}$

$$\tan(A + B) = \frac{\tan A + \tan B}{1 - \tan A \tan B}$$

$$= \frac{\left(-\dfrac{3}{4}\right) + \sqrt{3}}{1 - \left(-\dfrac{3}{4}\right) \cdot \sqrt{3}}$$

$$= \frac{\left(-3 + 4\sqrt{3}\right)\left(4 - 3\sqrt{3}\right)}{\left(4 + 3\sqrt{3}\right)\left(4 - 3\sqrt{3}\right)}$$

$$= \frac{48 - 25\sqrt{3}}{11}$$

45. $\sin^2 \dfrac{\theta}{2} = \dfrac{\csc \theta - \cot \theta}{2 \csc \theta}$

$$= \dfrac{\dfrac{1}{\sin \theta} - \dfrac{\cos \theta}{\sin \theta}}{\dfrac{2}{\sin \theta}}$$

$$= \frac{1 - \cos \theta}{\sin \theta} \cdot \frac{\sin \theta}{2}$$

$$= \frac{1 - \cos \theta}{2}$$

$$= \sin^2 \frac{\theta}{2}$$

47.
$$\left(\cos\frac{\beta}{2} - \sin\frac{\beta}{2}\right)^2 = 1 - \sin\beta$$

$$\cos^2\frac{\beta}{2} - 2\sin\frac{\beta}{2}\cos\frac{\beta}{2} + \sin^2\frac{\beta}{2} =$$

$$1 - 2\sin\frac{\beta}{2}\cos\frac{\beta}{2} =$$

$$1 - \sin\beta =$$

49.
$$\tan\frac{x}{2} = \csc x - \cot x$$

$$= \frac{1}{\sin x} - \frac{\cos x}{\sin x}$$

$$= \frac{1 - \cos x}{\sin x}$$

$$= \tan\frac{x}{2}$$

51.
$$1 - \tan^2\frac{A}{2} = \frac{2\cos A}{1 + \cos A}$$

$$1 - \frac{1 - \cos A}{1 + \cos A} =$$

$$\frac{1 + \cos A}{1 + \cos A} - \frac{1 - \cos A}{1 + \cos A} =$$

$$\frac{1 + \cos A - (1 - \cos A)}{1 + \cos A} =$$

$$\frac{2\cos A}{1 + \cos A} =$$

53.
$$\sin^2\frac{x}{2} = \frac{\sec x - 1}{2\sec x}$$

$$= \frac{\dfrac{1}{\cos x} - 1}{\dfrac{2}{\cos x}}$$

$$= \left(\frac{1 - \cos x}{\cos x}\right)\left(\frac{\cos x}{2}\right)$$

$$= \frac{1 - \cos x}{2}$$

$$= \sin^2\frac{x}{2}$$

55. Using the product-to-sum formula:

$$\sin A \cos B = \frac{1}{2}\left[\sin(A + B) + \sin(A - B)\right], \text{ we get}$$

$$\sin 16° \cos 44° = \frac{1}{2}\left[\sin 60° + \sin(-28°)\right], \text{ where } A = 16°, B = 44°$$

$$= \frac{1}{2}\left[\sin 60° - \sin 28°\right]$$

57. Using the product-to-sum formula:

$$\sin A \sin B = \frac{1}{2}\left[\cos(A - B) - \cos(A + B)\right], \text{ we get}$$

$$\sin 2x \sin 10x = \frac{1}{2}\left[\cos 8x - \cos 12x\right], \text{ where } A = 2x, B = 10x, \text{ and } \cos(-8x) = \cos 8x$$

59. Using the product-to-sum formula:

$$\cos A \cos B = \frac{1}{2}\left[\cos(A + B) + \cos(A - B)\right], \text{ we get}$$

$$\cos 5° \cos(-3°) = \frac{1}{2}\left[\cos 2° + \cos 8°\right]$$

So, $10\cos 5° \cos(-3°) = 5\left[\cos 2° + \cos 8°\right]$.

61. Using the sum-to-product formula:

$$\cos A + \cos B = 2 \cos \left(\frac{A+B}{2} \right) \cos \left(\frac{A-B}{2} \right), \text{ we get}$$

$\cos 75° + \cos 15° = 2 \cos 45° \cos 30°$, where $A = 75°$ and $B = 15°$

$$= 2 \cdot \frac{\sqrt{2}}{2} \cdot \frac{\sqrt{3}}{2}$$

$$= \frac{\sqrt{6}}{2}$$

63. $\sin A + \sin B = 2 \sin \left(\frac{A+B}{2} \right) \cos \left(\frac{A-B}{2} \right)$

$\sin 2y + \sin 4y = 2 \sin 3y \cos y$, where $A = 2y$, $B = 4y$ and $\cos(-y) = \cos y$

65. $\cos A - \cos B = -2 \sin \left(\frac{A+B}{2} \right) \sin \left(\frac{A-B}{2} \right)$

$\cos 5x - \cos x = -2 \sin 3x \sin 2x$, where $A = 5x$ and $B = x$

Chapter 4 Review Exercises, p. 286

1. $1 - \sin^2 x = \underline{\cos^2 x}$

2. $1 - 2\sin^2 x = \underline{\cos 2x}$

3. $1 + \tan^2 x = \underline{\sec^2 x}$

4. $2 \sin x \cos x = \underline{\sin 2x}$

5. $\sec(-x) = \dfrac{1}{\underline{\cos x}}$

6. $\dfrac{1}{\tan x} = \underline{\cot x}$

7. $\cos^2 x - \sin^2 x = \underline{\cos 2x}$

8. $\cos^2 x + \sin^2 x = \underline{1}$

9. $\pm \sqrt{\dfrac{1 + \cos 2x}{2}} = \underline{\cos x}$

10. $\pm \sqrt{\dfrac{1 - \cos 2x}{2}} = \underline{\sin x}$

11. $\cos(x - y) = \underline{\cos x \cos y + \sin x \sin y}$

12. $\sin x \csc x = \underline{1}$

13. $\sin(x + y) = \underline{\sin x \cos y + \cos x \sin y}$

14. $1 + \cot^2 x = \underline{\csc^2 x}$

15. $\cos(\pi + x) = \underline{-\cos x}$

16. $\sin(90° - x) = \underline{\cos x}$

17. $2 \csc x \sin 2x$

$= 2 \left(\dfrac{1}{\sin x} \right) 2 \sin x \cos x$

$= 4 \cos x$

18. $2 \sec x \sin 2x$

$= 2 \left(\dfrac{1}{\cos x} \right) 2 \sin x \cos x$

$= 4 \sin x$

19. $\sin^2 x + \cos 2x$

$= \sin^2 x + \cos^2 x - \sin^2 x$

$= \cos^2 x$

20. $\sec(-x) \cot(-x)$

$= \dfrac{1}{\cos(-x)} \cdot \dfrac{\cos(-x)}{\sin(-x)}$

$= \dfrac{1}{\sin(-x)} = \dfrac{1}{-\sin x}$

$= -\csc x$

21. $2 \sin 5x \cos 5x$

$= \sin 2(5x)$

$= \sin 10x$

22. $1 - 2\sin^2 10x$

$= \cos 2(10x)$

$= \cos 20x$

23. $\cos 7x \cos 6x + \sin 7x \sin 6x$

$= \cos(7x - 6x)$

$= \cos x$

24. $\sin 5x \cos 3x + \cos 5x \sin 3x$

$= \sin(5x + 3x)$

$= \sin 8x$

25. $\sqrt{\dfrac{1 - \cos 8x}{2}}$

$= \sin\left(\dfrac{8x}{2}\right)$

$= \sin 4x$

26. $\dfrac{\sin 4x}{1 + \cos 4x} = \tan\left(\dfrac{4x}{2}\right)$

$= \tan 2x$

27. $\cos^2 x(\sec^2 x - 1) = \sin^2 x$

$\cos^2 x(\tan^2 x) = \;\vdots$

$\cos^2 x\left(\dfrac{\sin^2 x}{\cos^2 x}\right) = \;\vdots$

$\sin^2 x = \;\downarrow$

28. $\tan^2 A \csc^2 A - \tan^2 A = 1$

$\tan^2 A(\csc^2 A - 1) = \;\vdots$

$\tan^2 A(\cot^2 A) = \;\vdots$

$1 = \;\downarrow$

29. $\dfrac{\cos y \tan y}{\sin y} = 1$

$\dfrac{\cos y \dfrac{\sin y}{\cos y}}{\sin y} = \;\vdots$

$\dfrac{\sin y}{\sin y} = \;\vdots$

$1 = \;\downarrow$

30. $\cot \alpha - \tan \alpha = \dfrac{\cos 2\alpha}{\sin \alpha \cos \alpha}$

$= \dfrac{\cos^2 \alpha - \sin^2 \alpha}{\cos \alpha \sin \alpha}$

$= \dfrac{\cos^2 \alpha}{\cos \alpha \sin \alpha} - \dfrac{\sin^2 \alpha}{\cos \alpha \sin \alpha}$

$= \dfrac{\cos \alpha}{\sin \alpha} - \dfrac{\sin \alpha}{\cos \alpha}$

$= \cot \alpha - \tan \alpha$

31. $\dfrac{1 + \sin \theta}{\cos \theta} = \dfrac{\cos \theta}{1 - \sin \theta}$

$= \left(\dfrac{\cos \theta}{1 - \sin \theta}\right) \cdot \left(\dfrac{1 + \sin \theta}{1 + \sin \theta}\right)$

$= \dfrac{\cos \theta(1 + \sin \theta)}{\cos^2 \theta}$

$= \dfrac{1 + \sin \theta}{\cos \theta}$

32. $\csc t = 2 \cos t \csc 2t$

$= 2 \cos t \dfrac{1}{\sin 2t}$

$= 2 \cos t \dfrac{1}{2 \sin t \cos t}$

$= \dfrac{1}{\sin t}$

$= \csc t$

33. $\sin 2x = 2 \sin^2 x \cos x \csc x$

$= 2 \sin^2 x \cos x \dfrac{1}{\sin x}$

$= 2 \sin x \cos x$

$= \sin x$

34. $\cos^4 \beta - \sin^4 \beta = \cos 2\beta$

$(\cos^2 \beta - \sin^2 \beta)(\cos^2 \beta + \sin^2 \beta) = \;\vdots$

$(\cos^2 \beta - \sin^2 \beta) \cdot 1 = \;\vdots$

$\cos 2\beta = \;\downarrow$

35. $\tan y + \sec y = \dfrac{1}{\sec y - \tan y}$

$$= \left(\dfrac{1}{\sec y - \tan y}\right)\left(\dfrac{\sec y + \tan y}{\sec y + \tan y}\right)$$

$$= \dfrac{\sec y + \tan y}{\sec^2 y - \tan^2 y}$$

$$= \dfrac{\sec y + \tan y}{1}$$

$$= \tan y + \sec y$$

36.

$$\dfrac{\cos x}{1 - \tan x} + \dfrac{\sin x}{1 - \cot x} = \cos x + \sin x$$

$$\dfrac{\cos x}{1 - \dfrac{\sin x}{\cos x}} + \dfrac{\sin x}{1 - \dfrac{\cos x}{\sin x}} =$$

$$\left(\dfrac{\cos x}{\cos x}\right)\left(\dfrac{\cos x}{1 - \dfrac{\sin x}{\cos x}}\right) + \left(\dfrac{\sin x}{\sin x}\right)\left(\dfrac{\sin x}{1 - \dfrac{\cos x}{\sin x}}\right) =$$

$$\dfrac{\cos^2 x}{\cos x - \sin x} + \left(\dfrac{\sin^2 x}{\sin x - \cos x}\right)\left(\dfrac{-1}{-1}\right) =$$

$$\dfrac{\cos^2 x - \sin^2 x}{\cos x - \sin x} =$$

$$\dfrac{(\cos x - \sin x)(\cos x + \sin x)}{\cos x - \sin x} =$$

$$\cos x + \sin x =$$

37.

$$\cos(90° + \theta) = -\sin\theta$$

$$\cos 90° \cos\theta - \sin 90° \sin\theta =$$

$$0 \cdot \cos\theta - 1 \cdot \sin\theta =$$

$$-\sin\theta =$$

38.

$$\sin(90° + x) = \cos x$$

$$\sin 90° \cos x + \cos 90° \sin x =$$

$$1 \cdot \cos x + 0 \cdot \sin x =$$

$$\cos x =$$

39.

$$\tan\left(\alpha - \dfrac{\pi}{4}\right) = \dfrac{\tan\alpha - 1}{1 + \tan\alpha}$$

$$\dfrac{\tan\alpha - \tan\dfrac{\pi}{4}}{1 + \tan\alpha \tan\dfrac{\pi}{4}} =$$

$$\dfrac{\tan\alpha - 1}{1 + \tan\alpha} =$$

40.

$$\tan\dfrac{A}{2} = \dfrac{\sec A \sin A}{\sec A + 1}$$

$$= \left(\dfrac{\sec A \sin A}{\sec A + 1}\right)\left(\dfrac{\cos A}{\cos A}\right)$$

$$= \dfrac{\sin A}{1 + \cos A}$$

$$= \tan\dfrac{A}{2}$$

41. Let $A = \dfrac{\pi}{4}$.

$$\tan \frac{\pi}{4} \cos \frac{\pi}{4} \sin \frac{\pi}{4} \neq \sec \frac{\pi}{4}$$

$$1 \cdot \frac{1}{\sqrt{2}} \cdot \frac{1}{\sqrt{2}} \neq \sqrt{2}$$

$$\frac{1}{2} \neq \sqrt{2}$$

42. Let $x = \dfrac{\pi}{2}$.

$$\cos 2\left(\frac{\pi}{2}\right) \neq 1 + 2\left(\cos \frac{\pi}{2}\right)^2$$

$$\cos \pi \neq 1 + 2 \cdot 0$$

$$-1 \neq 1$$

43. The statement is not an identity.

Let $x = \pi$.

$$\left(\sin \frac{\pi}{2}\right)^2 \neq \frac{(\cos \pi)^2}{2 - 2\cos \pi}$$

$$1 \neq \frac{1}{4}$$

44. The statement is not an identity.

Let $x = \dfrac{\pi}{4}$.

$$\left(\cot \frac{\pi}{4}\right)^2 \neq \frac{1 - \left(\cos 2\left(\frac{\pi}{4}\right)\right)^2}{\sin \frac{\pi}{4}}$$

$$1 \neq \sqrt{2}$$

45.

$$\cos\left(-\frac{5\pi}{12}\right) = \cos\left(\frac{5\pi}{12}\right)$$

$$= \cos\left(\frac{3\pi}{12} + \frac{2\pi}{12}\right) = \cos\left(\frac{\pi}{4} + \frac{\pi}{6}\right)$$

$$= \cos \frac{\pi}{4} \cos \frac{\pi}{6} - \sin \frac{\pi}{4} \sin \frac{\pi}{6} \qquad \text{Use the cosine sum identity.}$$

$$= \frac{\sqrt{2}}{2} \cdot \frac{\sqrt{3}}{2} - \frac{\sqrt{2}}{2} \cdot \frac{1}{2}$$

$$= \frac{\sqrt{6} - \sqrt{2}}{4}$$

46.

$$\sin(105°)$$

$$= \sin(60° + 45°)$$

$$= \sin 60° \cos 45° + \cos 60° \sin 45° \qquad \text{Use the sine sum identity.}$$

$$= \frac{\sqrt{3}}{2} \cdot \frac{\sqrt{2}}{2} + \frac{1}{2} \cdot \frac{\sqrt{2}}{2}$$

$$= \frac{\sqrt{6} + \sqrt{2}}{4}$$

47.

$$\cos 77° \cos 32° - \sin 77° \sin 32°$$

$$= \cos(77° + 32°) \qquad \text{Use the cosine sum identity.}$$

$$= \cos(109°) \neq \frac{\sqrt{2}}{2}, \quad \text{False}$$

48. $\sin 30° \cos 60° + \cos 30° \sin 60°$

$= \sin(30° + 60°)$

$= \sin 90° = 1,$ True

49. $\cos(60° + 45°)$

$= \cos 60° \cos 45° - \sin 60° \sin 45°$ Use the cosine sum identity.

$= \dfrac{1}{2} \cdot \dfrac{\sqrt{2}}{2} - \dfrac{\sqrt{3}}{2} \cdot \dfrac{\sqrt{2}}{2}$

$= \dfrac{\sqrt{2} - \sqrt{6}}{4} \neq \dfrac{\sqrt{6} - \sqrt{2}}{4},$ False

50. $\tan\left(\dfrac{\pi}{3} - \dfrac{\pi}{4}\right)$

$= \dfrac{\tan \dfrac{\pi}{3} - \tan \dfrac{\pi}{4}}{1 + \tan \dfrac{\pi}{3} \tan \dfrac{\pi}{4}}$ Use the tangent difference identity.

$= \dfrac{\left(\sqrt{3} - 1\right)}{\left(1 + \sqrt{3}\right)} \cdot \dfrac{\left(1 - \sqrt{3}\right)}{\left(1 - \sqrt{3}\right)}$

$= \dfrac{-4 + 2\sqrt{3}}{-2} = 2 - \sqrt{3},$ True

51.   By the half-angle identity for $\sin \dfrac{x}{2}$:

$$\sin \dfrac{x}{2} = \pm\sqrt{\dfrac{1 - \cos x}{2}}, \text{ we get}$$

$\sin 22.5° = \sqrt{\dfrac{1 - \cos 45°}{2}},$ for $x = 45° \to \dfrac{x}{2}$ in QI. True

52. $4 \sin 8x \cos 8x$

$= 2(2 \sin 8x \cos 8x)$

$= 2(\sin 2(8x))$ Use the sine dougle-angle identity.

$= 2 \sin 16x \neq 2 \sin 4x,$ False

53.   Using the cosine double-angle identity, we get:

$2 \cos^2 15x - 1$

$= \cos 2(15x) = \cos 30x.$ True

54. $\cos\left(\arccos \dfrac{1}{2} - \arcsin \dfrac{1}{2}\right)$

$= \cos(30° - 60°)$

$= \cos(-30°)$

$= \cos 30° = \dfrac{\sqrt{3}}{2},$ True

55. Since amplitude $= 1$, period $= \pi = \dfrac{2\pi}{|B|} \rightarrow B = 2$, using the cosine form, we get:

$$y = \cos 2x, \text{ which is equivalent to}$$
$$y = \cos^2 x - \sin^2 x \qquad \text{Use the cosine double-angle identity.}$$

56. Since amplitude $= \dfrac{1}{2}|1 - 0| = \dfrac{1}{2}$, period $= \pi = \dfrac{2\pi}{|B|} \rightarrow B = 2$, using the cosine form shifted up one-half unit, we get:

$$y = \frac{1}{2}\cos 2x + \frac{1}{2}$$
$$\text{or } y = \frac{1 + \cos 2x}{2}, \text{ which is equivalent to}$$
$$y = \cos^2 x \qquad \text{Use the cosine half-angle identity.}$$

57. Since $A = 1$, period $= \pi = \dfrac{2\pi}{|B|} \rightarrow B = 2$, and using the sine form, we get:

$$y = \sin 2x, \text{ which is equivalent to}$$
$$y = \sin 15x \cos 13x - \cos 15x \sin 13x \qquad \text{Use the sine difference identity.}$$

58. Using the tangent form, where period $= \dfrac{\pi}{2} = \dfrac{\pi}{|B|} \rightarrow B = 2$, we get:

$$y = \tan 2x \text{ which is equivalent to}$$
$$y = \frac{2\tan x}{1 - \tan^2 x} \qquad \text{Use the tangent double-angle identity.}$$
$$\text{or } y = -\cot 2\left(x + \frac{\pi}{4}\right) \quad \text{Reflect the cotangent across the } x\text{-axis and shift left } \frac{\pi}{4}.$$

59. If $\cos A = \dfrac{1}{2}$, we know that $\sin A = \dfrac{\sqrt{3}}{2}$ since A is in QI (these are recognizable common angle functional values).

60. If $\sin B = -\dfrac{12}{13}$:

$$\cos^2 B + \sin^2 B = 1$$
$$\cos^2 B + \left(-\frac{12}{13}\right)^2 = 1$$
$$\cos^2 B = 1 - \frac{144}{169}$$
$$\cos B = -\frac{5}{13}, B \text{ in QIII}$$

61–68.

	QI	QIII
	$\cos A = \dfrac{1}{2}$	$\cos B = -\dfrac{5}{13}$
	$\sin A = \dfrac{\sqrt{3}}{2}$	$\sin B = -\dfrac{12}{13}$
	$0 \le A \le 90°$	$180° \le B \le 270°$

61. $\cos(A + B) = \cos A \cos B - \sin A \sin B$

$$= \frac{1}{2} \cdot \left(-\frac{5}{13}\right) - \frac{\sqrt{3}}{2} \cdot \left(-\frac{12}{13}\right)$$

$$= \frac{-5 + 12\sqrt{3}}{26}$$

62. $\sin(A - B) = \sin A \cos B - \cos A \sin B$

$$= \frac{\sqrt{3}}{2} \cdot \left(-\frac{5}{13}\right) - \frac{1}{2} \cdot \left(-\frac{12}{13}\right)$$

$$= \frac{-5\sqrt{3} + 12}{26}$$

63. $\sin 2B = 2 \sin B \cos B$

$$= 2 \left(-\frac{12}{13}\right)\left(-\frac{5}{13}\right)$$

$$= \frac{120}{169}$$

64. $\tan 2A = \dfrac{2 \tan A}{1 - \tan^2 A}$

$$= \frac{2\sqrt{3}}{1 - \left(\sqrt{3}\right)^2} = -\sqrt{3}$$

65. $\cos \dfrac{A}{2} = \sqrt{\dfrac{1 + \cos A}{2}},\ \dfrac{A}{2}$ in QI

$$= \sqrt{\frac{1 + \dfrac{1}{2}}{2}}$$

$$= \frac{\sqrt{3}}{2}$$

66. $\sin \dfrac{B}{2} = \sqrt{\dfrac{1 - \cos B}{2}},\ \dfrac{B}{2}$ in QII

$$= \sqrt{\frac{1 + \dfrac{5}{13}}{2}}$$

$$= \frac{3\sqrt{13}}{13}$$

67. $\sin^2 \dfrac{A}{2} = \dfrac{1 - \cos A}{2}$

$$= \frac{\left(1 - \dfrac{1}{2}\right)}{2}$$

$$= \frac{1}{4}$$

68. $\cos^2 \dfrac{B}{2} = \dfrac{1 + \cos B}{2}$

$$= \frac{\left(1 - \dfrac{5}{13}\right)}{2}$$

$$= \frac{4}{13}$$

69. If $\sin A = \dfrac{3}{5}$ and A is in QII, then

$$\cos^2 A + \sin^2 A = 1$$

$$\cos^2 A + \left(\frac{3}{5}\right)^2 = 1$$

$$\cos^2 A = 1 - \frac{9}{25} = \frac{16}{25}$$

$$\cos A = -\frac{4}{5}.$$

70. If $\tan B = -\dfrac{4}{3} = \dfrac{y}{x}$ and B is in QIV,

then $x = 3,\ y = -4$

and $r = \sqrt{x^2 + y^2} = 5.$

So, $\sin B = \dfrac{y}{r} = -\dfrac{4}{5}.$

71–78.

QII	QIV
$\cos A = -\dfrac{4}{5}$	$\cos B = \dfrac{3}{5}$
$\sin A = \dfrac{3}{5}$	$\sin B = -\dfrac{4}{5}$
$90° \le A \le 180°$	$270° \le B \le 360°$

71. $\sin(A + B) = \sin A \cos B + \cos A \sin B$

$$= \frac{3}{5} \cdot \frac{3}{5} + \left(-\frac{4}{5}\right)\left(-\frac{4}{5}\right)$$

$$= 1$$

72. $\cos(A - B) = \cos A \cos B + \sin A \sin B$

$$= \left(-\frac{4}{5}\right) \cdot \frac{3}{5} + \frac{3}{5} \cdot \left(-\frac{4}{5}\right)$$

$$= -\frac{24}{25}$$

73. $\cos 2A = \cos^2 A - \sin^2 A$

$$= \left(-\frac{4}{5}\right)^2 - \left(\frac{3}{5}\right)^2$$

$$= \frac{7}{25}$$

74. $\tan 2B = \dfrac{2 \tan B}{1 - \tan^2 B}$

$$= \frac{2\left(-\frac{4}{3}\right)}{1 - \left(-\frac{4}{3}\right)^2}, \quad \tan B = -\frac{4}{3}$$

$$= \frac{\left(-\frac{8}{3}\right)}{\left(-\frac{7}{9}\right)} = \frac{24}{7}$$

75. $\sin \dfrac{B}{2} = \sqrt{\dfrac{1 - \cos B}{2}}, \ \dfrac{B}{2}$ in QII

$$= \sqrt{\frac{1 - \frac{3}{5}}{2}}$$

$$= \frac{\sqrt{5}}{5}$$

76. $\cos \dfrac{A}{2} = \sqrt{\dfrac{1 + \cos A}{2}}, \ \dfrac{A}{2}$ in QI

$$= \sqrt{\frac{1 - \frac{4}{5}}{2}}$$

$$= \frac{\sqrt{10}}{10}$$

77. $\tan \dfrac{A}{2} = \dfrac{\sin A}{1 + \cos A}$

$$= \frac{\frac{3}{5}}{\left(1 - \frac{4}{5}\right)}$$

$$= 3$$

78. $\sin(A - B)$

$= \sin A \cos B - \cos A \sin B$

$$= \frac{3}{5} \cdot \frac{3}{5} - \left(-\frac{4}{5}\right)\left(-\frac{4}{5}\right)$$

$$= -\frac{7}{25}$$

79. Using the cosine double-angle identity, we get:

$$\cos 2x = 2\cos^2 x - 1$$

$$0.8 = 2\cos^2 x - 1$$

$$\frac{1.8}{2} = \cos^2 x$$

$$0.9 = \cos^2 x$$

$$\cos x = -\sqrt{0.9}, \qquad 135° \leq x \leq 180° \rightarrow x \text{ in QII}$$

$$\text{or} \quad \cos x = -\frac{3\sqrt{10}}{10}$$

80. If $\sec B = \sqrt{5} \rightarrow \cos B = \frac{1}{\sqrt{5}}$.

$$\cos^2 B + \sin^2 B = 1$$

$$\sin^2 B = 1 - \frac{1}{5} = \frac{4}{5}$$

$$\sin B = \frac{2}{\sqrt{5}}, B \text{ in QI}$$

So, $\sin 2B = 2\sin B \cos B$

$$= 2 \cdot \frac{2}{\sqrt{5}} \cdot \frac{1}{\sqrt{5}} = \frac{4}{5}.$$

81. $\cos\left(\arctan\sqrt{3} + \tan^{-1} 1\right)$

$= \cos(60° + 45°)$, since $\arctan\sqrt{3} = 60°$, and $\tan^{-1} 1 = 45°$

$= \cos 60° \cos 45° - \sin 60° \sin 45°$

$= \frac{1}{2} \cdot \frac{\sqrt{2}}{2} - \frac{\sqrt{3}}{2} \cdot \frac{\sqrt{2}}{2}$

$= \frac{\sqrt{2} - \sqrt{6}}{4}$

82. $\sin\left(\sin^{-1}\frac{\sqrt{3}}{2} + \sin^{-1}(-1)\right)$

$= \sin(60° - 90°)$, since $\sin^{-1}\frac{\sqrt{3}}{2} = 60°$, and $\sin^{-1}(-1) = -90°$

$= \sin(-30°)$

$= -\frac{1}{2}$

83. $\tan\left(\csc^{-1} 2 + \arccos\dfrac{1}{2}\right)$

$= \tan(30° + 60°)$, since $\csc^{-1} 2 = \sin^{-1}\left(\dfrac{1}{2}\right) = 30°$, $\arccos\dfrac{1}{2} = 60°$

$= \tan(90°)$, which is undefined

84. $\cos(\mathrm{arcsec}(-2) + \mathrm{arccot}\,0)$

$= \cos(120° + 90°)$, since $\mathrm{arcsec}(-2) = \arccos\left(-\dfrac{1}{2}\right) = 120°$, and $\mathrm{arccot}\,0 = 90°$

$= \cos(210°)$

$= -\cos 30° = -\dfrac{\sqrt{3}}{2}$

85. $\cos 10x + \cos 3x = 2\cos\left(\dfrac{10x + 3x}{2}\right)\cos\left(\dfrac{10x - 3x}{2}\right)$

$\qquad\qquad\qquad = 2\cos\dfrac{13x}{2}\cos\dfrac{7x}{2}$ Use sum-to-product identity.

86. $\cos 5x - \cos 3x = -2\sin\left(\dfrac{5x + 3x}{2}\right)\sin\left(\dfrac{5x - 3x}{2}\right)$

$\qquad\qquad\qquad = -2\sin 4x \sin x$ Use sum-to-product identity.

87. $\sin 6x \sin 8x = \dfrac{1}{2}[\cos(6x - 8x) - \cos(6x + 8x)]$

$\qquad\qquad\quad = \dfrac{1}{2}[\cos 2x - \cos 14x]$ Use product-to-sum identity.

88. $\cos 9x \sin 5x = \dfrac{1}{2}[\sin(9x + 5x) - \sin(9x - 5x)]$

$\qquad\qquad\quad = \dfrac{1}{2}[\sin 14x - \sin 4x]$ Use product-to-sum identity.

Chapter 4 Test, p. 289

1. $\tan(-x) = \underline{-\tan x}$

2. $\cos x \cos y - \sin x \sin y = \underline{\cos(x + y)}$

3. $\sin^2 x = 1 - \underline{\cos^2 x}$

4. $1 + \tan^2 x = \underline{\sec^2 x}$

5. $\cos 2x = \underline{\cos^2 x - \sin^2 x}, \underline{2\cos^2 x - 1}$, or $\underline{1 - 2\sin^2 x}$

6. $\pm\sqrt{\dfrac{1 - \cos x}{2}} = \sin\dfrac{x}{2}$

7. $\cos^2 15x + \sin^2 15x = \underline{1}$

8. $2\cos x \sin x = \underline{\sin 2x}$

9. $\sin^2 x(1 + \cot^2 x) = 1$

$$\sin^2 x(\csc^2 x) = \vdots$$

$$\sin^2 x\left(\frac{1}{\sin^2 x}\right) = \vdots$$

$$1 = \downarrow$$

10.

$$\cot x + \tan x = \sec x \csc x$$

$$\frac{\cos x}{\sin x} + \frac{\sin x}{\cos x} = \vdots$$

$$\left(\frac{\cos x}{\sin x}\right)\left(\frac{\cos x}{\cos x}\right) + \left(\frac{\sin x}{\cos x}\right)\left(\frac{\sin x}{\sin x}\right) = \vdots$$

$$\frac{\cos^2 x + \sin^2 x}{\cos x \sin x} = \vdots$$

$$\frac{1}{\cos x} \cdot \frac{1}{\sin x} = \vdots$$

$$\sec x \csc x = \downarrow$$

11. $\cos 2x - \cos^2 x = -\sin^2 x$

$$(\cos^2 x - \sin^2 x) - \cos^2 x = \vdots$$

$$-\sin^2 x = \downarrow$$

12. $\sin 2x = 2\sin^2 x \cos x \csc x$

$$= 2\sin^2 x \cos x \frac{1}{\sin x}$$

$$= 2\sin x \cos x$$

$$= \sin 2x$$

13. $2\sin^2 \dfrac{x}{2} - 1 = -\cos x$

$$2\left(\frac{1 - \cos x}{2}\right) - 1 = \vdots$$

$$1 - \cos x - 1 = \vdots$$

$$-\cos x = \downarrow$$

14. $\cos^2 \dfrac{x}{2} = \dfrac{\sin^2 x}{2(1 - \cos x)}$

$$= \left(\frac{\sin^2 x}{2(1 - \cos x)}\right)\left(\frac{1 + \cos x}{1 + \cos x}\right)$$

$$= \frac{\sin^2 x(1 + \cos x)}{2\sin^2 x}$$

$$= \frac{1 + \cos x}{2}$$

$$= \cos^2 \frac{x}{2}$$

15.   The statement is not an identity. As a possible counterexample, let $x = \dfrac{\pi}{3}$.

$$1 - \sin\left(2 \cdot \frac{\pi}{3}\right) \neq \frac{1 - \left(\tan \dfrac{\pi}{3}\right)^2}{1 + \left(\tan \dfrac{\pi}{3}\right)^2}$$

$$1 - \frac{\sqrt{3}}{2} \neq \frac{1 - \left(\sqrt{3}\right)^2}{1 + \left(\sqrt{3}\right)^2}$$

$$1 - \frac{\sqrt{3}}{2} \neq -\frac{1}{2}$$

16. The statement is not an identity. As a possible counterexample, let $x = \dfrac{\pi}{2}$.

$$\left(\cos\left(2 \cdot \frac{\pi}{2}\right)\right)^2 + 2\left(\sin\frac{\pi}{2}\right)^2 \neq 1$$
$$(-1)^2 + 2 \neq 1$$
$$3 \neq 1$$

17. $\cos 105° = \cos(60° + 45°)$

$\quad = \cos 60° \cos 45° - \sin 60° \sin 45°$ Use the cosine sum identity.

$\quad = \dfrac{1}{2} \cdot \dfrac{\sqrt{2}}{2} - \dfrac{\sqrt{3}}{2} \cdot \dfrac{\sqrt{2}}{2}$

$\quad = \dfrac{\sqrt{2} - \sqrt{6}}{4}$

18. $\sin \dfrac{\pi}{12} = \sin\left(\dfrac{4\pi}{12} - \dfrac{3\pi}{12}\right)$

$\quad = \sin\dfrac{\pi}{3}\cos\dfrac{\pi}{4} - \cos\dfrac{\pi}{3}\sin\dfrac{\pi}{4}$ Use the sine difference identity.

$\quad = \dfrac{\sqrt{3}}{2} \cdot \dfrac{\sqrt{2}}{2} - \dfrac{1}{2} \cdot \dfrac{\sqrt{2}}{2}$

$\quad = \dfrac{\sqrt{6} - \sqrt{2}}{4}$

19. $\sin 12° \cos 48° + \cos 12° \sin 48°$

$\quad = \sin(12° + 48°)$ Use the sine sum identity.

$\quad = \sin(60°)$

$\quad = \dfrac{\sqrt{3}}{2}$

20. $\cos 75° \cos 75° - \sin 75° \sin 75°$

$\quad = \cos(75° + 75°)$ Use the cosine sum identity.

$\quad = \cos(150°)$

$\quad = -\dfrac{\sqrt{3}}{2}$

21. $\dfrac{\tan 47° - \tan 17°}{1 + \tan 47° \tan 17°}$

$\quad = \tan(47° - 17°)$ Use the tangent difference identity.

$\quad = \tan 30°$

$\quad = \dfrac{\sqrt{3}}{3}$

22. $\tan(\pi + x) = \dfrac{\tan \pi + \tan x}{1 - \tan \pi \tan x}$ Use the tangent sum identity.

$\qquad\qquad = \dfrac{0 + \tan x}{1 - (0)\tan x}$

$\qquad\qquad = \tan x$

23.   If $\cos A = -\dfrac{1}{2}$, then $\sin A = -\dfrac{\sqrt{3}}{2}$ (A is in QIII).

24. $\cos 2B = 1 - 2\sin^2 B$ Use the cosine double-angle identity.

$\qquad\quad = 1 - 2\left(\dfrac{4}{5}\right)^2$ $\sin B = \dfrac{4}{5}$

$\qquad\quad = -\dfrac{7}{25}$

25.   To find $\sin(A + B)$, we need $\cos B$.

$\cos^2 B + \sin^2 B = 1$

$\cos^2 B + \left(\dfrac{4}{5}\right)^2 = 1$

$\qquad\quad \cos^2 B = 1 - \dfrac{16}{25} = \dfrac{9}{25}$

$\qquad\qquad \cos B = -\dfrac{3}{5}, \ B \text{ is in QII}$

So, $\sin(A + B) = \sin A \cos B + \cos A \sin B$

$\qquad\qquad\qquad = \left(-\dfrac{\sqrt{3}}{2}\right)\left(-\dfrac{3}{5}\right) + \left(-\dfrac{1}{2}\right)\cdot\dfrac{4}{5}$

$\qquad\qquad\qquad = \dfrac{3\sqrt{3} - 4}{10}$

26.   We use the form

$\sin\dfrac{A}{2} = \sqrt{\dfrac{1 - \cos A}{2}}$, since $180° \le A \le 270°$, $90° \le \dfrac{A}{2} \le 135° \rightarrow \dfrac{A}{2}$ is in QII.

$\sin\dfrac{A}{2} = \sqrt{\dfrac{1 + \dfrac{1}{2}}{2}}$

$\qquad = \dfrac{\sqrt{3}}{2}$

27.   Using the sine form with amplitude $= 1$, period $= \pi = \dfrac{2\pi}{|B|} \rightarrow B = 2$, we get:

(c) $y = \sin 2x$, which is equivalent to

(a) $y = 2\sin x \cos x$ Use the sine double-angle identity.

or (f) $y = \sin 5x \cos 3x - \cos 5x \sin 3x$ Use the sine difference identity.

28. Using the cosine form with amplitude $= 1$, period $= 4\pi = \dfrac{2\pi}{|B|} \rightarrow B = \dfrac{1}{2}$, we get:

(b) $y = \cos \dfrac{1}{2} x$, which is equivalent to

(h) $y = \cos x \cos \dfrac{x}{2} + \sin x \sin \dfrac{x}{2}$ Use the cosine difference identity.

29. $\cos \left(\tan^{-1} \sqrt{3} - \sin^{-1} \dfrac{\sqrt{2}}{2} \right)$

$= \cos(60° - 45°)$ $\tan^{-1} \sqrt{3} = 60°$ and $\sin^{-1} \dfrac{\sqrt{2}}{2} = 45°$

$= \cos 60° \cos 45° + \sin 60° \sin 45°$

$= \dfrac{1}{2} \cdot \dfrac{\sqrt{2}}{2} + \dfrac{\sqrt{3}}{2} \cdot \dfrac{\sqrt{2}}{2}$

$= \dfrac{\sqrt{2} + \sqrt{6}}{4}$

30. $\sin 3x + \sin 5x$

$= 2 \sin \left(\dfrac{3x + 5x}{2} \right) \cos \left(\dfrac{3x - 5x}{2} \right)$ Use the sum-to-product identity.

$= 2 \sin(4x) \cos(-x)$

$= 2 \sin 4x \cos x$ $\cos(-x) = \cos x$

Chapter 5   Trigonometry Student's Solutions Manual

Exercise Set 5.1, p. 295

Answers to problems are listed as they are found in the solution rather than in numerical order.

1. **a.** When $\cos x = \dfrac{1}{2}$, we know that $\hat{x} = \dfrac{\pi}{3}$ and

$\cos x > 0$ (positive) in QI and QIV.

So, $x = \dfrac{\pi}{3}$ and $x = 2\pi - \dfrac{\pi}{3} = \dfrac{5\pi}{3}$.

b. $x = \dfrac{\pi}{3} + k \cdot 2\pi,\ x = \dfrac{5\pi}{3} + k \cdot 2\pi$ (The period of the cosine is 2π.)

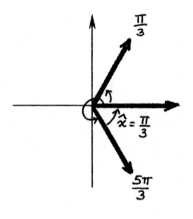

3. **a.** When $\sin x = -\dfrac{\sqrt{2}}{2}$, we know that $\hat{x} = \dfrac{\pi}{4}$ and

$\sin x < 0$ (negative) in QIII and QIV.

So, $x = \pi + \dfrac{\pi}{4} = \dfrac{5\pi}{4}$ and $x = 2\pi - \dfrac{\pi}{4} = \dfrac{7\pi}{4}$.

b. $x = \dfrac{5\pi}{4} + k \cdot 2\pi,\ x = \dfrac{7\pi}{4} + k \cdot 2\pi$ (The period of the sine is 2π.)

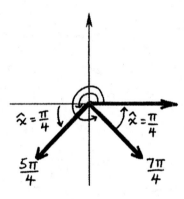

5. **a.** When $\tan x = \dfrac{\sqrt{3}}{3}$, we know that $\hat{x} = \dfrac{\pi}{6}$ and

$\tan x > 0$ in QI and QIII.

So, $x = \dfrac{\pi}{6}$ and $x = \pi + \dfrac{\pi}{6} = \dfrac{7\pi}{6}$.

b. $x = \dfrac{\pi}{6} + k \cdot \pi$ (The period of the tangent is π.)

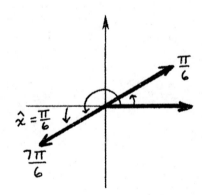

7. **a.** When $\sec x = 1$, we know that $\cos x = 1$, and that $x = 0$.
  b. $x = k \cdot 2\pi$

9. **a.** When $\csc x = -2$, we know that $\sin x = -\dfrac{1}{2}$, that $\hat{x} = \dfrac{\pi}{6}$ and $\sin x < 0$ in QIII and QIV.

  So, $x = \pi + \dfrac{\pi}{6} = \dfrac{7\pi}{6}$ and $x = 2\pi - \dfrac{\pi}{6} = \dfrac{11\pi}{6}$.

  b. $x = \dfrac{7\pi}{6} + k \cdot 2\pi,\ x = \dfrac{11\pi}{6} + k \cdot 2\pi$

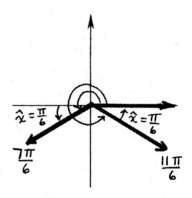

11. **a.** When $\cot x = -1$, we know that $\tan x = -1$, that $\hat{x} = \dfrac{\pi}{4}$ and $\cot x < 0$ in QII and QIV.

  So, $x = \pi - \dfrac{\pi}{4} = \dfrac{3\pi}{4}$ and $x = 2\pi - \dfrac{\pi}{4} = \dfrac{7\pi}{4}$.

  b. $x = \dfrac{3\pi}{4} + k \cdot \pi$

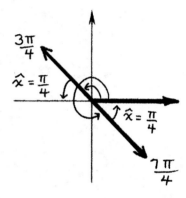

13. **a.** When $\tan \alpha = 1$, we know that $\hat{\alpha} = 45°$ and $\tan \alpha > 0$ in QI and QIII.
   So, $\alpha = 45°$ and $\alpha = 180° + 45° = 225°$.

  b. $\alpha = 45° + k \cdot 180°$

15. **a.** When $\csc \alpha = -\dfrac{2\sqrt{3}}{3}$, we know that $\sin \alpha = -\dfrac{\sqrt{3}}{2}$, that $\hat{\alpha} = 60°$ and $\csc \alpha < 0$ in QIII and QIV.
   So, $\alpha = 180° + 60° = 240°$ and $\alpha = 360° - 60° = 300°$.

  b. $\alpha = 240° + k \cdot 360°,\ \alpha = 300° + k \cdot 360°$

17. **a.** When $\cos \alpha = 0$, we know that $\alpha = 90°$ and $\alpha = 270°$.
  b. $\alpha = 90° + k \cdot 180°$

19. **a.** We know that $\cot \alpha = \dfrac{\cos \alpha}{\sin \alpha}$ is undefined when $\sin \alpha = 0$, or when $\alpha = 0°$ and $\alpha = 180°$.

  b. $\alpha = k \cdot 180°$

21, 23, 25, 27, and 29. *Use radian mode.*

21. For $\sin t = \dfrac{7}{25}$, $\sin t > 0$ in QI and QII, and

$$\hat{t} = \sin^{-1}\left(\dfrac{7}{25}\right) \approx 0.2838.$$

So, $t \approx 0.2838$ and $t \approx \pi - 0.2838 = 2.8578$.

23. For $\tan t = 5\dfrac{1}{2}$, $\tan t > 0$ in QI and QIII, and

$$\hat{t} = \tan^{-1}(5.5) \approx 1.3909.$$

So, $t \approx 1.3909$ and $t \approx \pi + 1.3909 = 4.5325$.

25. For $\cos t = -0.75$, $\cos t < 0$ in QII and QIII, and

$$\hat{t} = \cos^{-1}(0.75) \approx 0.7227.$$

So, $t \approx \pi - 0.7227 = 2.4189$ and $t \approx \pi + 0.7227 = 3.8643$.

27. For $\csc t = -1.28766$, $\csc t < 0$ in QIII and QIV, and

$$\hat{t} = \csc^{-1}(1.28766)$$

$$\hat{t} = \sin^{-1}\left(\dfrac{1}{1.28766}\right) \approx 0.8893.$$

So, $t \approx \pi + 0.8893 = 4.0308$ and $t \approx 2\pi - 0.8893 = 5.3939$.

29. For $\cot t = -0.0075$, $\cot t < 0$ in QII and QIV, and

$$\hat{t} = \cot^{-1}(0.0075)$$

$$= \tan^{-1}\left(\dfrac{1}{0.0075}\right) \approx 1.5633.$$

So, $t \approx \pi - 1.5633 = 1.5783$ and $t \approx 2\pi - 1.5633 = 4.7199$.

31, 33, 35, 37, and 39. *Use degree mode.*

31. For $\sin x = \pm 1$, we recognize the common angle functional values for:

$$x = 90° \text{ and } x = 270°$$

33. For $\cos x = -0.45$, $\cos x < 0$ in QII and QIII, and

$$\hat{x} = \cos^{-1}(0.45) \approx 63.3°.$$

So, $x \approx 180° - 63.3° = 116.7°$ and $x \approx 180° + 63.3° = 243.3°$.

35. For $\tan x = 1.59$, $\tan x > 0$ in QI and QIII, and

$$\hat{x} = \tan^{-1}(1.59) \approx 57.8°.$$

So, $x \approx 57.8°$ and $x \approx 180° + 57.8° = 237.8°$.

37. For $\cot x = \pm\sqrt{3}$, we know that $\hat{x} = 30°$. Since we want the angles for which $\cot x$ is both positive and negative, we use all four quadrants:
So, $x = 30°$, $x = 180° - 30° = 150°$, $x = 180° + 30° = 210°$, and $x = 360° - 30° = 330°$.

39. $\sec x = -\dfrac{1}{2}$ (or $\cos x = -2$) is not possible because $|\sec x| \geq 1$ (or $|\cos x| \leq 1$). This equation has no solution.

41. a. $y = 0.6$ (represents the horizontal line) and **b.** $\cos x = 0.6$
    $y = \cos x$

  c. $x = 0.9273$
    To verify, use a calculator in radian mode.

$$\cos 0.9273 \approx 0.6$$

43. a. $y = 5$ **b.** $\csc x = 5$ **c.** $x = 0.2014$
    $y = \csc x$

Exercise Set 5.2, p. 302

Answers to problems are listed as they are found in the solution rather than in numerical order.

1. Let $\sin x = u$.

$3u + 5 = 15u - 1$, first degree

3. Let $\cos x = u$.

$3u - 2u^2 + 1 = 0$

$2u^2 - 3u - 1 = 0$, second degree

5. Let $\sin x = u$.

$u(u - 5) = 6$

$u^2 - 5u - 6 = 0$, second degree

7. $2 \sin x = \sqrt{3}$

$\sin x = \dfrac{\sqrt{3}}{2}$ Divide by 2.

So, $x = \dfrac{\pi}{3}$ and $x = \dfrac{2\pi}{3}$.

9. $5 \sec x + 8 = 9 \sec x$

$8 = 4 \sec x$ Subtract $5 \sec x$.

$\sec x = 2$ Divide by 4.

$\cos x = \dfrac{1}{2}$ Use the reciprocal definition.

So, $x = \dfrac{\pi}{3}$ and $x = \dfrac{5\pi}{3}$.

11. $4 \cos^2 x = 3$

$\cos^2 x = \dfrac{3}{4}$ Divide by 4.

$\cos x = \pm\dfrac{\sqrt{3}}{2}$ Take the square root.

So, $x = \dfrac{\pi}{6}$, $x = \dfrac{5\pi}{6}$, $x = \dfrac{7\pi}{6}$, and $x = \dfrac{11\pi}{6}$.

13. $15 \tan^2 x = 5$

$\tan^2 x = \dfrac{1}{3}$ Divide by 15.

$\tan x = \pm\dfrac{1}{\sqrt{3}}$ Take the square root.

So, $x = \dfrac{\pi}{6}$, $x = \dfrac{5\pi}{6}$, $x = \dfrac{7\pi}{6}$, and $x = \dfrac{11\pi}{6}$.

15. $\cos x \sin x - \cos x = 0$

$\cos x(\sin x - 1) = 0$ Factor out $\cos x$.

$\cos x = 0$ or $\sin x - 1 = 0$ Set each factor to zero.

$\cos x = 0$ or $\sin x = 1$

So, $x = \dfrac{\pi}{2}$ and $x = \dfrac{3\pi}{2}$.

17.

$$2\cos^2 x + \cos x = 1$$

$$2\cos^2 x + \cos x - 1 = 0 \qquad \text{Write in standard form.}$$

$$(2\cos x - 1)(\cos x + 1) = 0 \qquad \text{Factor.}$$

$$2\cos x - 1 = 0 \quad \text{or} \quad \cos x + 1 = 0 \qquad \text{Set each factor to zero.}$$

$$\cos x = \frac{1}{2} \quad \text{or} \quad \cos x = -1$$

So, $x = \dfrac{\pi}{3}$, $x = \dfrac{5\pi}{3}$, and $x = \pi$.

19.

$$\tan^2 x = \tan x$$

$$\tan^2 x - \tan x = 0 \qquad \text{Write in standard form.}$$

$$\tan x (\tan x - 1) = 0 \qquad \text{Factor.}$$

$$\tan x = 0 \quad \text{or} \quad \tan x - 1 = 0 \qquad \text{Set each factor to zero.}$$

$$\tan x = 0 \quad \text{or} \quad \tan x = 1$$

So, $x = 0$, $x = \pi$, $x = \dfrac{\pi}{4}$, and $x = \dfrac{5\pi}{4}$.

21.

$$(\tan^2 x - 3)(\tan x - 1) = 0$$

$$\tan^2 x - 3 = 0 \quad \text{or} \quad \tan x - 1 = 0 \qquad \text{Set each factor to zero.}$$

$$\tan^2 x = 3 \quad \text{or} \quad \tan x = 1$$

$$\tan x = \pm\sqrt{3} \quad \text{or} \quad \tan x = 1$$

So, $x = \dfrac{\pi}{3}$, $x = \dfrac{2\pi}{3}$, $x = \dfrac{4\pi}{3}$, $x = \dfrac{5\pi}{3}$, $x = \dfrac{\pi}{4}$, and $x = \dfrac{5\pi}{4}$.

23.

$$4\sin^3 x - 3\sin x = 0$$

$$\sin x (4\sin^2 x - 3) = 0 \qquad \text{Factor out } \sin x.$$

$$\sin x = 0 \quad \text{or} \quad 4\sin^2 x - 3 = 0 \qquad \text{Set each factor to zero.}$$

$$\sin x = 0 \quad \text{or} \quad \sin x = \pm\frac{\sqrt{3}}{2}$$

So, $x = 0, \pi, \dfrac{\pi}{3}, \dfrac{2\pi}{3}, \dfrac{4\pi}{3}$, and $\dfrac{5\pi}{3}$.

25.

$$5\cos^2 x - 11\cos x + 6 = 0$$

$$(5\cos x - 6)(\cos x - 1) = 0 \qquad \text{Factor.}$$

$$5\cos x - 6 = 0 \quad \text{or} \quad \cos x - 1 = 0 \qquad \text{Set each factor to zero.}$$

$$\cos x = \frac{6}{5} \quad \text{or} \quad \cos x = 1$$

$$\text{(no solution)} \qquad \text{So, } x = 0.$$

27.
$$4 \csc^2 x + 3 \csc x - 1 = 0$$
$$(4 \csc x - 1)(\csc x + 1) = 0 \qquad \text{Factor.}$$
$$4 \csc x - 1 = 0 \quad \text{or} \quad \csc x + 1 = 0 \qquad \text{Set each factor to zero.}$$
$$\csc x = \frac{1}{4} \quad \text{or} \quad \csc x = -1$$
$$\sin x = 4 \quad \text{or} \quad \sin x = -1$$
(no solution)
$$\text{So, } x = \frac{3\pi}{2}.$$

29. Since the equation is already set to zero and factored, we set each factor equal to zero.
$$2 \sin \theta \cos \theta = 0$$
$$2 \sin \theta = 0 \quad \text{or} \quad \cos \theta = 0$$
$$\sin \theta = 0 \quad \text{or} \quad \cos \theta = 0$$
So, $\theta = 0°, 180°, 90°,$ and $270°$.

31. $2 \cos^2 \theta - 1 = 0$
$$\cos^2 \theta = \frac{1}{2}$$
$$\cos \theta = \pm \frac{1}{\sqrt{2}}$$
So, $\theta = 45°, 135°, 225°,$ and $315°$.

33.
$$2 \sin^2 \theta + \sin \theta - 1 = 0 \qquad \text{Write in standard form.}$$
$$(2 \sin \theta - 1)(\sin \theta + 1) = 0 \qquad \text{Factor.}$$
$$2 \sin \theta - 1 = 0 \quad \text{or} \quad \sin \theta + 1 = 0 \qquad \text{Set each factor to zero.}$$
$$\sin \theta = \frac{1}{2} \quad \text{or} \quad \sin \theta = -1$$
So, $\theta = 30°, 150°,$ and $270°$.

35.
$$\sec^2 \theta \tan \theta - \tan \theta = 0 \qquad \text{Set the equation equal to zero.}$$
$$\tan \theta (\sec^2 \theta - 1) = 0 \qquad \text{Factor.}$$
$$\tan \theta = 0 \quad \text{or} \quad \sec^2 \theta - 1 = 0$$
$$\tan \theta = 0 \quad \text{or} \quad \sec \theta = \pm 1$$
$$\tan \theta = 0 \quad \text{or} \quad \cos \theta = \pm 1$$
So, $\theta = 0°$ and $180°$.

37, 39, 41, and 43. *Use the radian mode.*

37. $8 \sin^2 t - 5 \sin t - 2 = 0$ Rewrite in standard form.

Since the equation does not factor, we use the quadratic formula:
$$\sin t = \frac{-(-5) \pm \sqrt{(-5)^2 - 4(8)(-2)}}{2(8)}$$
$$\sin t \approx 0.9021 \qquad \text{or} \quad \sin t \approx -0.2771$$
$$\hat{t} \approx \sin^{-1}(0.9021) \quad \text{or} \quad \hat{t} \approx \sin^{-1}(0.2771)$$
$$\hat{t} \approx 1.1247 \qquad\qquad \hat{t} \approx 0.2808$$

So: $t \approx 1.1247, t \approx \pi - 1.1247$ or $t \approx \pi + 0.2808, t \approx 2\pi - 0.2808$
$$\to t \approx 1.1247, 2.0169 \qquad \text{or} \quad t \approx 3.4224, 6.0024$$

39.
$$4\cos^2 t = \cos(-t)$$
$$4\cos^2 t - \cos t = 0 \qquad \text{Rewrite in standard form; } \cos(-t) = \cos t.$$
$$\cos t(4\cos t - 1) = 0 \qquad \text{Factor.}$$

$$\cos t = 0 \qquad \text{or} \quad \cos t = \frac{1}{4}$$

$$\cos t = 0 \qquad \text{or} \quad \hat{t} = \cos^{-1}\left(\frac{1}{4}\right) \approx 1.3181$$

$$\cos t = 0 \qquad \text{or} \quad t \approx 1.3181, t \approx 2\pi - 1.3181$$

$$\text{So, } t = \frac{\pi}{2}, \frac{3\pi}{2}, \qquad t \approx 1.3181, 4.9651.$$

41.
$$3\sin^2 t + 10\sin t - 8 = 0 \qquad \text{Rewrite in standard form; } \sin(-t) = -\sin t.$$
$$(3\sin t - 2)(\sin t + 4) = 0$$

$$3\sin t - 2 = 0 \qquad \text{or} \quad \sin t + 4 = 0$$

$$\sin t = \frac{2}{3} \qquad \text{or} \qquad \sin t = -4$$

$$\hat{t} \approx 0.7297 \qquad \text{(no solution)}$$

$$\text{So: } t \approx 0.7297, t \approx \pi - 0.7297$$
$$\rightarrow t \approx 0.7297, 2.4119$$

43.
$$\tan^2 t - 5\tan t + 3 = 0$$

$$\tan t = \frac{-(-5) \pm \sqrt{(-5)^2 - 4(1)(3)}}{2(1)}$$

$$\tan t \approx 4.3028 \quad \text{or} \quad \tan t \approx 0.6972$$
$$\hat{t} \approx 1.3424 \quad \text{or} \qquad \hat{t} \approx 0.6089$$

$$\text{So: } t \approx 1.3424, t \approx \pi + 1.3424 \quad \text{or} \quad t \approx 0.6089, t \approx 0.6089 + \pi$$
$$\rightarrow t \approx 1.3424, 4.4840, 0.6089, 3.7505$$

45, 47, and 49. *Use degree mode.*

45. $2\cos^2 \alpha - 4\cos \alpha + 1 = 0$ $\qquad\qquad\qquad\qquad$ Rewrite in standard form.

$$\cos \alpha = \frac{-(-4) \pm \sqrt{(-4)^2 - 4(2)(1)}}{2(2)}$$

$$\cos \alpha \approx 1.7071 \quad \text{or} \quad \cos \alpha \approx 0.2929$$
$$\text{(no solution)} \qquad \hat{\alpha} \approx 73.0°$$

$$\text{So: } \alpha \approx 73.0°, \alpha \approx 360° - 73.0°$$
$$\rightarrow \alpha \approx 73.0°, 287.0°$$

47. $2\sin^2 \alpha - 5\sin \alpha - 5 = 0$ $\qquad\qquad\qquad\qquad$ Rewrite in standard form.

$$\sin \alpha = \frac{-(-5) \pm \sqrt{(-5)^2 - 4(2)(-5)}}{2(2)}$$

$$\sin \alpha \approx 3.2656 \quad \text{or} \quad \sin \alpha = -0.7656$$
$$\text{(no solution)} \qquad \hat{\alpha} \approx 50.0°$$

$$\text{So: } \alpha \approx 180° + 50.0°, \alpha \approx 360° - 50.0°$$
$$\rightarrow \alpha \approx 230.0°, 310.0°$$

49. $5\tan^2\alpha + 16\tan\alpha - 40 = 0$ Rewrite in standard form.

$$\tan\alpha = \frac{-16 \pm \sqrt{(16)^2 - 4(5)(-40)}}{2(5)}$$

$\tan\alpha \approx 1.6496$ or $\tan\alpha \approx -4.8496$

$\hat{\alpha} \approx 58.8°$ $\hat{\alpha} \approx 78.3°$

So: $\alpha \approx 58.8°, \alpha \approx 180°+58.8°$ or $\alpha \approx 180° - 78.3°, \alpha \approx 360° - 78.3°$

$\rightarrow \alpha \approx 58.8°, 238.8°, 101.7°, 281.7°$

51. From Exercise 11, where the solutions were $x = \dfrac{\pi}{6}, \dfrac{5\pi}{6}, \dfrac{7\pi}{6}$, and $\dfrac{11\pi}{6}$, all solutions can be expressed as

$$x = \frac{\pi}{6} + k \cdot \pi, \quad x = \frac{5\pi}{6} + k \cdot \pi.$$

53. From Exercise 35, where the solutions were $x = 0°$ and $180°$, all solutions can be expressed as

$$x = k \cdot 180°.$$

55. From Exercise 47, where the solutions were $x \approx 230.0°$ and $310.0°$, all solutions can be expressed as

$$x \approx 230.0° + k \cdot 360°, \quad x \approx 310.0° + k \cdot 360°.$$

57. For $d(t) = 3.6\cos t$, where $d(t)$ is in cm and t is in sec:

$-2 = 3.6\cos t$ Let $d(t) = -2$.

$\dfrac{-2}{3.6} = \cos t$

$\hat{t} = \cos^{-1}\left(\dfrac{2}{3.6}\right) \approx 0.9818$ Use radian mode.

So: $t \approx \pi - 0.9818, t \approx \pi + 0.9818$ $(0 \le t < 6.3)$
To the nearest tenth of a second,

$$t = 2.2\,\text{sec} \quad \text{and} \quad t = 4.1\,\text{sec}.$$

59. For $T(t) = 98.9 + 5\sin t$, where t is in days and $T(t)$ is in degrees:

a. $103.9 = 98.9 + 5\sin t$, since $T(t) = 103.9°$

$5 = 5\sin t$

$\sin t = 1$

$t = \dfrac{\pi}{2} \approx 1.5708$ Use radian mode: $0 \le t \le 6$.

The temperature will spike at approximately 1.6 days into the illness.

b. $101 = 98.9 + 5\sin t$

$\dfrac{2.1}{5} = \sin t$

$\hat{t} = \sin^{-1}\left(\dfrac{2.1}{5}\right)$

$t \approx 0.4334, t \approx \pi - 0.4334 = 2.7082$ $(0 \le t \le 6)$

The temperature will be at $101°$ in approximately 0.4 days and 2.7 days.

61. **a.** For $h = -16t^2 + (v_0 \sin \theta)t$, when $\theta = 45°$, $v_0 = 200$ ft/sec and $t = 2$ sec, we get:

$$h = -16(2)^2 + (200 \sin 45°)(2)$$

$$h \approx 218.8427 \qquad \text{Use degree mode.}$$

To the nearest foot, after 2 sec the height of the cannonball will be 219 ft.

b. If $h = 0$:

$$0 = -16t^2 + (200 \sin 45°)t$$

$$0 = -16t^2 + 100\sqrt{2}\,t$$

$$0 = -4t(4t - 25\sqrt{2})$$

$$-4t = 0 \qquad \qquad \text{or} \quad 4t - 25\sqrt{2} = 0$$

$$t = 0 \text{ (time of release)} \quad \text{or} \qquad \qquad t = \frac{25\sqrt{2}}{4} \approx 8.8388$$

To the nearest tenth of a second, the cannonball will be back on the ground after 8.8 sec.

c. If $h = 100$, $t = 1$, $v_0 = 200$:

$$h = -16t^2 + (v_0 \sin \theta)t$$

$$100 = -16(1)^2 + (200 \sin \theta)(1)$$

$$\frac{116}{200} = \sin \theta$$

$$\theta = \sin^{-1}\left(\frac{116}{200}\right)$$

$$\theta \approx 35.4505° \qquad \qquad 0 \le \theta < 90°$$

The angle of elevation that should be used is 35.5°.

Exercise Set 5.3, p. 311

Answers to problems are listed as they are found in the solution rather than in numerical order.

Note: The symbol (∗) indicates which step causes you to check your answers and the answers that need to be checked.

1.

$$\sin^2 - \cos^2 x = 0$$

$$\sin^2 x - (1 - \sin^2 x) = 0 \qquad \text{Obtain one function.}$$

$$2\sin^2 x - 1 = 0$$

$$\sin^2 x = \frac{1}{2}$$

$$\sin x = \pm\frac{1}{\sqrt{2}}$$

So, $x = \dfrac{\pi}{4}, \dfrac{3\pi}{4}, \dfrac{5\pi}{4},$ and $\dfrac{7\pi}{4}$.

3.

$$4\cos x = 3 \sec x$$

$$4\cos x = \frac{3}{\cos x} \qquad \text{Obtain one function.}$$

$$4\cos^2 x = 3 \qquad \text{∗Assume } \cos x \neq 0.$$

$$\cos x = \pm\frac{\sqrt{3}}{2}$$

So, $x = \dfrac{\pi}{6}, \dfrac{5\pi}{6}, \dfrac{7\pi}{6},$ and $\dfrac{11\pi}{6}$. ∗No solution is discarded since $\cos x \neq 0$.

5.　　　　　$\cos^2 x + 2 \sin x + 2 = 0$

　　　　$(1 - \sin^2 x) + 2 \sin x + 2 = 0$　　　　Obtain one function.

　　　　　　$\sin^2 x - 2 \sin x - 3 = 0$　　　　Rewrite in standard form.

　　　　　$(\sin x - 3)(\sin x + 1) = 0$

　　$\sin x - 3 = 0$　or　$\sin x + 1 = 0$

　　　$\sin x = 3$　or　　　$\sin x = -1$

　　(no solution)　　　　$x = \dfrac{3\pi}{2}$

7.　　　$\tan x + \cot x + 2 = 0$

　　$\tan x + \dfrac{1}{\tan x} + 2 = 0$　　　　Obtain one function.

　$\tan^2 x + 2 \tan x + 1 = 0$　　　　*Assume $\tan x \neq 0$.

　　　　$(\tan x + 1)^2 = 0$

　　　　　$\tan x + 1 = 0$

　　　　　　　$\tan x = -1$

So, $x = \dfrac{3\pi}{4}$ and $\dfrac{7\pi}{4}$.　　　　*No solution is discarded since $\tan x \neq 0$.

9.　　　　　　　$\tan^2 x = 1 - \sec x$

　　　　　　$(\sec^2 x - 1) = 1 - \sec x$　　　　Obtain one function.

　　　　$\sec^2 x + \sec x - 2 = 0$

　　　　$(\sec x + 2)(\sec x - 1) = 0$

　$\sec x + 2 = 0$　　or　$\sec x - 1 = 0$

　　$\sec x = -2$　or　　　$\sec x = 1$

　$\cos x = -\dfrac{1}{2}$　or　　　$\cos x = 1$

So, $x = \dfrac{2\pi}{3}, \dfrac{4\pi}{3}, 0$

11.　　　　　　$\cos 2x - \sin x = 0$

　　　　$(1 - 2 \sin^2 x) - \sin x = 0$　　　　Obtain the same multiple of x and the same function.

　　　　　$2 \sin^2 x + \sin x - 1 = 0$

　　　　　$(2 \sin x - 1)(\sin x + 1) = 0$

　$2 \sin x - 1 = 0$　or　$\sin x + 1 = 0$

　　　$\sin x = \dfrac{1}{2}$　or　　　$\sin x = -1$

So, $x = 30°, 150°,$ and $270°$.

13.　　　　　　$\sin x - \sin 2x = 0$

　　　　$\sin x - 2 \sin x \cos x = 0$　　　　Obtain the same multiple of x.

　　　　　$\sin x (1 - 2 \cos x) = 0$

　$\sin x = 0$　or　$1 - 2 \cos x = 0$

　$\sin x = 0$　or　　　$\cos x = \dfrac{1}{2}$

So, $x = 0°, 180°, 60°,$ and $300°$.

15. $\sin 2x = \cos 2x$

$\quad (\sin 2x)^2 = (\cos 2x)^2$ *Since we already have the same multiple of x,

$\quad \sin^2 2x = \cos^2 2x$ we square both sides in order to obtain one function.

$\quad \sin^2 2x = 1 - \sin^2 2x$

$\quad 2\sin^2 2x = 1$

$\quad \sin^2 2x = \dfrac{1}{2}$

$\quad \sin 2x = \pm\dfrac{1}{\sqrt{2}}$ If $0 \leq x < 360°$, then $0 \leq 2x < 720°$.

$\rightarrow 2x = 45°, 135°, 225°, 315°, 405°, 495°, 585°, 675°$
and $x = 22.5°, 67.5°, 112.5°, 157.5°, 202.5°, 247.5°, 292.5°, 337.5°$

∗ After checking the solutions (as a result of squaring both sides of the equation), we get

$$x = 22.5°, \ 112.5°, \ 202.5°, \ \text{and} \ 292.5°.$$

17. $2\cos^2 \dfrac{x}{2} = 2\cos x$

$\quad 2\left(\dfrac{1 + \cos x}{2}\right) = 2\cos x$ Obtain the same multiple of x.

$\quad\quad 1 + \cos x = 2\cos x$

$\quad\quad\quad \cos x = 1$

So, $x = 0°$.

19. $\cos 2x = 2 + 3\sin x$

$\quad 1 - 2\sin^2 x = 2 + 3\sin x$ Obtain the same multiple of X.

$\quad 2\sin^2 x + 3\sin x + 1 = 0$

$\quad (2\sin x + 1)(\sin x + 1) = 0$

$2\sin x + 1 = 0 \quad \text{or} \quad \sin x + 1 = 0$

$\quad \sin x = -\dfrac{1}{2} \quad \text{or} \quad \sin x = -1$

So, $x = 210°, 330°,$ and $270°$.

21. $\sqrt{3}\cos x = 1 + \sin x$

$\quad \left(\sqrt{3}\cos x\right)^2 = (1 + \sin x)^2$ ∗ Square both sides.

$\quad\quad 3\cos^2 x = 1 + 2\sin x + \sin^2 x$

$\quad 3(1 - \sin^2 x) = 1 + 2\sin x + \sin^2 x$

$\quad 4\sin^2 x + 2\sin x - 2 = 0$

$\quad 2(2\sin x - 1)(\sin x + 1) = 0$

$\quad 2\sin x - 1 = 0 \quad \text{or} \quad \sin x + 1 = 0$

$\quad\quad \sin x = \dfrac{1}{2} \quad \text{or} \quad \sin x = -1$

$\rightarrow x = 30°, 150°, 270°$

∗ After checking the solutions (as a result of squaring both sides of the equation), we get:

$$x = 30°, \ 270°$$

23. $\cos\theta - \sin\theta = 1$

$(\cos\theta)^2 = (1+\sin\theta)^2$ * Square both sides.

$\cos^2\theta = 1 + 2\sin\theta + \sin^2\theta$

$1 - \sin^2\theta = 1 + 2\sin\theta + \sin^2\theta$

$2\sin^2\theta + 2\sin\theta = 0$

$2\sin\theta(\sin\theta + 1) = 0$

$2\sin\theta = 0$ or $\sin\theta + 1 = 0$

$\sin\theta = 0$ or $\sin\theta = -1$

$\to \theta = 0°,\ 180°, 270°.$

* After checking the solutions (as a result of squaring both sides of the equation), we get:

$$\theta = 0°,\ 270°$$

25. $\sin\dfrac{\theta}{2} + \cos\theta = 0$

$\pm\sqrt{\dfrac{1-\cos\theta}{2}} + \cos\theta = 0$ Obtain the same multiple of θ.

$\left(\pm\sqrt{\dfrac{1-\cos\theta}{2}}\right)^2 = (-\cos\theta)^2$ * Square both sides.

$\dfrac{1-\cos\theta}{2} = \cos^2\theta$

$0 = 2\cos^2\theta + \cos\theta - 1$

$0 = (2\cos\theta - 1)(\cos\theta + 1)$

$2\cos\theta - 1 = 0$ or $\cos\theta + 1 = 0$

$\cos\theta = \dfrac{1}{2}$ or $\cos\theta = -1$

$\to \theta = 60°,\ 300°,\ 180°$

* After checking the solutions (as a result of squaring both sides of the equation), we get:

$$\theta = 180°$$

27. $\cos 2\theta = 1 - 2\sin\theta$

$1 - 2\sin^2\theta = 1 - 2\sin\theta$ Obtain the same multiple of θ and the same functions.

$2\sin^2\theta - 2\sin\theta = 0$

$2\sin\theta(\sin\theta - 1) = 0$

$2\sin\theta = 0$ or $\sin\theta - 1 = 0$

$\sin\theta = 0$ or $\sin\theta = 1$

$\theta = 0°,\ 180°,\ 90°$

29. $\cos^2\dfrac{\theta}{2} - \cos\theta = 1$

$\dfrac{1+\cos\theta}{2} - \cos\theta = 1$ Obtain the same multiple of θ and the same function.

$1 + \cos\theta - 2\cos\theta = 2$

$-\cos\theta = 1$

$\cos\theta = -1$

$\theta = 180°$

31. $\cos 8\theta \cos 6\theta + \sin 8\theta \sin 6\theta = \cos \theta$

$\qquad\qquad \cos(8\theta - 6\theta) = \cos \theta$ Use the cosine difference formula.

$\qquad\qquad\qquad \cos 2\theta = \cos \theta$

$\qquad\qquad 2\cos^2 \theta - 1 = \cos \theta$ Obtain the same multiple of θ and the same function.

$\qquad 2\cos^2 \theta - \cos \theta - 1 = 0$

$\quad (2\cos \theta + 1)(\cos \theta - 1) = 0$

$2\cos \theta + 1 = 0 \qquad \text{or} \quad \cos \theta - 1 = 0$

$\cos \theta = -\dfrac{1}{2} \quad \text{or} \qquad \cos \theta = 1$

$\theta = 120°, \ 240°, \ 0°$

33. Adding multiples of 2π to the solutions we obtained (within one revolution) gives us:

$$x = k \cdot 2\pi, \quad \frac{2\pi}{3} + k \cdot 2\pi, \quad \frac{4\pi}{3} + k \cdot 2\pi$$

35. Adding multiples of 360° to the solutions we obtained (within one revolution) gives us:

$$x = 30° + k \cdot 360°, \quad 270° + k \cdot 360°$$

37. $\qquad 10\cos^2 x + 23\cos x = 5$

$\qquad 10\cos^2 x + 23\cos x - 5 = 0$

$\qquad (5\cos x - 1)(2\cos x + 5) = 0$

$5\cos x - 1 = 0 \qquad\qquad \text{or} \quad 2\cos x + 5 = 0$

$\quad \cos x = \dfrac{1}{5} \qquad\qquad \text{or} \qquad \cos x = -\dfrac{5}{2} = -2.5$

$\quad \hat{x} = \cos^{-1}\left(\dfrac{1}{5}\right) \qquad\qquad \text{(no solution)}$

$\quad x \approx 1.3694$

Since $\cos x$ is positive in QI, QIV

$\rightarrow x \approx 1.3694, x = 2\pi - \hat{x} \approx 4.9137.$

39. $\qquad \cos^2 x + \sin x = 0$

$\quad 1 - \sin^2 x + \sin x = 0$ Obtain the same function.

$\quad \sin^2 x - \sin x - 1 = 0$

$$\sin x = \frac{-(-1) \pm \sqrt{(-1)^2 - 4(1)(-1)}}{2(1)} \qquad \text{Use the quadratic formula.}$$

$\sin x \approx 1.6180 \quad \text{or} \quad \sin x \approx -0.6180$

$\text{(no solution)} \qquad\qquad \hat{x} \approx \sin^{-1}(0.6180)$

$\qquad\qquad\qquad\qquad \hat{x} \approx 0.6662$

Since $\sin x$ is negative in QIII, QIV

$\qquad x = \pi + \hat{x}, \qquad\qquad x = 2\pi - \hat{x}$

$\qquad \approx \pi + 0.6662, \qquad\qquad \approx 2\pi - 0.6662$

$\rightarrow x \approx 3.8078, \qquad\qquad x \approx 5.6169.$

41. $2\sec^2 x - 7\sec x + 3 = 0$

$(2\sec x - 1)(\sec x - 3) = 0$

$2\sec x - 1 = 0 \quad$ or $\quad \sec x - 3 = 0$

$\sec x = \dfrac{1}{2} \quad$ or $\quad \sec x = 3$

(no solution) $\qquad\quad \cos x = \dfrac{1}{3}$

$\hat{x} = \cos^{-1}\left(\dfrac{1}{3}\right)$

$\hat{x} \approx 1.2310$

$\to x \approx 1.2310,\ x \approx 2\pi - 1.2310 \approx 5.0522$

43. $\sin(2x) = \dfrac{1}{2}$ $\qquad\qquad\qquad\qquad\qquad 0 \le x < 2\pi$

$(2x) = \dfrac{\pi}{6}, \dfrac{5\pi}{6}, \dfrac{\pi}{6} + 2\pi, \dfrac{5\pi}{6} + 2\pi \qquad 0 \le 2x < 4\pi$

$2x = \dfrac{\pi}{6}, \dfrac{5\pi}{6}, \dfrac{13\pi}{6}, \dfrac{17\pi}{6}$

$x = \dfrac{\pi}{12}, \dfrac{5\pi}{12}, \dfrac{13\pi}{12}, \dfrac{17\pi}{12} \qquad\qquad$ Multiply by $\dfrac{1}{2}$.

45. $\tan(2x) = -\sqrt{3}$ $\qquad\qquad\qquad\qquad 0 \le x < 2\pi$

$(2x) = \dfrac{2\pi}{3}, \dfrac{5\pi}{3}, \dfrac{2\pi}{3} + 2\pi, \dfrac{5\pi}{3} + 2\pi \qquad 0 \le 2x < 4\pi$

$2x = \dfrac{2\pi}{3}, \dfrac{5\pi}{3}, \dfrac{8\pi}{3}, \dfrac{11\pi}{3}$

$x = \dfrac{\pi}{3}, \dfrac{5\pi}{6}, \dfrac{4\pi}{3}, \dfrac{11\pi}{6} \qquad\qquad$ Multiply by $\dfrac{1}{2}$.

47. $\sin 5x \cos 3x - \cos 5x \sin 3x = -\dfrac{\sqrt{2}}{2} \qquad\qquad 0 \le x < 2\pi$

$\sin(5x - 3x) = -\dfrac{\sqrt{2}}{2} \qquad\qquad$ Use sine difference formula.

$\sin(2x) = -\dfrac{\sqrt{2}}{2} \qquad\qquad 0 \le 2x < 4\pi$

$2x = \dfrac{5\pi}{4}, \dfrac{7\pi}{4}, \dfrac{5\pi}{4} + 2\pi, \dfrac{7\pi}{4} + 2\pi$

$2x = \dfrac{5\pi}{4}, \dfrac{7\pi}{4}, \dfrac{13\pi}{4}, \dfrac{15\pi}{4}$

$x = \dfrac{5\pi}{8}, \dfrac{7\pi}{8}, \dfrac{13\pi}{8}, \dfrac{15\pi}{8} \qquad\qquad$ Multiply by $\dfrac{1}{2}$.

49. $\cos^2 2x - 8\cos 2x - 9 = 0,$ $0 \le x < 2\pi$

$(\cos 2x - 9)(\cos 2x + 1) = 0$

$\cos 2x - 9 = 0$ or $\cos 2x + 1 = 0$

   $\cos 2x = 9$ or $\cos 2x = -1,$ $0 \le 2x < 4\pi$

   (no solution) $2x = \pi, 3\pi$

                            $x = \dfrac{\pi}{2}, \dfrac{3\pi}{2}$

51, 53, and 55. *Use substitution to solve the system.*

51. $y = 4\cos^2 x + 2\sin^2 x,\; y = 3$

   $\rightarrow$ $4\cos^2 x + 2\sin^2 x = 3$

   $4(1 - \sin^2 x) + 2\sin^2 x = 3$ Obtain the same function.

               $2\sin^2 x = 1$

               $\sin^2 x = \dfrac{1}{2}$

               $\sin x = \pm\dfrac{1}{\sqrt{2}}$

          $x = 45°, 135°, 225°, 315°$

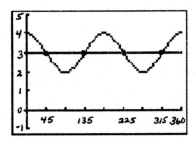

Substituting the value of x in either equation gives $y = 3$.
So the solutions to the system are:

   $(45°, 3), (135°, 3), (225°, 3), (315°, 3)$

53. $y = \sec x - \tan x,\; y = \cos x$

   $\rightarrow$ $\sec x - \tan x = \cos x$

      $\dfrac{1}{\cos x} - \dfrac{\sin x}{\cos x} = \cos x$

               $1 - \sin x = \cos^2 x$ *Assume $\cos x \ne 0$.

               $1 - \sin x = 1 - \sin^2 x$ Obtain one function.

          $\sin^2 x - \sin x = 0$

          $\sin x(\sin x - 1) = 0$

$\sin x = 0$ or $\sin x = 1$

   $x = 0°, 180°$ or $x = \cancel{90}°$

               * When $x = 90°, \cos x = 0$, so we discard this solution.

To find the corresponding values of y for each x:

If $x = 0°$: $y = \cos x$ If $x = 180°$: $y = \cos x$

          $y = \cos(0°)$ $y = \cos(180°)$

          $y = 1$ $y = -1$

So the solutions to the system are:

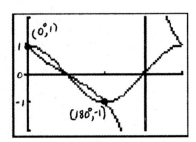

                $(0°, 1), (180°, -1)$

55. $y = \sin^2 x + \sin x,\; y = \cos^2 x$

$\quad\quad \rightarrow \sin^2 x + \sin x = \cos^2 x$

$\quad\quad\quad \sin^2 x + \sin x = 1 - \sin^2 x$ Obtain one function.

$\quad\quad 2\sin^2 x + \sin x - 1 = 0$

$\quad\quad (2\sin x - 1)(\sin x + 1) = 0$

$\quad\quad\; 2\sin x - 1 = 0$ or $\sin x + 1 = 0$

$\quad\quad\quad\quad \sin x = \dfrac{1}{2}$ or $\sin x = -1$

$\quad\quad\quad\quad x = 30°,\, 150°$ or $x = 270°$

If $x = 30°$: $y = \cos^2(30°)$

$\quad\quad\quad\quad\quad = \dfrac{3}{4}$ $\rightarrow \left(30°, \dfrac{3}{4}\right)$

If $x = 150°$: $y = \cos^2(150°)$

$\quad\quad\quad\quad\quad = \dfrac{3}{4}$ $\rightarrow \left(150°, \dfrac{3}{4}\right)$

If $x = 270°$: $y = \cos^2(270°)$

$\quad\quad\quad\quad\quad = 0$ $\rightarrow (270°, 0)$

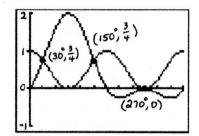

So, the solutions to the system are:

$$\left(30°, \frac{3}{4}\right),\; \left(150°, \frac{3}{4}\right),\; (270°, 0)$$

57. $H = \dfrac{v_0^2 \sin(2\alpha)}{32 \text{ ft/sec}^2}$

$\quad 350 = \dfrac{(110)^2 \sin(2\alpha)}{32}$

$\quad \sin(2\alpha) = \dfrac{(350)(32)}{(110)^2}$

$\quad \sin(2\alpha) \approx 0.9256$

$\quad\quad \widehat{(2\alpha)} \approx \sin^{-1}(0.9256)$

$\quad\quad \widehat{(2\alpha)} \approx 67.8°$

$\quad\quad 2\alpha \approx 67.8°$ or $2\alpha \approx 180 - 67.8°$

$\quad\quad \rightarrow \alpha \approx 33.9°,\, \alpha \approx 56.1°$

So, use an angle of elevation of $33.9°$ or $56.1°$.

Exercise Set 5.4, p. 320

Answers to problems are listed as they are found in the solution rather than in numerical order.

1. Since the parametric equations involve both sine and cosine, we use the Pythagorean identity to eliminate the parameter.

$$\cos^2 t + \sin^2 t = 1$$
$$(y)^2 + (-x)^2 = 1 \quad\quad\quad\quad\quad y = \cos t,\; -x = \sin t$$
$$\text{or } x^2 + y^2 = 1, \text{ which represents a circle}$$

3. Since the parametric equations involve both sine and cosine, we use the Pythagorean identity to eliminate the parameter, where

$$\frac{x}{4} = \cos t \text{ and } \frac{y}{5} = \sin t.$$

$$\cos^2 t + \sin^2 t = 1$$
$$\left(\frac{x}{4}\right)^2 + \left(\frac{y}{5}\right)^2 = 1$$

or $\frac{x^2}{16} + \frac{y^2}{25} = 1$, which represents an ellipse.

5. Since the parametric equations do not involve both sine and cosine, use the substitution method.

$$y = \cos t + 4$$
$$y = x + 4, \qquad\qquad x = \cos t$$

which represents a line.

7. Solving $\quad x = 2t - 4 \quad$ for t, we get

$$\frac{x+4}{2} = t, \quad \text{and substituting it into the parametric equation for } y$$

$$y = 4t$$
$$y = 4\left(\frac{x+4}{2}\right)$$

gives $y = 2x + 8$, which represents a line.

9. Solving $x = 2t$ for t, we get

$$t = \frac{x}{2}, \quad \text{and substituting it into}$$

$$y = 12t^2$$
$$\text{gives } y = 12\left(\frac{x}{2}\right)^2$$

or $y = 3x^2$, which represents a parabola.

11. Since the parametric equations involve secant and tangent, we use the identity

$$1 + \tan^2 t = \sec^2 t.$$

and substitute $\sec t = x$ and $\tan^2 t = y$ to get:

$$1 + \tan^2 t = \sec^2 t$$
$$1 + y = x^2$$
$$\text{or } y = x^2 - 1, \text{ which represents a parabola.}$$

13. $\left.\begin{array}{l} x = -\cos t \\ y = \sin t \end{array}\right\} x^2 + y^2 = 1$

t	x	y
0	-1	0
$\dfrac{\pi}{2}$	0	1
π	1	0
2π	-1	0

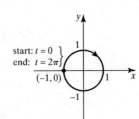

start: $t = 0$
end: $t = 2\pi$
$(-1, 0)$

15. $\left.\begin{array}{l} x = 3\sin t \\ y = 2\cos t \end{array}\right\}$ $\left(\dfrac{x}{3}\right)^2 + \left(\dfrac{y}{2}\right)^2 = 1 \rightarrow \dfrac{x^2}{9} + \dfrac{y^2}{4} = 1$

t	x	y
0	0	2
$\dfrac{\pi}{2}$	3	0
π	0	-2
2π	0	2

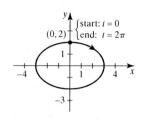

17. $\left.\begin{array}{l} x = \sin 2t \\ y = -\cos 2t \end{array}\right\}$ $x^2 + y^2 = 1$

t	x	y
0	0	-1
$\dfrac{\pi}{4}$	1	0
$\dfrac{\pi}{2}$	0	1
π	0	-1

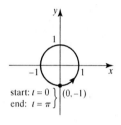

19. $\left.\begin{array}{l} x = 4t \\ y = 4t - 3 \end{array}\right\}$ $y = x - 3$

t	x	y
0	0	-3
1	4	1
2	8	5

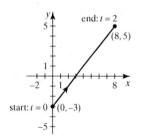

21. $\left.\begin{array}{l} x = \cos t \\ y = 5\cos t \end{array}\right\}$ $y = 5x$

t	x	y
0	1	5
$\dfrac{\pi}{2}$	0	0
π	-1	-5

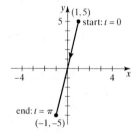

23. $\left.\begin{array}{l} x = 2t \\ y = 4t^2 + 1 \end{array}\right\}$ $y = x^2 + 1$

t	x	y
0	0	1
1	2	5
3	6	37

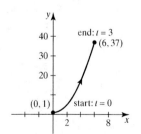

25. For $x = 5 - 2t$, $y = 6t$ $(0 \le t \le 3)$,   to find the value of t that gives the point

$$(1, 12) \rightarrow x = 1, y = 12,$$

we let $x = 1$ in the parametric equation for x, and then solve for t:

$$1 = 5 - 2t$$
$$\text{so } t = 2.$$

(We could have let $y = 12$ in the parametric equation for y:

$$12 = 6t, \quad \text{which would also give}$$
$$t = 2.)$$

27. For $x = 6 - t^2$, $y = 2t$ $(0 \le t \le 7)$,   to find the value of t that gives $(-10, 8) \rightarrow x = -10, y = 8$, we let:

$$-10 = 6 - t^2$$
$$t^2 = 16$$
$$t = 4.$$

29. a. $x = (48\cos 60°)t = 24t$
$\quad\ y = -16t^2 + (48\sin 60°)t$
$\quad\ y = -16t^2 + (24\sqrt{3})t$

b.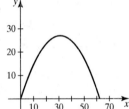

c. When the ball returns to the ground, $y = 0$. So:

$$0 = -16t^2 + (24\sqrt{3})t$$
$$0 = -4t(4t - 6\sqrt{3})$$
$$-4t = 0 \qquad \text{or} \quad 4t - 6\sqrt{3} = 0$$
$$t = 0 \text{ (start time)} \quad \text{or} \qquad t = \frac{3\sqrt{3}}{2} \approx 2.6$$

It takes 2.6 sec for the ball to return to the ground.

To find the distance it travels horizontally when $t = \dfrac{3\sqrt{3}}{2} \approx 2.6$, solve

$$x = 24t.$$

$$x = 24\left(\frac{3\sqrt{3}}{2}\right) = 36\sqrt{3} \approx 62$$

The ball has moved horizontally 62 ft.

31. a. $x = (120\cos 75°)t$
$\quad\ y = -16t^2 + (120\sin 75°)t$

b.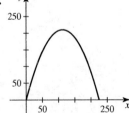

c. When the missile returns to the ground, $y = 0$. So:

$$0 = 16t^2 + (120\sin 75°)t$$

$$0 = -8t(2t - 15\sin 75°)$$

$$-8t = 0 \qquad \text{or} \quad 2t - 15\sin 75° = 0$$

$$t = 0 \text{ (start time)} \quad \text{or} \qquad t = \frac{15\sin 75°}{2} \approx 7.2$$

The missile returns to the ground in 7.2 sec.

To find the horizontal distance when $t = \dfrac{15\sin 75°}{2}$, solve

$$x = (120\cos 75°)t.$$

$$x = (120\cos 75°)\left(\frac{15\sin 75°}{2}\right)$$

$$= 225$$

The missile has moved horizontally 225 ft.

33 and 35. *Many answers are possible.*

33. $x = t,\ y = 4t + 1;$
$\quad x = \cos t,\ y = 4\cos t + 1$

35. Rewrite as: $x^2 + 4y^2 = 1$

So: $x = \cos t,\ y = \dfrac{1}{2}\sin t;$

$$x = \sin t,\ y = \frac{1}{2}\cos t$$

Chapter 5 Review Exercises, p. 323

Answers to problems are listed as they are found in the solution rather than in numerical order.

1. $\sqrt{2}\cos x + 1 = 0$

$$\cos x = -\frac{1}{\sqrt{2}},$$

$$\hat{x} = 45°$$

$$x = 135°, 225°$$

2. $2\sin(-x) = \sqrt{3}$

$$-2\sin x = \sqrt{3}$$

$$\sin x = -\frac{\sqrt{3}}{2}$$

$$\hat{x} = 60°$$

$$x = 240°, 300°$$

3.
$$\cos x \sin x = 2\sin x$$
$$\cos x \sin x - 2\sin x = 0$$
$$\sin x(\cos x - 2) = 0$$
$$\sin x = 0 \qquad \text{or} \quad \cos x - 2 = 0$$
$$\sin x = 0 \qquad \text{or} \qquad \cos x = 2$$
$$\text{(no solution)}$$
$$x = 0°, 180°$$

4.
$$\tan^3 x - 3\tan x = 0$$
$$\tan x(\tan^2 x - 3) = 0$$
$$\tan x = 0 \quad \text{or} \quad \tan^2 x - 3 = 0$$
$$\tan x = \pm\sqrt{3}$$
$$\hat{x} = 60°$$
$$x = 0°, 180°, 60°, 120°, 240°, 300°$$

5. $\dfrac{1 - \sin x}{1 + \sin x} = 3$

   $1 - \sin x = 3(1 + \sin x)$ *Assume $\sin x \neq -1$.

   $1 - \sin x = 3 + 3\sin x$

   $4\sin x = -2$

   $\sin x = -\dfrac{1}{2},$

   $\hat{x} = 30°$

   $x = 210°, 330°$ *No solution is discarded since $\sin x \neq -1$.

6. $3\sec^2 x - 4 = 0$

   $\sec^2 x = \dfrac{4}{3}$

   $\cos^2 x = \dfrac{3}{4}$

   $\cos x = \pm\dfrac{\sqrt{3}}{2},$

   $\hat{x} = 30°$

   $x = 30°, 150°, 210°, 330°$

7. $2\sin^2 x = 2\cos^2 x - 1$

   $2(1 - \cos^2 x) = 2\cos^2 x - 1$

   $3 = 4\cos^2 x$

   $\cos^2 x = \dfrac{3}{4}$

   $\cos x = \pm\dfrac{\sqrt{3}}{2},$

   $\hat{x} = 30°$

   $x = 30°, 150°, 210°, 330°$

8. $\sin x + 2\cot x = 2\csc x$

   $\sin x + 2\dfrac{\cos x}{\sin x} = \dfrac{2}{\sin x}$

   $\sin^2 x + 2\cos x = 2$ *Assume $\sin x \neq 0$.

   $(1 - \cos^2 x) + 2\cos x = 2$ Obtain one function.

   $\cos^2 x - 2\cos x + 1 = 0$

   $(\cos x - 1)(\cos x - 1) = 0$

   $\cos x - 1 = 0$

   $\cos x = 1$

   $x = \cancel{0}°,$ *This solution must be discarded since $\sin 0° = 0$.

   There is no solution.

9. $\sin x - \cos x = \sqrt{2}$

   $(\sin x - \cos x)^2 = \left(\sqrt{2}\right)^2$ *

   $\sin^2 x - 2\sin x \cos x + \cos^2 x = 2$

   $1 - 2\sin x \cos x = 2$

   $2\sin x \cos x = -1$

   $\sin 2x = -1$ $\quad 0 \leq 2x < 720°$

   $2x = 270°, 270° + 360°$

   $x = 135°, 315°$

   * After checking both answers (as a result of squaring both sides), we get

   $x = 135°.$

10.
$$4\cos^2 x - 4\sin x - 5 = 0$$
$$4(1 - \sin^2 x) - 4\sin x - 5 = 0$$
$$4 - 4\sin^2 x - 4\sin x - 5 = 0$$
$$4\sin^2 x + 4\sin x + 1 = 0$$
$$(2\sin x + 1)^2 = 0$$
$$2\sin x + 1 = 0$$
$$\sin x = -\frac{1}{2},$$
$$\hat{x} = 30°$$
$$x = 210°, 330°$$

11.
$$\cos^2 x - \cos 2x = \sin^2 x + \sin 2x$$
$$\cos^2 x - \sin^2 x - \cos 2x = \sin 2x$$
$$\cos 2x - \cos 2x = \sin 2x$$
$$0 = \sin 2x, \qquad\qquad 0° \le 2x < 720°$$
$$2x = 0°, 180°, 360°, 540°$$
$$x = 0°, 90°, 180°, 270°$$

12.
$$8\sin^4 x - 10\sin^2 x + 3 = 0$$
$$(4\sin^2 x - 3)(2\sin^2 x - 1) = 0$$
$$4\sin^2 x - 3 = 0 \qquad \text{or} \quad 2\sin^2 x - 1 = 0$$
$$\sin x = \pm\frac{\sqrt{3}}{2} \quad \text{or} \qquad \sin x = \pm\frac{1}{\sqrt{2}}$$
$$x = 60°, 120°, 240°, 300°, 45°, 135°, 225°, 315°$$

13.
$$\csc^2 x = \cot x + 1$$
$$1 + \cot^2 x = \cot x + 1$$
$$\cot^2 x - \cot x = 0$$
$$\cot x(\cot x - 1) = 0$$
$$\cot x = 0 \quad \text{or} \quad \cot x - 1 = 0$$
$$\cot x = 1, \hat{x} = 45°$$
$$x = 90°, 270°, 45°, 225°$$

14. $\sin\dfrac{x}{2} = \dfrac{\sqrt{3}}{2}$
$$\frac{x}{2} = 60°, 120° \qquad 0 \le \frac{x}{2} < 180°$$
$$x = 120°, 240°$$

15. $\tan 2x = 1 \qquad\qquad\qquad 0 \le 2x < 4\pi$
$$2x = \frac{\pi}{4}, \frac{5\pi}{4}, \frac{\pi}{4} + 2\pi, \frac{5\pi}{4} + 2\pi$$
$$x = \frac{\pi}{8}, \frac{5\pi}{8}, \frac{9\pi}{8}, \frac{13\pi}{8}$$

16. $2\cos 3x + 3 = 1$

$$\cos 3x = -1 \qquad\qquad\qquad 0 \le 3x < 6\pi$$

$$3x = \pi, \pi + 2\pi, \pi + 2\cdot 2\pi$$

$$x = \frac{\pi}{3}, \pi, \frac{5\pi}{3}$$

17.

$$\cos 2x - \cos x = 0$$
$$2\cos^2 x - 1 - \cos x = 0$$
$$2\cos^2 x - \cos x - 1 = 0$$
$$(2\cos x + 1)(\cos x - 1) = 0$$
$$2\cos x + 1 = 0 \quad \text{or} \quad \cos x - 1 = 0$$
$$\cos x = -\frac{1}{2} \quad \text{or} \quad \cos x = 1$$
$$x = \frac{2\pi}{3}, \frac{4\pi}{3}, 0$$

18.

$$2\sin x + \sqrt{2}\sin 2x = 0$$
$$2\sin x + \sqrt{2}(2\sin x \cos x) = 0$$
$$2\sin x(1 + \sqrt{2}\cos x) = 0$$
$$\sin x = 0 \text{ or } 1 + \sqrt{2}\,\cos x = 0$$
$$\cos x = -\frac{1}{\sqrt{2}}$$
$$x = 0, \pi, \frac{3\pi}{4}, \frac{5\pi}{4}$$

19.

$$2\sin^2 x - 11\cos x = 7$$
$$2(1 - \cos^2 x) - 11\cos x = 7$$
$$2\cos^2 x + 11\cos x + 5 = 0$$
$$(2\cos x + 1)(\cos x + 5) = 0$$
$$2\cos x + 1 = 0 \quad \text{or} \quad \cos x + 5 = 0$$
$$\cos x = -\frac{1}{2} \quad \text{or} \quad \cos x = -5$$
$$\text{(no solution)}$$
$$x = \frac{2\pi}{3}, \frac{4\pi}{3}$$

20.

$$\sin 2x - \sqrt{2}\cos x = 0$$
$$2\sin x \cos x - \sqrt{2}\cos x = 0$$
$$\cos x \left(2\sin x - \sqrt{2}\right) = 0$$
$$\cos x = 0 \text{ or } 2\sin x - \sqrt{2} = 0$$
$$\sin x = \frac{\sqrt{2}}{2}$$
$$x = \frac{\pi}{2}, \frac{3\pi}{2}, \frac{\pi}{4}, \frac{3\pi}{4}$$

21. $\left(\cos\frac{x}{2}\right)^2 + \frac{\sqrt{2}}{2}\cos x = 1 + \frac{1}{2}\cos x$

$$\frac{1 + \cos x}{2} + \frac{\sqrt{2}}{2}\cos x = 1 + \frac{1}{2}\cos x$$
$$1 + \cos x + \sqrt{2}\cos x = 2 + \cos x$$
$$\sqrt{2}\cos x = 1$$
$$\cos x = \frac{1}{\sqrt{2}}$$
$$x = \frac{\pi}{4}, \frac{7\pi}{4}$$

22.
$$13 \cot x + 11 \csc x = 6 \sin x$$
$$13 \frac{\cos x}{\sin x} + \frac{11}{\sin x} = 6 \sin x$$
$$13 \cos x + 11 = 6 \sin^2 x \qquad \qquad \text{*Assume } \sin x \neq 0.$$
$$13 \cos x + 11 = 6(1 - \cos^2 x)$$
$$6 \cos^2 x + 13 \cos x + 5 = 0$$
$$(3 \cos x + 5)(2 \cos x + 1) = 0$$

$$3 \cos x + 5 = 0 \qquad \text{or} \quad 2 \cos x + 1 = 0$$
$$\cos x = -\frac{5}{3} \qquad \qquad \cos x = -\frac{1}{2}$$
(no solution)

$$x = \frac{2\pi}{3}, \frac{4\pi}{3} \qquad \qquad \text{*No solution is discarded since } \sin x \neq 0.$$

23. $(\sin \theta + 1)(\sin \theta - 1) = 0$

$\sin \theta + 1 = 0 \quad$ or $\quad \sin \theta - 1 = 0$

$\quad \sin \theta = -1 \quad$ or $\qquad \sin \theta = 1$

$\qquad \theta = 270°, 90°$

24. $(2 \cos \theta + \sqrt{2})(\cos \theta + 1) = 0$

$$\cos \theta = -\frac{\sqrt{2}}{2} \quad \text{or} \quad \cos \theta = -1$$

$$\theta = 135°, 225°, 180°$$

25. $\sqrt{2} \sin 2\theta \tan 2\theta - \tan 2\theta = 0$

$\tan 2\theta \left(\sqrt{2} \sin 2\theta - 1 \right) = 0$

$\tan 2\theta = 0 \qquad \qquad$ or $\quad \sin 2\theta = \dfrac{1}{\sqrt{2}} \qquad \qquad 0° \leq 2\theta < 720°$

$2\theta = 0°, 180°, 360°, 540° \quad$ or $\qquad 2\theta = 45°, 135°, 405°, 495°$

$$\theta = 0°, 90°, 180°, 270°, 22.5°, 67.5°, 202.5°, 247.5°$$

26.
$$\sin 2\theta + 2 \sin^2 \theta = 0$$
$$2 \sin \theta \cos \theta + 2 \sin^2 \theta = 0 \qquad \qquad \text{Obtain the same multiple of } \theta.$$
$$2 \sin \theta (\cos \theta + \sin \theta) = 0$$
$$2 \sin \theta = 0 \quad \text{or} \quad \cos \theta + \sin \theta = 0$$
$$\sin \theta = -\cos \theta$$
$$\sin \theta = 0 \quad \text{or} \qquad \tan \theta = -1 \qquad \qquad \text{*Assume } \cos \theta \neq 0.$$
$$\theta = 0°, 180°, 135°, 315° \qquad \qquad * \cos \theta \neq 0$$

27. $2 \cos \theta \sin \theta + \sin 2\theta = 2$

$\qquad \sin 2\theta + \sin 2\theta = 2 \qquad \qquad$ Obtain the same multiple of θ.

$\qquad \qquad 2 \sin 2\theta = 2$

$\qquad \qquad \sin 2\theta = 1 \qquad \qquad 0° \leq 2\theta < 720°$

$\qquad \qquad 2\theta = 90°, 450°$

$\qquad \qquad \theta = 45°, 225°$

28. $\sqrt{3}\sec^2 2\theta - 2\sec 2\theta = 0$

$\sec 2\theta \left(\sqrt{3}\sec 2\theta - 2\right) = 0$ $0° \le 2\theta < 720°$

$\sec 2\theta = 0$ or $\sqrt{3}\sec 2\theta - 2 = 0$

(no solution) $\sec 2\theta = \dfrac{2}{\sqrt{3}}$

$\cos 2\theta = \dfrac{\sqrt{3}}{2}$

$2\theta = 30°, 330°, 390°, 690°$

$\theta = 15°, 165°, 195°, 345°$

29. $3\sin^2 x = 1$

$\sin^2 x = \dfrac{1}{3}$

$\sin x = \pm\dfrac{1}{\sqrt{3}}$

$\hat{x} = \sin^{-1}\left(\dfrac{1}{\sqrt{3}}\right) \approx 35.3°$

$x \approx 35.3°, 144.7°, 215.3°, 324.7°$

30. $\cos^2 x - 2 = 0$

$\cos^2 x = 2$

$\cos x = \pm\sqrt{2} \approx \pm 1.4142$

no solution ($|\cos x| \not> 1$)

31. $\cos^2 x = 3\sin x + 2$

$1 - \sin^2 x = 3\sin x + 2$

$\sin^2 x + 3\sin x + 1 = 0$

$\sin x = \dfrac{-3 \pm \sqrt{3^2 - 4(1)(1)}}{2(1)}$

$\sin x \approx -0.3820$ or $\sin x = -2.6180$

$\hat{x} \approx \sin^{-1}(0.3820)$ (no solution)

$\hat{x} \approx 22.5°$

$x \approx 202.5°, 337.5°$

32. $5\sin^3 x = 2\sin x$

$5\sin^3 x - 2\sin x = 0$

$\sin x(5\sin^2 x - 2) = 0$

$\sin x = 0$ or $5\sin^2 x - 2 = 0$

$\sin x = \pm\sqrt{\dfrac{2}{5}}$

$\hat{x} = \sin^{-1}\left(\sqrt{\dfrac{2}{5}}\right)$

$\hat{x} \approx 39.2°$

$x = 0°, 180°, x \approx 39.2°, 140.8°, 219.2°, 320.8°$

33.
$$2\sec^2 x - 5\tan x = 0$$
$$2(1 + \tan^2 x) - 5\tan x = 0$$
$$2\tan^2 x - 5\tan x + 2 = 0$$
$$(2\tan x - 1)(\tan x - 2) = 0$$

$$2\tan x - 1 = 0 \qquad \text{or} \quad \tan x - 2 = 0$$
$$\tan x = \frac{1}{2} \qquad\qquad\qquad \tan x = 2$$

$$\hat{x} = \tan^{-1}\left(\frac{1}{2}\right) \qquad\qquad \hat{x} = \tan^{-1}(2)$$

$$\hat{x} \approx 26.6° \qquad\qquad\qquad \hat{x} \approx 63.4°$$

$$x \approx 26.6°,\, 206.6°,\, 63.4°,\, 243.4°$$

34.
$$6\cot^2 x - 13\cot x + 5 = 0$$
$$(3\cot x - 5)(2\cot x - 1) = 0$$

$$3\cot x - 5 = 0 \qquad \text{or} \quad 2\cot x - 1 = 0$$
$$\cot x = \frac{5}{3} \qquad\qquad\qquad \cot x = \frac{1}{2}$$

$$\tan x = \frac{3}{5} \qquad\qquad\qquad \tan x = 2$$

$$\hat{x} = \tan^{-1}\left(\frac{3}{5}\right) \qquad\qquad \hat{x} = \tan^{-1}(2)$$

$$\hat{x} \approx 31.0° \qquad\qquad\qquad \hat{x} \approx 63.4°$$

$$x \approx 31.0°,\, 211.0°,\, 63.4°,\, 243.4°$$

35.
$$\sec^2 x = \frac{1}{2}\sec x$$

$$\sec^2 x - \frac{1}{2}\sec x = 0$$

$$\sec x\left(\sec x - \frac{1}{2}\right) = 0$$

$$\sec x = 0 \qquad \text{or} \quad \sec x - \frac{1}{2} = 0$$
$$\text{(no solution)} \qquad\qquad \sec x = \frac{1}{2}$$
$$\qquad\qquad\qquad\qquad \text{(no solution)}$$

36.
$$\csc^2 x = 5$$
$$\sin^2 x = \frac{1}{5}$$
$$\sin x = \pm\sqrt{\frac{1}{5}}$$
$$\hat{x} = \sin^{-1}\left(\sqrt{\frac{1}{5}}\right)$$
$$\hat{x} \approx 26.6°$$
$$x \approx 26.6°,\, 153.4°,\, 206.6°,\, 333.4°$$

37. $210° + k \cdot 360°,\ 330° + k \cdot 360°$

38. $30° + k \cdot 180°,\ 150° + k \cdot 180°$

39. $\dfrac{2\pi}{3} + k \cdot 2\pi,\ \dfrac{4\pi}{3} + k \cdot 2\pi$

40. $\dfrac{\pi}{2} + k \cdot \pi,\ \dfrac{\pi}{4} + k \cdot 2\pi,\ \dfrac{3\pi}{4} + k \cdot 2\pi$

41. $35.3° + k \cdot 180°,\ 144.7° + k \cdot 180°$

42. $15° + k \cdot 180°,\ 165° + k \cdot 180°$

43. For $y = 1 + \sin x$, $y = 2\cos^2 x$, we use substitution:

$$1 + \sin x = 2\cos^2 x$$
$$1 + \sin x = 2(1 - \sin^2 x)$$
$$2\sin^2 x + \sin x - 1 = 0$$
$$(2\sin x - 1)(\sin x + 1) = 0$$
$$2\sin x - 1 = 0 \quad \text{or} \quad \sin x + 1 = 0$$
$$\sin x = \frac{1}{2} \quad \text{or} \quad \sin x = -1$$
$$\text{So, } x = \frac{\pi}{6}, \frac{5\pi}{6}, \frac{3\pi}{2}.$$

If $x = \dfrac{\pi}{6}$, $y = 1 + \sin\dfrac{\pi}{6} = 1 + \dfrac{1}{2} = \dfrac{3}{2} \rightarrow \left(\dfrac{\pi}{6}, \dfrac{3}{2}\right)$.

If $x = \dfrac{5\pi}{6}$, $y = 1 + \sin\dfrac{5\pi}{6} = 1 + \dfrac{1}{2} = \dfrac{3}{2} \rightarrow \left(\dfrac{5\pi}{6}, \dfrac{3}{2}\right)$.

If $x = \dfrac{3\pi}{2}$, $y = 1 + \sin\dfrac{3\pi}{2} = 1 - 1 = 0 \rightarrow \left(\dfrac{3\pi}{2}, 0\right)$.

Therefore, the solutions to the system are:

$$\left(\frac{\pi}{6}, \frac{3}{2}\right), \left(\frac{5\pi}{6}, \frac{3}{2}\right), \left(\frac{3\pi}{2}, 0\right)$$

44. For $y = \sin x$, $y = \csc x$

$$\rightarrow \quad \sin x = \csc x$$
$$\sin x = \frac{1}{\sin x} \qquad \text{*Assume } \sin x \neq 0.$$
$$\sin^2 x = 1$$
$$\sin x = \pm 1$$

$$x = \frac{\pi}{2}, \frac{3\pi}{2} \qquad {}^* \sin x \neq 0$$

If $x = \dfrac{\pi}{2}$, $y = \sin\dfrac{\pi}{2} = 1 \rightarrow \left(\dfrac{\pi}{2}, 1\right)$.

If $x = \dfrac{3\pi}{2}$, $y = \sin\dfrac{3\pi}{2} = -1 \rightarrow \left(\dfrac{3\pi}{2}, -1\right)$.

45. For $y = \tan^2 x$, $y = \frac{3}{2}\sec x$

$$\rightarrow \qquad \tan^2 x = \frac{3}{2}\sec x$$

$$\sec^2 x - 1 = \frac{3}{2}\sec x$$

$$2\sec^2 x - 3\sec x - 2 = 0$$

$$(2\sec x + 1)(\sec x - 2) = 0$$

$2\sec x + 1 = 0 \qquad$ or $\quad \sec x - 2 = 0$

$$\sec x = -\frac{1}{2} \qquad\qquad \sec x = 2$$

(no solution) $\qquad\qquad \cos x = \frac{1}{2}$

$$x = \frac{\pi}{3}, \frac{5\pi}{3}$$

If $x = \frac{\pi}{3}$, $y = \tan^2\frac{\pi}{3} = 3 \rightarrow \left(\frac{\pi}{3}, 3\right)$.

If $x = \frac{5\pi}{3}$, $y = \tan^2\frac{5\pi}{3} = 3 \rightarrow \left(\frac{5\pi}{3}, 3\right)$.

46. If $y = \cos^2 x$, $y = \tan x - \sin^2 x$

$$\rightarrow \qquad \cos^2 x = \tan x - \sin^2 x$$

$$\cos^2 x + \sin^2 x = \tan x$$

$$1 = \tan x$$

$$x = \frac{\pi}{4}, \frac{5\pi}{4}$$

If $x = \frac{\pi}{4}$, $y = \cos^2\frac{\pi}{4} = \frac{1}{2} \rightarrow \left(\frac{\pi}{4}, \frac{1}{2}\right)$.

If $x = \frac{5\pi}{4}$, $y = \cos^2\frac{5\pi}{4} = \frac{1}{2} \rightarrow \left(\frac{5\pi}{4}, \frac{1}{2}\right)$.

47–48. *Graphing calculator screens demonstrate "graph intersection method" for one solution.*

47. $x \approx 0.5988, 3.7404$

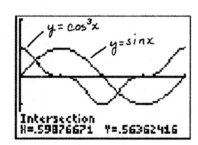

48. $x \approx 1.0182, 5.2650$

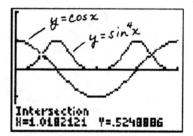

49.

$$x = \sin\frac{1}{2}t$$

$$y = \cos\frac{1}{2}t$$

$$\cos^2\left(\frac{1}{2}t\right) + \sin^2\left(\frac{1}{2}t\right) = 1$$

$$y^2 + x^2 = 1$$

or $x^2 + y^2 = 1$

t	x	y
0	0	1
π	1	0
2π	0	-1

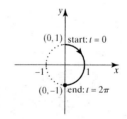

50.
$$\left.\begin{array}{l} \dfrac{x}{3} = \cos t \\[2mm] -\dfrac{y}{2} = \sin t \end{array}\right\} \left(\dfrac{x}{3}\right)^2 + \left(-\dfrac{y}{2}\right)^2 = 1 \text{ or } \dfrac{x^2}{9} + \dfrac{y^2}{4} = 1$$

t	x	y
0	3	0
$\dfrac{\pi}{2}$	0	-2
π	-3	0
2π	3	0

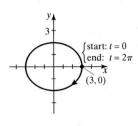

51.
$$\left.\begin{array}{l} x = \tan t \\ y = \tan^2 t \end{array}\right\} y = x^2$$

t	x	y
0	0	0
$\dfrac{\pi}{4}$	1	1

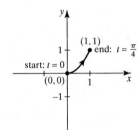

52.
$$\left.\begin{array}{l} x = \cos t \\ y = 1 - \sin^2 t = \cos^2 t \end{array}\right\} y = x^2$$

t	x	y
0	1	1
$\dfrac{\pi}{2}$	0	0

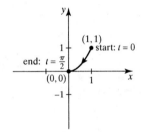

53.
$$\left.\begin{array}{l} x = 4t - 3 \\ y = 6 - 8t = 2(3 - 4t) \end{array}\right\} y = -2x$$

t	x	y
-2	-11	22
0	-3	6
2	5	-10

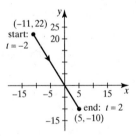

54.
$$\left.\begin{array}{l} x = 2 - \dfrac{1}{2}t \\[2mm] y = 6t \end{array}\right\} y = 6(4 - 2x) \text{ or } y = -12x + 24$$

t	x	y
-4	4	-24
0	2	0
4	0	24

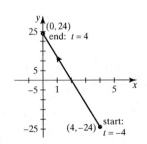

55. $d(t) = 9.5\cos(\pi t)$

$0 = 9.5\cos(\pi t)$, where displacement $d = 0$

$0 = \cos(\pi t)$

$\pi t = \dfrac{\pi}{2}, \dfrac{3\pi}{2}$

$t = \dfrac{1}{2}, \dfrac{3}{2}, 0 \le t < 2$

The displacement is 0 cm at times $\dfrac{1}{2}$ sec and $\dfrac{3}{2}$ sec.

56. For $h = -16t^2 + (1500\sin\alpha)t$, if $h = 1200$ and $t = 2$, then

$$1200 = -16(2)^2 + (1500\sin\alpha) \cdot 2$$

$$\frac{1200 + 64}{3000} = \sin\alpha$$

$$\hat{\alpha} = \sin^{-1}\left(\frac{1264}{3000}\right) \approx 25°$$

The angle of elevation, to the nearest degree to reach a height of 1200 ft in 2 seconds, is 25°.

Chapter 5 Test, p. 325

Answers to problems are listed as they are found in the solution rather than in numerical order.

1. $\sqrt{2}\sin(-x) - 1 = 0$

$-\sqrt{2}\sin x = 1$

$\sin x = -\dfrac{1}{\sqrt{2}}$,

$\hat{x} = \dfrac{\pi}{4}$

$x = \dfrac{5\pi}{4}, \dfrac{7\pi}{4}$

2. $2\cos^2 x - \cos x = 0$

$\cos x(2\cos x - 1) = 0$

$\cos x = 0$ or $2\cos x - 1 = 0$

$\cos x = \dfrac{1}{2}$

$\hat{x} = \dfrac{\pi}{3}$

$x = \dfrac{\pi}{2}, \dfrac{3\pi}{2}, \dfrac{\pi}{3}, \dfrac{5\pi}{3}$

3. $\sin^2 x + 8\sin x = 9$

$\sin^2 x + 8\sin x - 9 = 0$

$(\sin x + 9)(\sin x - 1) = 0$

$\sin x + 9 = 0$ or $\sin x - 1 = 0$

$\sin x = -9$ $\quad\quad$ $\sin x = 1$

(no solution) $\quad\quad$ $x = \dfrac{\pi}{2}$

4. $\sin 2x + \sin x = 0$

$2\sin x\cos x + \sin x = 0$

$\sin x(2\cos x + 1) = 0$

$\sin x = 0$ or $2\cos x + 1 = 0$

$\cos x = -\dfrac{1}{2}$,

$\hat{x} = \dfrac{\pi}{3}$

$x = 0, \pi, \dfrac{2\pi}{3}, \dfrac{4\pi}{3}$

5.
$$\cos \frac{x}{2} = -\cos x$$

$$\pm\sqrt{\frac{1 + \cos x}{2}} = -\cos x$$

$$\left(\pm\sqrt{\frac{1 + \cos x}{2}}\right)^2 = (-\cos x)^2 \qquad *\text{Square both sides.}$$

$$\frac{1 + \cos x}{2} = \cos^2 x$$

$$2\cos^2 x - \cos x - 1 = 0$$

$$(2\cos x + 1)(\cos x - 1) = 0$$

$$2\cos x + 1 = 0 \quad \text{or} \quad \cos x - 1 = 0$$

$$\cos x = -\frac{1}{2} \quad \text{or} \quad \cos x = 1$$

$$x = \frac{2\pi}{3}, \frac{4\pi}{3}, 0$$

$*$ As a result of checking the answers (since we squared both sides of the equation), we get:

$$x = \frac{2\pi}{3}.$$

6. $4\sin x - \csc x = 0$

$$4\sin x - \frac{1}{\sin x} = 0$$

$$4\sin^2 x - 1 = 0 \qquad *\text{Assume } \sin x \neq 0.$$

$$\sin^2 x = \frac{1}{4}$$

$$\sin x = \pm\frac{1}{2}$$

$$x = \frac{\pi}{6}, \frac{5\pi}{6}, \frac{7\pi}{6}, \frac{11\pi}{6} \qquad * \sin x \neq 0$$

7.
$$\frac{\tan 2\theta - \tan \theta}{1 + \tan 2\theta \tan \theta} = -\sqrt{3}$$

$$\tan(2\theta - \theta) = -\sqrt{3}$$

$$\tan \theta = -\sqrt{3}$$

$$\theta = 120°, 300°$$

8. $\cos 2\theta \cos 4\theta + \sin 2\theta \sin 4\theta = \dfrac{1}{2}$

$$\cos(2\theta - 4\theta) = \frac{1}{2}$$

$$\cos(2\theta) = \frac{1}{2}$$

$$2\theta = 60°, 300°, 420°, 660° \qquad 0° \leq 2\theta < 720°$$
$$\theta = 30°, 150°, 210°, 330°$$

9.
$$\cos 2\theta + 2 = 3\cos\theta$$
$$2\cos^2\theta - 1 + 2 = 3\cos\theta$$
$$2\cos^2\theta - 3\cos\theta + 1 = 0$$
$$(2\cos\theta - 1)(\cos\theta - 1) = 0$$
$$2\cos\theta - 1 = 0 \quad \text{or} \quad \cos\theta - 1 = 0$$
$$\cos\theta = \frac{1}{2} \quad \text{or} \quad \cos\theta = 1$$
$$\theta = x = 60°, 300°, 0°$$

10.
$$2\cos^2\theta - \sqrt{2}\sin\theta = 2$$
$$2(1 - \sin^2\theta) - \sqrt{2}\sin\theta = 2$$
$$2\sin^2\theta + \sqrt{2}\sin\theta = 0$$
$$\sin\theta\left(2\sin\theta + \sqrt{2}\right) = 0$$
$$\sin\theta = 0 \quad \text{or} \quad 2\sin\theta + \sqrt{2} = 0$$
$$\sin\theta = 0 \quad \text{or} \quad \sin\theta = -\frac{\sqrt{2}}{2}$$
$$\theta = 0°, 180°, 225°, 315°$$

11.
$$\tan^2 x + 4\tan x = 4$$
$$\tan^2 x + 4\tan x - 4 = 0$$
$$\tan x = \frac{-4 \pm \sqrt{4^2 - 4(1)(-4)}}{2(1)}$$

$$\tan x \approx 0.8284 \qquad \text{or} \quad \tan x \approx -4.8284$$
$$\hat{x} \approx \tan^{-1}(0.8284) \qquad \hat{x} \approx \tan^{-1}(4.8284)$$
$$\hat{x} \approx 39.6° \qquad\qquad \hat{x} \approx 78.3°$$
$$x = 39.6°, 219.6°, 101.7°, 281.7°$$

12.
$$\left(\sin\frac{x}{2}\right)^2 - \cos x = 0.4$$
$$\frac{1 - \cos x}{2} - \cos x = 0.4$$
$$1 - \cos x - 2\cos x = 0.8$$
$$-3\cos x = -0.2$$
$$\cos x = \frac{0.2}{3}$$
$$\hat{x} = \cos^{-1}\left(\frac{0.2}{3}\right)$$
$$\hat{x} \approx 86.2°$$
$$x \approx 86.2°, 273.8°$$

13.
$$10\sin x = 5\csc x + 10$$
$$10\sin x = \frac{5}{\sin x} + 10$$
$$10\sin^2 x = 5 + 10\sin x \qquad\qquad *\text{Assume } \sin x \neq 0.$$
$$10\sin^2 x - 10\sin x - 5 = 0$$
$$5(2\sin^2 x - 2\sin x - 1) = 0$$
$$\sin x = \frac{2 \pm \sqrt{(-2)^2 - 4(2)(-1)}}{2(2)}$$
$$\sin x \approx 1.3660 \quad \text{or} \quad \sin x \approx -0.3660$$
$$\text{(no solution)} \qquad \hat{x} \approx \sin^{-1}(0.3660)$$
$$\hat{x} \approx 21.5°$$
$$x \approx 201.5°, 338.5° \qquad\qquad\qquad *\sin x \neq 0$$

14. $\cot^3 2x = \dfrac{1}{27}$

$\cot 2x = \sqrt[3]{\dfrac{1}{27}} = \dfrac{1}{3}$

$(\widehat{2x}) = \tan^{-1}(3) \approx 71.6°$

$(2x) \approx 71.6°, 251.6°, 431.6°, 611.6°$

$x \approx 35.8°, 125.8°, 215.8°, 305.8°$

15. $y = 3 - 5\sin x, \ y = \cos 2x$

$\rightarrow \qquad\qquad 3 - 5\sin x = \cos 2x$

$\qquad\qquad 3 - 5\sin x = 1 - 2\sin^2 x$

$\qquad 2\sin^2 x - 5\sin x + 2 = 0$

$\qquad (2\sin x - 1)(\sin x - 2) = 0$

$2\sin x - 1 = 0 \quad \text{or} \quad \sin x - 2 = 0$

$\qquad \sin x = \dfrac{1}{2} \quad \text{or} \qquad \sin x = 2$

$\qquad\qquad\qquad\qquad \text{(no solution)}$

$\qquad\qquad x = \dfrac{\pi}{6}, \dfrac{5\pi}{6}$

If $x = \dfrac{\pi}{6}, y = \cos 2\left(\dfrac{\pi}{6}\right) = \dfrac{1}{2} \rightarrow \left(\dfrac{\pi}{6}, \dfrac{1}{2}\right)$.

If $x = \dfrac{5\pi}{6}, y = \cos 2\left(\dfrac{5\pi}{6}\right) = \dfrac{1}{2} \rightarrow \left(\dfrac{5\pi}{6}, \dfrac{1}{2}\right)$.

16. $y = \sqrt{3}\tan x, \ y = \sec^2 x - 1$

$\rightarrow \qquad\qquad \sqrt{3}\tan x = \sec^2 x - 1$

$\qquad\qquad \sqrt{3}\tan x = \tan^2 x$

$\qquad\qquad \tan^2 x - \sqrt{3}\tan x = 0$

$\qquad\qquad \tan x\left(\tan x - \sqrt{3}\right) = 0$

$\tan x = 0 \quad \text{or} \quad \tan x - \sqrt{3} = 0$

$\tan x = 0 \quad \text{or} \qquad\qquad \tan x = \sqrt{3}$

$x = 0, \pi, \dfrac{\pi}{3}, \dfrac{4\pi}{3}$

If $x = 0, y = \sqrt{3}\tan 0 = 0 \rightarrow (0, 0)$.

If $x = \pi, y = \sqrt{3}\tan \pi = 0 \rightarrow (\pi, 0)$.

If $x = \dfrac{\pi}{3}, y = \sqrt{3}\tan\dfrac{\pi}{3} = 3 \rightarrow \left(\dfrac{\pi}{3}, 3\right)$.

If $x = \dfrac{4\pi}{3}, y = \sqrt{3}\tan\dfrac{4\pi}{3} = 3 \rightarrow \left(\dfrac{4\pi}{3}, 3\right)$.

17. **a.** $\qquad\qquad \cos^4 x - \sin^4 x = \dfrac{1}{2}$

$(\cos^2 x + \sin^2 x)(\cos^2 x - \sin^2 x) = \dfrac{1}{2}$

$\qquad\qquad\qquad (1)(\cos 2x) = \dfrac{1}{2}, \qquad\qquad 0 \leq 2x < 4\pi$

$\qquad\qquad\qquad 2x = \dfrac{\pi}{3}, \dfrac{5\pi}{3}, \dfrac{7\pi}{3}, \dfrac{11\pi}{3}$

$\qquad\qquad\qquad x = \dfrac{\pi}{6}, \dfrac{5\pi}{6}, \dfrac{7\pi}{6}, \dfrac{11\pi}{6}$

b. $x = \dfrac{\pi}{6} + k \cdot \pi, \dfrac{5\pi}{6} + k \cdot \pi$

18. **a.** $\cot^2 x = 2\csc^2 x - 2$

$\cot^2 x = 2(1 + \cot^2 x) - 2$

$\cot^2 x = 0$

$\cot x = 0$

$x = \dfrac{\pi}{2}, \dfrac{3\pi}{2}$

b. $x = \dfrac{\pi}{2} + k \cdot \pi$

19. $x = -4\cos t \quad \rightarrow \quad -\dfrac{x}{4} = \cos t$

$\quad y = 4\sin t \qquad\qquad \dfrac{y}{4} = \sin t$ $\left.\begin{array}{c} \\ \\ \end{array}\right\}$ $\left(-\dfrac{x}{4}\right)^2 + \left(\dfrac{y}{4}\right)^2 = 1$, or $x^2 + y^2 = 16$

t	x	y
0	-4	0
$\dfrac{\pi}{2}$	0	4
π	4	0

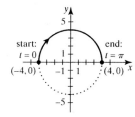

20. $\left.\begin{array}{c} x = t + 1 \\ y = 4t^2 \end{array}\right\} \rightarrow y = 4(x-1)^2$

t	x	y
0	1	0
1	2	4
2	3	16

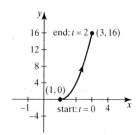

21.   For $d(t) = 2\sin t + \cos 2t - 1$, if displacement is 0, for $0 \le t \le 3$,

$0 = 2\sin t + \cos 2t - 1$

$0 = 2\sin t + (1 - 2\sin^2 t) - 1$

$0 = 2\sin^2 t - 2\sin t$

$0 = 2\sin t(\sin t - 1)$

$2\sin t = 0 \quad \text{or} \quad \sin t - 1 = 0$

$\qquad t = 0 \quad \text{or} \qquad \sin t = 1$

$\qquad\qquad\qquad\qquad t = \dfrac{\pi}{2} \approx 1.57$

The displacement is 0 at times (to the nearest tenth)

$\qquad t = 0\,\text{sec} \ \text{and}\ t = 1.6\,\text{sec}\,.$

22.   The projectile strikes the ground when $y = 0$. So:

$y = -16t^2 + (80\sin 40°)t$

$0 = -16t^2 + (80\sin 40°)t$

$0 = -16t(t - 5\sin 40°)$

$-16t = 0 \qquad\qquad\qquad \text{or} \quad t - 5\sin 40° = 0$

$\quad t = 0\ \text{(start time)} \quad \text{or} \qquad\qquad t = 5\sin 40°$

$\qquad\qquad\qquad\qquad\qquad\qquad\qquad t \approx 3.2$

To the nearest tenth of a second, it strikes the ground in 3.2 seconds.

Chapter 6   Trigonometry Student's Solutions Manual

Exercise Set 6.1, p. 336

1. The triangle method connects the terminal point of **b** with the initial point of **a**; the resultant is determined by the initial point of **b** and the terminal point of **a**.

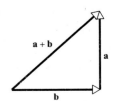

3. The parallelogram method connects the initial points of **b** and **a**; the resultant **a** + **b** has the same initial point and coincides with the diagonal.

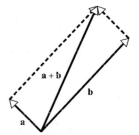

5.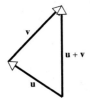

7.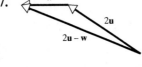

9.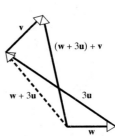

11.

13.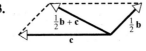

15. We use the parallelogram method and label c the magnitude of the resultant, and the angle the resultant forms with the 6-lb force we label α.
To find c, we use the Pythagorean Theorem.

$$c^2 = a^2 + b^2$$
$$c^2 = 6^2 + 8^2 = 100$$
$$c = 10$$

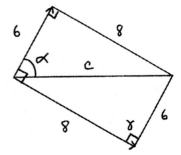

To find α: $\tan \alpha = \dfrac{\text{opp}}{\text{adj}}$

$$\tan \alpha = \frac{8}{6}$$

$$\alpha = \tan^{-1}\left(\frac{4}{3}\right) \approx 53.1°$$

So, the magnitude of the resultant is 10 lb, and it makes an angle of 53.1° with the 6-lb force.

17. We first find β:
$$16.8^2 = 8^2 + 13^2 - 2(8)(13)\cos\beta$$
$$\beta \approx 103.7°$$

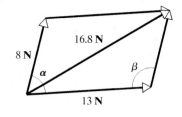

We want α, the angle between the vectors, which is supplementary to β:
$$\alpha + \beta = 180°$$
$$\alpha \approx 180° - 103.7°$$
$$\alpha \approx 76.3°$$

The angle between the 8-N and 13-N forces is 76.3°.

19. We first find β by using the law of sines.
$$\frac{\sin\beta}{30} = \frac{\sin 120°}{50}$$
$$\beta \approx 31.3°$$

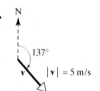

Then $\alpha = 180° - \beta - \gamma$
$$\alpha \approx 180° - 31.3° - 120°$$
$$\alpha \approx 28.7°$$

To find the other force a, we use the law of sines.
$$\frac{a}{\sin 28.7°} = \frac{30}{\sin 31.3°}$$
$$a \approx 27.7$$

So, the force is 27.7 N, and the angle it makes with the resultant is $\beta \approx 31.3°$.

21.

23.

25.

27. We let a represent the speed of the current, and since we have a right triangle, we use the tangent function.
$$\tan 8° = \frac{a}{20}$$
$$a \approx 2.8108$$

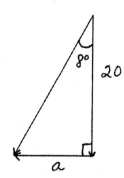

To the nearest tenth of a mph, the current is 2.8 mph.

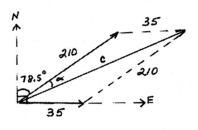

29. We start by drawing the parallelogram in which the magnitude c of the diagonal represents the ground speed and the direction of the diagonal represents the true course.

The angle between the heading of the airplane and the wind is:

$$90° - 78.5° = 11.5°,$$

which means that the adjacent angle in the parallelogram γ is:

$$\gamma = 180° - 11.5° = 168.5°.$$

To find c, we use the law of cosines.

$$c^2 = 35^2 + 210^2 - 2(35)(210)\cos 168.5°$$
$$c \approx \sqrt{59729.8932}$$
$$c \approx 244.4$$

So the ground speed of the airplane is approximately 244.4 mph.
The actual course of the airplane is $78.5° + \alpha$, and we find α using the law of sines:

$$\frac{\sin \alpha}{35} = \frac{\sin 168.5°}{244.4}$$
$$\alpha \approx 1.6361°$$

Thus, the true course bearing is $78.5° + 1.6361° \approx 80.1°$.

31. The heading of the airplane will be determined by $360° - \alpha$, and the air speed will be c:

$$c^2 = 20^2 + 330^2 - 2(20)(330)\cos 45°$$
$$c \approx \sqrt{99966.1905}$$
$$c \approx 316.2$$

So, the air speed should be 316.2 mph.

$$\frac{\sin \alpha}{20} = \frac{\sin 45°}{316.2}$$
$$\alpha \approx 2.6°$$

So, the heading of the airplane should be

$$360° - \alpha \approx 360° - 2.6°$$
$$\text{or } 357.4°.$$

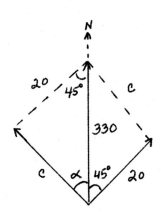

33. We let a represent the magnitude of the force that pulls the car down the ramp.

$$\sin 30° = \frac{a}{4200}$$
$$a = 4200 \sin 30°$$
$$a = 2100$$

So, the magnitude of the force is 2100 lb.

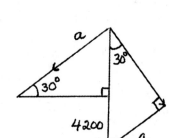

35. To find α: $\sin \alpha = \dfrac{75}{120}$

$\qquad\qquad\quad \alpha \approx 38.7°$

The angle the bench makes with the
horizontal is 38.7°.

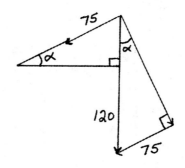

Exercise Set 6.2, p. 348

1. Since $v_1 = 1$ and $v_2 = 1$,

$|\mathbf{v}| = \sqrt{v_1^2 + v_2^2}$

$\qquad = \sqrt{1^2 + 1^2} = \sqrt{2}$

To find θ: $\cos \theta = \dfrac{v_1}{|\mathbf{v}|} = \dfrac{1}{\sqrt{2}}$

$\qquad\qquad \theta = 45°$, since $\mathbf{v}$ is in QI

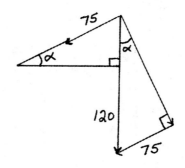

3. For $-6\mathbf{i} - 3\mathbf{j}$, $v_1 = -6$, $v_2 = -3$ and

$|\mathbf{v}| = \sqrt{v_1^2 + v_2^2}$

$\qquad = \sqrt{(-6)^2 + (-3)^2}$

$\qquad = 3\sqrt{5}$

To find θ: $\cos \theta = \dfrac{v_1}{|\mathbf{v}|} = \dfrac{-2}{\sqrt{5}}$

$\qquad\qquad \hat{\theta} = \cos^{-1}\left(\dfrac{2}{\sqrt{5}}\right) \approx 26.6°$

$\qquad\qquad \theta \approx 206.6°$, since $\mathbf{v}$ is in QIII

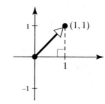

5. $|\mathbf{v}| = \sqrt{v_1^2 + v_2^2}$

$\qquad = \sqrt{(-3)^2 + (4)^2}$

$\qquad = 5$

$\cos \theta = \dfrac{v_1}{|\mathbf{v}|} = \dfrac{-3}{5}$

$\quad \hat{\theta} = \cos^{-1}\left(\dfrac{3}{5}\right) \approx 53.1°$

$\quad \theta \approx 126.9°$, since $\mathbf{v}$ is in QII

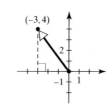

7. $\left.\begin{array}{l} v_1 = |\mathbf{v}|\cos\theta = 3\cos 50° \approx 1.9 \\ v_2 = |\mathbf{v}|\sin\theta = 3\sin 50° \approx 2.3 \end{array}\right\} \rightarrow \mathbf{v} = \langle 1.9, 2.3 \rangle$

9. $\left.\begin{array}{l} v_1 = |\mathbf{v}|\cos\theta = 42\cos 205° \approx -38.1 \\ v_2 = |\mathbf{v}|\sin\theta = 42\sin 205° \approx -17.7 \end{array}\right\} \rightarrow \mathbf{v} = \langle -38.1, -17.7 \rangle$

11. $\left.\begin{array}{l} v_1 = |\mathbf{v}|\cos\theta = 8\cos 60° = 4 \\ v_2 = |\mathbf{v}|\sin\theta = 8\sin 60° = 4\sqrt{3} \end{array}\right\} \rightarrow \mathbf{v} = 4\mathbf{i} + 4\sqrt{3}\mathbf{j}$

13. $\left.\begin{array}{l} v_1 = |\mathbf{v}|\cos\theta = 11\cos 270° = 0 \\ v_2 = |\mathbf{v}|\sin\theta = 11\sin 270° = -11 \end{array}\right\} \rightarrow \mathbf{v} = -11\mathbf{j}$

15. $\left.\begin{array}{l} v_1 = |\mathbf{v}|\cos\theta = 12\cos 225° = -6\sqrt{2} \\ v_2 = |\mathbf{v}|\sin\theta = 12\sin 225° = -6\sqrt{2} \end{array}\right\} \rightarrow \mathbf{v} = -6\sqrt{2}\mathbf{i} - 6\sqrt{2}\mathbf{j}$

17. $\mathbf{v} + \mathbf{w} = (2\mathbf{i} + \mathbf{j}) + (\mathbf{i} - \mathbf{j}) = (2\mathbf{i} + \mathbf{i}) + (\mathbf{j} - \mathbf{j}) = 3\mathbf{i}$
    $3\mathbf{w} - 2\mathbf{v} = 3(\mathbf{i} - \mathbf{j}) - 2(2\mathbf{i} + \mathbf{j}) = (3\mathbf{i} - 4\mathbf{i}) + (-3\mathbf{j} - 2\mathbf{j}) = -\mathbf{i} - 5\mathbf{j}$
    $|\mathbf{v} - \mathbf{w}| = |(2\mathbf{i} + \mathbf{j}) - (\mathbf{i} - \mathbf{j})| = |\mathbf{i} + 2\mathbf{j}| = \sqrt{1^2 + 2^2} = \sqrt{5}$
    $\mathbf{v} \cdot \mathbf{w} = (2\mathbf{i} + \mathbf{j}) \cdot (\mathbf{i} - \mathbf{j}) = (2)(1) + (1)(-1) = 2 - 1 = 1$

19. $\mathbf{v} + \mathbf{w} = \langle -1, 2 \rangle + \langle 0, 5 \rangle = \langle -1, 7 \rangle$
    $3\mathbf{w} - 2\mathbf{v} = 3\langle 0, 5 \rangle - 2\langle -1, 2 \rangle = \langle 2, 11 \rangle$
    $|\mathbf{v} - \mathbf{w}| = |\langle -1, 2 \rangle - \langle 0, 5 \rangle| = |\langle -1, -3 \rangle| = \sqrt{(-1)^2 + (-3)^2} = \sqrt{10}$
    $\mathbf{v} \cdot \mathbf{w} = \langle -1, 2 \rangle \cdot \langle 0, 5 \rangle = (-1)(0) + (2)(5) = 10$

21. $\mathbf{v} + \mathbf{w} = (6\mathbf{i} - 2\mathbf{j}) + (2\mathbf{i} + 6\mathbf{j}) = 8\mathbf{i} + 4\mathbf{j}$
    $3\mathbf{w} - 2\mathbf{v} = 3(2\mathbf{i} + 6\mathbf{j}) - 2(6\mathbf{i} - 2\mathbf{j}) = -6\mathbf{i} + 22\mathbf{j}$
    $|\mathbf{v} - \mathbf{w}| = |(6\mathbf{i} - 2\mathbf{j}) - (2\mathbf{i} + 6\mathbf{j})| = |4\mathbf{i} - 8\mathbf{j}| = \sqrt{4^2 + (-8)^2} = 4\sqrt{5}$
    $\mathbf{v} \cdot \mathbf{w} = (6\mathbf{i} - 2\mathbf{j}) \cdot (2\mathbf{i} + 6\mathbf{j}) = (6)(2) + (-2)(6) = 0$

23. $\mathbf{v} \cdot \mathbf{w} = |\mathbf{v}||\mathbf{w}|\cos\theta$, where θ is the angle between $\mathbf{v}$ and $\mathbf{w}$.
    $= (6)(4)\cos 30°$
    $= 12\sqrt{3} \approx 20.8$

25. The angle θ between the vectors is $130° - 22° = 108°$.
    $\mathbf{v} \cdot \mathbf{w} = |\mathbf{v}||\mathbf{w}|\cos\theta$
    $= (7)(14)\cos 108° \approx -30.3$

27, 29, 31, and 33. *To find θ the angle between the vectors $\mathbf{v}$ and $\mathbf{w}$ we use*

$$\cos\theta = \frac{\mathbf{v} \cdot \mathbf{w}}{|\mathbf{v}||\mathbf{w}|}.$$

27. $\cos\theta = \dfrac{\langle 7, 8 \rangle \cdot \langle -2, 10 \rangle}{|\langle 7, 8 \rangle||\langle -2, 10 \rangle|}$

    $= \dfrac{66}{\sqrt{113}\sqrt{104}}$

    $\theta = \cos^{-1}\left(\dfrac{66}{\sqrt{113}\sqrt{104}}\right) \approx 52.5°$

29. $\cos\theta = \dfrac{(6\mathbf{i} + 2\mathbf{j}) \cdot (4\mathbf{i})}{|6\mathbf{i} + 2\mathbf{j}||4\mathbf{i}|}$

    $\theta = \cos^{-1}\left(\dfrac{24}{\sqrt{40}\sqrt{16}}\right) \approx 18.4°$

31. $\cos\theta = \dfrac{\langle 0, -5\rangle \cdot \langle 9, 0\rangle}{|\langle 0, -5\rangle ||\langle 9, 0\rangle|}$

$\theta = \cos^{-1}\left(\dfrac{0}{45}\right) = 90°$

33. $\cos\theta = \dfrac{(-3\mathbf{i} + 2\mathbf{j}) \cdot (7\mathbf{i} - \mathbf{j})}{|-3\mathbf{i} + 2\mathbf{j}||7\mathbf{i} - \mathbf{j}|}$

$\theta = \cos^{-1}\left(\dfrac{-23}{\sqrt{13}\sqrt{50}}\right) \approx 154.4°$

35, 37, and 39. *The vectors will be orthogonal if their dot product is zero.*

35. $\langle 2, -1\rangle \cdot \langle 1, 2\rangle = (2)(1) + (-1)(2) = 0$
The vectors are orthogonal.

37. $(4\mathbf{i} + 6\mathbf{j}) \cdot (-10\mathbf{i}) = (4)(-10) + (6)(0) = -40$
The vectors are not orthogonal.

39. $(7\mathbf{i}) \cdot (-3\mathbf{j}) = (7\mathbf{i} + 0\mathbf{j}) \cdot (0\mathbf{i} - 3\mathbf{j}) = (7)(0) + (0)(-3) = 0$
The vectors are orthogonal.

41 and 43. $\text{comp}_{\mathbf{w}}\mathbf{v} = \dfrac{\mathbf{v} \cdot \mathbf{w}}{|\mathbf{w}|}$

41. $\text{comp}_{\mathbf{w}}\mathbf{v} = \dfrac{(-5\mathbf{i} + 2\mathbf{j}) \cdot (-2\mathbf{i} + 0\mathbf{j})}{|-2\mathbf{i}|} = \dfrac{10}{2} = 5$

43. $\text{comp}_{\mathbf{w}}\mathbf{v} = \dfrac{\langle 2, 6\rangle \cdot \langle -5, 4\rangle}{|\langle -5, 4\rangle|} = \dfrac{14}{\sqrt{41}} = \dfrac{14\sqrt{41}}{41}$

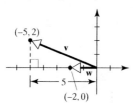

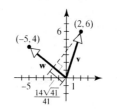

45, 47, and 49. $\text{comp}_{\mathbf{v}}\mathbf{w} = \dfrac{\mathbf{w} \cdot \mathbf{v}}{|\mathbf{v}|}$

45. $\text{comp}_{\mathbf{v}}\mathbf{w} = \dfrac{(-2\mathbf{i}) \cdot (-5\mathbf{i} + 2\mathbf{j})}{|-5\mathbf{i} + 2\mathbf{j}|} = \dfrac{10}{\sqrt{29}} = \dfrac{10\sqrt{29}}{29}$

47. $\text{comp}_{\mathbf{v}}\mathbf{w} = \dfrac{\langle -1, 3\rangle \cdot \langle -3, 4\rangle}{|\langle -3, 4\rangle|} = \dfrac{15}{5} = 3$

49. $\text{comp}_{\mathbf{v}}\mathbf{w} = \dfrac{(10\mathbf{i}) \cdot (3\mathbf{j})}{|3\mathbf{j}|} = \dfrac{0}{3} = 0$

51 and 53. $\overrightarrow{PQ} = \langle q_1 - p_1, q_2 - p_2\rangle = (q_1 - p_1)\mathbf{i} + (q_2 - p_2)\mathbf{j}$

51. For $P(-2, 6)$ and $Q(8, -5)$:

$\overrightarrow{PQ} = \langle (8) - (-2), (-5) - (6)\rangle = \langle 10, -11\rangle$
or $\overrightarrow{PQ} = (8 + 2)\mathbf{i} + (-5 - 6)\mathbf{j} = 10\mathbf{i} - 11\mathbf{j}$

53. For $P(2, -2)$ and $Q(-3, 12)$:

$\overrightarrow{PQ} = (-3 - 2)\mathbf{i} + (12 + 2)\mathbf{j} = -5\mathbf{i} + 14\mathbf{j}$

55. True

57. False; the magnitude of a vector is a scalar.

59. True

61. False; the vector **0** is not the same as the scalar 0.

63. True   **65.** True   **67.** True

69. $W = \mathbf{F} \cdot \mathbf{D}$

$= |\mathbf{F}||\mathbf{D}| \cos \theta$, where θ is the angle between $\mathbf{F}$ and $\mathbf{D}$

$W = (600 \text{ lb})(40 \text{ ft}) \cos 30°$

$\approx 20{,}785 \text{ ft} \cdot \text{lb}$

71. $W = |\mathbf{F}||\mathbf{D}| \cos \theta$, and since the force is being applied in the direction of the motion, $\theta = 0°$.

So, $W = (150 \text{ lb})(2.5 \text{ ft}) \cos 0°$

$= 375 \text{ ft} \cdot \text{lb}$.

73. $\mathbf{D} = \overrightarrow{PQ} = (19 - 2)\mathbf{i} + (25 - 7)\mathbf{j} = 17\mathbf{i} + 18\mathbf{j}$

$W = \mathbf{F} \cdot \mathbf{D}$, where $\mathbf{F} = \mathbf{v} = 2\mathbf{i} + 6\mathbf{j}$

$= (2\mathbf{i} + 6\mathbf{j}) \cdot (17\mathbf{i} + 18\mathbf{j})$

$= (2)(17) + (6)(18)$

$= 142$

So, the work done is $142 \text{ ft} \cdot \text{lb}$.

Exercise Set 6.3, p. 360

1. $(3, 120°)$

3. $(6, 315°)$

5. $\left(4, \dfrac{3\pi}{2}\right)$

7, 9, and 11. *Other answers are possible.*

7.

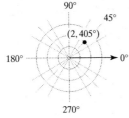

$(2, 45°), (2, -315°)$

9.

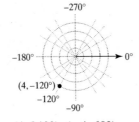

$(4, 240°), (-4, 60°)$

11.

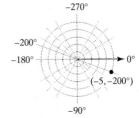

$(5, 340°), (5, -20°)$

13. $x = r \cos \theta$ and $y = r \sin \theta$

$x = 6 \cos \dfrac{\pi}{6}$, $y = 6 \sin \dfrac{\pi}{6}$

$x = 3\sqrt{3}$, $y = 3$

$(x, y) = \left(3\sqrt{3}, 3\right)$

15. $x = r \cos \theta$ and $y = r \sin \theta$

$x = -5 \cos 120°$ $y = -5 \sin 120°$

$x = -5\left(-\dfrac{1}{2}\right) = \dfrac{5}{2}$ $y = -5\left(\dfrac{\sqrt{3}}{2}\right)$

$(x, y) = \left(\dfrac{5}{2}, -\dfrac{5\sqrt{3}}{2}\right)$

17. $x = r \cos \theta$ and $y = r \sin \theta$

$x = 0 \cos 221°$ $y = 0 \sin 221°$

$x = 0$ $y = 0$

$(x, y) = (0, 0)$

19. Point $(5, 0)$, $x = 5$, $y = 0$, is on the positive side of the x-axis.

$$r = \pm\sqrt{x^2 + y^2}$$
$$= \pm\sqrt{5^2 + 0^2} = \pm 5$$

We select $r = 5$.

For θ: $\tan\theta = \dfrac{y}{x} = \dfrac{0}{5} = 0$

$$\hat{\theta} = 0.$$

Since the point is on the positive side of the x-axis, $\theta = 0$

and $(r, \theta) = (5, 0)$.

21. Point $(7, 7)$, $x = 7$ and $y = 7$, is in QI.

$$r = \sqrt{(7)^2 + (7)^2}$$
$$= 7\sqrt{2}$$

For θ: $\tan\theta = \dfrac{y}{x} = \dfrac{7}{7} = 1$

$$\hat{\theta} = \dfrac{\pi}{4}.$$

Since the point is in QI,

$$(r, \theta) = \left(7\sqrt{2}, \dfrac{\pi}{4}\right).$$

23. Point $(-\sqrt{3}, 1)$, $x = -\sqrt{3}$ and $y = 1$, is in QII.

$$r = \sqrt{x^2 + y^2}$$
$$r = \sqrt{(-\sqrt{3})^2 + (1)^2}$$
$$r = 2$$

For θ: $\tan\theta = \dfrac{y}{x} = \dfrac{1}{-\sqrt{3}}$

$$\hat{\theta} = \dfrac{\pi}{6}.$$

Since the point is in QII,

$$(r, \theta) = \left(2, \dfrac{5\pi}{6}\right).$$

25.
$$x^2 + y^2 = 16 \qquad\qquad$$
$$r^2 = 16 \qquad\qquad x^2 + y^2 = r^2$$
$$r = 4$$

27.
$$y = 10$$
$$r\sin\theta = 10 \qquad\qquad y = r\sin\theta$$
$$r = \dfrac{10}{\sin\theta} \qquad\qquad \text{Solve for } r.$$
$$r = 10\csc\theta$$

29. $x^2 + y^2 - 8y = 0$

$$r^2 - 8r\sin\theta = 0 \qquad\qquad x^2 + y^2 = r^2 \text{ and } y = r\sin\theta$$
$$r(r - 8\sin\theta) = 0$$
$$r = 0 \quad\text{or}\quad r - 8\sin\theta = 0$$
$$\rightarrow r = 8\sin\theta \qquad\qquad \text{Contains } r = 0 \text{ when } \theta = 0.$$

31. $r\cos\theta = 8$

$$x = 8 \qquad\qquad x = r\cos\theta$$

33.
$$\theta = \frac{\pi}{6}$$
$$\tan\theta = \frac{y}{x}$$
$$\tan\frac{\pi}{6} = \frac{y}{x}$$
$$\frac{1}{\sqrt{3}} = \frac{y}{x}$$
$$y = \frac{x}{\sqrt{3}} = \frac{\sqrt{3}}{3}x$$

35.
$$r^2 = \csc 2\theta$$
$$r^2 = \frac{1}{\sin 2\theta}$$
$$r^2 \sin 2\theta = 1$$
$$r^2(2\sin\theta\cos\theta) = 1$$
$$2r\sin\theta\, r\cos\theta = 1$$
$$2yx = 1$$
$$y = \frac{1}{2x}$$

$$\theta = \frac{\pi}{6}$$
$$\tan\frac{\pi}{6} = \frac{1}{\sqrt{3}}$$

37.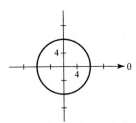

39.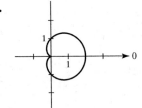

41.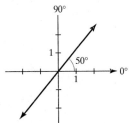

67.
$$r = \cos 3\theta$$
$$r = \frac{1}{2}$$

$$\rightarrow \cos 3\theta = \frac{1}{2}, 0 \le \theta < 2\pi$$

$$3\theta = \frac{\pi}{3}, \frac{5\pi}{3}, \frac{7\pi}{3}, \frac{11\pi}{3}, \frac{13\pi}{3}, \frac{17\pi}{3}, \text{ for } 0 \le 3\theta < 6\pi$$

$$\theta = \frac{\pi}{9}, \frac{5\pi}{9}, \frac{7\pi}{9}, \frac{11\pi}{9}, \frac{13\pi}{9}, \frac{17\pi}{9}$$

For each value of θ, $r = \frac{1}{2}$, so the solutions are (r, θ):

$$\left(\frac{1}{2}, \frac{\pi}{9}\right), \left(\frac{1}{2}, \frac{5\pi}{9}\right), \left(\frac{1}{2}, \frac{7\pi}{9}\right), \left(\frac{1}{2}, \frac{11\pi}{9}\right), \left(\frac{1}{2}, \frac{13\pi}{9}\right), \left(\frac{1}{2}, \frac{17\pi}{9}\right)$$

Exercise Set 6.4, p. 421

1 and 3. *To solve for x and y, for the two equal complex numbers we set the real parts equal, and the imaginary parts equal.*

1. $2x = 2 + x$ and $3y = -4$
   $x = 2$ and $y = -\frac{4}{3}$

3. $6x^2 = 24$ and $-15y = 3 - 2y$
   $x^2 = 4$
   $x = \pm 2$ and $y = -\frac{3}{13}$

5. $(4 - 6i) + (2 - 5i) = (4 + 2) + (-6 - 5)i = 6 - 11i$

7. $(12 - 2i) - (9 - 3i) = (12 - 9) + (-2 + 3)i = 3 + i$

9. $(6 + 6i) - (2 + 9i) = 4 - 3i$

11. $(2 + 5i) + (6) + (2 - i) = 10 + 4i$

13. $(a + bi) + (a - bi) = 2a$

15. $2i(9 - 6i) = 2i(9) + 2i(-6i)$
$$= 18i - 12i^2$$
$$= 12 + 18i \qquad (i^2 = -1)$$

17. $(4 - i)(2 + 6i) = 8 + 24i - 2i - 6i^2$ Use FOIL method.
$$= 8 + 6 + 22i \qquad\qquad\quad i^2 = -1$$
$$= 14 + 22i$$

19. $(2 - 5i)^2 = (2 - 5i)(2 - 5i)$
$$= 4 - 10i - 10i + 25i^2$$
$$= 4 - 25 - 20i$$
$$= -21 - 20i$$

21. $(3 - 2i)(3 + 2i) = 9 + 6i - 6i - 4i^2$
$$= 9 + 4$$
$$= 13$$

23. $(a + bi)(a - bi) = a^2 - abi + abi - b^2 i^2$
$$= a^2 + b^2$$

25. Since $(1 - i)^2 = (1 - i)(1 - i)$
$$= 1 - 2i + i^2$$
$$= 1 - 2i - 1 = -2i,$$
then $(1 - i)^4 = (1 - i)^2 (1 - i)^2$
$$= (-2i)(-2i)$$
$$= 4i^2$$
$$= -4$$

27, 29, and 31. *Rationalize the denominator.* $(i^2 = -1)$

27. $\dfrac{(2 + 3i)}{(4i)} \cdot \dfrac{(-i)}{(-i)} = \dfrac{-2i - 3i^2}{-4i^2} = \dfrac{3}{4} - \dfrac{2i}{4} = \dfrac{3}{4} - \dfrac{1}{2}i$

29. $\dfrac{3i}{(2 - i)} \cdot \dfrac{(2 + i)}{(2 + i)} = \dfrac{6i + 3i^2}{2^2 + 1^2} = -\dfrac{3}{5} + \dfrac{6}{5}i$

31. $\dfrac{(2 + i)}{(2 - i)} \cdot \dfrac{(2 + i)}{(2 + i)} = \dfrac{4 + 4i + i^2}{4 + 1} = \dfrac{3}{5} + \dfrac{4}{5}i$

33. $i^{17} = (i^4)^4 \cdot i^1 = 1 \cdot i = i$

35. $i^{19} = (i^4)^4 \cdot i^3 = 1(-i) = -i$

37. $i^{40} = (i^4)^{10} = 1$

39, 41, 43, 45, 47, and 49. *Using the definition* $\sqrt{-b} = i\sqrt{b}, b > 0$, *rewrite the expressions.*

39. $\sqrt{-81} = i\sqrt{81} = 9i$

41. $\sqrt{-49} + \sqrt{-4} + \sqrt{25} = 7i + 2i + 5 = 5 + 9i$

43. $\sqrt{-9}\left(1 - 2\sqrt{-4}\right) = 3i(1 - 4i) = 3i - 12i^2 = 12 + 3i$

45. $\left(7 - \sqrt{-4}\right)\left(3 + 2\sqrt{-4}\right) = (7 - 2i)(3 + 4i)$
$$= 21 + 28i - 6i - 8i^2$$
$$= 29 + 22i$$

47. $\dfrac{9\sqrt{4}}{\sqrt{-16}} = \dfrac{9 \cdot 2}{4i} = \dfrac{(9)}{(2i)} \cdot \dfrac{(-i)}{(-i)} = \dfrac{-9i}{2} = -\dfrac{9}{2}i$

49. $\dfrac{6}{2 + \sqrt{-9}} = \dfrac{6}{(2 + 3i)} \cdot \dfrac{(2 - 3i)}{(2 - 3i)} = \dfrac{12 - 18i}{4 + 9} = \dfrac{12}{13} - \dfrac{18}{13}i$

51, 53, 55, 57, and 59. *The modulus of* $a + bi = |a + bi| = \sqrt{a^2 + b^2}$.

51. $-1 + 4i \rightarrow a = -1, b = 4$

$|-1 + 4i| = \sqrt{(-1)^2 + 4^2} = \sqrt{17}$

53. $4 + 7i \rightarrow a = 4, b = 7$

$|4 + 7i| = \sqrt{4^2 + 7^2} = \sqrt{65}$

55. $8 - i \rightarrow a = 8, b = -1$

$|8 - i| = \sqrt{8^2 + (-1)^2} = \sqrt{65}$

57. $-8i \rightarrow a = 0, b = -8$

$|-8i| = \sqrt{0^2 + (-8)^2} = 8$

59. $7 \rightarrow a = 7, b = 0$

$|7| = 7$

Exercise Set 6.5, p. 381

1. $r = |\sqrt{3} + i| = \sqrt{\left(\sqrt{3}\right)^2 + 1^2} = 2$

$\tan \theta = \dfrac{1}{\sqrt{3}}$

$\theta = 30°$ θ is in QI

Therefore, $\sqrt{3} + i = 2(\cos 30° + i \sin 30°)$

or $= 2 \operatorname{cis} 30°$.

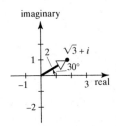

3. $r = |-7 + 7i| = \sqrt{(-7)^2 + (7)^2} = 7\sqrt{2}$

$\tan \theta = \dfrac{7}{-7} = -1$

$\theta = 135°$ θ is in QII

Therefore, $-7 + 7i = 7\sqrt{2} \operatorname{cis} 135°$.

5. $r = |-2 - 2\sqrt{3}i| = \sqrt{(-2)^2 + \left(-2\sqrt{3}\right)^2} = 4$

$\tan\theta = \dfrac{-2\sqrt{3}}{-2} = \sqrt{3}$

$\theta = 240°$ $\qquad\qquad$ θ is in QIII

Therefore, $-2 - 2\sqrt{3}i = 4$ cis $240°$.

7. $r = |-4i| = \sqrt{0^2 + (-4)^2} = 4$

$\tan\theta = \dfrac{4}{0} \to$ undefined

$\theta = 270°$

Therefore, $-4i = 4$ cis $270°$.

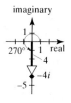

9. $r = |5| = 5$

$\theta = 0°$

Therefore, $5 = 5$ cis $0°$.

imaginary

$5 + 0i$

11. $5(\cos 60° + i\sin 60°)$

$= 5\left(\dfrac{1}{2} + i\left(\dfrac{\sqrt{3}}{2}\right)\right)$

$= \dfrac{5}{2} + \dfrac{5\sqrt{3}}{2}i$

13. $4\cos(135° + i\sin 135°)$

$= 4\left(\dfrac{-\sqrt{2}}{2} + i\left(\dfrac{\sqrt{2}}{2}\right)\right)$

$= -2\sqrt{2} + 2\sqrt{2}i$

15. $\cos 330° + i\sin 330°$

$= \dfrac{\sqrt{3}}{2} + i\left(-\dfrac{1}{2}\right)$

$= \dfrac{\sqrt{3}}{2} - \dfrac{1}{2}i$

17. $9(\cos 270° + i\sin 270°)$

$= 9(0 + i(-1))$

$= -9i$

19. $2(\cos 12° + i\sin 12°) \cdot 5(\cos 33° + i\sin 33°)$

$= 2 \cdot 5[\cos(12° + 33°) + i\sin(12° + 33°)]$

$= 10[\cos 45° + i\sin 45°]$

$= 10\left[\dfrac{\sqrt{2}}{2} + i\left(\dfrac{\sqrt{2}}{2}\right)\right]$

$= 5\sqrt{2} + 5\sqrt{2}i$

21. $3(\cos 200° + i\sin 200°) \cdot \dfrac{1}{3}(\cos 70° + i\sin 70°)$

$= 3 \cdot \dfrac{1}{3}[\cos(200° + 70°) + i\sin(200° + 70°)]$

$= \cos 270° + i\sin 270°$

$= 0 + i(-1)$

$= -i$

23. $8(\cos 110° + i \sin 110°) \cdot 2(\cos 130° + i \sin 130°)$

$= 8 \cdot 2[\cos(110° + 130°) + i \sin(110° + 130°)]$

$= 16[\cos 240° + i \sin 240°]$

$= -8 - 8\sqrt{3}i$

25. $\dfrac{9(\cos 241° + i \sin 241°)}{3(\cos 16° + i \sin 16°)}$

$= \dfrac{9}{3}[\cos(241° - 16°) + i \sin(241° - 16°)]$

$= 3[\cos 225° + i \sin 225°]$

$= -\dfrac{3\sqrt{2}}{2} - \dfrac{3\sqrt{2}}{2}i$

27. $\dfrac{2(\cos 97° + i \sin 97°)}{3(\cos 7° + i \sin 7°)}$

$= \dfrac{2}{3}[\cos(97° - 7°) + i \sin(97° - 7°)]$

$= \dfrac{2}{3}[\cos 90° + i \sin 90°]$

$= \dfrac{2}{3}i$

29. $\dfrac{3(\cos 80° + i \sin 80°)}{7(\cos 140° + i \sin 140°)}$

$= \dfrac{3}{7}[\cos(80° - 140°) + i \sin(80° - 140°)]$

$= \dfrac{3}{7}[\cos(-60°) + i \sin(-60°)]$

$= \dfrac{3}{14} - \dfrac{3\sqrt{3}}{14}i$

31. $[2(\cos 12° + i \sin 12°)]^5$

$= 2^5[\cos(5 \cdot 12°) + i \sin(5 \cdot 12°)]$

$= 32[\cos 60° + i \sin 60°]$

$= 16 + 16\sqrt{3}i$

33.   First we put $1 - i$ in trigonometric form.

$r = |1 - i| = \sqrt{1^2 + (-1)^2} = \sqrt{2}$

$\tan \theta = \dfrac{-1}{1} = -1$

$\theta = 135°$ θ is in QII

So: $(1 - i)^6 = \left[\sqrt{2}(\cos 135° + i \sin 135°)\right]^6$

$= \left(\sqrt{2}\right)^6 [\cos(6 \cdot 135°) + i \sin(6 \cdot 135°)]$

$= 8[\cos 810° + i \sin 810°]$

$= 8[\cos 90° + i \sin 90°]$

$= 8i$

35. $(1 - \sqrt{3}i)^4 \Rightarrow r = 2, \theta = 300°$

$= [2(\cos 300° + i \sin 300°)]^4$

$= 2^4[\cos(4 \cdot 300°) + i \sin(4 \cdot 300°)]$

$= 16[\cos 1200° + i \sin 1200°]$

$= 16[\cos 120° + i \sin 120°]$

$= -8 + 8\sqrt{3}i$

37. $[25(\cos 75° + i \sin 75°)]^{-2}$

$= 25^{-2}[\cos(-2 \cdot 75°) + i \sin(-2 \cdot 75°)]$

$= \dfrac{1}{625}[\cos(-150°) + i \sin(-150°)]$

$= -\dfrac{\sqrt{3}}{1250} - \dfrac{1}{1250}i$

39. $(-2 + 2i)^{-4} \Rightarrow r = 2\sqrt{2}, \theta = 135°$

$= [2\sqrt{2}(\cos 135° + i \sin 135°)]^{-4}$

$= \left(2\sqrt{2}\right)^{-4} [\cos(-4 \cdot 135°) + i \sin(-4 \cdot 135°)]$

$= \dfrac{1}{64}[\cos(-540°) + i \sin(-540°)]$

$= \dfrac{1}{64}[\cos 180° + i \sin 180°]$

$= -\dfrac{1}{64}$

41.   The two square roots of $16(\cos 90° + i \sin 90°)$:

For $k = 0$: $\sqrt{16}\left[\cos\left(\dfrac{90° + 0 \cdot 360°}{2}\right) + i \sin\left(\dfrac{90° + 0 \cdot 360°}{2}\right)\right]$

$= 4[\cos 45° + i \sin 45°] = 4 \operatorname{cis} 45°$

For $k = 1$: $\sqrt{16}\left[\cos\left(\dfrac{90° + 1 \cdot 360°}{2}\right) + i \sin\left(\dfrac{90° + 1 \cdot 360°}{2}\right)\right]$

$= 4 \operatorname{cis} 225°$

43.   The two square roots of $\dfrac{1}{2} + \dfrac{\sqrt{3}}{2}i = 1 \operatorname{cis} 60°$:

For $k = 0$: $\sqrt{1}\left[\operatorname{cis}\left(\dfrac{60° + 0 \cdot 360°}{2}\right)\right] = \operatorname{cis} 30°$

For $k = 1$: $\sqrt{1}\left[\operatorname{cis}\left(\dfrac{60° + 1 \cdot 360°}{2}\right)\right] = \operatorname{cis} 210°$

45.   The three cube roots of $8(\cos 135° + i \sin 135°)$:

For $k = 0$: $\sqrt[3]{8}\left[\operatorname{cis}\left(\dfrac{135°}{3}\right)\right] = 2 \operatorname{cis} 45°$

For $k = 1$: $\sqrt[3]{8}\left[\operatorname{cis}\left(\dfrac{135° + 360°}{3}\right)\right] = 2 \operatorname{cis} 165°$

For $k = 3$: $\sqrt[3]{8}\left[\operatorname{cis}\left(\dfrac{135° + 720°}{3}\right)\right] = 2 \operatorname{cis} 285°$

47.   The five fifth roots of $\left(\dfrac{1}{2} - \dfrac{\sqrt{3}}{2}i\right) = 1 \operatorname{cis} 300°$:

For $k = 0$: $\sqrt[5]{1}\left[\operatorname{cis}\left(\dfrac{300°}{5}\right)\right] = \operatorname{cis} 60°$

For $k = 1$: $\sqrt[5]{1}\left[\operatorname{cis}\left(\dfrac{300° + 360°}{5}\right)\right] = \operatorname{cis} 132°$

For $k = 2$: $\sqrt[5]{1}\left[\operatorname{cis}\left(\dfrac{300° + 2 \cdot 360°}{5}\right)\right] = \operatorname{cis} 204°$

For $k = 3$: $\sqrt[5]{1}\left[\operatorname{cis}\left(\dfrac{300° + 3 \cdot 360°}{5}\right)\right] = \operatorname{cis} 276°$

For $k = 4$: $\sqrt[5]{1}\left[\operatorname{cis}\left(\dfrac{300° + 4 \cdot 360°}{5}\right)\right] = \operatorname{cis} 348°$

49. The two square roots of $100(\cos 100° + i \sin 100°)$:

For $k = 0$: $\sqrt{100}\left[\text{cis}\left(\dfrac{100°}{2}\right)\right] = 10 \text{ cis } 50°$

For $k = 1$: $\sqrt{100}\left[\text{cis}\left(\dfrac{100° + 360°}{2}\right)\right] = 10 \text{ cis } 230°$

51. The four fourth roots of $\left(\dfrac{1}{2} - \dfrac{\sqrt{3}}{2}i\right) = 1 \text{ cis } 300°$:

For $k = 0$: $\sqrt[4]{1}\left[\text{cis}\left(\dfrac{300°}{4}\right)\right] = \text{ cis } 75°$

For $k = 1$: $\sqrt[4]{1}\left[\text{cis}\left(\dfrac{300° + 360°}{4}\right)\right] = \text{ cis } 165°$

For $k = 2$: $\sqrt[4]{1}\left[\text{cis}\left(\dfrac{300° + 2 \cdot 360°}{4}\right)\right] = \text{cis } 255°$

For $k = 3$: $\sqrt[4]{1}\left[\text{cis}\left(\dfrac{300° + 3 \cdot 360°}{4}\right)\right] = \text{cis } 345°$

53. For Exercise 41,

a. $4 \text{ cis } 45° = 4\left[\dfrac{\sqrt{2}}{2} + \dfrac{\sqrt{2}}{2}i\right] = 2\sqrt{2} + 2\sqrt{2}i$

b. $4 \text{ cis } 225° = 4\left[-\dfrac{\sqrt{2}}{2} - \dfrac{\sqrt{2}}{2}i\right] = -2\sqrt{2} - 2\sqrt{2}i$

55. a. $2 \text{ cis } 45° = 2\left[\dfrac{\sqrt{2}}{2} + \dfrac{\sqrt{2}}{2}i\right] = \sqrt{2} + \sqrt{2}i$

b. $2 \text{ cis } 165° = 2[\cos 165° + i \sin 165°] \approx -1.93 + 0.52i$

c. $2 \text{ cis } 285° = 2[\cos 285° + i \sin 285°] \approx 0.52 - 1.93i$

57. To solve $x^4 + 1 = 0$ or $x^4 = -1$, we need four fourth roots of -1.
We first find the trigonometric form:
$$-1 = 1[\cos 180° + i \sin 180°],$$

and then use the extension of DeMoivre's Theorem.

For $k = 0$: $\sqrt[4]{1}\left[\text{cis}\left(\dfrac{180°}{4}\right)\right] = \text{cis } 45° = \dfrac{\sqrt{2}}{2} + \dfrac{\sqrt{2}}{2}i$

For $k = 1$: $\sqrt[4]{1}\left[\text{cis}\left(\dfrac{180° + 360°}{4}\right)\right] = \text{cis } 135° = -\dfrac{\sqrt{2}}{2} + \dfrac{\sqrt{2}}{2}i$

For $k = 2$: $\sqrt[4]{1}\left[\text{cis}\left(\dfrac{180° + 2 \cdot 360°}{4}\right)\right] = \text{cis } 225° = -\dfrac{\sqrt{2}}{2} - \dfrac{\sqrt{2}}{2}i$

For $k = 3$: $\sqrt[4]{1}\left[\text{cis}\left(\dfrac{180° + 3 \cdot 360°}{4}\right)\right] = \text{cis } 315° = \dfrac{\sqrt{2}}{2} - \dfrac{\sqrt{2}}{2}i$

59. Since the equation $x^4 - 2x^2 + 4 = 0$ has quadratic form, we use the quadratic formula to find x^2:

$$x^2 = \frac{-(-2) \pm \sqrt{(-2)^2 - 4(1)(4)}}{2(1)}$$

$$x^2 = \frac{2 \pm \sqrt{-12}}{2} = \frac{2 \pm 2\sqrt{3}i}{2} = 1 \pm \sqrt{3}i$$

For (a) $x^2 = 1 + \sqrt{3}i$ and (b) $x^2 = 1 - \sqrt{3}i$, we need to find the two square roots of each equation.

a. $1 + \sqrt{3}i = 2 \operatorname{cis} 60°$, the two square roots are:

For $k = 0$: $\quad \sqrt{2}\left[\operatorname{cis}\left(\frac{60°}{2}\right)\right] = \sqrt{2}\operatorname{cis}30°$

$$= \frac{\sqrt{6}}{2} + \frac{\sqrt{2}}{2}i$$

For $k = 1$: $\quad \sqrt{2}\left[\operatorname{cis}\left(\frac{60° + 360°}{2}\right)\right] = \sqrt{2}\operatorname{cis}210°$

$$= -\frac{\sqrt{6}}{2} - \frac{\sqrt{2}}{2}i$$

b. $1 - \sqrt{3}i = 2 \operatorname{cis} 300°$, the two square roots are:

For $k = 0$: $\quad \sqrt{2}\left[\operatorname{cis}\left(\frac{300°}{2}\right)\right] = \sqrt{2}\operatorname{cis}150°$

$$= -\frac{\sqrt{6}}{2} + \frac{\sqrt{2}}{2}i$$

For $k = 1$: $\quad \sqrt{2}\left[\operatorname{cis}\left(\frac{300° + 360°}{2}\right)\right] = \sqrt{2}\operatorname{cis}330°$

$$= \frac{\sqrt{6}}{2} - \frac{\sqrt{2}}{2}i$$

So, the four solutions are: $\dfrac{\sqrt{6}}{2} + \dfrac{\sqrt{2}}{2}i, \ -\dfrac{\sqrt{6}}{2} - \dfrac{\sqrt{2}}{2}i, \ -\dfrac{\sqrt{6}}{2} + \dfrac{\sqrt{2}}{2}i, \ \dfrac{\sqrt{6}}{2} - \dfrac{\sqrt{2}}{2}i.$

61. False; $a + bi$ is standard form.

63. True

65. False; $0 + 0i = 0 \operatorname{cis} 0°$.

67. True

69. True

Chapter 6 Review Exercises, p. 389

1. We use the parallelogram method.

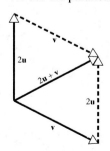

2. We use the parallelogram method.

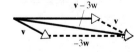

3. We use the triangle method.

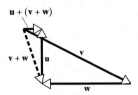

4. We use the triangle method.

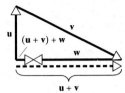

5.

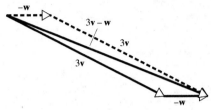

6.

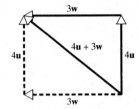

7. To find α, we use the law of sines.

$$\frac{\sin \alpha}{6} = \frac{\sin 135°}{14}$$

$$\alpha = \sin^{-1}\left(\frac{6 \sin 135°}{14}\right)$$

$$\alpha \approx 17.6°$$

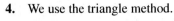

To find the force b, where $\quad \beta = 180° - \alpha - \gamma$

$$\approx 180° - 17.6° - 135°$$

$$\approx 27.4°,$$

we use the law of sines.

$$\frac{b}{\sin 27.4°} = \frac{14}{\sin 135°}$$

$$b \approx 9.10$$

So, the other force is 9.10N, and it makes an angle of 17.6° with the resultant.

8. $\cos 15° = \dfrac{a}{7}$

$$a = 7 \cos 15°$$

$$a \approx 6.8$$

The speed of the swimmer in still water is 6.8 mph.

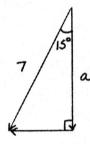

9. Let w represent the magnitude of the wind.

$$w^2 = 430^2 + 400^2 - 2(430)(400)\cos 12°$$
$$w \approx \sqrt{8417.2253}$$
$$\approx 91.75$$

So, the wind speed is 91.75 mph.

To find the wind direction:

$$172° + \beta$$

we use the law of cosines to find β.

$$400^2 = 91.75^2 + 430^2 - 2(91.75)(430)\cos \beta$$
$$\cos \beta \approx 0.4223$$
$$\beta \approx 65.0°$$

So, the wind direction (to the nearest tenth of a degree) is

$$172° + 65.0° = 237.0°.$$

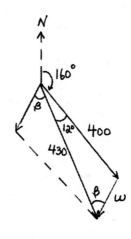

10. $|\langle 7, -7 \rangle| = \sqrt{(7)^2 + (-7)^2} = 7\sqrt{2}$

$\tan \theta = \dfrac{y}{x} = \dfrac{-7}{7} = -1,$

$\hat{\theta} = 45°$

$\theta = 315°$, since θ is in QIV.

11. $|\langle 6\sqrt{2}, 6\sqrt{2} \rangle| = \sqrt{\left(6\sqrt{2}\right)^2 + \left(6\sqrt{2}\right)^2} = 12$

$\tan \theta = \dfrac{y}{x} = \dfrac{6\sqrt{2}}{6\sqrt{2}} = 1$

$\theta = 45°$, since θ is in QI

12. $|-3\mathbf{i} + 6\mathbf{j}| = \sqrt{(-3)^2 + 6^2} = 3\sqrt{5}$

$\tan \theta = \dfrac{y}{x} = \dfrac{6}{-3} = -2$

$\hat{\theta} = \tan^{-1}(2) \approx 63.4°$

$\theta \approx 116.6°$, since θ is in QII

13. $|5\mathbf{i} - 12\mathbf{j}| = \sqrt{(5)^2 + (-12)^2} = 13$

$\tan \theta = \dfrac{y}{x} = \dfrac{-12}{5}$

$\hat{\theta} = \tan^{-1}\left(\dfrac{12}{5}\right) \approx 67.4°$

$\theta \approx 292.6°$, since θ is in QIV

14. $v_1 = |\mathbf{v}|\cos \theta \quad$ and $\quad v_2 = |\mathbf{v}|\sin \theta$
$v_1 = 9\cos 100° \qquad v_2 = 9\sin 100°$
$\approx -1.6 \qquad\qquad \approx 8.9$

So, $\mathbf{v} = -1.6\mathbf{i} + 8.9\mathbf{j}$.

15. $v_1 = |\mathbf{v}|\cos \theta \quad$ and $\quad v_2 = |\mathbf{v}|\sin \theta$
$= 12\cos 310° \qquad = 12\sin 310°$
$\approx 7.7 \qquad\qquad \approx -9.2$

So, $\mathbf{v} = 7.7\mathbf{i} - 9.2\mathbf{j}$.

16. $v_1 = |\mathbf{v}|\cos \theta \quad$ and $\quad v_2 = |\mathbf{v}|\sin \theta$
$= 1\cos 90° \qquad = 1\sin 90°$
$= 0 \qquad\qquad = 1$

So, $\mathbf{v} = \mathbf{j}$.

17. $v_1 = |\mathbf{v}|\cos \theta \quad$ and $\quad v_2 = |\mathbf{v}|\sin \theta$
$= 7\cos 180° \qquad = 7\sin 180°$
$= -7 \qquad\qquad = 0$

So, $\mathbf{v} = -7\mathbf{i}$.

18. $2\mathbf{v} + \mathbf{w} = 2\langle 2, -5 \rangle + (\mathbf{i} + \mathbf{j})$
$= (4\mathbf{i} - 10\mathbf{j}) + (\mathbf{i} + \mathbf{j}) = 5\mathbf{i} - 9\mathbf{j}$
$|2\mathbf{v} + \mathbf{w}| = |5\mathbf{i} - 9\mathbf{j}| = \sqrt{(5)^2 + (-9)^2} = \sqrt{106}$

19. $2\mathbf{v} + \mathbf{w} = 2(6\mathbf{i} + 2\mathbf{j}) + \langle -3, 4 \rangle$
$= 12\mathbf{i} + 4\mathbf{j} - 3\mathbf{i} + 4\mathbf{j} = 9\mathbf{i} + 8\mathbf{j}$
$|2\mathbf{v} + \mathbf{w}| = |9\mathbf{i} + 8\mathbf{j}| = \sqrt{9^2 + 8^2} = \sqrt{145}$

20. $2\mathbf{v} + \mathbf{w} = 2(\mathbf{i} + 4\mathbf{j}) + (9\mathbf{i} - 9\mathbf{j})$
$= 2\mathbf{i} + 8\mathbf{j} + 9\mathbf{i} - 9\mathbf{j} = 11\mathbf{i} - \mathbf{j}$
$|2\mathbf{v} + \mathbf{w}| = |11\mathbf{i} - \mathbf{j}| = \sqrt{(11)^2 + (-1)^2} = \sqrt{122}$

21. $2\mathbf{v} + \mathbf{w} = 2(-3\mathbf{i} + \mathbf{j}) + (\mathbf{i} - 7\mathbf{j})$
$= -6\mathbf{i} + 2\mathbf{j} + \mathbf{i} - 7\mathbf{j} = -5\mathbf{i} - 5\mathbf{j}$
$|2\mathbf{v} + \mathbf{w}| = |-5\mathbf{i} - 5\mathbf{j}| = \sqrt{(-5)^2 + (-5)^2} = 5\sqrt{2}$

22. $\mathbf{v} \cdot \mathbf{w} = \langle 3, -3 \rangle \cdot \langle 10, -8 \rangle$
$= (3)(10) + (-3)(-8) = 54$

23. $\mathbf{v} \cdot \mathbf{w} = (-2\mathbf{i} - 4\mathbf{j}) \cdot (5\mathbf{i} + 7\mathbf{j})$
$= (-2)(5) + (-4)(7) = -38$

24. $\mathbf{v} \cdot \mathbf{w} = |\mathbf{v}||\mathbf{w}|\cos\theta$
$= (10)(4)\cos(107° - 55°)$
$= 40\cos 52°$
≈ 24.6

25. $\mathbf{v} \cdot \mathbf{w} = |\mathbf{v}||\mathbf{w}|\cos\theta$
$= (5)(26)\cos 78°$
≈ 27.0

26. $\cos\theta = \dfrac{\mathbf{v} \cdot \mathbf{w}}{|\mathbf{v}||\mathbf{w}|}$
$\cos\theta = \dfrac{\langle 7, -3 \rangle \cdot \langle -1, -3 \rangle}{|\langle 7, -3 \rangle||\langle -1, -3 \rangle|}$
$\theta = \cos^{-1}\left(\dfrac{2}{\sqrt{58}\sqrt{10}}\right) \approx 85.2°$

27. $\cos\theta = \dfrac{\mathbf{v} \cdot \mathbf{w}}{|\mathbf{v}||\mathbf{w}|}$
$\cos\theta = \dfrac{(-6\mathbf{i} - 2\mathbf{j}) \cdot (10\mathbf{i} - \mathbf{j})}{|-6\mathbf{i} - 2\mathbf{j}||10\mathbf{i} - \mathbf{j}|}$
$\theta = \cos^{-1}\left(\dfrac{-58}{\sqrt{40}\sqrt{101}}\right) \approx 155.9°$

28. $\text{comp}_\mathbf{v}\mathbf{u} = \dfrac{\mathbf{u} \cdot \mathbf{v}}{|\mathbf{v}|}$ and $\text{comp}_\mathbf{u}\mathbf{v} = \dfrac{\mathbf{v} \cdot \mathbf{u}}{|\mathbf{u}|}$

$= \dfrac{(-5\mathbf{i} + 3\mathbf{j}) \cdot (-6\mathbf{i} - 4\mathbf{j})}{|-6\mathbf{i} - 4\mathbf{j}|}$ $= \dfrac{(-6\mathbf{i} - 4\mathbf{j}) \cdot (-5\mathbf{i} + 3\mathbf{j})}{|-5\mathbf{i} + 3\mathbf{j}|}$

$\text{comp}_\mathbf{v}\mathbf{u} = \dfrac{18}{\sqrt{52}} = \dfrac{9\sqrt{13}}{13}$ $\text{comp}_\mathbf{u}\mathbf{v} = \dfrac{18}{\sqrt{34}} = \dfrac{9\sqrt{34}}{17}$

29. $\text{comp}_\mathbf{v}\mathbf{u} = \dfrac{\mathbf{u} \cdot \mathbf{v}}{|\mathbf{v}|}$ and $\text{comp}_\mathbf{u}\mathbf{v} = \dfrac{\mathbf{v} \cdot \mathbf{u}}{|\mathbf{u}|}$

$= \dfrac{(10\mathbf{i} + 4\mathbf{j}) \cdot (8\mathbf{i} - 3\mathbf{j})}{|8\mathbf{i} - 3\mathbf{j}|}$ $= \dfrac{(8\mathbf{i} - 3\mathbf{j}) \cdot (10\mathbf{i} + 4\mathbf{j})}{|10\mathbf{i} + 4\mathbf{j}|}$

$\text{comp}_\mathbf{v}\mathbf{u} = \dfrac{68}{\sqrt{73}} = \dfrac{68\sqrt{73}}{73}$ $\text{comp}_\mathbf{u}\mathbf{v} = \dfrac{68}{\sqrt{116}} = \dfrac{34\sqrt{29}}{29}$

30. $R(-2, 4)$ and $S(7, 12)$

$\overrightarrow{RS} = (7 - (-2))\mathbf{i} + (12 - 4)\mathbf{j}$
$= 9\mathbf{i} + 8\mathbf{j}$

31. $R(8, -2)$ and $S(-6, -3)$

$\overrightarrow{RS} = (-6 - 8)\mathbf{i} + (-3 - (-2))\mathbf{j}$
$= -14\mathbf{i} - \mathbf{j}$

32. $W = |\mathbf{F}||\mathbf{D}|\cos\theta$

$\quad = (50\text{ lb})(200\text{ ft})\cos 35°$

$\quad \approx 8191.52\text{ ft}\cdot\text{lb}$

33.

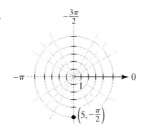

$x = r\cos\theta = 5\cos\left(-\dfrac{\pi}{2}\right) = 0$

$y = r\sin\theta = 5\sin\left(-\dfrac{\pi}{2}\right) = -5$ $\quad\Bigg\} \to (x, y) = (0, -5)$

34.

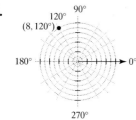

$x = r\cos\theta = 8\cos 120° = -4$

$y = r\sin\theta = 8\sin 120° = 4\sqrt{3}$ $\quad\Bigg\} \to (x, y) = \left(-4, 4\sqrt{3}\right)$

35.

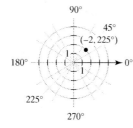

$x = r\cos\theta = (-2)\cos 225° = \sqrt{2}$

$y = r\sin\theta = (-2)\sin 225° = \sqrt{2}$ $\quad\Bigg\} \to (x, y) = (\sqrt{2}, \sqrt{2})$

36.

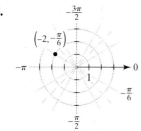

$x = r\cos\theta = (-2)\cos\left(-\dfrac{\pi}{6}\right) = -\sqrt{3}$

$y = r\sin\theta = (-2)\sin\left(-\dfrac{\pi}{6}\right) = 1$ $\quad\Bigg\} \to (x, y) = (-\sqrt{3}, 1)$

37. $(x, y) = \left(-3, \sqrt{3}\right)$, which is in QII.

$\quad r = \pm\sqrt{(-3)^2 + \left(\sqrt{3}\right)^2} = 2\sqrt{3} \qquad (r > 0)$

$\quad \tan\theta = \dfrac{y}{x} = \dfrac{\sqrt{3}}{-3} = -\dfrac{\sqrt{3}}{3}$

$\quad\quad \hat{\theta} = 30°$

$\quad\quad \theta = 150°,\ \theta \text{ is in QII}$

$\quad\text{or } \theta = -210°, \text{ since } -360° < \theta \leq 360°$

$\quad \text{So, } (r, \theta) = \left(2\sqrt{3}, 150°\right), \left(2\sqrt{3}, -210°\right)$

38. $(x, y) = (1, -1)$, which is in QIV.

$\quad r = \sqrt{(1)^2 + (-1)^2} = \sqrt{2}$

$\quad \tan\theta = \dfrac{y}{x} = -1$

$\quad\quad \hat{\theta} = 45°$

$\quad\quad \theta = 315°,\ \theta \text{ is in QIV}$

$\quad\text{or } \theta = -45°, \text{ since } -360° < \theta \leq 360°$

$\quad \text{So, } (r, \theta) = \left(\sqrt{2}, 315°\right), \left(\sqrt{2}, -45°\right).$

39. $(x, y) = (7, 0)$

$r = 7$

$\theta = 0°, 360°$

So, $(r, \theta) = (7, 0°), (7, 360°)$.

40. For $(x, y) = (0, -9)$

$r = 9$

$\theta = 270°, -90°$

So, $(r, \theta) = (9, -90°), (9, 270°)$.

41. $3x^2 + 3y^2 = 12y$

$3(x^2 + y^2) = 12y$

$3r^2 = 12r \sin \theta$ $x^2 + y^2 = r^2, y = r \sin \theta$

$3r(r - 4 \sin \theta) = 0$

$r = 0$ or $r = 4 \sin \theta$

Since $r = 4 \sin \theta$ includes $r = 0$ when $\theta = 0°$, $\Rightarrow r = 4 \sin \theta$.

42. $y = -2$

$r \sin \theta = -2$ $y = r \sin \theta$

$r = -2 \csc \theta$

43. $\theta = \dfrac{7\pi}{4}$

$\tan \theta = \dfrac{y}{x}$

$\tan \dfrac{7\pi}{4} = \dfrac{y}{x}$

$-1 = \dfrac{y}{x}$

$y = -x$

44. $r \cos \theta = 7r \sin \theta + 12$

$x = 7y + 12$ $x = r \cos \theta, y = r \sin \theta$

$x - 7y - 12 = 0$

45. 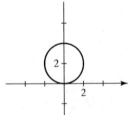 $r = 4 \sin \theta$

46. 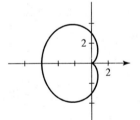 $r = 3 - 3 \cos \theta$

47. 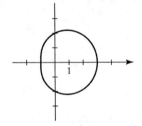 $r = 2 + \cos \theta$

48. 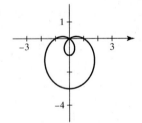 $r = 1 - 2 \sin \theta$

49. $(-3 + 4i) + 6(2 - 5i) = 9 - 26i$

50. $\dfrac{(6 - i)}{(2 + 2i)} \cdot \dfrac{(2 - 2i)}{(2 - 2i)} = \dfrac{12 - 14i + 2i^2}{4 + 4} = \dfrac{10 - 14i}{8} = \dfrac{5}{4} - \dfrac{7}{4}i$

51. $(1 + i)^2 = 1 + 2i + i^2 = 2i$

52. $\left(\sqrt{-4} + \sqrt{25}\right)\left(\sqrt{-9} + 3\right)$
$= (2i + 5)(3i + 3)$
$= 15 + 21i + 6i^2 = 9 + 21i$

53. $i^{33} + i^2 - i^{11}$
$= (i^4)^8 i + i^2 - (i^4)^2 i^3$
$= i - 1 - (-i) = -1 + 2i$

54. $\dfrac{-4}{\left(1 + \sqrt{2}i\right)} \cdot \dfrac{\left(1 - \sqrt{2}i\right)}{\left(1 - \sqrt{2}i\right)} = \dfrac{-4 + 4\sqrt{2}i}{1 + 2} = -\dfrac{4}{3} + \dfrac{4\sqrt{2}}{3}i$

55. $|1 - i| = \sqrt{(1)^2 + (-1)^2} = \sqrt{2}$

56. $|-\sqrt{3} + i| = \sqrt{\left(-\sqrt{3}\right)^2 + (1)^2} = 2$

57. $|-3 - 4i| = \sqrt{(-3)^2 + (-4)^2} = 5$

58. $|-5 + 12i| = \sqrt{(-5)^2 + (12)^2} = 13$

59. $|6 + \sqrt{2}i| = \sqrt{(6)^2 + \left(\sqrt{2}\right)^2} = \sqrt{38}$

60. $|3 - \sqrt{5}i| = \sqrt{(3)^2 + \left(-\sqrt{5}\right)^2} = \sqrt{14}$

61. From Exercise 55, $|1 - i| = \sqrt{2}$.

$\tan \theta = -1$
$\quad \theta = 315°, \theta$ is in QIV

So, $1 - i = \sqrt{2} \operatorname{cis} 315°$.

62. $|-\sqrt{3} + i| = 2$　　　　　See Exercise 56.
$\quad \tan \theta = -\dfrac{1}{\sqrt{3}}$
$\quad\quad \theta = 150°, \theta$ is in QII

So, $-\sqrt{3} + i = 2 \operatorname{cis} 150°$.

63. $|-2 - 2\sqrt{3}i| = \sqrt{(-2)^2 + \left(-2\sqrt{3}\right)^2} = 4$
$\quad\quad \tan \theta = \sqrt{3}$
$\quad\quad\quad \theta = 240°,$ since θ is in QIII

So, $-2 - 2\sqrt{3}i = 4 \operatorname{cis} 240°$.

64. $|-8i| = 8$

$\theta = 270°$

So, $-8i = 8 \operatorname{cis} 270°$.

65. $7(\cos 150° + i \sin 150°)$

$= 7\left(-\dfrac{\sqrt{3}}{2} + \dfrac{1}{2}i\right)$

$= -\dfrac{7\sqrt{3}}{2} + \dfrac{7}{2}i$

66. $\cos 240° + i \sin 240°$

$= -\dfrac{1}{2} - \dfrac{\sqrt{3}}{2}i$

67. $6(\cos 315° + i \sin 315°)$

$= 6\left(\dfrac{\sqrt{2}}{2} + i\left(-\dfrac{\sqrt{2}}{2}\right)\right)$

$= 3\sqrt{2} - 3\sqrt{2}i$

68. $2(\cos 180° + i \sin 180°)$

$= 2(-1 + i(0))$

$= = -2$

69. $3(\cos 88° + i \sin 88°) \cdot 5(\cos 32° + i \sin 32°)$

$= 3 \cdot 5[\cos(88° + 32°) + i \sin(88° + 32°)]$

$= 15[\cos 120° + i \sin 120°]$

$= 15\left[-\dfrac{1}{2} + \dfrac{\sqrt{3}}{2}i\right]$

$= -\dfrac{15}{2} + \dfrac{15\sqrt{3}}{2}i$

70. $7(\cos 40° + i \sin 40°) \cdot 8(\cos 350° + i \sin 350°)$

$= 7 \cdot 8[\cos(40° + 350°) + i \sin(40° + 350°)]$

$= 56[\cos 30° + i \sin 30°]$

$= 28\sqrt{3} + 28i$

71. $\dfrac{15(\cos 209° + i \sin 209°)}{25(\cos 29° + i \sin 29°)}$

$= \dfrac{15}{25}[\cos(209° - 29°) + i \sin(209° - 29°)]$

$= \dfrac{3}{5}[\cos 180° + i \sin 180°]$

$= -\dfrac{3}{5}$

72. $\dfrac{34(\cos 315° + i \sin 315°)}{17(\cos 270° + i \sin 270°)}$

$= \dfrac{34}{17}[\cos(315° - 270°) + i \sin(315° - 270°)]$

$= 2[\cos 45° + i \sin 45°]$

$= \sqrt{2} + \sqrt{2}i$

73. $[3(\cos 45° + i \sin 15°)]^6$

$= 3^6[\cos(6 \cdot 15°) + i \sin(6 \cdot 15°)]$

$= 729[\cos 90° + i \sin 90°]$

$= 729i$

74. $\left(\sqrt{3} - i\right)^6 = [2(\cos 330° + i \sin 330°)]^6$

$= 2^6[\cos(6 \cdot 330°) + i \sin(6 \cdot 330°)]$

$= 64[\cos 180° + i \sin 180°]$

$= -64$

75. $[5(\cos 120° + i \sin 120°)]^{-2}$

$= 5^{-2}[\cos(-2 \cdot 120°) + i \sin(-2 \cdot 120°)]$

$= \dfrac{1}{25}[\cos(-240°) + i \sin(-240°)]$

$= \dfrac{1}{25}\left[-\dfrac{1}{2} + \dfrac{\sqrt{3}}{2}i\right]$

$= -\dfrac{1}{50} + \dfrac{\sqrt{3}}{50}i$

76. $(6 + 6i)^{-3} = \left[6\sqrt{2}(\cos 45° + i \sin 45°)\right]^{-3}$

$= \left(6\sqrt{2}\right)^{-3}[\cos(-3 \cdot 45°) + i \sin(-3 \cdot 45°)]$

$= \dfrac{1}{432\sqrt{2}}[\cos(-135°) + i \sin(-135°)]$

$= \dfrac{1}{432\sqrt{2}}\left[-\dfrac{\sqrt{2}}{2} - \dfrac{\sqrt{2}}{2}i\right]$

$= -\dfrac{1}{864} - \dfrac{1}{864}i$

77.   The three cube roots of $216(\cos 27° + i \sin 27°)$:

For $k = 0$: $\sqrt[3]{216}\left[\text{cis}\left(\dfrac{27°}{3}\right)\right] = 6\text{cis}9°$

For $k = 1$: $\sqrt[3]{216}\left[\text{cis}\left(\dfrac{27° + 360°}{3}\right)\right] = 6\text{ cis } 129°$

For $k = 2$: $\sqrt[3]{216}\left[\text{cis}\left(\dfrac{27° + 2 \cdot 360°}{3}\right)\right] = 6\text{ cis } 249°$

78.   The two square roots of $\dfrac{1}{2} - \dfrac{\sqrt{3}}{2}i = \text{cis } 300°$:

For $k = 0$: $\text{cis}\left(\dfrac{300°}{2}\right) = \text{cis } 150°$

For $k = 1$: $\text{cis}\left(\dfrac{300° + 360°}{2}\right) = \text{cis } 330°$

79. $x^2 + 4i = 0$

      $x^2 = -4i$

We need two square roots of $-4i = 4\text{ cis } 270°$:

For $k = 0$: $\sqrt{4}\text{ cis}\left(\dfrac{270°}{2}\right) = 2\text{ cis } 135°$

For $k = 1$: $\sqrt{4}\text{ cis}\left(\dfrac{270° + 360°}{2}\right) = 2\text{ cis } 315°$

80. $x^3 = 1$

We need three cube roots of $1 = 1 \text{ cis } 0°$:

For $k = 0$: $\sqrt[3]{1}\left[\text{cis}\left(\dfrac{0°}{3}\right)\right] = 1 \text{ cis } 0° = 1$

For $k = 1$: $\sqrt[3]{1}\left[\text{cis}\left(\dfrac{0° + 360°}{3}\right)\right] = \text{cis } 120°$

$$= -\frac{1}{2} + \frac{\sqrt{3}}{2}i$$

For $k = 2$: $\sqrt[3]{1}\left[\text{cis}\left(\dfrac{0° + 2 \cdot 360°}{3}\right)\right] = \text{cis } 240°$

$$= -\frac{1}{2} - \frac{\sqrt{3}}{2}i$$

Chapter 6 Test, p. 391

1. a.

b.

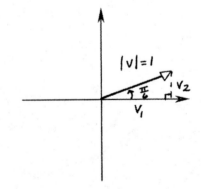

2. a. $\left|4\mathbf{i} - 6\mathbf{j}\right| = \sqrt{(4)^2 + (-6)^2} = 2\sqrt{13}$

$$\tan\theta = \frac{-6}{4}$$

$$\hat{\theta} = \tan^{-1}\left(\frac{3}{2}\right) \approx 56.3°$$

$$\theta \approx 303.7°, \theta \text{ is in QIV}$$

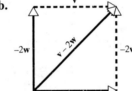

b. $\left|\langle -3, 6\rangle\right| = \sqrt{(-3)^2 + 6^2} = 3\sqrt{5}$

$$\tan\theta = \frac{6}{-3} = -2$$

$$\hat{\theta} = \tan^{-1}(2) \approx 63.4°$$

$$\hat{\theta} \approx 116.6°, \theta \text{ is in QII}$$

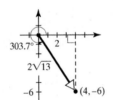

3. a. $v_1 = |\mathbf{v}|\cos\theta$ and $v_2 = |\mathbf{v}|\sin\theta$

$$= (1)\cos\frac{\pi}{6} \qquad = (1)\sin\frac{\pi}{6}$$

$$= \frac{\sqrt{3}}{2} \qquad\qquad = \frac{1}{2}$$

So, $\mathbf{v} = \dfrac{\sqrt{3}}{2}\mathbf{i} + \dfrac{1}{2}\mathbf{j}$

$$\approx 0.9\mathbf{i} + 0.5\mathbf{j}.$$

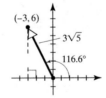

b. $v_1 = |\mathbf{v}| \cos\theta$ and $v_2 = |\mathbf{v}| \sin\theta$

$\qquad = (5) \cos 138°$ $\qquad = (5) \sin 138°$

$\qquad \approx -3.7$ $\qquad \approx 3.3$

So, $\mathbf{v} \approx -3.7\mathbf{i} + 3.3\mathbf{j}$.

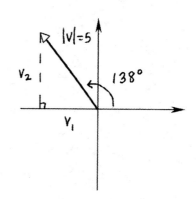

4. a. $2\mathbf{v} - 4(\mathbf{u} + \mathbf{w})$

$\qquad = 2(2\mathbf{i} - \mathbf{j}) - 4((4\mathbf{i} + 8\mathbf{j}) + (-3\mathbf{j}))$

$\qquad = 4\mathbf{i} - 2\mathbf{j} - 4(4\mathbf{i} + 5\mathbf{j})$

$\qquad = -12\mathbf{i} - 22\mathbf{j}$

b. $\mathbf{v} \cdot \mathbf{w} = (2\mathbf{i} - \mathbf{j}) \cdot (-3\mathbf{j})$

$\qquad = (2)(0) + (-1)(-3)$

$\qquad = 3$

c. $\cos\theta = \dfrac{\mathbf{u} \cdot \mathbf{w}}{|\mathbf{u}||\mathbf{w}|}$

$\qquad \cos\theta = \dfrac{(4\mathbf{i} + 8\mathbf{j}) \cdot (-3\mathbf{j})}{|4\mathbf{i} + 8\mathbf{j}||-3\mathbf{j}|}$

$\qquad \theta = \cos^{-1}\left(\dfrac{-24}{\sqrt{80 \cdot 3}}\right) \approx 153.4°$

d. $\text{comp}_{\mathbf{v}}\mathbf{w} = \dfrac{\mathbf{w} \cdot \mathbf{v}}{|\mathbf{v}|}$

$\qquad = \dfrac{(-3\mathbf{j}) \cdot (2\mathbf{i} - \mathbf{j})}{|2\mathbf{i} - \mathbf{j}|}$

$\qquad = \dfrac{3}{\sqrt{5}} = \dfrac{3\sqrt{5}}{5}$

e. $|\mathbf{v} - \mathbf{u}| = |(2\mathbf{i} - \mathbf{j}) - (4\mathbf{i} + 8\mathbf{j})|$

$\qquad = |-2\mathbf{i} - 9\mathbf{j}|$

$\qquad = \sqrt{(-2)^2 + (-9)^2}$

$\qquad = \sqrt{85}$

5. $\mathbf{v} \cdot \mathbf{w} = |\mathbf{v}||\mathbf{w}| \cos\theta$

$\qquad = (8)(3) \cos 120°$

$\qquad = -12$

6. To find c, use the law of cosines.

$\qquad c^2 = 12^2 + 3^2 - 2(12)(3) \cos 160°$

$\qquad c \approx \sqrt{220.6579}$

$\qquad \approx 14.9$

So the resultant is a 14.9-lb force.

To find β, use the law of sines.

$\qquad \dfrac{\sin\beta}{12} = \dfrac{\sin 160°}{14.9}$

$\qquad \sin\beta \approx 0.2755$

$\qquad \beta \approx 16.0°$

The resultant makes an angle of 16.0° with the 3-lb force.

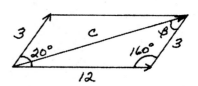

7. $c^2 = 500^2 + 100^2 - 2(500)(100) \cos 150°$

$c \approx \sqrt{346602.5404}$

$c \approx 588.7$

So the ground speed, to the nearest mile, is 589 mph.

To find the true course of the airplane, $180° + \alpha$, we find α using the law of sines.

$$\frac{\sin \alpha}{500} = \frac{\sin 150°}{588.7}$$

$$\sin \alpha \approx 0.4247$$

$$\alpha \approx 25.1°$$

Therefore, the true course (to the nearest tenth of a degree) is

$$180° + 25.1° = 205.1°.$$

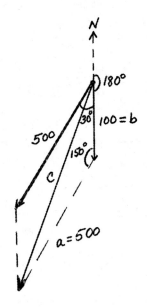

8. a. If $(r, \theta) = (3, 120°)$:

$x = r \cos \theta$ and $y = r \sin \theta$

$x = (3) \cos 120°$ $\qquad = (3) \sin 120°$

$\quad = -\dfrac{3}{2}$ $\qquad\qquad = \dfrac{3\sqrt{3}}{2}$

So, $(x, y) = \left(-\dfrac{3}{2}, \dfrac{3\sqrt{3}}{2}\right)$.

b. If $(r, \theta) = (-4, 45°)$:

$x = r \cos \theta$ and $y = r \sin \theta$

$\quad = (-4) \cos 45°$ $\qquad = (-4) \sin 45°$

$\quad = -2\sqrt{2}$ $\qquad\qquad = -2\sqrt{2}$

So, $(x, y) = \left(-2\sqrt{2}, -2\sqrt{2}\right)$.

9. *Other answers are possible.*

a. If $(x, y) = (10, -10)$, the point is in QIV.

$$r = \pm\sqrt{(10)^2 + (-10)^2} = \pm10\sqrt{2}$$

We select $r = 10\sqrt{2}$.

$$\tan \theta = \frac{-10}{10} = -1$$

$$\hat{\theta} = 45°$$

$\theta = 315°, -45°$, since $-360° < \theta \leq 360°$

So, $(r, \theta) = \left(10\sqrt{2}, 315°\right), \left(10\sqrt{2}, -45°\right)$.

b. If $(x, y) = \left(5\sqrt{3}, 5\right)$, the point is in QI.

$$r = \pm\sqrt{\left(5\sqrt{3}\right)^2 + 5^2} = \pm10$$

We select $r = 10$.

$$\tan \theta = \frac{5}{5\sqrt{3}} = \frac{1}{\sqrt{3}}$$

$$\hat{\theta} = 30°$$

$\theta = 30°, -330°$, since $-360° < \theta \leq 360°$

So, $(r, \theta) = (10, 30°), (10, -330°)$.

10. a. $x^2 + y^2 = 25$
$$r^2 = 25$$
$$r = 5 \text{ (or } r = -5)$$

b. $y = -1$
$$r \sin \theta = -1$$
$$r = -\csc \theta$$

11. a. $r = 3 \cos \theta$
$$r^2 = 3r \cos \theta$$
$$x^2 + y^2 = 3x$$
$$x^2 + y^2 - 3x = 0$$

b. $r = \dfrac{5}{\cos \theta}$
$$r \cos \theta = 5$$
$$x = 5$$

12. a. $(-4 + 2i) - 3(2 + i)$
$$= -4 + 2i - 6 - 3i$$
$$= -10 - i$$

b. $\sqrt{-25}(4 - 2i)$
$$= 5i(4 - 2i)$$
$$= 20i - 10i^2$$
$$= 10 + 20i$$

13. a. $2 - 2i \rightarrow r = \sqrt{(2)^2 + (-2)^2} = 2\sqrt{2}$
$$\tan \theta = \frac{-2}{2} = -1$$
$$\hat{\theta} = 45°$$
$$\theta = 315°, \text{ since } \theta \text{ is in QIV}$$
So, $2 - 2i = 2\sqrt{2} \text{ cis } 315°$.

b. $6i = 6 \text{ cis } 90°$

14. a. $4(\cos 45° + i \sin 45°)$
$$= 4\left(\frac{\sqrt{2}}{2} + \frac{\sqrt{2}}{2}i\right)$$
$$= 2\sqrt{2} + 2\sqrt{2}i$$

b. $\sqrt{3}(\cos 60° + i \sin 60°)$
$$= \sqrt{3}\left(\frac{1}{2} + \frac{\sqrt{3}}{2}i\right)$$
$$= \frac{\sqrt{3}}{2} + \frac{3}{2}i$$

c. $9(\cos 90° + i \sin 90°) \cdot \dfrac{1}{3}(\cos 180° + i \sin 180°)$
$$= 9 \cdot \frac{1}{3}[\cos(90° + 180°) + i \sin(90° + 180°)]$$
$$= 3[\cos 270° + i \sin 270°]$$
$$= -3i$$

d. $\dfrac{12(\cos 217° + i \sin 217°)}{6(\cos 67° + i \sin 67°)}$
$$= \frac{12}{6}[\cos(217° - 67°) + i \sin(217° - 67°)]$$
$$= 2[\cos 150° + i \sin 150°]$$
$$= 2\left[-\frac{\sqrt{3}}{2} + \frac{1}{2}i\right]$$
$$= -\sqrt{3} + i$$

15. a. $[2(\cos 30° + i \sin 30°)]^6$

$= 2^6[\cos(6 \cdot 30°) + i \sin(6 \cdot 30°)]$

$= 64[\cos 180° + i \sin 180°]$

$= -64$

b. $(1 + \sqrt{3}i)^9 = [2(\cos 60° + i \sin 60°)]^9$

$= 2^9[\cos(9 \cdot 60°) + i \sin(9 \cdot 60°)]$

$= 512[\cos 180° + i \sin 180°]$

$= -512$

16. a. $x^2 + 9i = 0$

$\qquad x^2 = -9i$

We need the two square roots of $-9i = 9 \text{ cis } 270°$.

For $k = 0$: $\sqrt{9} \text{ cis } \left(\dfrac{270°}{2}\right) = 3 \text{ cis } 135°$

For $k = 1$: $\sqrt{9} \text{ cis } \left(\dfrac{270° + 360°}{2}\right) = 3 \text{ cis } 315°$

b. $x^4 + 1 = 0$

$\qquad x^4 = -1$

We need the four fourth roots of $-1 = 1 \text{ cis } 180°$.

For $k = 0$: $\sqrt[4]{1} \text{ cis } \left(\dfrac{180°}{4}\right) = \text{cis } 45°$

For $k = 1$: $\sqrt[4]{1} \text{ cis } \left(\dfrac{180° + 360°}{4}\right) = \text{cis } 135°$

For $k = 2$: $\sqrt[4]{1} \text{ cis } \left(\dfrac{180° + 2 \cdot 360°}{4}\right) = \text{cis } 225°$

For $k = 3$: $\sqrt[4]{1} \text{ cis } \left(\dfrac{180° + 3 \cdot 360°}{4}\right) = \text{cis } 315°$

Trigonometry Student's Solutions Manual, Chapters 1–6

Cumulative Review, p. 393

1. a. Values are given counterclockwise from $(1, 0)$:

$$\left(\frac{\sqrt{3}}{2}, \frac{1}{2}\right), \left(\frac{\sqrt{2}}{2}, \frac{\sqrt{2}}{2}\right), \left(\frac{1}{2}, \frac{\sqrt{3}}{2}\right), (0, 1), (-1, 0), (0, -1)$$

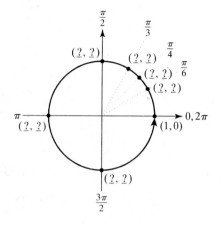

b.

x	$\cos x$	$\csc x$	$\tan x$
0	1	undefined	0
$\dfrac{\pi}{6}$	$\dfrac{\sqrt{3}}{2}$	2	$\dfrac{\sqrt{3}}{3}$
$45°$	$\dfrac{\sqrt{2}}{2}$	$\sqrt{2}$	1
$60°$	$\dfrac{1}{2}$	$\dfrac{2\sqrt{3}}{3}$	$\sqrt{3}$
$\dfrac{\pi}{2}$	0	1	undefined
π	-1	undefined	0
$\dfrac{3\pi}{2}$	0	-1	undefined
$360°$	1	undefined	0

2. a. QIV   **b.** $\dfrac{5}{3}$ **c.** -1 **d.** $-\dfrac{7}{25}$

   e. $\dfrac{24}{7}$ **f.** $-\dfrac{7\sqrt{2}}{10}$ **g.** QII   **h.** $-\dfrac{2\sqrt{5}}{5}$

3. a. $P = 4\pi,\ A = 3$ **b.** $P = \dfrac{\pi}{2}$, asymptotes: $x = \dfrac{\pi}{4} + k \cdot \dfrac{\pi}{2}$

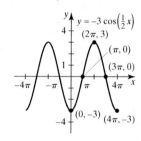

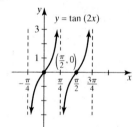

4. a. $y = -4\sin(2x),\ y = 4\sin\left[2\left(x - \dfrac{\pi}{2}\right)\right]$ **b.** $y = 3\sec(2x),\ y = 3\csc\left[2\left(x + \dfrac{\pi}{4}\right)\right]$

5. a. $y = \arcsin x$ **b.** $y = \tan^{-1} x$ **c.** $y = \arccos x$

6. a. $\dfrac{\sqrt{2}}{2}$ **b.** $-\dfrac{\sqrt{3}}{2}$ **c.** $-\dfrac{\sqrt{2}}{2}$ **d.** $-\dfrac{2\sqrt{3}}{3}$

e. 1 **f.** $-\dfrac{\pi}{4}$ **g.** $\dfrac{1}{2}$ **h.** $78.9°$

i. $\dfrac{3\sqrt{3}-2\sqrt{2}}{2}$ **j.** $\dfrac{4}{5}$ **k.** $120°$ or $\dfrac{2\pi}{3}$ **l.** $45°$ or $\dfrac{\pi}{4}$

7. 13.1 in.

8. a. -4.5 cm   **b.** 1.8 sec

9. $\dfrac{\tan 360° - \tan x}{1 + \tan 360° \tan x} = -\tan x$

$\dfrac{0 - \tan x}{1 + 0} =$

$-\tan x =$

10. $\dfrac{\sqrt{2+\sqrt{3}}}{2}$ or $\dfrac{\sqrt{6}+\sqrt{2}}{4}$

11. a. $\sin^2 x = 1 - \cos^2 x$ **b.** $\sec^2 x = 1 + \tan^2 x$ **c.** $\cos^2 \dfrac{x}{2} = \dfrac{1+\cos x}{2}$

d. $\sin 2x = 2\sin x \cos x$ **e.** $2\cos^2 x - 1 = \cos 2x$ **f.** $\tan(-x) = -\tan x = \dfrac{-1}{\cot x}$

12. a.

$2\left(\cos \dfrac{x}{2}\right)^2 - \cos x = 1$

$2\left(\dfrac{1+\cos x}{2}\right) - \cos x =$

$1 + \cos x - \cos x =$

$1 =$

b.

$\dfrac{\sin 5x \cos 3x - \cos 5x \sin 3x}{\cos 2x + 1} = \sin x \sec x$

$\dfrac{\sin(5x - 3x)}{(2\cos^2 x - 1) + 1} =$

$\dfrac{2\sin x \cos x}{2\cos^2 x} =$

$\dfrac{\sin x}{\cos x} =$

$\sin x \sec x =$

c.

$\sec^2 \theta + \csc^2 \theta = \sec^2 \theta \csc^2 \theta$

$\dfrac{1}{\cos^2 \theta} + \dfrac{1}{\sin^2 \theta} =$

$\dfrac{\sin^2 \theta + \cos^2 \theta}{\sin^2 \theta \cos \theta} =$

$\dfrac{1}{\sin^2 \theta \cos^2 \theta} =$

$\dfrac{1}{\sin^2 \theta} \cdot \dfrac{1}{\cos^2 \theta} =$

$\sec^2 \theta \csc^2 \theta =$

d. Let $x = \pi$.

$\sin x + \cos x = 1$

$\sin \pi + \cos \pi \neq 1$

$0 + (-1) \neq 1$

13. a. $60°, 300°$ **b.** $0°, 180°$ **c.** $0°, 90°, 180°, 270°$

d. $36.2°, 143.8°$ **e.** $60°, 300°$ **f.** $90°, 180°$

g. $90°, 210°, 330°$

14. a. $\dfrac{3\pi}{4}, \dfrac{5\pi}{4}$ **b.** $\dfrac{\pi}{8}, \dfrac{5\pi}{8}, \dfrac{9\pi}{8}, \dfrac{13\pi}{8}$ **c.** $\dfrac{\pi}{2}$

15. 6.70 ft

16. $a = 5, b = 10, c = 5\sqrt{3}, \alpha = 30°, \beta = 90°, \gamma = 60°$

17.

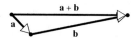

Triangle method

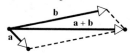

Parallelogram method

18. a. $-5\mathbf{i} + 5\mathbf{j}$ **b.**   **c.** Yes

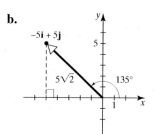

19. a. $4\mathbf{i} + 10\mathbf{j}$ **b.** 0   **c.** 90°

   d. 8.1°   **e.** 5   **f.** $\dfrac{\sqrt{2}}{2}$

20. 10.6 lb, 40.9°   **21.** 346.0 mph, 3.5°

22. a.   **b.** $(2, 315°), (-2, 135°)$ **c.** $\left(\sqrt{2}, -\sqrt{2}\right)$

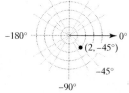

23. a. $(12, 120°)$ **b.** $r^2 + 6r \sin\theta = 7$

24. $x^2 + y^2 - 3x = 0$

25. a. $r = 1 + \sin\theta$ **b.** $r = \sin 2\theta$

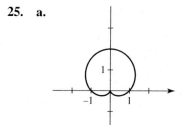

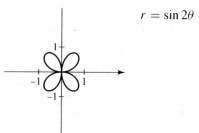

26. a. $r = 2$ **b.** $r = 2\cos\theta$ **c.** $r = 1 + 2\cos\theta$

27. $\left(\dfrac{x}{2}\right)^2 + \left(\dfrac{y}{3}\right)^2 = 1$

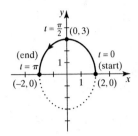

28. a. $-1 + 3i$ **b.** $-\dfrac{3}{5} + \dfrac{6}{5}i$ **c.** $2\sqrt{17}$

d. $3\sqrt{2}\,\text{cis}\,45°$ **e.** -324 **f.** $\sqrt[4]{18}\,\text{cis}\,22.5°,\ \sqrt[4]{18}\,\text{cis}\,202.5°$

29. False; the angle terminates in QIV.   **30.** False; t is in QIV.

31. False; the argument must be the same: $\cos^2 x + \sin^2 x = 1$ or $\cos^2 y + \sin^2 y = 1$ would be true.

32. False; $\csc x = \dfrac{1}{\sin x}$.   **33.** False; it could be the case that $\cos t = -\dfrac{\sqrt{3}}{2}$.

34. True   **35.** True   **36.** True   **37.** True

38. False; $\tan^2 x = \sec^2 x - 1$.   **39.** False; $\sin 2x = 2\sin x \cos x$.

40. False; $\dfrac{\sin 2x}{2} = \dfrac{2\sin x \cos x}{2} = \sin x \cos x$.   **41.** True

42. False; $(\sin x)^{-1} = \dfrac{1}{\sin x} = \csc x$, whereas $\sin^{-1} x = \arcsin x$ or the inverse sine.

43. True   **44.** True

45. True   **46.** False; $\theta = \arcsin y$ only for $-90° \le \theta \le 90°$.

47. False; the period is $\dfrac{\text{pure period}}{|B|} = \dfrac{2\pi}{3}$.   **48.** True

49. False; $\tan x = \dfrac{\sin x}{\cos x}$, $\tan 2x = \dfrac{\sin 2x}{\cos 2x}$.

50. True   **51.** True   **52.** True   **53.** True

54. False; answers can be expressed in many ways. For example, $2\sin x \cos x$ could be expressed as $\sin 2x$.

55. False; $\sin(x + y) = \sin x \cos y + \cos x \sin y$.

56. True   **57.** True

58. False; $\cos^2 x - \sin^2 x = \cos 2x$.   **59.** True

60. False; the equation could have many solutions, depending on the interval for x.

61. True   **62.** False; rectangular coordinates are unique.

63. False; $r = 7 \cos \theta$ represents a circle.

64. False; the sum of two vectors is a vector.

65. True

66. True

67. True

68. True

69. True

70. False; $|1 - 6i| = \sqrt{1^2 + (-6)^2} = \sqrt{37}$.

Answers to
Appendix Exercises

Appendix Exercises Solutions

A.1 Real Number System

1–6 State the property of the real numbers demonstrated by the statement.

1. $6 + 7 = 7 + 6$

Commutative property of addition

2. $5(x + 2) = 5x + 10$

Distributive property

3. $9 + (2 + y) = (9 + 2) + y$

Associative property of addition

4. $12 \cdot 2 = 2 \cdot 12$

Commutative property of multiplication

5. $(81 - t)2 = 162 - 2t$

Distributive property

6. $2 \cdot (5 \cdot 7) = (2 \cdot 5) \cdot 7$

Associative property of multiplication

7–16 Simplify the expressions.

7. $4^2 \div 2 + 3(5 - 4)$

$= 4^2 \div 2 + 3(1)$

$= 16 \div 2 + 3$

$= 8 + 3 = 11$

8. $1 - \left(\dfrac{1}{2}\right)^2$

$= 1 - \dfrac{1}{4}$

$= \dfrac{4}{4} - \dfrac{1}{4} = \dfrac{3}{4}$

9. $\sqrt{8^2 + 6^2}$

$= \sqrt{64 + 36}$

$= \sqrt{100}$

$= 10$

10. $\left|\dfrac{-3}{2}\right| - \dfrac{6(4 - 5)}{5}$

$= \dfrac{3}{2} - \dfrac{6(-1)}{5}$

$= \dfrac{3}{2} + \dfrac{6}{5} = \dfrac{15}{10} + \dfrac{12}{10} = \dfrac{27}{10}$

11. $\dfrac{1 + \dfrac{1}{2}}{2}$

$= \dfrac{\left(\dfrac{3}{2}\right)}{\left(\dfrac{2}{1}\right)} = \dfrac{3}{2} \cdot \dfrac{1}{2} = \dfrac{3}{4}$

12. $8^2 + 5^2 - 2 \cdot 8 \cdot 5 \cdot \dfrac{1}{2}$

$= 64 + 25 - 40$

$= 49$

13. $\dfrac{9^2 - 4^2 - 6^2}{-2(4)(6)}$

$= \dfrac{81 - 16 - 36}{-48}$

$= \dfrac{29}{-48} = -\dfrac{29}{48}$

14. $-33.9 \div 10 + |0.61 - 8|$

$= -33.9 \div 10 + 7.39$

$= -3.39 + 7.39$

$= 4$

15. $2\left(-\dfrac{12}{13}\right)\left(\dfrac{5}{13}\right)$

$\quad = \dfrac{2}{1}\left(-\dfrac{60}{169}\right)$

$\quad = -\dfrac{120}{169}$

16. $\dfrac{1-\dfrac{3}{5}}{\dfrac{1}{2}}$

$\quad = \dfrac{\dfrac{5}{5}-\dfrac{3}{5}}{\left(\dfrac{1}{2}\right)} = \dfrac{\left(\dfrac{2}{5}\right)}{\left(\dfrac{1}{2}\right)}$

$\quad = \dfrac{2}{5}\cdot\dfrac{2}{1} = \dfrac{4}{5}$

17–18 Find the distance d between the two points on the real number line.

17. $25, -17$

$\quad d(25, -17) = |25-(-17)|$

$\qquad\qquad\quad = |42| = 42$

18. $-9.5, -2.7$

$\quad d(-9.5, -2.7) = |-9.5-(-2.7)|$

$\qquad\qquad\qquad = |-6.8|$

$\qquad\qquad\qquad = 6.8$

A.2 Exponents and Radicals

1–6 Simplify the expressions and eliminate any negative exponent(s).

1. $(-2)^0 - 100^0$

$\quad = 1 - 1$

$\quad = 0$

2. $3^4 3^{-2} + \dfrac{3^2}{2^{-2}}$

$\quad = 3^{4+(-2)} + 3^2 \cdot 2^2$

$\quad = 3^2 + 3^2 \cdot 2^2$

$\quad = 9 + 9 \cdot 4 = 9 + 36$

$\quad = 45$

3. $\left(\dfrac{1}{7}\right)^{-3}\left(\dfrac{7}{5}\right)^{-2}$

$\quad = \left(\dfrac{7}{1}\right)^3 \cdot \left(\dfrac{5}{7}\right)^2 = \dfrac{7^3}{1}\cdot\dfrac{5^2}{7^2} = 7^{3-2}\cdot 5^2$

$\qquad\qquad\qquad\qquad\qquad = 7\cdot 25$

$\qquad\qquad\qquad\qquad\qquad = 175$

4. $\dfrac{4x^3 y^7}{16xy^{-2}} = \dfrac{x^{3-1}y^{7-(-2)}}{4}$

$\quad = \dfrac{x^2 y^9}{4}$

5. $\left(\dfrac{a^2 b^{-3}}{x^{-1}b^4}\right)^2\left(\dfrac{a^{-3}b}{x^3}\right)$

$\quad = \left(\dfrac{a^2 x}{b^7}\right)^2\left(\dfrac{b}{a^3 x^3}\right)$

$\quad = \dfrac{a^4 x^2}{b^{14}}\cdot\dfrac{b}{a^3 x^3}$

$\quad = a^{4-3}x^{2-3}b^{1-14}$

$\quad = \dfrac{a}{b^{13}x}$

6. $\dfrac{(a^3 b^2)^4 (ab^4)^{-2}}{a^2 b} = \dfrac{a^{12}b^8 a^{-2}b^{-8}}{a^2 b}$

$\quad = a^{12+(-2)-2}b^{8+(-8)-1} = a^8 b^{-1}$

$\qquad\qquad\qquad\qquad\quad = \dfrac{a^8}{b}$

7–14 Simplify each radical expression. Assume all variables represent positive numbers.

7. $\sqrt{\dfrac{4}{9}} = \dfrac{\sqrt{4}}{\sqrt{9}} = \dfrac{2}{3}$

8. $\sqrt{2}\sqrt{6} = \sqrt{2 \cdot 6} = \sqrt{4 \cdot 3}$
$= 2\sqrt{3}$

9. $3\sqrt{8} - \sqrt{32}$
$= 3\sqrt{4 \cdot 2} - \sqrt{16 \cdot 2}$
$= 3 \cdot 2\sqrt{2} - 4\sqrt{2}$
$= 6\sqrt{2} - 4\sqrt{2}$
$= 2\sqrt{2}$

10. $\dfrac{1}{\sqrt{3}} \cdot \dfrac{\sqrt{3}}{\sqrt{3}} = \dfrac{\sqrt{3}}{3}$

11. $\sqrt[3]{56} = \sqrt[3]{8 \cdot 7}$
$= 2\sqrt[3]{7}$

12. $\dfrac{1}{\left(1 + \sqrt{2}\right)} \dfrac{(1 - \sqrt{2})}{(1 - \sqrt{2})} = \dfrac{1 - \sqrt{2}}{1 - 2} = \dfrac{1 - \sqrt{2}}{-1}$
$= \sqrt{2} - 1$

13. $\dfrac{\left(\sqrt{3} + 1\right)\left(\sqrt{3} + 1\right)}{\left(\sqrt{3} - 1\right)\left(\sqrt{3} + 1\right)}$
$= \dfrac{3 + \sqrt{3} + \sqrt{3} + 1}{3 - 1}$
$= \dfrac{4 + 2\sqrt{3}}{2}$
$= \dfrac{\cancel{2}\left(2 + \sqrt{3}\right)}{\cancel{2}}$
$= 2 + \sqrt{3}$

14. $\sqrt{\dfrac{2}{3}} = \dfrac{\sqrt{2}}{\sqrt{3}} \cdot \dfrac{\sqrt{3}}{\sqrt{3}} = \dfrac{\sqrt{6}}{3}$

15. $\sqrt[4]{x^5 y^8}$
$= \sqrt[4]{x^4 x (y^4)^2}$
$= xy^2 \sqrt[4]{x}$

16. $\sqrt[3]{a^2 b}\,\sqrt[3]{ab^5}$
$= \sqrt[3]{a^2 b \cdot ab^5}$
$= \sqrt[3]{a^3 b^6}$
$= ab^2$

17–20 Write each expression in radical form. Then, simplify the radical expression.

17. $x^{\frac{3}{2}} = \sqrt{x^3}$
$= \sqrt{x^2 x}$
$= x\sqrt{x}$

18. $a^{-\frac{3}{2}} = \dfrac{1}{\sqrt{a^3}}$
$= \dfrac{1}{a\sqrt{a}} \cdot \dfrac{\sqrt{a}}{\sqrt{a}}$
$= \dfrac{\sqrt{a}}{a^2}$

19. $z^{-\frac{1}{5}} = \dfrac{1}{\sqrt[5]{z}}$

$= \dfrac{1}{\sqrt[5]{z}} \cdot \dfrac{\sqrt[5]{z^4}}{\sqrt[5]{z^4}}$

$= \dfrac{\sqrt[5]{z^4}}{z}$

20. $5y^{\frac{3}{4}} = 5\sqrt[4]{y^3}$

21–26 Simplify the expression and eliminate any negative exponent(s). Assume all variables represent positive numbers.

21. $\left(\dfrac{25}{16}\right)^{-\frac{1}{2}}$

$= \left(\dfrac{16}{25}\right)^{\frac{1}{2}}$

$= \sqrt{\dfrac{16}{25}}$

$= \dfrac{4}{5}$

22. $(-32)^{\frac{3}{5}}$

$= \left(\sqrt[5]{-32}\right)^3$

$= (-2)^3$

$= -8$

23. $\left(\dfrac{1+\dfrac{4}{5}}{2}\right)^{\frac{1}{2}} = \left(\dfrac{\dfrac{5}{5}+\dfrac{4}{5}}{2}\right)^{\frac{1}{2}}$

$= \left(\dfrac{\dfrac{9}{5}}{2}\right)^{\frac{1}{2}} = \left(\dfrac{9}{10}\right)^{\frac{1}{2}} = \dfrac{3}{\sqrt{10}} \cdot \dfrac{\sqrt{10}}{\sqrt{10}}$

$= \dfrac{3\sqrt{10}}{10}$

24. $\left(\dfrac{1-\dfrac{8}{9}}{9}\right)^{-\frac{1}{2}} = \left(\dfrac{\dfrac{9}{9}-\dfrac{8}{9}}{9}\right)^{-\frac{1}{2}} = \left(\dfrac{\dfrac{1}{9}}{9}\right)^{-\frac{1}{2}}$

$= \left(\dfrac{1}{81}\right)^{-\frac{1}{2}} = \left(\dfrac{81}{1}\right)^{\frac{1}{2}}$

$= \sqrt{81}$

$= 9$

25. $\left(\dfrac{x^6 y}{y^4}\right)^{\frac{1}{2}}$

$= \sqrt{\dfrac{x^6 y}{y^4}} = \dfrac{x^3\sqrt{y}}{y^2}$

26. $(4b)^{\frac{1}{2}}(8b^3)^{\frac{2}{3}}$

$\sqrt{4b} \cdot \left(\sqrt[3]{8b^3}\right)^2$

$= 2\sqrt{b}\,(2b)^2$

$= 2\sqrt{b} \cdot 4b^2$

$= 8b^2\sqrt{b}$

A.3 Algebraic Expressions

1–8 Simplify each expression.

1. $x^5 + 3x - 5 + 8x^5 - 4x^2 - 3x + 10$

$= 9x^5 - 4x^2 + 5$

2. $(4a - 2b + c) - (a - 3b + 2c)$

$= 4a - 2b + c - a + 3b - 2c$

$= 3a + b - c$

3. $\left(-3x^2y^3z\right)\left(-x^4z^2\right)$

$= 3 \cdot x^{2+4}y^3z^{1+2}$

$= 3x^6y^3z^3$

4. $-3s(5s-6)$

$= -3s(5s) - 3s(-6)$

$= -15s^2 + 18s$

5. $2x^2(x^2-3x-2)$

$= 2x^2x^2 - 2x^2 \cdot 3x - 2x^2 \cdot 2$

$= 2x^4 - 6x^3 - 4x^2$

6. $(t+2)(t-4)$

$= t^2 - 4t + 2t - 8$

$= t^2 - 2t - 8$

7. $(a+b)^2$

$= (a+b)(a+b)$

$= a^2 + 2ab + b^2$

8. $(2x-5)^2$

$= (2x-5)(2x-5)$

$= 4x^2 - 20x + 25$

9–16 Factor each expression.

9. $9x + 36$

$= 9(x+4)$

10. $25x^2 - 36y^2$

$= (5x-6y)(5x+6y)$

11. $4x^2 - 8x + 2$

$= 2(2x^2 - 4x + 1)$

12. $3x^2 - 3$

$= 3(x^2 - 1)$

$= 3(x+1)(x-1)$

13. $k^2 - 4k + 3$

$= (k-3)(k-1)$

14. $3y^2 - 2y - 1$

$= (3y+1)(y-1)$

15. $uv - v^2$

$= v(u-v)$

16. $ax + bx - ay - by$

$= x(a+b) - y(a+b)$

$= (a+b)(x-y)$

17–24 Simplify each rational expression.

17. $\dfrac{x^2-1}{x-1}$

$= \dfrac{(x+1)(x-1)}{(x-1)}$

$= x + 1$

18. $= \dfrac{2\sqrt{2} - 4x}{2}$

$= \dfrac{2\left(\sqrt{2} - 2x\right)}{2}$

$= \sqrt{2} - 2x$

19. $\dfrac{4}{\left(4-\sqrt{2}\right)}\dfrac{\left(4+\sqrt{2}\right)}{\left(4+\sqrt{2}\right)}$

$= \dfrac{4\left(4+\sqrt{2}\right)}{16-2} = \dfrac{4\left(4+\sqrt{2}\right)}{14}$

$= \dfrac{2\left(4+\sqrt{2}\right)}{7}$

$= \dfrac{8+2\sqrt{2}}{7}$

20. $\sqrt{\dfrac{1+\frac{1}{2}}{2}} = \sqrt{\dfrac{\frac{2}{2}+\frac{1}{2}}{\left(\frac{2}{1}\right)}} = \sqrt{\dfrac{3}{2}\cdot\dfrac{1}{2}}$

$= \sqrt{\dfrac{3}{4}} = \dfrac{\sqrt{3}}{2}$

21. $\dfrac{x^2-5x-14}{7-x}$

$= \dfrac{(x-7)(x+2)}{-1(x-7)} = \dfrac{x+2}{-1}$

$= -x-2$

22. $\dfrac{1}{1-a}+\dfrac{1}{1+a} = \dfrac{1}{(1-a)}\dfrac{(1+a)}{(1+a)}+\dfrac{1}{(1+a)}\dfrac{(1-a)}{(1-a)}$

$= \dfrac{1+a+1-a}{(1-a)(1+a)}$

$= \dfrac{2}{(1-a)(1+a)}$

23. $-\sqrt{\dfrac{1-\dfrac{\sqrt{3}}{2}}{2}}$

$= -\sqrt{\dfrac{\dfrac{2-\sqrt{3}}{2}}{\left(\dfrac{2}{1}\right)}} = -\dfrac{\sqrt{2-\sqrt{3}}}{\sqrt{4}}$

$= -\dfrac{\sqrt{2-\sqrt{3}}}{2}$

24. $\dfrac{x+\dfrac{1}{\sqrt{3}}}{1-(x)\left(\dfrac{1}{\sqrt{3}}\right)} = \dfrac{\left(x+\dfrac{1}{\sqrt{3}}\right)\dfrac{\sqrt{3}}{\sqrt{3}}}{\left(1-\dfrac{x}{\sqrt{3}}\right)}$

$= \dfrac{\left(x\sqrt{3}+1\right)\left(\sqrt{3}+x\right)}{\left(\sqrt{3}-x\right)\left(\sqrt{3}+x\right)}$

$= \dfrac{x^2\sqrt{3}+4x+\sqrt{3}}{3-x^2}$

A.4 Solving Equations

1–22 Solve the following equations.

1. $3x+2 = 4(x-6)$

$3x+2 = 4x-24$

$2 = x-24$

$x = 26$

2. $ab = a$

$ab-a = 0$

$a(b-1) = 0$

$a = 0 \quad \text{or} \quad b-1 = 0$

$a = 0 \quad \text{or} \quad b = 1$

3. $4x^2 = 1$

$x^2 = \dfrac{1}{4}$

$x = \pm\sqrt{\dfrac{1}{4}}$

$x = \pm\dfrac{1}{2}$

4. $25y^2 = 9$

$y^2 = \dfrac{9}{25}$

$y = \pm\sqrt{\dfrac{9}{25}}$

$y = \pm\dfrac{3}{5}$

5.
$$10x^2 - 13x = -3$$
$$10x^2 - 13x + 3 = 0$$
$$(10x - 3)(x - 1) = 0$$
$$10x - 3 = 0 \quad \text{or} \quad x - 1 = 0$$
$$x = \frac{3}{10} \quad \text{or} \quad x = 1$$

6. $\quad c^2 = 5^2 + 6^2 - 2(5)(6)\left(\dfrac{1}{2}\right)$
$$c^2 = 25 + 36 - 30$$
$$c^2 = 31$$
$$c = \pm\sqrt{31}$$

7.
$$\frac{x}{5} = \frac{3}{7}$$
$$5\left(\frac{x}{5}\right) = 5\left(\frac{3}{7}\right)$$
$$x = \frac{15}{7}$$

8.
$$\frac{21}{4} = \frac{8}{x}$$
$$21x = 32 \quad (x \neq 0)$$
$$x = \frac{32}{21}$$

9.
$$4 + 3x = \frac{14}{2x}$$
$$2x(4 + 3x) = 14 \qquad (x \neq 0)$$
$$8x + 6x^2 = 14$$
$$6x^2 + 8x - 14 = 0$$
$$2(3x^2 + 4x - 7) = 0$$
$$2(3x + 7)(x - 1) = 0$$
$$3x + 7 = 0 \quad \text{or} \quad x - 1 = 0$$
$$x = -\frac{7}{3} \quad \text{or} \quad x = 1$$

10. $\quad 10^2 = 5^2 + x^2 - 10x$
$$0 = x^2 - 10x - 75$$
$$0 = (x - 15)(x + 5)$$
$$x - 15 = 0 \quad \text{or} \quad x + 5 = 0$$
$$x = 15 \qquad \text{or} \quad x = -5$$

11. $\quad x^2 - 2 = 1$
$$x^2 = 3$$
$$x = \pm\sqrt{3}$$

12. $\quad 25 = -16t^2 + 40t$
$$16t^2 - 40t + 25 = 0$$
$$(4t - 5)(4t - 5) = 0$$
$$4t - 5 = 0$$
$$t = \frac{5}{4}$$

13. $\quad 2xy - \sqrt{3}y = 0$
$$y\left(2x - \sqrt{3}\right) = 0$$
$$y = 0 \quad \text{or} \quad 2x - \sqrt{3} = 0$$
$$y = 0 \quad \text{or} \quad x = \frac{\sqrt{3}}{2}$$

14.
$$4y^2 + 33y = 27$$
$$4y^2 + 33y - 27 = 0$$
$$(4y - 3)(y + 9) = 0$$
$$y = \frac{3}{4} \quad \text{or} \quad y = -9$$

15. $3x - \dfrac{1}{x} = 1$

$3x^2 - 1 = x \quad (x \neq 0)$

$3x^2 - x - 1 = 0$

$x = \dfrac{-(-1) \pm \sqrt{(-1)^2 - 4(3)(-1)}}{2(3)}$

$x = \dfrac{1 \pm \sqrt{13}}{6}$

16. $\sqrt{\dfrac{1+x}{2}} + x = 0$

$\left(\sqrt{\dfrac{1+x}{2}}\right)^2 = (-x)^2 \qquad$ (square both sides $\Rightarrow$ must check answers)

$\dfrac{1+x}{2} = x^2$

$0 = 2x^2 - x - 1$

$0 = (2x + 1)(x - 1)$

$2x + 1 = 0 \quad \text{or} \quad x - 1 = 0$

$x = -\dfrac{1}{2} \qquad\qquad \cancel{x = 1}$

17. $\sqrt{\dfrac{1-t}{2}} = \sqrt{\dfrac{1}{2} - t}$

$\left(\sqrt{\dfrac{1-t}{2}}\right)^2 = \left(\sqrt{\dfrac{1}{2} - t}\right)^2 \qquad$ (square both sides $\Rightarrow$ must check answers)

$\dfrac{1-t}{2} = \dfrac{1 - 2t}{2}$

$1 - t = 1 - 2t$

$t = 0$

18. $1 - 2r^2 = 1 - 2r$

$2r^2 - 2r = 0$

$2r(r - 1) = 0$

$2r = 0 \quad \text{or} \quad r - 1 = 0$

$r = 0 \quad \text{or} \quad r = 1$

19. $x + \dfrac{1}{x} + 2 = 0$

$x^2 + 2x + 1 = 0 \quad (x \neq 0)$

$(x + 1)(x + 1) = 0$

$x = -1$

20. $4x^2 = 4x$

$4x^2 - 4x = 0$

$4x(x - 1) = 0$

$4x = 0 \quad \text{or} \quad x - 1 = 0$

$x = 0 \quad \text{or} \quad x = 1$

21.
$$\dfrac{1}{x} + \dfrac{1}{x - 3} = \dfrac{9}{x^2 - 3x}$$

Multiply by LCD: $x(x - 3)$
where $x \neq 0, x \neq 3$

$$x(x - 3)\dfrac{1}{x} + x(x - 3)\dfrac{1}{x - 3} = x(x - 3)\dfrac{9}{x(x - 3)}$$

$$x - 3 + x = 9$$
$$\cancel{x = 3}$$

We discard the solution

$\Rightarrow$ This equation has no solution.

22. $\dfrac{3x}{x} = 3 \quad (x \neq 0)$

$3x = 3x \qquad\qquad$ Identity

$\Rightarrow x \in \mathbb{R}, x \neq 0$

A.5 The Coordinate Plane

1–6 Plot the points and state the quadrant that they are in.

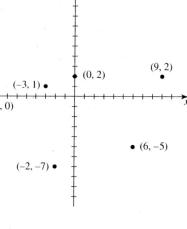

1. $(6, -5)$

QIV

2. $(9, 2)$

QI

3. $(-2, -7)$

QIII

4. $(0, 2)$

Not in a quadrant

5. $(-3, 1)$

QII

6. $(-8, 0)$

Not in a quadrant

7–14 Graph the equation in the xy-coordinate plane and indicate any intercepts.

7. $2x + y = 9$

x	y
0	9
4.5	0

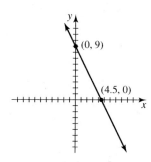

8. $y = \dfrac{1}{2}x + 6$

x	y
0	6
-12	0

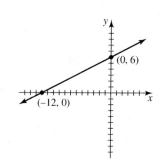

9. $y = 4x^2 - 2$

x	y
0	-2
$\pm\dfrac{\sqrt{2}}{2}$	0

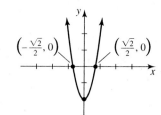

10. $x^2 + y^2 = 1$

x	y
0	±1
±1	0

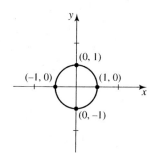

11. $16x^2 + 9y^2 = 144$

x	y
0	±4
±3	0

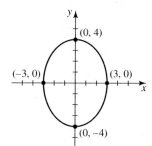

12. $y = -x^2 + 5$

x	y
0	5
$\pm\sqrt{5}$	0

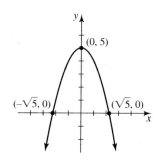

13. $4x^2 + 4y^2 = 16$

x	y
0	± 2
± 2	0

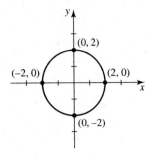

14. $x^2 + 25y^2 = 25$

x	y
0	± 1
± 5	0

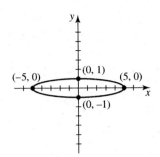

15–18 Find the distance between P and Q.

15. $P(5, -4)$, $Q(8, 0)$

$$d = \sqrt{(8-5)^2 + (0+4)^2}$$
$$= \sqrt{3^2 + 4^2}$$
$$= \sqrt{9 + 16}$$
$$= \sqrt{25} = 5$$

16. $P\left(\sqrt{2}, 5\right)$, $Q\left(3\sqrt{2}, 4\right)$

$$d = \sqrt{\left(3\sqrt{2} - \sqrt{2}\right)^2 + (4-5)^2}$$
$$= \sqrt{\left(2\sqrt{2}\right)^2 + (-1)^2}$$
$$= \sqrt{8 + 1}$$
$$= \sqrt{9} = 3$$

17. $P\left(\dfrac{\sqrt{3}}{2}, \dfrac{1}{2}\right)$, $Q(0, 1)$

$$d = \sqrt{\left(0 - \frac{\sqrt{3}}{2}\right)^2 + \left(1 - \frac{1}{2}\right)^2}$$
$$= \sqrt{\frac{3}{4} + \frac{1}{4}}$$
$$= \sqrt{\frac{4}{4}}$$
$$= 1$$

18. $P(3, 8)$, $Q(-2, 13)$

$$d = \sqrt{(-2 - 3)^2 + (13 - 8)^2}$$
$$= \sqrt{(-5)^2 + (5)^2}$$
$$= \sqrt{25 + 25}$$
$$= \sqrt{2 \cdot 25}$$
$$= 5\sqrt{2}$$

A.6 Relations and Functions

1–4 If $f(x) = -4.9x^2 + 18x + 2$, find the following.

1. $f(0)$

$$= -4.9(0)^2 + 18(0) + 2$$
$$= 2$$

2. $f(2)$

$$= -4.9(2)^2 + 18(2) + 2$$
$$= 18.4$$

3. $f(a)$

$$= -4.9a^2 + 18a + 2$$

4. $f(a + b)$

$$= -4.9(a + b)^2 + 18(a + b) + 2$$

5–8 Determine whether the graphs represent functions.

5. No.

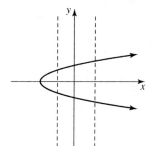

6. Yes.

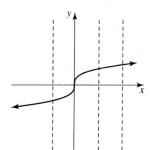

7. No.

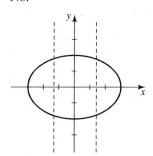

8. Yes.

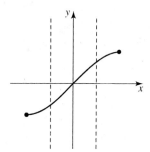

9–12 Determine by their graphs whether the functions are one-to-one functions.

9. Yes.

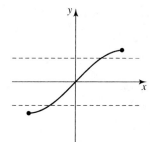

10. No.

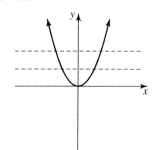

11. Yes.

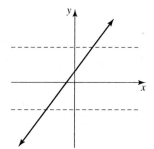

12. No.

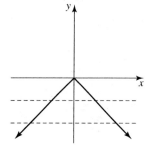

13–14 Find the inverse of the one-to-one function.

13. $f(x) = 3x + 4$

$y = 3x + 4$

Inverse:

$x = 3y + 4$

$y = \dfrac{x - 4}{3}$

$\Rightarrow f^{-1}(x) = \dfrac{x - 4}{3}$

14. $g(x) = \dfrac{1}{2x}$

$y = \dfrac{1}{2x}$

Inverse:

$x = \dfrac{1}{2y}$

$xy = \dfrac{1}{2}$

$y = \dfrac{1}{2x}$

$\Rightarrow g^{-1}(x) = \dfrac{1}{2x}$

15–16 Find the graph of the inverse of the one-to-one function.

15.

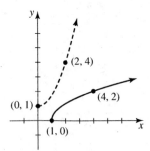

16.

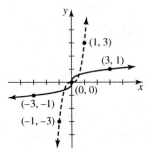

17–20 Determine whether the graphs are symmetric with respect to the y-axis, x-axis, and the origin.

17. origin, x-axis, y-axis

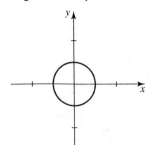

18. origin

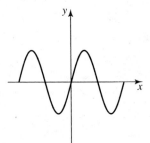

19. y-axis

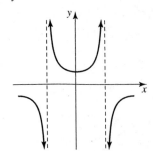

20. x-axis

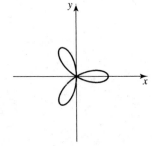